Sex, Sin, & Violence on Screen

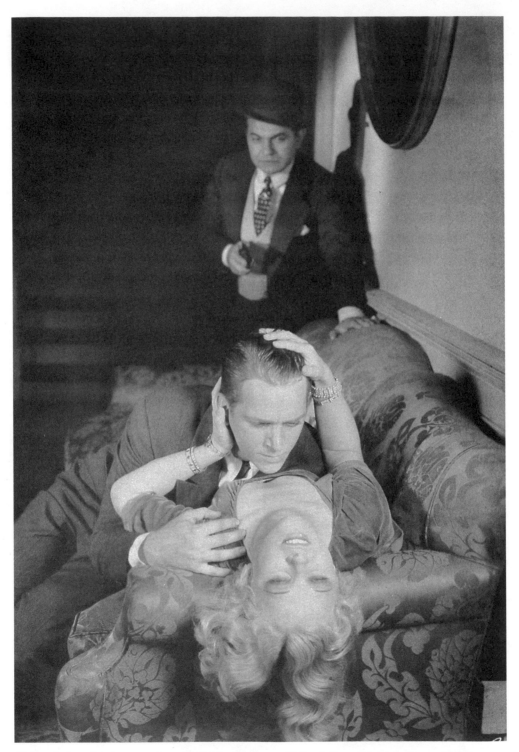

Although the affair between Douglas Fairbanks, Jr., and Glenda Farrell in Little Caesar *(1930) was tame even by contemporary standards, this publicity still for the Edward G. Robinson vehicle combines elements that would have made most censors of the day reach for their cutting shears.*

Sex, Sin, &
Violence on Screen

Frank Miller

Turner Publishing, Inc.

ATLANTA

This book is dedicated to my uncle,
Philip Collins,
who saw *The Outlaw* twenty-eight times in the forties
and has yet to show any ill effects for it.

Published by Turner Publishing, Inc.
A Subsidiary of Turner Broadcasting System, Inc.
1050 Techwood Drive, N.W.
Atlanta, Georgia 30318

First Edition 10 9 8 7 6 5 4 3 2 1

Library of Congress Cataloging-in-Publication Data

Miller, Frank
    Censored Hollywood: sex, sin & violence on screen / Frank Miller.
        — 1st. ed.
        p. cm.
    Includes bibliographical references and index.
    ISBN 1-57036-116-9: $24.95. — ISBN 1-878685-55-4 (pbk.) : $14.95
        1. Motion pictures—Censorship—United States. I. Title.
    PN1995.62.M55 1994
    384' .8' 0973—dc20   94-19982
                                                                        CIP

Distributed by Andrews and McMeel
A Universal Press Syndicate Company
4900 Main Street
Kansas City, Missouri 64112

Vice President, Editorial—Walton Rawls
Editor—Katherine Buttler
Vice President, Design—Michael Walsh
Art Director/Book Designer—Karen E. Smith
Production Manager—Anne Murdoch
Photo Research—Woosley Ackerman, Marty Moore
Photo Coordinator—Zodie Spain

Printed in the U.S.A.

Contents

The Dream Wars

Introduction

. . . It was often a case of inherited American standards—products of a Christian civilization—against alien customs variously described as "modern," "liberal," or "pagan." Hosts of Americans clung firmly to their own ideals and strongly resisted the alien invasion.[1]

When Will H. Hays, retired president of the Motion Picture Producers and Distributors of America (MPPDA), wrote those words in his memoirs, he was referring to the chaotic changes in American culture in the 1920s and the "invasion" of sophisticated ideas from Europe. With a shift to the present tense, however, his words could just as easily fit into a speech by Pat Buchanan or Dan Quayle on family values and a cultural war as old as the culture itself.

The first cave painter probably heard complaints that his or her images of bison and hunters somehow violated tribal traditions and community standards. Euripides's first version of *Hippolytus* was shouted off the stage in ancient Greece because of a scene in which Phaedra made romantic overtures to her stepson. When he rewrote the scene so that Phaedra merely eavesdropped as her nurse hinted at a possible liaison, Euripides may have been the first writer forced to revise a script for the censors.

The theater consistently has attracted the wrath of reformers and moralists. The early Christian church, having survived a ban on its own activities, didn't wait long after coming into power before it outlawed the theater—a ban that lasted from the later days of the Roman Empire through the Dark Ages.

In Shakespeare's England, most public theaters were located just outside London to escape the frequent bans imposed by the city's moralistic, middle-class government. Even then, the Bard's work, particularly the history plays, was diligently scrutinized for politically subversive content. Molière had to rewrite *Tartuffe* twice because his tale of a

A minor casualty of Hollywood's dream wars: This publicity still for Hollywood Party *(1934) was nixed by MPPDA staffers charged with keeping not only the movies but also their advertising from arousing impure thoughts.*

religious hypocrite bilking an old man of his estate was deemed too controversial.

Theatrical censorship moved into this century with attacks on the trailblazing works of such playwrights as Henrik Ibsen and George Bernard Shaw. But at the turn of the century, a new form of entertainment developed that would soon supplant the stage as the moralists' favorite whipping post—the movies.

The screen's attraction to would-be censors grows out of one of the characteristics that most clearly distinguishes it from the theater: its almost universal reach. Whereas a single stage performance can be presented to only one audience at a time, each individual film can travel around the world and reach millions of people—of all ages, races, nationalities, and social classes—without any major changes to its original form.

In addition, the screen has always possessed a special fascination for less sophisticated audiences. Early on, young people and the working classes, particularly immigrants, were drawn to the flickering images projected in small, dark, and often poorly ventilated rooms. And these were exactly the people that the reformers of the early twentieth century were most concerned with bringing into the light.

Finally, projected film—by its very size and the ease with which it manipulates images—may very well be the most persuasive of all modern media. While Hitler was building his Third Reich in Germany, he knew enough to enlist filmmaker Leni Riefenstahl to capture the dream of Aryan supremacy in *Triumph of the Will*. In America, the success of Thomas H. Ince's pacifist *Civilization* in 1916 was credited with helping Woodrow Wilson stay in the White House during a fiercely fought presidential campaign.

This very pervasiveness of film has both raised the stakes and clouded the issues. It's easy to look back on the censorship battles of centuries gone by and know who the villains are. History has shown many of the moralists' most fervent objections to be ultimately pointless and has proclaimed many a suppressed work a masterpiece. With film, however, the issues are thornier. The most repressive and intolerant would-be censors fight side by side with parents legitimately concerned about the influence of film on their children and minorities justifiably enraged when they are portrayed only in crude, potentially destructive stereotypes. Dedicated artists find their battles for freedom of expression joined by smut peddlers—and even the most perceptive cannot always tell the difference between the two.

Nor is it possible to place limits on the victories that either side enjoys. A little bit of censorship may mean raising necklines an inch or halving the amount of blood in a murder scene, but it almost always ends up regulating what ideas may or may not be represented on screen. Crack the barricades to allow freedom for a Roberto Rossellini or a David Lynch, and a Larry Flynt will slip through as well.

Censors come in all shapes and sizes but can be classified in two ways—by their general organization and by their approach to the materials they want to control. In terms of organization, institutional censors[2] are different from pressure groups. Institutional censorship is the work of groups with clearly established power to control film content. Inherently paternalistic, the institutional censor specializes in making decisions for others, screening films to determine their effects on other people's morals. (How the censors themselves escape contamination by objectionable material is a question that has long remained unanswered.) Institutional censorship may be imposed by the government (state and local censorship boards), organized religion (the Catholic Legion of Decency), or even by representatives of the medium to be censored (the MPPDA's Production Code Administration, or PCA).

Less formal are the efforts of various pressure groups. In general, these groups seek to advance more specific concerns about film content, ranging from a protest lodged by the National Fire Protection Association over Bette Davis's smoking in bed in *All About Eve* to more pressing concerns about the depiction of minorities on screen. Without institutional backing, these groups can only try to enforce their demands through economic and social pressure.

In their approach to material, censors can be either quantitative or qualitative. The quantitative censor works from a list of proscribed materials to snip shots, lines, and scenes considered harmful to audiences. Hollywood's Production Code included such a list, designed to render all films passed by the MPPDA "suitable for family viewing."

Qualitative censors deal with works as a whole, concentrating on a film's overall message rather than its individual elements. Pressure groups deal largely in this area. The National Association for the Advancement of Colored People (NAACP) and the Gay and Lesbian Alliance Against Defamation (GLAAD) have exerted strong pressure on Hollywood in their fight to see blacks and homosexuals, respectively, portrayed more favorably on-screen.

As admirable as those efforts may appear to many, qualitative censorship is potentially the most dangerous weapon in the cultural wars. In an effort to keep offensive materials off the screen, the Production Code also tried to stifle "unacceptable" ideas, most notably those that seriously questioned the status quo. In the fifties, suspected Communists were censored out of jobs by the Hollywood blacklist, while Charles Chaplin was censored right out of the country—simply because they were thought to have espoused the wrong ideas. In its most extreme form, the censoring impulse borders on the genocidal, whether the battleground is Nazi Germany or Renaissance Spain.

Most censorship never reaches such extreme levels, of course. At the same time, however, censorship's capacity to reach the level of cultural murder cannot be ignored.

All of these issues are reflected in Hollywood's efforts to censor its own work. Since the twenties, the MPPDA (now the Motion Picture Association of America, or MPAA) has tried to reconcile the work of Hollywood's, and sometimes the world's, filmmakers with the interests of institutional censors and pressure groups. In addition to managing the industry's own system of self-regulation—the Production Code and the ratings system—the MPAA has worked closely with other censors. In fact, the original purpose of Hollywood self-regulation was to smooth the way with local censors and fight the passage of additional censorship legislation.

The MPAA has generated a good deal of controversy lately over its ratings system and particularly over the financial difficulties posed by the NC-17 rating. This is nothing new. During the golden years of Hollywood, the Production Code Administration (PCA), which preceded the current ratings system, was frequently attacked for keeping certain subjects and literary properties off the screen. These complaints have often blinded critics to the positive work of the MPAA. By making Hollywood clean up its own act, both on- and off-screen, the MPAA has served as a powerful argument against federal censorship. The organization has provided a sounding board for smaller groups and individuals and has worked with civic groups to raise audience tastes and promote some of Hollywood's more ambitious undertakings.

Despite negative publicity about cuts and changes made in the name of the Production Code, particularly during Joe Breen's reign as head of the PCA, the Code had its positive side. Code restrictions forced writers to appeal to the audience's imagination, thus leading to some of the screen's most romantic moments. Some films even may have been improved by PCA recommendations.

At the same time, however, many of the attacks on the Code were fully justified. The PCA in general, and Breen in particular, often lagged far behind the rest of the country in terms of taste and standards. The American public may have needed to know about the rise of fascism in Europe, the spread of venereal disease, and the increasing prevalence of drug addition, but they didn't learn anything about those situations from the films regulated by Joe Breen.

This book focuses primarily on the history of Hollywood's self-regulation, from the first efforts by Will Hays to keep certain books and plays off the screen to the more recent battles over the MPAA's ratings system. In addition, sidebars will look at censorship in other countries and other media to place the MPAA's operations within a larger context. Special emphasis will also be given to the role of the courts in shaping the censorship wars. Solutions are hard to come by in this ever-more-complicated world we share. Solutions that everyone can agree on are next to impossible. What is possible is a look at the facts: the forces at work today; the way the past has shaped the present; and the way the same battles seem to be waged, often in almost the same words, time and time again.

"What Are You Going to Do, Charge Me with Smoking?"

Chapter One

Unlike Catherine Tramell in *Basic Instinct*'s infamous interrogation scene, director Paul Verhoeven was facing something much worse during the early months of 1992 than a fine for inappropriate nicotine use. After more than a year's work on the steamy thriller, with its nightmarish mixture of sex and violence, Verhoeven was threatened with an NC-17 rating.

Advance word on the picture, the story of a police detective obsessed with the key suspect in a series of ice-pick murders, was strong. According to Bernard Weinraub of the *New York Times*, the film was being touted as "'a guaranteed blockbuster,' 'the steamiest movie of the year' and 'hot, hot, hot.'"[1] With Michael Douglas bringing his proven box-office clout to the lead and Sharon Stone in what promised to be a breakthrough performance, Verhoeven and his studio, Carolco Pictures, seemed to have a winner on their hands.

Now, all of that could be in jeopardy. An NC-17 rating would do more than just restrict anyone under the age of seventeen from attending the film—a serious cut into potential profits. Hundreds of movie theaters routinely refuse to book films rated NC-17. In fact, many malls, which house a significant portion of U.S. movie screens, contractually bar their theaters from presenting such adult fare.

The first film rated NC-17, director Philip Kaufman's *Henry and June* (1990), played in only 307 theaters in the United States. *Basic Instinct*'s distributor, TriStar Pictures, was preparing to open the film in one thousand to twelve hundred theaters in March.

Mae West (pictured above in Belle of the Nineties) *was hardly the first sex goddess to burn up the screen, nor is Sharon Stone likely to be the last. The notoriety of both actresses proves that each generation, no matter how liberal, can still find something to be shocked about.*

13

The potential loss of nine hundred bookings was a serious threat to any film, especially one whose cost had been estimated as high as $49 million.

Of all those involved in the squabble over *Basic Instinct*'s rating, TriStar was in the best position. Like many other distribution deals in today's Hollywood, TriStar's contract for *Basic Instinct* demanded the delivery of an R-rated picture. If the MPAA's Classification and Ratings Administration (CARA) refused to award an R to the finished film, the distributor could legally require Verhoeven and Carolco to appeal or negotiate cuts to get the required rating.

Things were much more precarious for Carolco. Despite having produced the number-one box-office film of the previous year, *Terminator 2*, the studio was on the edge of bankruptcy from its investments in a series of big-budget flops. *Basic Instinct* was the first of four expensive projects on which Carolco was depending to get back into the black.

For Verhoeven, *Basic Instinct* marked a return to the stylized, cutting-edge stories he'd worked with at the start of his career. The Dutch director had won an Oscar nomination for Best Foreign Language Film in 1973 with *Turkish Delight*, and *The Fourth Man* had been a surprising box-office success in the U.S. Both films were extremely sensual; both went beyond the boundaries in delving into the darker side of sexual relations. After repeated attacks from Dutch critics, who charged him with misrepresenting his homeland's culture, Verhoeven broke into the film industry with two blockbusters—*Robocop* and *Total Recall*—whose only relation to his earlier work was their striking visual sense. With *Basic Instinct*, he was once more making a personal statement with his work, getting the chance to show the U.S. moneymen that he could do more than direct explosions and high-tech shootouts.

The stakes may have been even higher for costar Sharon Stone. At the time *Basic Instinct* came along, Stone had already been in Hollywood for ten years. She'd made her film debut in 1980 as the dream girl kissing the train window in Woody Allen's *Stardust Memories*. Horror fans remembered her as the woman with the spider in her mouth in Wes Craven's *Deadly Blessing*, and she had gotten good reviews as Ryan O'Neal's ambitious actress girlfriend in 1984's *Irreconcilable Differences*, but in the rest of her films, she was little more than a very attractive appendage to such heroes as Richard Chamberlain, Carl Weathers, and Steven Seagal.

Then she got the first role to make good use of her talents for chic villainy, Arnold Schwarzenegger's sexy, murderous wife in *Total Recall*. During filming she heard about the director's next project and launched a campaign to win the female lead in *Basic Instinct*. She even showed up at a looping session for *Total Recall* in the kind of formfitting dress and Grace Kelly hairdo she would end up wearing as Catherine Tramell.

Stone was the first actress Verhoeven tested for the role and his first choice throughout casting, but the studio and Michael Douglas demanded that he look for a bigger name. Over the course of five months, Verhoeven looked at other actresses but kept coming back to his tape of Stone. With major names like Geena Davis and Ellen Barkin turning down the part, reportedly because of the nudity and sex, Verhoeven finally got his way. If an NC-17 rating were to cost *Basic Instinct* 50 to 75 percent of its potential bookings, however, Stone's career-making role could easily fizzle.

For all the trouble CARA was causing for *Basic Instinct*, it had a lot at stake in the film as well. Liberal critics and filmmakers had long complained about the financial restrictions of the MPAA's X rating, the predecessor of the NC-17. Despite the fact that the NC-17 had been created to remove the stigma attached to the X, the complaints had not stopped. Several theaters still refused to book NC-17 films, just as they previously had with X-rated films. Some newspapers would not accept advertising for such pictures. And many video stores and chains—including the nation's largest video-rental chain, Blockbuster—had bowed to pressure from religious conservatives and refused to stock NC-17 movies.

Now, CARA was getting it from the right. Religious conservatives had been building a strong power base in the United States since the mid-seventies. Using an extensive media network and increasingly sophisticated organizational techniques, they had set out to influence public opinion and public policy on a broad spectrum of issues—from abortion rights and school curricula to defense spending and civil rights for sexual minorities. As religious leaders complained increasingly of a so-called "cultural elite" spreading liberal and secular humanist propaganda, conservative attacks on the entertainment and news media grew. Some groups, like the Reverand Donald Wildmon's American Family Association, threatened to boycott the sponsors of television programming that seemed to advocate liberal causes. Others simply called for a return to the family-oriented filmmaking of Hollywood's golden years.

In 1992, the Atlanta-based Christian Film and Television Commission announced work on an updated version of the old Production Code, which had governed film-industry self-regulation from the thirties until the adoption of the ratings system in 1968. In a speech on February 1, 1992, Cardinal Roger Mahony of Los Angeles took up the cry: "Perhaps the time is ripe for the entertainment industry to consider the advisability of having such a code. . . . I would encourage the media to look upon calls for reform not as a censorship issue, but, rather, as an issue of human rights and dignity."[2]

Mahony's remarks, coming in the midst of a heated campaign by the religious right to

While Hollywood was being attacked by conservatives over *Basic Instinct* and other films that stretched the boundaries of screen permissiveness, the movie capital was also under assault from a group whose concerns couldn't have been farther from those of the right. *Basic Instinct* became the rallying cry for gay rights groups whose members had long been fed up with Hollywood's sporadic, often stereotyped treatment of gay men and lesbians.

The battle had been building since 1969, when the Stonewall riots in New York's Greenwich Village officially launched the gay movement. The increasing visibility of homosexuals since then—coupled with the violent debate fostered by the AIDS crisis—had led to increasing fire from the right. It also had led to a dramatic increase in hate crimes against gay men and lesbians.

As far as most gay activists were concerned, Hollywood wasn't helping. There had been a few attempts to deal realistically with gay issues in films and on television, but most television treatments generated strong boycott threats from conservative groups, and positive treatments of lesbians and gay men on screen were mostly limited to such independent productions as *Desert Hearts* and *Parting Glances*. The AIDS crisis had inspired the award-winning television films *An Early Frost* and *Andre's Mother*, numerous television series episodes, and dozens of plays, but the only American film to focus on the issue was another independent production, *Longtime Companion*.

In place of serious consideration of gay issues, the screen offered stereotyped buffoons and killers. By the time *Basic Instinct* was ready for release, gay groups had already complained about the swishy wedding consultant played by Martin Short in *Father of the Bride;* the transsexual killer—complete with pierced nipple, pet poodle, and other stereotyped gay accoutrements—in *The Silence of the Lambs;* and the cartel of killer homosexuals director Oliver Stone placed behind the Kennedy assassination in *JFK.* Just as bad was the "straightening out" of gay characters from literature and history, like the young women played by Mary Stuart Masterson and Mary-Louise Parker in *Fried Green Tomatoes.*

The problems with *Basic Instinct* started in March of 1991, when somebody leaked the script to various gay groups, which were appalled at the depiction of Catherine Tramell as an ice-pick-wielding bisexual murderess and by such scenes as the confrontation between Nick and Catherine's snarling, leather-clad lesbian lover, Roxy. With one of Hollywood's top box-office stars in the lead and a hot action director at the helm, these negative images of gay life threatened to reach an even wider audience than before.

Groups like the Gay and Lesbian Alliance Against Defamation (GLAAD) initiated letter-writing campaigns to present their concerns to the filmmakers. When that didn't work, activists launched an organized campaign to disrupt filming in San Francisco. Protesters shouted and set off bullhorns near the locations. During the shooting of a car chase, they held up signs asking motorists to honk their horns in support of the San Francisco 49ers or U.S. troops, producing an impressive outpouring of noise that did little to disrupt the scene, which was being filmed without sound.

Initially, Eszterhas was unsympathetic to the protests, saying "minority groups of any kind have to accept the possibility that among them is a sociopath."[3] As the protests grew, however, they began to get to the Marin County resident, and he wrote to Verhoeven urging him to meet with the groups. But their meeting did little to solve the problems. Verhoeven was less than receptive to the groups' demands, which ranged from changing Nick's gender to eliminating a suggestion of date rape. When Eszterhas started siding with the protesters, he and the director exchanged heated words. The meeting ended with Eszterhas's promise to work on script revisions but no promises from Verhoeven to accept them.

A little over a week later, Eszterhas handed in seventeen pages of script changes, including a disclaimer to run with the opening credits, Nick asking his psychiatrist girlfriend permission to engage in rough sex, and a line in which Nick stated that all of the best people he'd met in San Francisco were gay. When Verhoeven and producer Alan Marshall rejected the changes on the grounds that they weakened the script and the characters, Eszterhas withdrew from the production.

Meanwhile, the protests continued. Marshall got an injunction to keep outsiders one hundred feet from any filming. When protesters violated that boundary, he made citizen's arrests of thirty-one of them. They were back on the street within hours. Carolco also issued a strong press statement: "Censorship by street action will not be tolerated. While these groups have a right to express their opinions, they have no right to threaten First Amendment guarantees of freedom of speech and expression. . . . The filmmakers are men and women of integrity and artistic vision, and we support their work unequivocally. They are dedicated to the rights of all people and to a life free of persecution, harassment and discrimination. We ask we be accorded the same privilege."[4]

As the film's March 20, 1992 premiere approached, rumors began spreading about plans to disrupt screenings around the country. Protesters supposedly planned to use airhorns to drown out the soundtrack or threatened to release hundreds of moths inside theaters in hopes they would fly toward the light from the projector and block out the film. One group, calling itself "Catherine Did It," revealed the killer's identity in hopes of discouraging attendance. Beyond that, there were rumors about planned demonstrations at the Oscar presentations later in the month, where it was feared protesters might even try to "out" some of the celebrities on national television.

Most of the tactics used against *Basic Instinct* were nothing new. Threats of boycotts, demonstrations, and public embarrassment had dogged the movies for years. But an appreciation of historical perspective wasn't going to help a $40-million-plus film turn a profit if the protests scared audiences away. ✂

change the focus of American media, were not well received by the Hollywood establishment. The American Civil Liberties Union and various media writers accused him of calling for a return to censorship. Critic Michael Medved spoke up in his defense, stating that all Cardinal Mahony wanted was what "an overwhelming majority of Americans"[5] wanted, a change in the values put forth by films and television. But the terms of debate had already been set by more sweeping condemnations of Hollywood, and there seemed to be no middle ground between filmmakers' demands for artistic freedom and the right's demands for a return to decency.

Either way, with Cardinal Mahony's statements rousing controversy, the timing was far from the best for a film like *Basic Instinct*. "'Cardinal Mahony was saying that Hollywood was polluting the world,' one source close to the film said. 'The last thing the ratings board wanted to see was this movie. They just didn't want to deal with it.'"[6]

The ratings controversy over *Basic Instinct* was only the latest in a series of battles involved in getting the film to the screen. *Basic Instinct* first made headlines in 1990, when Joe Eszterhas, the writer of such hits as *Flashdance* and *Jagged Edge*, sold his script to Carolco in a nine-studio bidding war that brought him a record $3 million. Carolco then brought in Michael Douglas to star and Paul Verhoeven to direct, a package with strong box-office potential but a hefty price tag.

Almost from the start, Verhoeven clashed with Eszterhas and producer Irwin Winkler, a frequent Eszterhas collaborator. Where Eszterhas had treated the love scenes only suggestively, indicating that they should be filmed largely in the dark, Verhoeven wanted to bring the characters' sex lives out into the open. "I told him that you have two pages of love-making, we can't shoot it all in the dark," said Verhoeven. "We have to light it so the audience can see something, otherwise it gets too boring."[7] This and Verhoeven's desire to add a lesbian love scene to the film were more than Eszterhas and Winkler would agree to. The producer-writer team tried unsuccessfully to buy back the script, then left the project, with some sources saying they quit and others suggesting they were fired.

Verhoeven was under pressure from Douglas, who thought Nick, the film's police detective hero, was too passive, too much Catherine's tool. So Gary Goldman, who had done a successful rewrite of *Total Recall*, was brought in to work on the script. After three tries, however, Verhoeven decided that he couldn't improve on Eszterhas's work and staged a public reconciliation with the writer. He also went through the script with Douglas line by line, to show the actor how Verhoeven planned to give Nick more control of the action.

During location shooting in San Francisco, the uneasy relationships fell apart again.

Along with rumors about Douglas's and Stone's failure to hit it off on the set and stories about battles between the director and his leading lady, the film was plagued with protests from the local gay community, which brought about another, even more bitter split between Eszterhas and the production.

By the time Verhoeven delivered his director's cut for review by CARA, he'd already been through more problems than any film artist would want to face on a dozen pictures. Now he had another fight on his hands, a fight to preserve his personal vision of what *Basic Instinct* could be. This new battle came at the end of a year's work on the film, but its roots reached back much further. In truth, Paul Verhoeven's problems started seventy years earlier, at a wild party in San Francisco.

"Stop These Fiends
of Decadence!"

Chapter Two

All Roscoe Conkling Arbuckle wanted to do over Labor Day weekend in 1921 was have some fun. He'd just signed a $3 million contract with Paramount that marked a new high in his rise to become one of Hollywood's top stars, and he wanted to celebrate with a bunch of his drinking buddies—including future director Lowell Sherman—and some pretty girls.

Arbuckle was only twenty-one in 1908 when he began working as a film extra and minor comic at the Selig Polyscope Company. Although he weighed more than 250 pounds, Fatty Arbuckle, as he came to be called, was amazingly graceful, an attribute that made him one of the screen's greatest slapstick players. By 1913 he'd moved to Mack Sennett's Keystone Company, where he became a star in a series of popular shorts teaming him with Mabel Normand. He left Sennett in 1917 to establish his own production unit at Paramount. There he worked with the young Buster Keaton and became an even bigger box-office attraction. By 1921 he was ranked second only to Charlie Chaplin in both popularity and critical acclaim.

On September 3, 1921, Arbuckle led a caravan of friends up the coast to San Francisco for a lavish party that filled three adjoining suites at the Hotel St. Francis. Among the beautiful women along for the fun was Virginia Rappe, a starlet with a questionable reputation. On Labor Day, September 5, she was discovered in one of the bedrooms at the St. Francis, nearly unconscious and with her clothes torn. Five days later, she died of peritonitis brought on by a ruptured bladder.

This orgy scene from Erich Von Stroheim's The Merry Widow *(1925) is typical of the decadent excesses on-screen that, coupled with wild off-screen living, made Hollywood a frequent target for moralists and would-be censors.*

According to Bambina Maude Delmont, the sometime actress who'd brought Virginia on the trip, Rappe had been fine until Arbuckle pulled her into one of the bedrooms and locked the door. Suddenly there was a piercing shriek followed by Virginia's moans. When Arbuckle opened the door, Delmont discovered the now-ailing girl moaning, "I'm dying, I'm dying. . . . He hurt me." Later, at the hospital, Rappe told a nurse, "Fatty Arbuckle did this to me. Please see that he doesn't get away with it!"[1]

What had Fatty done to Virginia Rappe in that locked hotel room? Some said that he'd staged a lover's leap onto her prone body, thus rupturing her bladder. Others insisted he'd assaulted the girl in more perverse ways. The newspapers, particularly those owned by publishing tycoon William Randolph Hearst, trumpeted the story almost daily, headlining each new speculation. There was talk of trying Arbuckle for rape and murder, but manslaughter was the only charge on which the San Francisco district attorney could build a case.

Even that failed to hold up in court. The prosecution didn't dare call on Fatty's chief accuser for fear that Delmont's checkered past would discredit anything she might say. Few of the other guests had been sober enough to recall many details. In addition, Rappe's medical history had included internal problems that led to screaming fits and the tearing of her clothing. Two juries failed to return a verdict. A third not only acquitted Arbuckle but issued a statement of sympathy for the beleaguered star: "Acquittal is not enough for Roscoe Arbuckle. We feel a grave injustice has been done him, and there was not the slightest proof to connect him in any way with the commission of any crime."[2]

Neither the jury's statement nor all the work of Paramount's publicity department could undo the damage to Fatty's image. Between trials, the studio released his Christmas films. They had no trouble attracting audiences, but protests from religious and civic leaders led to the films' withdrawal. To make matters worse, reformers used the case to renew their attacks on Hollywood in general, calling for the dismissal of all morally suspect film stars and the creation of a national censorship office.

The Fatty Arbuckle case, however, was only the latest in a string of scandals, which started with Mary Pickford's move to Minden, Nevada, to obtain a quickie divorce from Owen Moore in 1920. When word leaked out, Pickford claimed that she was considering a quieter life in Nevada, but as soon as the divorce became final she was back in Hollywood. A month later she married another recent divorcé, Douglas Fairbanks. Pickford shared headlines with Arbuckle when the attorney general of Nevada tried to have her divorce decree overturned, which would have made America's Sweetheart a bigamist.

Scandal stayed in the family when Pickford's sister-in-law, Olive Thomas, committed suicide in Paris on September 10, 1920. Olive's fresh-faced beauty had made her a Ziegfeld Follies star and an instant hit in Hollywood. When she married the equally wholesome Jack Pickford, the press dubbed them "the Ideal Couple." They didn't seem all that ideal, however, after investigators linked her to a notorious drug dealer operating in Hollywood.

Thomas was only one of the hundreds of young women who fell prey to sin and degradation in Hollywood. An odyssey had started a few years before, in 1915, when young people began moving west to fulfill their dreams of film stardom. Men made the trek as well, but the young women, whose new mobility marked a decided break from the post-Victorian norm, made the headlines. Many of these innocents fell into the hands of crooked talent agents or simply fell on hard times. Competition for jobs was fierce, leading some to turn to the streets to pay the rent. These unfortunate women joined the already swelling ranks of Los Angeles prostitutes, drawn to the city by the oil and real-estate booms as well as the growth of the movies. Even those with no dreams of stardom would sign on at talent agencies so they could list "actress" as their profession in case they got busted. Each time the police hauled in a bunch of these "actresses," the story inspired horrified headlines throughout small-town America.

Arbuckle himself added to the wave of scandal. In 1917 he'd celebrated his first contract with Paramount by throwing a wild party in Boston. The party was raided, but Paramount executives paid the district attorney and mayor close to $100,000 to cover up the incident. News of the cover-up broke four years later and almost ended the DA's career.

Those were just the off-screen shenanigans. On-screen, the movies managed to promote morality while exploiting any possible violation of American standards. Cecil B. DeMille was a master at this, directing a cycle of chic comedy-romances about divorce with titles like *Don't Change Your Husband* and *Why Change Your Wife?* His films flirted coyly with adultery, made Gloria Swanson a star, and inspired hordes of imitations. A cycle of venereal-disease films came out during and just after World War I, but they came to a halt under pressure from the Catholic Church. Prior to that, there had been a spate of films about prostitution, starting with *Traffic in Souls* in 1913. Equally horrifying to the moralists were the nude and near-nude scenes that popped up in everything from D. W. Griffith's *Intolerance* to DeMille's *Male and Female*.

Crime and violence were also a problem. Early films featuring actual executions were decried as morbid influences on the young. Later, producers exploited headline-grabbing murders with fictionalized versions, often starring the cases' real-life participants. Evelyn

Many historians place the official birth of the movies in 1894, the year the first Kinetescope parlor opened on Broadway. If that's the case, then film censorship actually precedes the medium's birth.

In 1893, Thomas Edison prepared a special Kinetoscope preview for the Chicago World's Fair. Among the moving pictures he created for these early peep-show boxes was one featuring a noted turn-of-the-century exotic dancer named Fatima. Her gyrations were too much for some, however, so Edison prepared a censored version in which white cross-hatchings were etched across the image. In 1896, an Atlantic City minister was struck by the long lines waiting to get into a penny arcade on the boardwalk. When he learned that the gentlemen were all waiting for the same picture, *Dolorita's Passion Dance,* he shared his disapproval with the authorities and had the picture banned.

Projected film elicited equally strong reactions. Two months after Edison premiered his Vitascope system on Broadway in 1896, technicians at his studios filmed the highlight of the current Broadway hit *The Widow Jones.* The scene, officially called *The May Irwin-John C. Rice Kiss,* had been merely titillating on stage. On film, it created a furor. In the words of one critic: "Such things demand police interference. Our cities from time to time have spasms of morality, when they arrest people for displaying lithographs of ballet-girls; yet they permit, night after night, a performance which is infinitely more degrading. . . . While we tolerate such things, what avails all the talk of American Puritanism and the filthiness of imported English and French stage shows?"[3]

Such complaints had little effect on the first great audience of movie lovers, the working class. As projectors became available, shopkeepers in poorer neighborhoods discovered that they could make a nice profit by converting a backroom or the entire establishment into a nickelodeon. Before long, families could spend an entire day going from theater to theater, often without leaving a single city block. By 1910 twenty-six million people attended the movies every week.

As word of the movies' popularity spread, the reformers, a powerful political force at the time, started looking into the situation. They were shocked at the hot, barely ventilated theaters in which the poor spent their hard-earned leisure time, appalled at the number of children who passed their days at the movies, and outraged at the content of early films.

Broad comedy, often with a hint of the risqué, did very well. So did action films, particularly those with a focus on crime. This added to the reformers' complaints. Along with being shocked at titillating displays of leggy chorus girls and artists' models, they feared that the popularity of crime films would inspire imitation. When a young boy was killed in 1912 attempting a train robbery in Pennsylvania, the *Philadelphia Record* claimed he'd been inspired by a screening of *The Great Train Robbery* in Scranton, even though it hadn't been showing there at the time.

The reformers got their first toehold in Chicago. By 1907, there were 116 nickelodeons in the city, serving an estimated hundred thousand customers a day. The *Chicago Tribune* attacked these theaters as "ministering to the lowest passions of childhood"[4] and cited such objectionable titles as *Cupid's Barometer, Child Robbers,* and *Beware, My Husband Comes.* In response, the Chicago City Council gave censorship power to the chief of police in 1907. Two years later, the law was contested in the first legal battle over film censorship in U.S. history. In *Block* v. *Chicago,* two hundred theater owners sued the city over the ban of two early westerns, *The James Boys in Illinois* and *Night Riders,* claiming that their constitutional rights had been violated. As would happen in most cases during the first half-century of American film, the courts sided with the censors.

The other major censorship battle was fought in New York. In 1907, the Children's Society had a theater manager arrested for showing children *The Great Thaw Trial,* a film version of the notorious Harry K. Thaw–Stanford White–Evelyn Nesbit murder case. A month later, the police commissioner filed a report with Mayor George B. McClellan suggesting that all arcades and nickelodeons be closed. It took the mayor a year and a half to get around to it, but on December 23, 1908, he ordered the theaters closed at midnight on Christmas Eve. This prompted the theater owners to get together, in their first truly cooperative effort, to fight the decree. When they won an injunction, the mayor used blue laws to order that only educational programs could be shown on Sundays. So the theaters hired lecturers to stand up during films and announce "These are railroad tracks," "More railroad tracks," and "We are now passing a mountain."[5]

Finally, Charles Sprague Smith of the People's Institute suggested a solution. In cooperation with the film producers, the institute created the National Board of Censorship of Motion Pictures to review films and prepare lists of those recommended to parents and educators. The board would be supported by the film industry, which would pay a fee per foot of film reviewed, and films passed by the board would include a notification to that extent in their titles.

On March 26, 1909, the National Board of Censorship met for the first time to screen five hours of film. Out of eighteen thousand feet submitted, they cut four hundred. The only film they refused to pass was *Every Lass a Queen;* the story of a sailor with a girl in every port was banned for being "inartistic." At first the board was highly praised, and its influence grew. Its reports were widely circulated, and passage by the board was ruled a prerequisite for films exhibited in Chattanooga, St. Louis, and the state of Florida. Once the initial threat had passed, however, it became more and more difficult to enforce the board's decisions. Some filmmakers refused to make cuts. Others would add the board's seal of approval to films that had never even been screened for them. The board itself seemed more interested in singling out good films than in condemning bad ones. Finally, the group abandoned all pretense of censorship and changed its name in 1916. The new National Board of Review took as its slogan "Selection—not censorship—the Solution,"[6] but it lost many members and much of its credibility in the process. ✂

Nesbit scored a hit with *Redemption* (1917), a film filled with references to her off-screen involvements with Harry K. Thaw and Stanford White. Even Hollywood objected when acquitted murderess Clara Harmon played herself in *Fate* (1921): The American Society of Cinematographers forbade its members to work on the film and expelled André Barlatier when he defied the ban.

Of course, not all of these films were mere exploitation, and even the more exploitative ones may have served some social function. Several of the VD films were produced by the U.S. government to educate GIs going off to World War I. For all its melodramatic excess, *Traffic in Souls* dealt with a very real social problem—immigrant girls were being virtually kidnapped from the docks of New York and forced to work as

Speech or Commerce?

Despite opposition within the film industry, local censorship spread after 1910. Pennsylvania created the first state censorship board in 1911, followed two years later by Ohio and Kansas. Not only did the state and local boards ban and cut films with little regard for commerce or consistency, but they made distributors pay for the privilege of having their product damaged. Finally, the issue came up before the U.S. Supreme Court.

The Mutual Film Company did not want to pay screening fees to the Ohio Board and sued to have the censorship law overturned as a violation of the First Amendment and the Ohio Constitution. In 1915, the case reached the U.S. Supreme Court, whose unanimous decision to uphold the state law would influence film censorship in America for almost four decades.

There was no question of First Amendment rights. At the time, the Bill of Rights was held to apply solely to federal legislation. Dealing with the Ohio constitution, the Court refused to extend free-speech status to film: "The exhibition of motion pictures is a business pure and simple, originated and conducted for profit . . . not to be regarded, nor intended to be regarded by the Ohio Constitution, we think as part of the press of the country or as organs of public opinion. They are mere representations of events, of ideas and sentiments published or known; vivid, useful, and entertaining, no doubt, but . . . capable of evil, having power for it, the greater because of their attractiveness and manner of exhibition.⁷"

The Court's denial of protected speech status to film rested on three suppositions. First, they saw movies as strictly an entertainment medium rather than a vehicle for ideas. This is understandable given the nature of film at the time, even though the decision was issued only four days after the justices saw *The Birth of a Nation*. Second, the Court saw film as a business motivated by profit, an opinion suggesting that the justices only subscribed to newspapers that operated in the red. Finally, the Court, reflecting the opinions of contemporary moralists, feared film had a special

prostitutes. The Immigration Department even showed the film as a warning on boats headed for America.

As protests against "bad" films grew, the studios tried to give the appearance that they were doing something. They created the National Association of the Motion Picture Industry (NAMPI) in 1916 to preserve screen morals and, more importantly, to fight censorship bills and other legal sanctions against the industry. NAMPI put on a good show for a while. In 1921, the organization issued a list of thirteen points that were considered unsuitable for presentation on the screen, including nudity, prostitution, gambling, drunkenness, and any illicit love affair "which tends to make virtue odious and vice attractive."[8] Any member violating these thirteen points would be

capacity for evil, a special power to influence action. As evidence of the latter, the Court pointed to the fact that movies were shown to audiences in which men, women, and children mixed freely. Suspicion of the movies' special power to influence behavior has remained a part of judicial thinking to this day, justifying restrictions on film that have not been applied to the press.

The *Mutual Film* decision ushered in decades of court-sanctioned local censorship. One of the first films banned under its influence was *Birth Control*, a 1917 picture produced by and starring Margaret Sanger in a dramatization of her pioneering work in family planning. She is shown working as a nurse in the ghettos, where she witnesses the devastating effects of poverty, malnutrition, and overpopulation. When one of her patients dies trying to end an unwanted pregnancy, Sanger decides to defy the law and teach working-class women basic birth control methods.

This seeming glorification of Sanger's illegal activities led to a ban in New York City. Citing *Mutual Film* as a precedent, the Court of Appeals upheld the state's right to "censor such productions in order that they may be regulated and controlled in the interest of morality, decency, and public safety and welfare."[9]

Birth Control would not be the last film barred on those grounds. In 1922, Pathé Exchange contested a New York law subjecting newsreels to the state censorship board. Upholding the law, the state court leaned heavily on the medium's capacity to influence viewers: "The picture creates its own atmosphere so vividly, so attractively, that even the child and the illiterate adult may see and learn."[10] Later court decisions extended the *Mutual Film* decision to cover talking pictures. Free expression on screen was not totally stifled—there were too many differences among local censors and too many areas free from censorship for that—but it was considerably limited, even without Will Hays's growing influence on screen content. ✂

expelled from NAMPI—or at least that's what was said. In truth, the studios largely ignored the restrictions and continued with business as usual.

As a result, Hollywood was engaged in a serious battle against government censorship. By the twenties, five states—Ohio, Kansas, Virginia, Maryland, and Pennsylvania —had censorship boards. Well over a hundred cities and towns had censorship laws on the books. The first federal censorship bill was introduced in Congress in 1914. Though the industry had been successful in fighting off passage thus far, the uproar roused by the 1921 Arbuckle case made any lasting victory highly questionable.

To make matters worse, the studios were going through an economic crunch in the early twenties. A series of epidemics had cut into film attendance, as people became reluctant to risk exposure to crowds. As the problem subsided, however, the screen was hit with competition from a new medium—radio. With the decline in box-office sales, the threat from state censors became critical. When New York State set up its own censorship board in 1921, threatening the nation's largest film market, the studio heads knew that they had to do something before it was too late.

So they created a new trade association, the Motion Picture Producers and Distributors of America (MPPDA), and looked for someone to front the organization. Baseball had dealt with some scandals of its own—including the throwing of the 1919 World Series by the Chicago White Sox—by appointing a conservative judge to act as baseball commissioner, or, as the press dubbed him, "baseball czar." Now, the movie industry needed a czar of its own.

The MPPDA members considered Herbert Hoover but decided he was too rich and might be too difficult to control. Then they remembered Will Hays, a prominent Republican who had made a good impression on Hollywood during Warren G. Harding's successful presidential campaign. Hays was Middle America personified. He was a Presbyterian elder from Indiana who also belonged to the Masons, the Knights of Pythias, the Kiwanians, the Rotarians, the Moose, and the Elks. He had risen through the ranks of the state's Republican Party, then made the leap to chairman of the Republican National Committee. Not only had Hays helped push through Harding's nomination at the political convention for which the phrase "smoke-filled rooms" was coined, but he had enlisted Hollywood to help win the election.

Hays had noted the beneficial influence of Thomas Ince's pacifist epic *Civilization* on Woodrow Wilson's reelection campaign in 1916. Why couldn't the screen do the same for a Republican? Charles C. Pettijohn, a childhood friend who was a lawyer working for Exhibitors Mutual, provided an entree to the studio heads, who helped Hays generate extensive newsreel coverage of Harding's campaign. Hays made such a good impression on Hollywood that William Fox even offered him an executive position.

Instead, Hays chose a spot on Harding's cabinet as postmaster general. Hays's new job gave him a chance to demonstrate his organizational skills by putting the chaotic postal service in order. In addition, he got his first experience as a censor, supervising enforcement of the Comstock Act, which barred the shipment of indecent materials through the mails.

On December 8, 1921, Lewis J. Selznick and Saul Rogers offered Hays the MPPDA presidency for $100,000 a year (some sources say $150,000; either figure would make him one of the highest-paid men in the U.S.). Over the Christmas holiday he considered the deal. What made up his mind—in a story that exemplifies the man's small-town appeal—was waking up Christmas morning to the sound of his son and nephews arguing over who would get to be western star William S. Hart when they played cowboys. He would later write in his memoirs: "I realized on that Christmas morning that motion pictures had become as strong an influence on our children and on countless adults, too, as the daily press. The juvenile argument which I had overheard confirmed my feeling and my fears that the great motion picture industry might as easily become a corrupting as a beneficial influence on our future generations."[11]

There may have been another reason for Hays's decision to move to Hollywood. The Harding administration has been called one of the most corrupt in U.S. history. Hays may not have transgressed on the same level as some other cabinet members, but he had accepted a $75,000 gift and a $185,000 loan from oilman Harry Sinclair to help push through Harding's nomination. When this was revealed by a Senate investigation in 1928, the former postmaster general narrowly escaped prosecution. By jumping ship for Hollywood when he did, Hays may have been making a propitious getaway.

In press conferences, Hays described his new role as the conscience of the industry, noting that he would work both to encourage self-regulation in Hollywood and to increase public support of quality films. The press gave him a few titles of their own, including "Family Doctor of the Movies," "Doctor of Celluloid," and "the Little White Father of the Cinema."[12] But the best description was one offered by industrialist George Eastman, who called Hays "the Cat's Whiskers."[13]

Hays's first major challenge came on February 2, 1922, when film director William Desmond Taylor was found murdered in his Hollywood bungalow, creating another major Hollywood scandal. Police found a secret collection of pornographic photos, some featuring the fifty-year-old director with a few of Hollywood's better-known leading ladies. In the toe of a boot were found love letters from comic queen Mabel Normand. Between the pages of a book was found a note traced to Mary Miles Minter,

W hen D. W. Griffith created *The Birth of a Nation* in 1915, his goal was to bring the American movie to the same level of sophistication and respectability that had been achieved by the new feature films being imported from Europe. He did that and more, creating what most critics consider the single most important film in American movie history. With his choice of subject matter, he also created the screen's first major censorship battle.

Griffith based his American epic on *The Clansman*, a novel and play by the Reverend Thomas Dixon. To Griffith's genteel, unconscious racism—the feeling that only he and other white southerners truly understood "the Negro problem"—was added Dixon's more virulent bigotry. Dixon hoped to create a polemic against the move toward Negro equality and the repeal of laws forbidding intermarriage, and Griffith, however unthinkingly, gave him exactly that.

The Birth of a Nation is one of the most maddening films in history. Coupled with Griffith's still impressive presentation of epic scenes of battle and devastation, his effective use of story-telling, and the often thrilling editing, particularly during the gathering of the Ku Klux Klan, are some of the most virulently racist messages ever included in a major American film. The depredations wrought on the South during Reconstruction are blamed on the fictional Senator Austin Stoneman (based on real-life Thaddeus Stevens) acting under the influence of his vengeful mulatto mistress. The mulatto politician whom Stoneman brings to power in the South lusts after the senator's daughter (Lillian Gish) and tries to force her into marriage.

The fate of white southerners is personified in the Cameron family, which loses two sons in the war, then suffers insults from its former slaves. When a black militiaman tries to rape daughter Elsie (Mae Marsh), she jumps to her death. This leads the remaining son, Benjamin (Henry B. Walthall), to found a local Klan chapter to avenge her death and punish the South's despoilers. As an added insult, all of the major black roles in the film, including the senator's mistress, the politician, and the two freed slaves who stay faithful to the Camerons, are played by white actors in blackface.

The film got an early boost when Dixon arranged a private screening for President Woodrow Wilson, who issued his famous statement comparing it to "writing history with lightning."[14] Dixon also set up screenings for Congress and the Supreme Court (Chief Justice Edward Douglass White had been a Klan member himself).

Their praise was balanced by complaints from social reformers. Jane Addams called it a "pernicious caricature of the Negro race . . . unjust and untrue,"[15] while Oswald Garrison Villard, grandson of the noted abolitionist, decried it as "a deliberate attempt to humiliate ten million American citizens and portray them as nothing but beasts."[16]

The recently formed National Association for the Advancement of Colored People led the battle, pressuring the National Board of Censorship (see "Film Censorship Before Will Hays," p. 24) to deny approval to the film. In an effort to appease the NAACP, Griffith cut two scenes—a love scene between Stoneman and his mistress and one fight—but it simply wasn't enough. In New York, Mayor John Mitchell assured protesters that more scenes had been cut. They weren't, but Dixon used the enthusiastic response to his Washington screenings to convince theater owners to open the film.

There were more protests in Boston. In a public meeting there, Griffith offered ten thousand dollars to anyone who could find a single historical inaccuracy in the film, but apparently he wasn't listening when NAACP President Moorfield Storey asked "when a mulatto lieutenant-governor of any southern state had tied up, gagged and locked in a room a young white woman in an attempt to force her marriage to him."[17] After the meeting, Storey refused to shake Griffith's hand.

A week after the Boston meetings, pioneering black publisher William Monroe Trotter led a march on the Tremont Theatre, where two hundred protesters demanded tickets to the film. A fight broke out with the Pinkerton security guards who had been hired to protect the theater, and Trotter and ten other blacks were arrested. Four days later, two thousand blacks marched on the state house.

Protests and censorship action followed *The Birth of a Nation* around the country. Five hundred blacks marched on Philadelphia's Forest Theatre. Chicago's mayor delayed the film's opening until the state legislature could pass a ban on racially inflammatory materials that was clearly aimed at *The Birth of a Nation*. Other bans were enforced in Minneapolis, Denver, Pittsburgh, St. Louis, and the state of Ohio.

Despite the bans and protests, or maybe because of them, *The Birth of a Nation* was the first great hit of the silent screen. Estimates place its grosses at $10 million, which, adjusted for inflation, would be well over $100 million today. It would hold its place as the screen's biggest hit until Walt Disney released *Snow White and the Seven Dwarfs* in 1938.

The controversy was one of the first large-scale protests against U.S. racism and helped established the NAACP as a major national organization. It also had a lasting effect on Griffith, who issued pamphlets decrying censorship, then sank most of his earnings into a cinematic reply to the critics, *Intolerance*. The 1916 epic also has been hailed as one of the greatest films of all time, but its box-office failure plunged Griffith into debt for years.

The Birth of a Nation continued to face censorship battles when reissued in 1924, 1931, and 1938. In later years, local censors frequently banned the film to prevent the Ku Klux Klan from using it as a recruiting tool. Following the decline of local censorship, a Klan screening in 1978 triggered a riot in Oxnard, California. Even eight decades later, the battle over *The Birth of a Nation* continues. When the film was added to the National Film Registry in 1993, black leaders complained anew about its racist content. ✄

a twenty-two-year-old actress Paramount was grooming to be a threat to Mary Pickford. The police also uncovered connections between Taylor and the Los Angeles underground's gay bars and dope dens. One neighbor had seen Normand leave the house late on the night of the murder. Ten minutes later, there were gunshots and another figure, apparently a man, but one who walked like a woman, fled the scene. Once again the rumors flew. Some said Taylor had been involved in a three-way affair with Normand, Minter, and Minter's mother, Charlotte Shelby, and one of them had shot him. Or the possessive Mrs. Shelby had shot him to keep him from running off with her daughter. Or Taylor was running drugs and had been shot by a rival dealer. Or Taylor was trying to end the drug traffic in Hollywood, and the underworld had gotten rid of him.

The case was never solved. When the furor died down, however, Minter was finished on screen forever. Normand, too, was out of favor for a while, particularly when word of her cocaine habit got out.

The one winner in all of this was Hays. Although it was too late to save the principals

Over There: The Birth of Film Censorship in England

As the United States developed its own forms of film censorship, other governments were dealing with the issue as well. Whether the goal was to weed out political subversion or to curb indecency, nations around the globe developed their own approaches to regulating film content. None had more impact on the U.S. film industry than the development of censorship in Great Britain.

Initially, Parliament simply wanted to make sure theaters were safe from fires. The Cinematograph Act of 1910 was intended to give local authorities the right to make cinemas adhere to fire laws, but it was so loosely worded it actually opened the doors to local censorship as well. The censor boards that sprang up around England rarely agreed on decency standards. By 1912 the situation had become so chaotic that members of the industry created the British Board of Film Censors (BBFC), preceding Hollywood's first attempts at self-regulation by a decade.

The BBFC used a rudimentary rating system. Films that weren't banned outright were graded either U, for universal exhibition, or A, not recommended for children. In addition, the censors evaluated scripts prior to shooting and advised producers on probable ratings.

With no control over local boards, however, the BBFC did little at first to relieve the chaos. Local censors could ban or cut films approved by the industry or allow showings of banned pictures. Occasionally, the producer of a questionable film would obtain local clearances first to pressure the BBFC into passing his picture. Gradually, however, the local boards came around,

in the case, he could still save Hollywood. Hays supervised all public relations efforts related to the case, keeping strict control over every piece of information that went out. From now on, Hollywood would be just another good, clean, all-American small town. As a result, the studios' press departments became experts at keeping stories out of the papers—at least if the star was big enough to warrant such protection.

The Taylor case wasn't the only challenge facing Hays in his new job. In his first days he was confronted with a ten-point program for improving industry relations:

> *Internal Disorders*, such as bad trade practices and scandals
> *Censorship* and other threatened restrictions
> *Mexican Diplomatic Crisis* over American films
> Building a more perfect *union* in the industry, and one that would
>   be self-governing
> Improving the *Quality* of pictures quickly
> Securing the *Practical Co-operation of Educators*
> Helping *Distributors* to overcome fraud and loss

and by 1921 the London County Council had made passage by the BBFC a prerequisite for playing within the city.

Unlike the MPPDA, the BBFC never developed a written code stating what could and could not be done on-screen. The traditions they developed over the years were consistent enough, however, to allow producers to anticipate their demands. Operating-room scenes were forbidden, so American producers made protection shots set in hospital corridors to prevent the loss of essential dialogue. British sensibilities also precluded the presentation of religious rituals of any kind, so church weddings were routinely cut from American films.

The most pervasive effect the BBFC had on Hollywood filmmaking was in the depiction of marital bliss. For some reason, the British censors did not want people to know that married couples often slept in the same bed. The problem first surfaced with the 1938 comedy *The Mad Miss Manton*, in which a caretaker and his wife are shown waking up in a double bed. When the BBFC objected, RKO Studios had to darken the scene so viewers could barely discern the sleeping arrangements.

After that, American producers were routinely advised to put married couples in twin beds, thus giving rise to the legend that the MPPDA forbade double beds. Columbia Pictures tried to get around the BBFC in 1948 by creating the "Hollywood bed"—twin beds pushed together and sharing the same headboard—for *Her Husband's Affairs,* but the BBFC wasn't buying. The studio had to reshoot the scenes with properly British beds at the added cost of $30,000. ✂

Helping *Exhibitors* adjust contract problems

Improving the quality of *Advertising*.[18]

Hays solved trade problems with Mexico by getting the MPPDA to pass a resolution forbidding negative portrayals of the country and its people. He created standardized distribution and exhibition contracts (later declared restraint of trade by the Supreme Court), and hired the Burns Detective Agency to track down lost prints and discourage film piracy. In response to complaints about the abuse of talent, he launched studies that led to the creation of studio schools for juvenile performers and the Central Casting Corporation, which had exclusive control of extra casting and put many a crooked agent out of business. In 1925 the MPPDA started a title registry, initially to prevent films with similar titles from confusing audiences but also to get rid of what Hays called the "sex title." When Hollywood needed financial credit, Hays used his political pull and powers of persuasion to get the East Coast banks to back the studios.

The biggest triumph of Hays's early years was the defeat of Massachusetts's proposed censorship bill. The bill already had passed the state legislature but needed to go through a public ballot in November 1922. Hays hired spokesmen to visit small-town papers and argue Hollywood's case. He also enlisted exhibitors, who flashed slides between movies urging patrons to "vote NO on the amendments."[19] As a result, the bill was defeated by a three-to-one margin.

Hays also turned his eye to Hollywood's off-screen behavior, with dramatic and sometimes tragic results. Fatty Arbuckle was banned from the screen for a year, after which Hays created a new scandal by allowing him to work behind the camera. Arbuckle directed and wrote gags under the name William B. Goodrich, "Will B. Good," until his death in 1933.

To cut down on stories of young women led astray by Hollywood, Hays launched a press campaign to discourage people from joining the Hollywood odyssey. To deal with stars' behavior, he urged the studios to add morals clauses to their contracts. To fore- stall future scandals, he issued what Hollywood unofficially called "the Doom Book," a list of 117 actors deemed unfit for the movies because of their involvement in drugs, illicit sex, or other transgressions. According to Gloria Swanson, fear of the Doom Book led her to get a clandestine abortion and even forced her to settle a messy divorce trial at her own expense rather than allow soon-to-be-ex-husband Herbert Somborn to smear her in court.

Fear of the Doom Book also led Paramount, already ravaged by scandal, to rush star Wallace Reid into a drug treatment program that may have cost him his life. Reid had never really wanted to be a star. He had come to Hollywood with his father, playwright

James Hallek Reid, hoping to become a cameraman. One look at the tall, handsome young man, however, and it was the front of the camera for him, often in various states of undress.

Reid was beginning to add writing and directing credits to his resumé when his performance as the battling blacksmith in *The Birth of a Nation* brought him a contract at Paramount, where he became the epitome of dashing youth, the small-town boy made good. Sometime around 1919, he began taking morphine—according to the official story, he got hooked after he was injured in a train accident that left him with chronic back pain. Just as likely is the possibility that, like many a Hollywood actor, he started taking drugs to keep up his energy in the face of the killing production schedules of the day. When he collapsed on the set of *Thirty Days* in 1922, studio executives, fearing that he would be blacklisted, ordered him to kick the habit.

Reid's treatment, though successful, left him with a seriously damaged immune system. A case of the flu turned into pneumonia, and he died on January 18, 1923. Initially, the press was willing to let the matter drop, but his wife, actress Dorothy Davenport, wasn't. With Hays at her side she announced that she would produce and star in a film designed to tell America about the evils of drug addiction. Hays even waived the MPPDA's recent ban on drug stories (see next chapter) so that she could make it.

The result was *Human Wreckage*, released in 1923, and it was one of the biggest hits of the year. Davenport (billed as "Mrs. Wallace Reid") starred as a lawyer's wife who witnesses drug use first in the slums (where low-income mother Bessie Love spikes her baby's formula to keep it from crying, as some mothers did at the time). Then she discovers that her husband has turned to morphine to help him deal with a heavy case load. What Mrs. Reid could not do in real life her character accomplishes on screen— she saves her husband for a happy ending.

At least one person threatened by the Doom Book found a happy ending of her own. When investigators uncovered her drug habit, comedienne and serial queen Juanita Hansen was blacklisted, but she bounced back. Not only did Hansen get herself off drugs, but she created the Juanita Hansen Foundation "to help the thousands of narcotic addicts now living in darkness—alone, ashamed, abandoned, bewildered."[20]

Juanita Hansen's story would have made a great movie—if anyone in Hollywood could have made it. By the time she launched her foundation, however, Hays had reinstated his ban on drug stories. That was only one of the several subjects he tried to keep off the screen during the early years of Hollywood's self-censorship.

"No Law but Her Own Desire"

Chapter Three

From a title card for Erich Von Stroheim's *Queen Kelly* (1928), the above line describes the decadent Queen Regina (Seena Owen), who parades about the palace in the nude and takes a horsewhip to leading lady Gloria Swanson. Considering the director's legendary excesses, the title could easily have been autobiographical. He was far from the only filmmaker of the era, however, who lived by no law but his own desire, as Will Hays would discover when he tried to introduce the concept of self-regulation to Hollywood.

Initially, Hays and the studios belonging to the MPPDA reached a gentlemen's agreement on thirteen elements to be avoided on screen. These were similar to NAMPI's thirteen points and pertained to films that:

1. dealt with sex in an improper manner;
2. were based on white slavery;
3. made vice attractive;
4. exhibited nakedness;
5. had prolonged passionate love scenes;
6. were predominantly concerned with the underworld;
7. made gambling and drunkenness attractive;
8. might instruct the weak in methods of committing crime;
9. ridiculed public officials;
10. offended religious beliefs;

Wearing more clothing than usual, the wicked Queen Regina (Seena Owen) drives out Patricia Kelly (Gloria Swanson) in Queen Kelly *(1928). Producer Joseph P. Kennedy abandoned the film in part because he feared its sex-charged story would rouse protests from the Catholic Church.*

11. emphasized violence;

12. portrayed vulgar postures and gestures; and

13. used salacious subtitles or advertising.[1]

At least that was the idea. In reality, the studios did little to change on-screen content. Drug stories and real-life murder cases were abandoned; but as for the rest of the issues, Hollywood simply put on a pious face.

With his gentlemen's agreement in place, if not necessarily in action, Hays tackled the problem of offensive pictures from the other end, by dealing with the medium's critics. During his first year in office, he met in New York with the leaders of various volunteer groups that had been promoting quality films and criticizing the screen's excesses. Out of this meeting emerged the Executive Committee of Twenty, a group of civic leaders supervised by Colonel Jason S. Joy, whom Hays met when Joy worked in the War Department's public relations office. The Executive Committee of Twenty was such a success that in 1925 Hays made it a part of the MPPDA's corporate structure, changing its name to the Public Relations Committee.

Through his contacts with civic groups, Hays set up advance screenings in many of the larger cities in order to promote better films. He also created an open-door policy, making the MPPDA a sounding board for anyone with a complaint about the movies. Eventually, some of the leading groups even sent representatives to Hollywood to advise Hays on films, scripts, and issues as they came up.

Hays's contacts with civic organizations gave him an idea for carrying self-regulation further. In 1923, Jesse Lasky asked Hays to assess public reaction to a proposed film version of Homer Croy's controversial best-seller *West of the Water Tower*. The book had created an uproar with its scathing look at small-town scandals, including illegitimacy and a drunken clergyman. Hays brought back a negative report. His contacts felt that even a sanitized adaptation would promote sales of the objectionable book. When Lasky made the film anyway, the National Council of Parents and Teachers severed all ties with the MPPDA. But it got Hays thinking. In his opinion, the problem lay not in Hollywood itself but in the more sophisticated worlds of publishing and the theater: "During the 1920s the licentious mood of current books and stage plays was another important factor. . . . Our industry has always been dependent on published works for much of its raw material, and if it became less 'raw'—in a salacious sense—when presented in our medium we decided that our responsibility had been fulfilled. Incidentally, it has often seemed to me that a little self-regulation would do no harm in the book industry."[2]

The result was the "Hays Formula," adopted in 1924. Members agreed to submit all materials considered for screen adaptation to MPPDA readers, who would review and advise on censorship issues. This would allow producers to revise stories before filming or to cancel production altogether if a work was deemed too objectionable for the screen. Hays also reserved the right to demand a new title if a property required too many changes or was considered too controversial. The Hays Formula was administered by Colonel Joy through the Public Relations Committee. By 1926, Hays decided to move the committee and Joy to Hollywood so that they would be closer to the film studios.

In the first year of the Hays Formula, sixty-seven properties were rejected. The numbers dropped in later years as studios learned what not to submit (though not necessarily what not to film). By the time the Formula was abandoned in 1930, 125 books, stories, articles, and plays had been kept off the screen, including Theodore Dreiser's classic novel *An American Tragedy* and Ferenc Molnár's *The Guardsman*.

After their initial show of support for the Formula, however, the studios soon tired of this limit on their sovereignty. Before long, production heads started withholding material from the Public Relations Committee; on other occasions they simply ignored its recommendations. When the hit military drama *What Price Glory?* failed to pass the Formula, Fox filmed it anyway, scoring one of the biggest hits of 1926.

As the studios increasingly ignored the Hays Formula, complaints and threats of legislation grew. Realizing that the industry needed a stronger self-regulation system, Hays sent Joy to meet with local censors and learn what they cut most often. In 1927 Hays incorporated Joy's findings in a speech to the MPPDA's West Coast membership. The result was the "Don'ts and Be Carefuls," a list of thirty-six subjects to be avoided or handled with care if the studios wanted to ease censorship problems:

Resolved, that those things which are included in the following list shall not appear in pictures produced by members of this Association, irrespective of the manner in which they are treated:

1. Pointed profanity—by either title or lip—this includes the words "God," "Lord," "Jesus," "Christ" (unless used reverently in connection with proper religious ceremonies), "hell," "damn," "Gawd," and every other profane and vulgar expression, however it may be spelled.
2. Any licentious or suggestive nudity—in fact or in silhouette; and any lecherous or licentious notice thereof by other characters in the picture.
3. The illegal traffic in drugs.
4. Any inference of sex perversion.
5. White slavery.

6. Miscegenation (sex relationships between white and black races).

7. Sex hygiene and venereal diseases.

8. Scenes of actual childbirth—in fact or in silhouette.

9. Children's sex organs.

10. Ridicule of the clergy.

11. Willful offense to any nation, race or creed.

And be it further resolved that special care be exercised in the manner in which the following subjects are treated, to the end that vulgarity and suggestiveness may be eliminated and that good taste be emphasized:

1. The use of the flag.

2. International relations (avoiding picturization in an unfavorable light another country's religion, history, institutions, prominent people, and citizenry).

3. Arson.

4. The use of firearms.

5. Theft, robbery, safecracking, and dynamiting of trains, mines, buildings, etc. (having in mind the effect which a too-detailed description of these may have upon the moron).

6. Brutality and possible gruesomeness.

7. Technique of committing murder by whatever method.

8. Methods of smuggling.

9. Third-degree methods.

10. Actual hangings or electrocutions as legal punishment for crime.

11. Sympathy for criminals.

12. Attitude toward public characters and institutions.

13. Sedition.

14. Apparent cruelty to children and animals.

15. Branding of people or animals.

16. The sale of women, or of a woman selling her virtue.

17. Rape or attempted rape.

18. First-night scenes.

19. Man and woman in bed together.

20. Deliberate seduction of girls.

21. The institution of marriage.

22. Surgical operations.

23. The use of drugs.

24. Titles or scenes having to do with the law enforcement or law-enforcing officers.

25. Excessive or lustful kissing, particularly when one character or the other is a "heavy."[3]

The Public Relations Committee continued to review scripts and applied this new set of restrictions to their administration of the Hays Formula. In addition, the committee reviewed finished films. This increasing emphasis on self-regulation brought a name change as well—in 1927 the committee became the Studio Relations Committee. The overall purpose was to advise studios of material likely to be cut by local censors, and in that area Joy maintained an impressive track record. Scripts that he edited were cut only 1.9 percent by local censors; scripts he did not edit were cut by as much as 6 percent.

For all of its new exactness, however, the system didn't really have any teeth. There was no way to enforce Joy's judgments. Producers unhappy with his cuts could appeal to a rotating panel of three producers that came to be called "the Hollywood Jury." Since producers on the panel knew that they might be making appeals of their own at some time, they tended to side with their own against Joy. Once Joy's cuts were turned down, he had no appeals process. The word of the producers was final.

Films made under the Hays Formula and the Don'ts and Be Carefuls are a paradoxical mix of restraint and license. Producers honored judgments on the hottest issues but often cheated on details. Frequently, a film would depict an hour's worth of sinning, recorded in lavish detail, followed by a few minutes of speedy repentance before the final fade-out. In *Our Dancing Daughters* (1928), *Our Modern Maidens* (1929), and *Our Blushing Brides* (1930), MGM titillated audiences with the amorous adventures of a trio of young women played by Joan Crawford, Anita Page, and Dorothy Sebastian. Despite some hot dancing by Crawford and intimations of premarital sex, the films all end with the girls happily married or paying for their transgressions. In response to these and other films, *Collier's* magazine dubbed the Don'ts and Be Carefuls "Don't forget to stop before you have gone too far" and "If you can't be good, be careful."[4]

Studios also continued to film books and plays that were too hot for the screen, though often with major alterations, some of which worked, and some of which left the finished film making little or no sense. MGM wanted to turn Anthony McGuire's *Twelve Miles Out* into a vehicle for John Gilbert in 1927. The play follows the adventures of a swashbuckling bootlegger who kidnaps a flapper (Joan Crawford) and her boyfriend, then wins the girl's heart with his nobility. Hays wouldn't hear of a story that glorified a criminal who defied Prohibition laws. So the writers changed the ending: After successfully saving Crawford from the unwanted attentions of a less scrupulous bootlegger (Ernest Torrence), Gilbert dies in her arms from wounds received in the battle. According to historian Kevin Brownlow, the ending came out of the blue, but that

One reason Hollywood needed to censor its own product until well into the sixties was the existence of state and local censorship boards. When Will Hays signed on with the MPPDA in 1922, there were six state boards: Kansas, Maryland, New York, Ohio, Pennsylvania, and Virginia. In 1932 Massachusetts slipped into censorship by using a Lord's Day observance statute to regulate films shown on Sundays (which was actually the same as regulating them throughout the week; few exhibitors prepared special bills or prints just for Sunday showings). In addition, Louisiana passed a censorship law in the thirties that was never enforced, and Florida barred all films not passed by the National Board of Review. Colonel Joy estimated that 50 percent of the nation and 60 percent of potential revenues were affected by local censors.

Each board charged a fee per foot of film screened. Some also had a smaller fee for each print distributed within the state. Since each regional exchange distributed films to several states, cuts made for a single state board would usually apply to all of the states within a given region. In addition, some states without their own censorship boards passed laws requiring that films be distributed in the form passed by a neighboring state.

In the early days of local censorship, each of the state boards developed its own special sensibilities. Kansas, which had strong prohibition laws before and after the Volstead Act, routinely cut all drinking scenes. For a while the Maryland board was headed by a druggist, who insisted that all scenes of poisoning be eliminated, even when essential to the plot. The most powerful of the state boards was New York's, which controlled films exhibited in the largest market and import center, New York City. The New York censors' blind spot was government corruption. Even an unsuccessful attempt to bribe a police officer on-screen could not get by them.

Pennsylvania had the most entertaining of the state boards. Pennsylvania's censors usually saw films after they had been cut for New York and then cut them a little more just to show that they could. In 1914, chief censor J. Louis Breitinger banned a film version of Jack London's tale of the evils of drink, *John Barleycorn*. He backed down, however, after the local press revealed his financial connections to the liquor industry.

The Pennsylvania board routinely cut any reference to pregnancy—even the sight of a married woman knitting baby clothes—no matter how important to the plot. Cecil B. DeMille's 1915 *Kindling* was a heartrending study of the plight of the poor. When the heroine learns she is pregnant, she steals from her employer to get money to move her family to a healthier environment out west. Not only was her pregnancy the key factor motivating the crime, but its revelation prompted her employer to drop all charges and finance the trip. The Pennsylvania censors cut all references to it nonetheless, leaving the film essentially nonsensical. When the distributor complained, they responded, "The movies are patronized by thousands of children who believe that babies are brought by the stork, and it would be criminal to undeceive them."[5]

Matching the work of state censors were numerous local boards. Although no census of local censors was ever attempted, their number during Hollywood's golden years has been estimated at between 90 and 150. Few localities had actual prescreening boards. Instead, local laws allowed for censorship action whenever a complaint was filed.

Of the local boards, the oldest and most powerful was Chicago's, which practically controlled film content in the Midwest. The Chicago board was run by two police officers supervising a committee of political appointees, all of them women, who often were referred to inaccurately as the "police widows."

Like most censors, the Chicago board could ban or cut a film for immorality. Chicago also allowed the imposition of an age limit on certain films and, unique among censorship boards, cut or banned racially insulting material. Not too surprisingly, the Chicago censorship board was particularly sensitive to crime pictures, especially those set in the Windy City. Howard Hughes produced an adaptation of the stage play *The Racket* in 1928. The film showed a Chicago police officer (Thomas Meighan) fighting the city's corrupt administration to bring in a notorious gangster (Louis Wolheim) modeled on Al Capone. The mob tried to block production, sending death threats to key players. When that didn't work, it used political influence to have the film banned in Chicago, as well as in Dallas and Portland, Oregon, while New York and Pennsylvania cut it severely.

Equally damning was the work of Lloyd Binford in Memphis, Tennessee. Binford ruled the Memphis censorship board from 1927 into the fifties, using his personal perspective on God and the universe to determine what Memphians could see. He disagreed with Cecil B. DeMille's interpretation of scripture, so *King of Kings* was banned. He found Jean Renoir's 1945 classic *The Southerner* an unflattering picture of the South, so no one else in Memphis got to see it. There was too much shooting for his taste in *Destry Rides Again,* so it was kept out of town, along with dozens of other westerns.

Binford's place in the pantheon of the narrow-minded is guaranteed by his decisions on films with black characters. *Brewster's Millions* was banned in 1945 because the black servant played by Eddie "Rochester" Anderson was too familiar. *Curley* was banned in 1949 because it showed black children visiting a white school and "the South does not permit Negroes in white schools nor recognize social equality among the races even in children." Lena Horne may have been one of the most gifted singers on-screen, but Binford routinely eliminated her musical numbers "because there are plenty of good white singers."[6]

Usually, however, when a film was banned outright, the distributor booked it into the nearest theater outside the censors' jurisdiction. Films banned in Cincinnati played across the Ohio River in Kentucky. If Binford didn't want Memphians to see a picture, they could just drive across the Mississippi to West Memphis, Arkansas—which they generally did in impressive numbers. ✂

didn't discourage Gilbert's devoted fans, who made the film a hit.

The tacked-on tragic ending still didn't satisfy Hays, and the film elicited more than a few protests. To appease Hays, MGM head Louis B. Mayer issued an open letter to the other studios urging them to stick to the rules. This bit of hypocrisy (*Photoplay* publisher James B. Quirk called Mayer "holier than none"[7]) wasn't all that unusual. Many of Hollywood's worst offenders often tried to get themselves off the hook by pointing at others' violations of the Formula.

A year later, Mayer would get into more trouble with Hays when he tried to film Michael Arlen's notorious novel *The Green Hat*. The story had enough censorable elements to guarantee its total rejection under the Hays Formula: Iris March's husband commits suicide on their wedding night because he has syphilis; her brother drinks himself to death because of repressed homosexual desire for Iris's husband; and Iris comes to a bad end herself after bearing an illegitimate child by a former suitor. As if the plot weren't questionable enough, the film had been slated as a vehicle for Greta Garbo, whose early Hollywood career was filled with shady-lady roles.

The first change Hays demanded was the film's title. Not only was the picture renamed *A Woman of Affairs*, but there was to be no reference to *The Green Hat* whatsoever. Instead, the film's ads and credits carried the line "From the story by Michael Arlen." Hays also demanded that the character names be changed. Ironically, that constituted a minor improvement. Garbo's character was renamed Diana, for the goddess of virginity and the hunt, which emphasizes her independence and the fact that, no matter how tarnished her reputation is, she radiates nobility throughout the story.

Then Hays began to sanitize the plot. The suicide was inescapable, but its cause was changed. Venereal disease was out—instead, Garbo's husband (Johnny Mack Brown) kills himself over the revelation that he's an embezzler. The brother's homosexuality is never mentioned. And Garbo's one night of illicit passion with former lover John Gilbert is played in such a way that less aware audience members might think they spent the evening talking. Instead of being hospitalized after the birth of an illegitimate child, Garbo becomes ill from grief over her brother's death and the loss of Gilbert.

The results were mixed. Douglas Fairbanks, Jr. was far from the world's most accomplished actor when he played Garbo's younger brother, but there's something touching about his unsureness on-screen; and even without any explicit titles, the character's adulation of his brother-in-law has a sexual edge. Changing the illegitimate pregnancy to an unspecified illness is no great loss, either, and still provides sufficient reason for Garbo's hospital scenes, which are some of the best in the picture.

Changing the motivation for Brown's suicide, however, was another matter. In both

Censored Hollywood

book and film, Iris/Diana refuses to reveal the reason for her husband's death. The scandal destroys her reputation, but she preserves her brother's image of his friend. Covering up the matter is simple in the novel: Only Iris, her dead husband, and an old family friend know about it. In the film, however, the husband's suicide involves several people. As a result, the cover-up seems contrived and robs the plot of believability.

The same year as *A Woman of Affairs*, a major star caused more trouble for Hays with her determination to play one of the shadiest ladies of all time—Sadie Thompson. The South Seas trollop was born in "Miss Thompson," a short story by W. Somerset Maugham that created a scandal with its attack on religious hypocrisy. The story concentrates on the Reverend Alfred Davidson, a South Seas missionary who converts prostitute Sadie Thompson, then suddenly commits suicide. At the story's end, Sadie reverts to her old ways and damns all men as "filthy, dirty pigs,"[8] a plot turn that strongly suggests she was raped by Davidson.

It didn't take long for somebody to seize on the dramatic possibilities of Maugham's story. In 1923, *Rain*, an adaptation by John Colton and Clemence Randolph, opened in London. In New York the following season, it became one of the great Broadway hits of the twenties, largely due to Jeanne Eagels's impassioned performance as Sadie.

In translating the story to the stage, Colton and Randolph put more focus on Sadie. They gave her a suitor, a U.S. Marine sergeant named O'Hara, who asks her to settle down with him in Sydney, and softened her reactions at the end. Sadie still returns to her old ways after the attack—she even uses Maugham's line about men being pigs—but her position changes when she learns of Davidson's suicide. The play ends with Davidson's wife returning to face Sadie after identifying her husband's body:

> MRS. DAVIDSON (*sadly*): I understand, Miss Thompson. I'm sorry for him and I'm sorry for you.
> (MRS. DAVIDSON *passes her, hastily, covers her face and walks upstairs. . . .*)
> SADIE (*in a low, sick voice*): I'm sorry for everybody in the world! Life's a quaint present from somebody, there's no doubt about that. (*Moving to O'HARA.*) Maybe it will be easier in Sydney.
> *She clutches O'HARA's arm and breaks into sobs as the* CURTAIN *falls.*[9]

With its impressive success record *Rain* was a natural for the movies—until it was banned under the Hays Formula. Gloria Swanson was determined to play the role, however, so she bought the rights to the original short story, which had never been submitted under the Formula. She even used the ban as leverage to acquire both story and play for sixty thousand dollars, forty thousand less than the asking price for the play alone.

To get around Hays, Swanson invited him to lunch to discuss a difficult property she was considering. Without mentioning either title, she told him she'd found a wonderful story about a fanatical minister persecuting a woman who was trying to build a new life. She knew she'd have to change the minister to a reformer to avoid the MPPDA stipulation against presenting religion in an unfavorable light, but she feared the author wouldn't grant her the rights under those circumstances. Could she use Hays's name to convince the writer that the change was in his best interests? Hays readily agreed.

When the story got out, the MPPDA's members, whom Hollywood had nicknamed "the Pinochle Club," were outraged. They wired their protest to Joseph Schenck, whose United Artists was backing the film:

> OUR REFUSAL TO PRODUCE SALACIOUS BOOKS AND PLAYS AGAINST WHICH THERE IS AN OVERWHELMING PUBLIC OPINION AT THIS TIME HAS BEEN THE CORNERSTONE UPON WHICH THE PRODUCERS ASSOCIATION HAS BEEN BUILT AND TO DESTROY THAT AT THIS TIME WOULD IN OUR OPINION BE AN ACTION UNFORGIVABLE AND UNWARRANTED AND A DIRECT VIOLATION OF PROMISES WE HAVE MADE THE PUBLIC THAT MATERIAL OF THIS KIND WOULD NOT BE MADE. . . .[10]

This enraged Swanson on two counts. First, in complaining to Schenck, the Pinochle Club was ignoring her role as producer. Second, almost all of the telegram's signers—including William Fox; Jesse L. Lasky and Adolph Zukor of Paramount; Marcus Loew of MGM; Abe Warner of Warner Bros.; and her future business partner, Joe Kennedy—had violated the Hays Formula at one time or another. She stood firm in her commitment to the film, arguing that Hays had approved the story because of her plans to change the character of the missionary. Months later, Swanson wrote to Maugham to inquire about sequel rights to "Miss Thompson," only to learn that William Fox had hired him to write a sequel before the Pinochle Club protested her production.

Swanson made several concessions to Hays in order to bring *Rain* to the screen. The Reverend Alfred Davidson became Mr. Atkinson (in the film's 1984 restoration his name is Davidson again). The title was changed to *Sadie Thompson*, and, as had happened with *A Woman of Affairs*, no reference was made to the original play or story. In fact, the word "rain" is used only in one title at the beginning: "Pago-Pago—in the sultry South Seas where there is no need for bed clothes—yet the rain comes down in sheets."

Hays was so concerned that there be nothing on screen to indicate the source material that he even hired lip readers to screen the film. They found no unnecessary references to *Rain,* but they must have been napping when Swanson mouthed the line "You'd yank wings off butterflies and claim you were saving their soul, you psalm-singing sonofabitch." For all the film's sexuality, however, the scene that concerned Hays most in the finished cut was Atkinson's suicide. Swanson had to remove shots of the razor he used on himself.

The result was a sturdy drama, though Swanson seems a little too ladylike when Sadie is supposed to be carrying on like a tramp. Some critics blamed that failing on the censors. Yet the performance is similar to Swanson's work in other films; she seems to be merely putting on the characterization for a lark. Her enjoyment of the part is infectious—you can't not like her as Sadie—and her conversion scenes are strong and convincing, but at other times the performance is so animated and high-spirited she seems to be doing her famous Charlie Chaplin imitation without the moustache.

Much stronger is Lionel Barrymore as Atkinson. Although he overplays occasionally, which was typical for Barrymore, he manages more subtlety in communicating the character's sexual repression, even though the play's references to Atkinson's sexless marriage and his erotic dreams about Sadie are cut. Unfortunately, the rape and suicide scenes have been lost forever. When Kino International restored the film in 1984, they had to use stills and title cards in place of the picture's missing last reel.

Sadie Thompson was a major hit, setting house records at the Rivoli–United Artists in New York and grossing more than $1 million. It also brought Swanson an Oscar nomination for Best Actress. The fact that it was made at all, however, points to the continuing problems with the Hays Formula and the Don'ts and Be Carefuls.

Complaints about film content continued. In 1928, the Federal Motion Picture Council met in Washington to push for federal censorship. Hays urged many civic-group contacts to attend and paid the way for six of them (when word of this leaked in 1930, he almost lost his job). Hays even staged a walkout on the last day of the conference so his public relations people could claim a major victory against censorship.

It must have worked. Hays successfully lobbied against passage of a bill to ban block booking and blind buying, two practices that theater owners said forced them to play objectionable films. His lobbyists even managed to prove that whenever theater owners had a choice, they booked sex films anyway.

But the threat still stood. In January 1929, Joy wrote to Hays to discuss problems with the system. Less than half the MPPDA's members were submitting stories. Some just sent scenes; others didn't send all their scripts. On average, only 20 percent of all Hollywood films were being reviewed by the Studio Relations Committee. The studios didn't always follow editing suggestions, and there was no way of checking up on them. And with the development of talking pictures, these problems were sure to get worse. Hays had to come up with a better way of making the studios behave themselves.

"Immorality May Be Fun, but..."

Chapter Four

Edward Everett Horton's condemnation of indecency in *Design for Living* (1933) could have been a rallying cry for Hollywood during the first years of talking pictures, as sex and crime were exploited as fully as possible to draw Depression-weary audiences into theaters. The above line's conclusion, "but it isn't fun enough to take the place of one hundred percent virtue and three square meals a day," would prove prophetic. As the studios finally fell victim to the changing economy, they would be forced to champion "one hundred percent virtue" if they wanted to survive.

No one was happy at the start of the thirties. Will Hays had heralded the birth of talking pictures when he spoke on camera to introduce Warner Bros.' first Vitaphone feature, *Don Juan*, in 1926, but soon he would be tempted to curse the new medium. The studios had done their best to defy the MPPDA without sound. Now the influx of talent from Broadway, vaudeville, and burlesque—imported because of their experience with spoken dialogue—meant new challenges to the Formula. Few of these new recruits had faced the kinds of restrictions the Hays Office was trying to enforce. To make matters worse, ad-libbing, which had never been a problem before, became a major pitfall. Joy would approve a script only to discover that the finished film was rife with objectionable elements.

As sound brought a new freedom to the screen, would-be censors sprang into action with renewed vigor. William Randolph Hearst, whose newspapers had cultivated many

With no way of enforcing the Production Code in the early thirties, Will Hays and his colleagues were as helpless as the naked Christian in this shot from Cecil B. De Mille's The Sign of the Cross, *one of many films defying Code restrictions on nudity.*

of Hollywood's recent scandals, threatened to throw his support behind federal censorship. Iowa's Senator Smith Brookhart, who earlier had tried to outlaw block booking and blind bidding, introduced a bill to place the film industry under control of the Federal Trade Commission.

Local censorship became an even greater problem with the advent of sound. During the early days of sound-on-disc, it was virtually impossible to cut a film once it was in release. With the development of sound-on-film techniques, cutting was easier but often embarrassingly obvious. Rather than inspiring the studios to adhere to the MPPDA's regulations, however, such problems led producers to complain that Hays wasn't doing enough to keep the censors at bay.

Hays was more than willing to accept his share of the blame. After three years, it was clear that the Don'ts and Be Carefuls weren't working. Joy felt the problem was that the list of thirty-six rules was too negative, and Hays agreed. The rules only told producers what not to do. That quantitative approach simply wasn't enough. What was needed was a philosophy, a qualitative statement of what messages the movies should be giving audiences.

The one man in Hollywood who could help Hays in this was Martin Quigley. The wealthy publisher of the *Motion Picture Herald* was also a devout Catholic with solid connections to the church hierarchy. During the summer of 1929, Hays was on the point of contacting Quigley when Quigley called him and arranged a meeting. Quigley had been equally disturbed with the screen's increasing immorality and had editorialized against it incessantly. Working with Father Daniel A. Lord, S.J., of St. Louis University, who had been one of the technical advisors on DeMille's *King of Kings*, Quigley had come up with a "Code to Govern the Making of Talking, Synchronized and Silent Motion Pictures."[1]

Quigley's code was exactly what Hays was looking for, an attempt to define the moral world in which movies should take place. When Hays presented it to the MPPDA board, it set up a committee headed by Irving J. Thalberg to put it all together. Quigley served as consultant to the committee and even arranged for Lord to come to Hollywood.

On February 17, 1930, the MPPDA's West Coast board of directors accepted the Production Code unanimously. This was no indication of a sudden rush to morality. As Leonard Leff and Jerold Simmons point out in *The Dame in the Kimono*, the Code's adoption only a few months after the stock-market crash may have been economically motivated, an attempt to put on a holy face and satisfy the beleaguered East Coast investors who stood to lose still more if Hollywood's films suddenly fell out of favor.

The Production Code, which remained virtually unchanged through Hays's reign and for a long while thereafter, consisted of two sections (see Appendix). "Particular Applications of the Code and the Reasons Therefore" was a more detailed version of the Don'ts and Be Carefuls and represented Hollywood's contribution to the document. The "Particular Applications" include all of the restrictions on screen content most often associated with the Code. They bar depictions of the techniques of crime, any representation of illegal drug traffic, justifications of adultery, sex perversion, white slavery, venereal disease, profanity, nudity, suggestive dances, and the ridicule of religion and other nationalities. Contrary to legend, however, the Code does not bar married couples from sharing the same bed or place time limits on kisses.

Both the guidelines and their application over the years placed greater emphasis on sex than on violence. Violence was most strongly condemned in specific contexts: the glorification of crime in many gangster films, the disturbing morbidity of the horror genre. Unlike sex, however, at the time violence was not considered distasteful in and of itself. Longtime MPPDA staffer Jack Vizzard explains this attitude in terms of the influence of such Irish-Americans as Martin Quigley and, later, Joe Breen on the Code. His reasoning could just as easily apply to the general attitudes towards sex and violence during the thirties: "To the Irish, violence was not necessarily connected with the debasing of human life. It was frequently a sign of manliness. . . . The Irish culture was infected with Jansenism, which dreaded sex as being identified with the darker forces, but which did not so fear brutality, since this was not as 'catching.' It contained its own remedy in that it hurt."[2]

The Particular Applications also include a brief statement of the General Principles underlying the Code:

1. No picture shall be produced which will lower the moral standards of those who see it. Hence the sympathy of the audience shall never be thrown to the side of crime, wrongdoing, evil or sin.
2. Correct standards of life, subject only to the requirements of drama and entertainment, shall be presented.
3. Law, natural or human, shall not be ridiculed, nor shall sympathy be created for its violation.

These statements were drawn from the work of Quigley and Lord, which constituted the other part of the Code, the General Principles. The General Principles recognize film as both entertainment and art but, in each case, distinguish between works that "improve the race" through enlightenment or recreation and those that "tend to degrade human beings." This is based on a definition of art as "the presentation of human thoughts, emotions and experiences, in terms of an appeal to the soul thru the senses."[3] Further, the General Principles find a moral value in art both as a reproduction of the morality of its creators and through its effect on the morals of the audience.

The moral center of the Code would come to be embodied in the phrase "compensating moral values," though those words never occur in the Code itself, only in the letters relating to its enforcement. Acknowledging that it is impossible to make films in which sin and crime are never represented, the Code simply requires that they be presented in a clear moral light. Evil should never be made to seem alluring, sympathetic, or successful, nor should good be ridiculed or painted unattractively. In addition, good and evil must be clearly delineated.

Sins that repel—such as murder, most theft, lying, hypocrisy, and cruelty—present no great problems, as they naturally arouse condemnation. The only danger is that their repetition and brutality may harden the audience to the evils they represent. But there are also sins that attract, including sex sins, banditry, daring thefts, leadership in evil, organized crime, and revenge. These must be placed in a clear moral framework, lest they inspire admiration or imitation. Other subjects—including homosexuality, venereal disease, and drug addiction—were barred completely for fear they would inspire morbid curiosity, which could lead to imitation.

In the real world, of course, such practices do exist; good and evil are not always clearly distinguished, and evil is not always punished. Nonetheless, Hays refused to accept any criticism of the Code as perpetuating an unrealistic view of the world. In his opinion, those who wished to depict life uncensored were not realists but "literalists." The true realist, in Hays's view, presented not just the facts of life but their moral framework. That moral framework, or at least Hays's and Quigley's vision of it, is what the Production Code was created to preserve.

The adoption of the Production Code did not herald any great change in the way the Studio Relations Committee worked. Staff members still evaluated source materials, story treatments, and script drafts, as well as song lyrics and costume tests. They also were available during filming to review rewrites or visit the set to advise on questionable scenes. At the end of filming, the Studio Relations Committee would view the final cut and either pass or reject it. Producers of rejected films could either recut them to MPPDA specifications or appeal to the Hollywood Jury. Once a film had been passed, the association would also help with local censors, negotiating cuts, using their own approval as an argument for the passage of questionable films, and soliciting expert opinion in their support.

The same year the Production Code was passed, the MPPDA also created an Advertising Code. Trailers, posters, newspaper ads, production stills, and other promotional materials were submitted to the newly created Advertising Code Administration.

News of the Production Code helped Hays fight off several censorship bills, but the studios quickly found their way around it. Initially, script submission was not required. As more and more studios kept questionable scripts to themselves, however, Hays got the board to pass a resolution in October of 1931 that made script submission compulsory.

Even with that, however, producers simply ignored any changes they didn't want to make. When a film came up for review, they could argue almost anything past the Studio Relations Committee. On the rare occasions (ten times in three and a half years) that the committee refused to pass a film, the Hollywood Jury overturned them. The jury could be counted on to demand token cuts, but on the whole they simply ignored the Code. When the childbirth scene in Paramount's 1932 version of *A Farewell to Arms* was deemed too graphic, the jury decided "because of the greatness of the picture and the excellence of direction and treatment that the childbirth sequence was not in violation of [the] Code."[4] They did, however, issue a stern warning to producers of lesser pictures not to attempt such sequences.

Instability at the top of the Studio Relations Committee compounded the problem. Joy finally tired of the battles and accepted a position at Fox in 1932. Ironically, his new position had been created in response to the Production Code. He would serve as Fox's Code liaison for years.

Hays went looking for somebody tougher. He thought he'd found him in Dr. James Wingate, who had spent five years as head of the New York censorship board; but even Wingate couldn't beat the studio heads at this game. It would take a stronger fighter than he, with a lot more backing from outside Hollywood, to bring the studio heads around.

Hollywood's refusal to toe the line on the new Production Code was nothing sinister. It was simply the executives' response to changing times and a changing medium. After all, the movie moguls weren't selling morality to America; they were simply selling movies. Much of what the moralists found objectionable in Hollywood product of the early thirties resulted from an attempt to meet audience tastes. The Depression was devastating the rest of America, but Hollywood seemed to be immune to its effects. The men who built the studios were determined to stay immune as long as possible.

With the coming of sound came a renewed interest in screen realism and a short-lived flowering of social-problem pictures. At Warner Bros. in particular, plots were taken from the headlines and filmed so quickly that they made it into theaters while the stories were still hot. Even at their worst, the pictures produced by this approach were fast-paced, gritty reflections of Depression life. They were so timely—and frequently so well done—that they often were hits with the critics and the audience, if not necessarily with the censors.

The studio's 1933 *Heroes for Sale* may not have been the best of the cycle, but it was probably the most comprehensive. Richard Barthelmess stars as Tom, a veteran addicted to morphine after treatment of a war injury. He helps an anarchist inventor (Robert Barrat) market a new, automated laundry system; sides with the laundry workers in a strike; and tries unsuccessfully to keep the strike from turning into a riot. After a prison stretch, he's hounded by police as a dangerous radical and joins the swelling ranks of the dispossessed, moving from one hobo jungle to another.

There was more than enough here to violate the Production Code. Commenting on the first draft, submitted under the title *Breadline*, Wingate objected to the depiction of drug addiction and cautioned that local censors would probably cut any references to communism. But the real problem was political: Wingate also objected to the film's unsympathetic portrayal of the police. Although such treatment was barred by the Code, Wingate dealt with it in terms of local censorship, possibly thinking that argument would carry more weight. He cautioned that censors might cut a sequence in which the police round up suspected radicals and a scene in which two officers harass Tom after his return from prison. Coupled with other negative portrayals of the authorities, this made the film seem to side with the strikers.

Despite Wingate's sensitivities, Warners got away with a lot on this one. The only states that made extensive cuts were Pennsylvania and New York. The former deleted some of Barrat's more extreme comments (e.g., "When you get to be my age, you'll have a bomb in every pocket"[5]). The latter removed some references to morphine and some of the more inflammatory shots in the riot scene. *Heroes for Sale* wasn't much of a target, though, for it ended up neither a critical success nor a box-office winner.

I Am a Fugitive from a Chain Gang was both, however, and excited a lot more activity among the censors. Real-life fugitive Robert Burns had recounted his experiences in a series of magazine articles, later published in book form as *I Am a Fugitive from a Georgia Chain Gang*. The book dealt with the unendurable conditions he experienced after being convicted of petty theft. After escaping, Burns fled to Chicago to build a new life and become a respected citizen. When his wife turned him over to the law, he struck a deal to return to Georgia in return for an early release. The state reneged on its promise, so he escaped again. From then on, he was forced to live on the run. Burns's book was a hot property in Hollywood, with several studios bidding for it before Warner Bros. obtained the rights. Initially, Colonel Joy had serious doubts about the story. On February 26, 1932, he warned Irving J. Thalberg at MGM and Darryl F. Zanuck at Warners that the story's major points—the prison camp conditions and Burns's two successful escapes—could not be shown in any great detail. In a letter to Hays written on the same day, Joy also worried about reactions in the South to such a blatant condemnation of the chain-gang system: "While it may be true that the systems are wrong, I very much doubt if it is our business as an entertainment force to clear it up, and thereby possibly get into trouble with the southern states who, as our southern representative puts it, can stand any criticism as long as it isn't directed at themselves." Zanuck bought the story anyway, assigning Paul Muni to star and Mervyn LeRoy to direct.

When a chain-gang scandal broke in Florida, Joy's concerns were somewhat relieved. He wrote Zanuck in July expressing the hope that viewers might think the film was set there rather than in Georgia. Just to be sure, he urged Zanuck to "reverse the number of white and black prisoners, as it is the preponderance of blacks makes the section unmistakably southern." Zanuck was not willing to do this, nor would he cut other scenes Joy objected to, including Muni's whipping and the scene after his first escape in which an old friend tries to set him up with a prostitute for the night (both would be cut by local censors). Oddly, Joy never complained about the film's lack of compensating moral values; nobody in the corrupt state government is punished for Muni's mistreatment.

Once the film was finished, Joy gave it his full support, commending it to Albert Howson of Warners as "one of the important pictures of the year." In the same letter, dated October 17, 1932, Joy suggests that the film's "strongly individualized story of one man's personal experiences arising from one particular miscarriage of justice" would rescue it from any charge of social activism.

This was merely damage control. Most audiences saw the film for exactly what it was: a strong indictment of prison conditions. *Daily Variety* mentioned walkouts at early previews and could recommend the film only "for those who enjoy suffering."[6] Most other reviews were more enthusiastic. Hearst columnist Arthur Brisbane set the tone, hailing *I Am a Fugitive from a Chain Gang* as both a good picture and a tool for social change: "You should see this picture, advise other men to see it, and thus help to arouse public opinion against a shameful prison system that exploits miserable criminals for private profit, and pushes vindictive torture even to murder."[7]

Public opinion was indeed aroused. The film was so popular and the outcry so strong that Georgia finally took the chains off its prisoners. At the same time, however, the state struck back—Georgia and two of its prison officials sued Warners for libel, suits the studio settled out of court. State officials also let it be known that Warners employees—particularly Jack Warner and Mervyn LeRoy—had better make sure to stay out of Georgia unless they wanted to sample the same variety of southern hospitality that had been extended to Burns. Efforts to extradite Robert Burns continued for more than a decade, until reform governor Ellis Arnell commuted his sentence to time served in 1945.

Crime Pays

More popular and more troublesome than the social-problem films was another genre "torn from the headlines"—the gangster picture. There had been films about organized crime since the earliest days of the movies; many historians cite D. W. Griffith's 1912 *The Musketeers of Pig Alley* as the first. The genre didn't take off, however, until the advent of sound.

Censorship boards had never been kind to these films, particularly in areas where the censors had close ties to the police. In 1913, Detroit banned any films depicting police corruption or the methods of crime. Chicago banned *The Racket* in 1928 and *Alibi* the following year, partly because of their negative treatment of the police. Warners' *Doorway to Hell* (1930) was criticized for casting the young, attractive Lew Ayres as a gangster. In addition, the New York and Ohio censors cut a scene showing how to hide a machine gun in a violin case.

The censors' objections to gangster films can be traced to a number of legitimate concerns. They feared that any realistic treatment of the subject would teach people —particularly the young and impressionable—how to commit crimes. Even though most movie gangsters ended up dead or in jail, moralists still complained that the pictures made crime attractive, particularly when the crooks spent their profits on fast cars and faster women.

In addition, the stories hit too close to home. Crime stories filled the headlines almost daily in the early thirties, giving criminals like Al Capone and John Dillinger nearly legendary status. Many films in the genre were based, in part, on actual stories of mob warfare and racketeering, leading some to fear that gangster films would help glorify their real-life models.

Most of the ill feeling toward the gangster film focused on three pictures of the genre: *Little Caesar* and *The Public Enemy*, both 1931 Warner Bros. releases, and Howard Hughes's production *Scarface* (1932). *Little Caesar* set the tone both in its record-breaking box-office performance and in its portrayal of a ruthless gangster's rise and fall.

W. R. Burnett had written the novel *Little Caesar* after hearing a Chicago radio broadcast that was disrupted by a gangland shootout, and he loosely based his lead character, Rico Bandello, on Al Capone. Initially, he had trouble finding a publisher; nobody wanted to touch a gangster story in 1929. When Dial Press published the book, however, it became a big hit. Mervyn LeRoy brought the story to Warner Bros. and sold production chief Darryl F. Zanuck on the idea of a totally evil protagonist, a role that would make Edward G. Robinson the first great gangster star.

There is little correspondence in the MPPDA files relating to the film's creation. Once it was ready for release, however, Colonel Joy had a major job getting it past the censors. The principal complaint was that the picture's treatment of crime was too strong and too detailed. Massachusetts censors cut all lines showing how Rico's gang planned its crimes. When the New York board, then run by Dr. Wingate, threatened to ban the film or cut it severely, Joy tried to justify the presentation on moral grounds: "The more ghastly, the more ruthless the criminal acts of these gangsters are shown on the screen, the stronger will be the audience reaction against men of their kind and organized crime in general. . . . To further reduce the portrayal of these details would, in our opinion, reduce and even destroy the moral value. . . ."

The argument must have worked. The New York censors let the film pass with relatively few cuts: some lines about planning crimes, some gunplay, and some shots of the stolen money.

Joy also had major problems with Canadian censors. Protesting that Canada had not suffered the effects of organized crime, police captain Robert Pearson, chief censor of motion pictures for Edmonton, Alberta, still argued that "a picture of this kind had two functions—one was to teach young criminals how to commit crime, and secondly to stimulate them to become heroes by doing these things." Joy was less successful here, advising Warners not to appeal the film's ban in Alberta.

The Public Enemy, released just three months later, was even more brutal. As Tom Powers—a character modeled on Capone's chief rival in Chicago, Deanie O'Bannion— James Cagney slaps and shoots his way to the top of the rackets, even taking vengeance on the horse that accidentally kills his boss. In the end, his dead body, wrapped up like Boris Karloff at the start of *The Mummy*, is delivered to his mother's doorstep. Originally the film was to have been even more brutal. Early script drafts called for Tom's brother, Mike (Donald Cook), to avenge his death, but Joy convinced Zanuck to drop the idea.

In addition to its violence, *The Public Enemy* raised problems with its treatment of

Tom's sexual activities. Most of these scenes tie in with the film's anticrime message. Tom's romantic involvements are, on the whole, rather pathetic, giving the impression that the same flaws that drove him to a life of crime make any sustained adult relationship impossible. In the film's most famous scene, Cagney assaults girlfriend Mae Clarke with a grapefruit at the breakfast table. You wouldn't have known about it had you lived in Ohio or Maryland, where the scene was cut. This did not mark an emerging sensitivity to violence against women. In fact, *The Public Enemy* created a mini-trend in that area, with Cagney and other leading men roughing up their on-screen partners in a series of early-thirties films. What the censors objected to was the scene's costuming. The fact that Cagney and Clarke were still in their pajamas clearly indicated they had spent the night together.

Even with local cuts, *The Public Enemy* was a big hit, breaking box-office records set by *Little Caesar* only a few months earlier. The combined success of these pictures spurred the production of still more gangster films, leading to still more complaints. Reformers urged Will Hays to put a stop to the genre, while pressure groups condemned the depiction of Italians as gangsters and buffoons.

None of this put Hays or Joy in a very receptive mood when Ben Hecht's script for the biggest, most brutal gangster film ever arrived at the Studio Relations Committee's office in May 1931. To begin with, the Howard Hughes production was called *Scarface*, one of Al Capone's nicknames, and the leading character, Tony Camonte, was clearly modeled on the Chicago vice lord. Camonte's mother was described by MPPDA consultant Dr. Carleton Simon as "a grasping virago," a characterization guaranteed to excite complaints from Italian-Americans. Tony came to a bad end in the script, but his exit, going out in a blaze of gunfire and taking his chief nemesis on the police force with him, left him in a heroic light. And adding to the script's problems, Tony was a loving family man who eluded the police until he shot the man who had dishonored his sister. At the end, she proudly helped her brother through the final shootout.

Joy wrote to E. B. Derr of Hughes's Caddo Company with a long list of changes, including having Tony's mother repudiate her son's criminal career, building up the role of law-enforcement officials in bringing about Tony's downfall, making Tony's devotion to his sister less sympathetic, and giving him a more cowardly ending. Hughes and director Howard Hawks went along with some of Joy's suggestions. They rewrote the role of Tony's mother and, to make his protectiveness of his sister less sympathetic, hinted that he had an incestuous yen for her. The one thing they would not change, however, was the ending. Although they allowed the police detective to survive, they refused to make Tony turn coward.

While Joy and Hughes went around over scene changes, opposition to the genre continued to grow. The New York Society for Suppression of Vice asked the state's censors to ban all gangster films, including the upcoming *Scarface*. When a twelve-year-old boy in Montclair, New Jersey, was shot playing cops and robbers with a friend, Warner Bros. promised that they would send the city no more gangster films.

On July 22, 1931, Joy wrote a memo to the files stating that everything objectionable had been taken out of *Scarface* and that the rushes for the first third of the picture were "very much in our favor." Joy felt Tony, as played by Paul Muni, was sufficiently unsympathetic that the audience would side with the police. Hughes still refused to change the ending, however.

As Hawks drew closer to completion, problems with the film returned. In August, Joy told Hughes and Derr that the picture would be unplayable in 50 percent of the U.S. He saw a rough cut in September and argued for an hour to get them to change the ending. "If this suggestion is accepted," he wrote in the files, "it will involve another five days' shooting and will really weaken the value of the picture, but it will relieve the picture of any nonconformance to the Code."

A member of Joy's staff, future writer and producer Lamar Trotti, had come up with an approach to the film that made Tony's cowardice acceptable to Hawks and Hughes. Tony would turn chicken because he didn't have a gun to hide behind anymore: "The Gangster is a great man as long as he has a gun; once without a gun, he is a yellow rat. The final message of the picture will be—not to let criminals get possession of guns."

The Hughes publicity machine went to work promoting the idea, claiming it had been Hughes's intention all along. New scenes were added to the film, including the revised ending. Derr suggested a scene in which children are shot in the course of one of Tony's crimes, but Trotti rejected that as simply adding to the problem. A reference to the incident remains in a strong speech given to Edwin Maxwell, who played the police commissioner: "Did you read what happened the other day? Car full of them chasing another down the street—broad daylight—three kiddies playing hopscotch on the sidewalk get lead poured in their little bellies. When I think what goes on in the minds of these lice I want to vomit."

The changes must have worked, at least in Hollywood. Joy screened the film for such industry leaders as Irving J. Thalberg, Douglas Fairbanks, and Harold Lloyd, and they all thought the film made a strong antigun statement. An October screening for law-enforcement officials brought more statements of support.

Once *Scarface* was shipped to New York, however, there was more trouble. After a screening for the MPPDA's East Coast office, Hays refused to pass it, insisting that it would never get by the New York censors. He demanded still more changes to make the antigun message stronger. In addition, he insisted that Tony survive the shootout so he could stand trial and face execution. He even wanted the title changed.

The new ending was shot over four days, but without the film's director or star. Hawks refused to shoot the additional scenes. Muni was working on Broadway, and Tony had to be played by a stand-in, who was seen only from the rear.

Hays still wasn't happy, feeling the film needed a stronger moral message. A relatively recent addition to the staff, Joe Breen, suggest a framing sequence in which a judge would tell the story to a group of delinquent children to scare them away from crime, but that was rejected. Finally, Hughes added a spoken prologue and epilogue featuring Maxwell and a newspaper editor played by Tully Marshall.

The title was an even bigger problem. At Hays's insistence, every possible reference to "Scarface" was cut from the soundtrack. The production company and the Hays Office came up with three possible titles: *Yellow, Man Is Still Savage*, and *The Shame of a Nation*. Hughes chose the last, even though he didn't want to make the change. Learning that there was a similar title registered, he switched it to *A Scar on a Nation*, then shortened it to *The Scar*. That had been copyrighted by somebody else, however, so Hughes insisted on a return to the original.

Even with its title unchanged, however, the film had been altered enough to satisfy Will Hays—but not the New York censors. Hays brought them the product of his handiwork, and they banned it entirely. Hughes was justifiably outraged. He had put one hundred thousand dollars into revisions that Hays insisted were necessary to pass the censors. Hughes announced plans to release the film in its original form, with or without Hays's approval, and sue any censorship board that dared to ban it. He also issued a press release claiming that state censors were "conniving with dishonest politicians to suppress the picture, or ruin it with unnecessary cuts because it reveals the truths about gangsterism in the United States."

The notoriety piqued public interest in the film, leading to record attendance in several cities. Eventually, Hughes would get back double his one million dollar investment. He also reached a compromise with the MPPDA. He would release the film as cut for Hays, but reverting to the ending Joy had requested, in which Tony turns yellow and is shot down by the police. When Hughes had tried releasing Hays's version, he had come up against several local bans on execution scenes.

On re-viewing *Scarface*, it's easy to see what all the excitement was about. It is not only the best of the big three gangster films but, thanks to Hawks's fluid direction, the least dated. Although most of the killings are done by suggestion—most notably mob leader Boris Karloff's execution in a bowling alley, symbolized by a single pin whirling, then toppling over—there is a great deal of gunplay. When Tony first tries out a tommy gun, his reaction, and the reaction of his mistress (Karen Morley), is almost sexual. "Get out of my way, Johnny," he shouts, "I'm gonna spit!"

Muni plays Tony as a human ape, an amoral, animalistic child living for nothing but quick gratification. Though the choice might have seemed unusual enough to prevent any glamorization of Tony, the actor's magic worked by Muni makes the character perversely appealing, putting emphasis on the naive innocence with which he approaches each new transgression.

One of the most interesting elements of the film is the way it appears to have benefited from Joy's initial suggestions. Most notable of these is his request to make Tony's devotion to his sister, Cesca, less sympathetic. This inspired one of the film's most memorable elements, the near-incestuous relationship between the two. Hawks would later say that he and Hecht modeled their scenes on stories of Cesare Borgia and his sister Lucrezia, who were rumored to have been lovers.

Muni and costar Ann Dvorak ran with the idea, bringing a special passion to their fight scenes. Best of all is the sequence in which Tony returns from a trip to discover Cesca living with his second-in-command (George Raft). In the original script, Tony simply shot a gangster who had seduced his sister. Joy had objected to that, so in the film Tony shoots the man, then learns from Cesca that the pair were secretly married. His reaction, mumbling "I didn't know" as he walks dazedly from the scene, is one of the film's highlights.

Yet, for all of the changes and all of the ways Hawks incorporated Code-approved moral lessons within the script, *Scarface* still roused protests. Even allowing for the effort to emphasize the destructive nature of crime, some critics worried that the message might be lost on younger viewers, who would focus only on Tony's daring rise to the top.

As the protests grew, Joy and Hays tried to convince producers to abandon the crime cycle. The Canadian provinces were banning almost all gangster films by this time. In England, American crime films inspired a campaign for the institution of governmental censorship. In the U.S., Hays still hadn't worked out a system to make the studios toe the line on this, or just about any other issue.

Sex Sells

Crime was far from the only problem facing the Hays Office in the early thirties. The horror cycle, which started with Universal's *Dracula* (1930) and *Frankenstein*, was also generating complaints. The British Board of Film Censors even had to create a new classification—H for horror—to deal with the genre. Although parents complained about the effect of such films on their children, Joy was less concerned about this cycle, certain it would peter out because of the relatively small supply of classic horror stories. What concerned him more was a genre that was causing as much trouble as the gangster film—the sex picture.

Sex had always been a staple of the screen, starting with *The May Irwin-John C. Rice Kiss* back in 1896. Vamps like Theda Bara and Barbara La Marr had defined the sex urge as something foreign and exotic during the silent era. An all-American school of sexual excess started with the flapper. Clara Bow embodied "It" until the coming of sound and a series of scandals ended her career. Then, Joan Crawford and Anita Page took over in a trio of MGM films—*Our Dancing Daughters*, *Our Modern Maidens*, and *Our Blushing Brides*—that drew people into theaters to learn the latest fashions and lovemaking techniques.

The flapper films heralded the new openness in Hollywood during the early thirties. *The Guardsman* and *An American Tragedy* finally made it to the screen, as works previously banned under the Hays Formula were suddenly allowable under, or in spite of, the Production Code.

Ferenc Molnár's lawyers convinced Hays that although *The Guardsman* might have been too risqué for the silent screen, spoken dialogue would allow a more subtle presentation of its story about a jealous husband who dons a disguise to test his wife's fidelity. Joy fought to make it crystal clear that the wife (Lynn Fontanne) knew all along that the Russian guardsman trying to seduce her was really her husband (Alfred Lunt), but MGM's Irving J. Thalberg insisted on maintaining the play's naughty ambiguity.

Hollywood inserted sex into almost every type of film. The historical genre took on a sexual dimension when Marlene Dietrich glorified adultery on her way to becoming *The Scarlet Empress* (1934), and Garbo strode about the Swedish palace in men's clothes in *Queen Christina* (1933). The Studio Relations Committee tried to cut one of the most famous scenes from the latter movie. Garbo sensuously memorizes the room in which she has enjoyed nights of passion with her Spanish lover (John Gilbert), then says, "This is how the Lord must have felt when he first beheld the finished world." They failed, but censors in New York, Virginia, Maryland, Kansas, Pennsylvania, and Ohio removed at least part of the scene, including the final line.

The much-protested horror genre moved into sexual territory when Paramount filmed its version of *Dr. Jekyll and Mr. Hyde* in 1932 with Fredric March. To illustrate Hyde's total depravity, the studio gave him a mistress, Ivy (Miriam Hopkins). Although

Colonel Joy succeeded in cutting the most pointed suggestions that Ivy was a prostitute, he couldn't get the studio to cut her first meeting with Jekyll. As the doctor examines her, Ivy slowly strips under her bedclothes, barely covering her breasts in one shot.

Even the religious epic could wallow in sensuality, particularly in the hands of a master of excess like Cecil B. DeMille, who went overboard dramatizing the decadence of ancient Rome in 1932's *The Sign of the Cross*. Because of the reputation he built on such high moral works as *King of Kings* and *The Ten Commandments*, he got away with it. Commenting on a pagan dance sequence, Joy wrote to Harold Hurley of Paramount: "Ordinarily we would have been concerned about those portions of the dance sequence in which the Roman dancer executes the 'Kootch' Movement. But since the director obviously used dancing to show the conflict between paganism and Christianity, we are agreed that there is justification for its use under the Code." In addition, Joy let DeMille get by with Claudette Colbert's bath in asses' milk, graphic shots of Christians being shot down by Roman archers, and a naked Christian awaiting execution in the gladiatorial ring. He also allowed a scene in which the film's hero (Fredric March) tries to warm up the Christian of his dreams (Elissa Landi) by having a lesbian procuress (Jobyna Howland) come on to her.

In pictures like *The Guardsman*, *Queen Christina*, *The Scarlet Empress*, and *Dr. Jekyll and Mr. Hyde*, sensuality was integral to the plots, giving an indication of how Hollywood might have developed the kind of mature approach to sex that for decades seemed confined to European films. In many other cases, however, the sex was simply gratuitous, a little extra spice to provide box-office insurance.

At the same time, the Hollywood studios developed an entire genre reflecting some of the harsher realities of sex in the early years of the Depression. As in other times of economic upheaval, there was a rise in prostitution during the early thirties. In addition, more women were entering or trying to enter the work force as traditional family roles fell prey to economic necessity. These two factors mix in the Hollywood sex film. While the studios rarely would focus an entire film on prostitution (though Josef von Sternberg shot some effective streetwalking scenes with Marlene Dietrich in 1932's *Blonde Venus*), the woman's picture of the era sidestepped the issue by linking sex and work.

The women in these films are trying to live a dream of feminist self-determination in a prefeminist era. They have to use their wits to get ahead. Failing that, however, they can use their bodies, though the latter recourse is rarely smiled upon. In *She Had to Say Yes* (1933), Loretta Young plays a buyers' girl, a garment-district worker hired to wine and dine customers and do anything necessary to keep them happy. Young barely survives with her honor intact, but manages to hold off her wolfish customers with style and grace (qualities she had in abundance in her earlier films). Only at the fadeout, when one of her most ardent clients (Lyle Talbot) proposes marriage, does she agree to spend the night with him in a surprising plot turn that Wingate tried to cut.

The Warners musicals proposed the same ethos. The gold-digging chorus girls played by Joan Blondell, Ginger Rogers, and Aline McMahon were working women trying to keep afloat in the rough seas of the Depression. They could tease—as Blondell and McMahon did with their wealthy suitors in *Gold Diggers of 1933*—but if they gave in, like Rogers's Anytime Annie in *42nd Street* (1933), they were permanently out of the running, doomed to remain in the chorus while more innocent workers like Ruby Keeler ascended to stardom.

These moral lessons were surrounded by as much titillation as the market could bear. *She Had to Say Yes* is filled with crude double entendres about what other buyers' girls have to do to sell the goods. The Warners musicals flashed all the flesh they could in dressing-room shots and Busby Berkeley's famous dance numbers. The latter roused more than a few problems of their own. Censors tried to cut the finish of "Shuffle Off to Buffalo" in *42nd Street* as Keeler's arm, reaching through the curtains of a railroad berth, reacts to her newlywed husband's initiation of lovemaking. In the "Petting in the Park" number from *Gold Diggers of 1933*, Keeler slips into a metal suit, thwarting Dick Powell's attempts at necking until a leering midget (Billy Barty) hands him a can opener.

The most genteel form taken by the women's picture of the early thirties was the confessional drama, and nobody had more to confess on-screen than Constance Bennett. Starting with *Common Clay* in 1930, Bennett specialized in playing working women who strayed. As a kept woman in *The Common Law* (1931), she posed nude for artist Joel McCrea, then moved in with him. The same year, she rebelled against poverty and became a high-living model in *Bought*. She sees her chance for happiness with playboy Ray Milland and allows him to seduce her. When he discovers that her parents were never married, however, he rejects her, and she goes back to her humble beginnings to wed aspiring writer Ben Lyon. Joy tried unsuccessfully to cut the seduction from *Bought* or at least render it ambiguous. Local censors, however, cut all references to seduction and illegitimacy, leaving the plot senseless.

But of all Bennett's films, the one that probably caused the most problems was *The Easiest Way* (1931). Eugene Walter's play had created a sensation on Broadway in 1909 with its tale of Laura Murdock, a failed actress who becomes the mistress of the wealthy Willard Brockton. After years of luxury, Laura falls in love with John Madison, a young writer who doesn't hold her past against her. She promises to leave Brockton while John makes his fortune, but it takes longer than they had expected. When Laura runs out of money, she goes back to Brockton, just two months before John returns, now a wealthy man. Realizing Laura's duplicity, both John and Brockton leave her for good. At the end of the play, Laura has no choice but to find another man to keep her: "Get my new hat, dress up my body and paint up my face. It's all they've left of me. They've taken my soul away with them. . . . Doll me up, Annie. . . . I'm going to Rector's to make a hit, and to hell with the rest."[8] The play was a scandalous success. According to Broadway legend, the final speech so tarnished the name of Rector's that the popular restaurant went bankrupt within five years.

Lewis J. Selznick had faced the Kansas censors unsuccessfully when he filmed *The Easiest Way* with Clara Kimball Young as Laura in 1917. The film made money, but by the time it was ripe for a remake, the Hays Formula was in effect. The property was considered so difficult that Hays and Joy discouraged producers from even submitting it. In March 1930, Harry Cohn wanted to pick it up for Columbia, but Joy talked him out of it "for the good of the industry." Several months later, Irving J. Thalberg defied Joy, optioning it for MGM and signing Bennett to star at the height of her popularity.

In adapting the play to the screen, Thalberg had the writers create a more sympathetic background for Laura. She is now a hardworking girl from the slums who first stumbles into modeling and then becomes the mistress of the wealthy William Brockton (Adolph Menjou) so she can help support her family. Despite the help she gives them, her mother refuses to see her. When her mother dies, Laura isn't even allowed to attend the funeral. In addition, her brother-in-law (Clark Gable, in his first MGM film) refuses to let her visit his family. Joy objected to all of this on the grounds that Laura's poverty gives her too convenient an excuse for accepting Brockton's propositions. He also felt that her constant rejection by her family made her too sympathetic. In addition, there was too much emphasis placed on the material benefits of her fallen state.

The biggest problem, however, came with the ending. Edith Ellis's shooting script, dated October 28, 1930, keeps the gist of Walter's original finale. After the two men leave Laura, "a slow, bitter hardness comes into her face. You realize that whatever was soft and sweet and tender in this girl's soul has perished. A prostitute is being born!" Laura then goes to a nightclub to find a new keeper, suffering in ermine as men flock about her for the final fadeout. The shooting script also has a notation suggesting a happier ending in which John (Robert Montgomery) and Laura meet at the club and reconcile.

The latter ending was impossible under the Code. The fallen woman could not win back the man she had wronged. The original ending was unacceptable, too. Joy would not allow an ending that left Laura with the fruits of her transgressions, no matter how much she was suffering inside. John V. Wilson of the MPPDA staff suggested having

Laura return to her sister's house and watch the happy family through the window before she "slinks off and is swallowed in the darkness." That may have inspired what wound up on screen. In the finished film, it is Laura who rejects Brockton after John leaves. Months later, she is standing outside her sister's house on Christmas Eve when Nick comes out and invites her in, signaling that she has finally paid for her sins. This still failed to satisfy Joy, who would have preferred for Laura to be left out in the cold (reportedly some prints ended that way), but the studio refused to make any more changes.

As Joy had predicted, the film generated protests and extensive local censorship action. Father Lord wrote to Joy, complaining that the film "made immorality alluring to young people before it reached its final lesson." Harry Cohn wanted to know why Joy had scared him off the play and then allowed MGM to film it. Local censors cut many of the key plot points, including Brockton's initial temptation of Laura, her father's taking money from her, and Laura's return to Brockton (which left the film making no sense at all). The Alberta censor wrote to Joy: "Yesterday, we ran a picture called *The Easiest Way*, that had been cut so badly to try to make it decent, before it reached us, that we had to stop in the middle of it, because we thought we were looking at the wrong reels."

While Constance Bennett was demonstrating the latest in genteel sex problems, Barbara Stanwyck showed Hollywood's leading ladies how to put a little grit into their suffering. In *Night Nurse* (1931), she and Joan Blondell went through nursing school taking their clothes off whenever possible before settling down to a job caring for two little girls being starved to death by their rich, drunken mother and her abusive chauffeur-lover (Gable again). The film also made a hash of compensating moral values when Stanwyck's bootlegger boyfriend (Ben Lyon) sets up a "happy" ending by having Gable bumped off. The same year, Stanwyck went from trial marriage to the real thing, with infidelity on both sides, in *Illicit*, a film that raised more than a few hackles with its excessive drinking and scenes of Stanwyck and boyfriend James Rennie lounging around in their pajamas.

When Stanwyck starred as a small-town girl determined to get to the top of the business world in *Baby Face* (1933), the censors went wild. In Darryl F. Zanuck's original story (written under the pen name Mark Canfield), Lily Powers (Stanwyck) is a poor girl in a rough steel town, forced by her father to dance almost naked in his speakeasy and entertain selected guests in the bedroom. When her father is killed by an exploding still, Lily takes off for the big city, seducing a brakeman so she can ride for free in an empty freight car. In New York, she sweet-talks her way into a job at the Old

Manhattan Trust Company, then works her way up through the bank's executives (including a young John Wayne), until she marries the president (George Brent). To keep Stanwyck in luxury, Brent skims money from the bank. When his embezzlement surfaces, he begs her to sacrifice her jewels to bail him out. Stanwyck refuses, but then realizes she truly loves Brent. She runs to his office with the jewels, only to discover that he's shot himself.

The script was submitted to the MPPDA late in 1932, after Dr. Wingate had replaced Colonel Joy. Wingate worried that this was yet another entry in the sex picture genre, but felt that Stanwyck's casting would mitigate against any problems "in view of her sincere and restrained acting." The few changes he suggested were designed to tone down the suggestion that Lily was using her body to bargain for favors and soften the indication that her father had pushed her into prostitution.

The New York censors were not as understanding as their former boss. On April 1, 1933, they rejected the film entirely, and Zanuck turned to Wingate for help in remaking the picture. There was only one problem: Neither Stanwyck nor Brent were available for retakes. Using Wingate's suggestions, Zanuck reshot the film around his two stars. Cutting was the easiest part. The brakeman scene was eliminated entirely, along with the rougher moments involving Lily and her father. More difficult was the task of giving the film a stronger moral tone. In the original cut, Lily's best friend is an elderly cobbler, described in the story outline as "a gnarled, twisted, old German, a cripple—with a bitter resentment of the world. His trade is shoe mending but he reads Nietzsche, and he is steeped in the philosophy of nature—contempt for the weak." Early in the film, he counsels her: "A woman, young, beautiful, like you, can get anything she wants in the world. Because you have power over men. But you must use men, not let them use you. You must be a master, not a slave. Look here. Nietzsche says: 'All life, no matter how we idealize it, is nothing more nor less than exploitation.' That's what I'm telling you. Exploit yourself. Go to some big city where you will find opportunities. Use men! Be strong! Defiant! Use men to get the things you want."

Zanuck turned the cobbler into the film's moral voice. He re-edited his scenes and had the actor, Alphonse Ethier, redub his dialogue over reaction shots of Stanwyck. The above speech was changed to: "A woman, young, beautiful, like you, can get anything she wants in the world. But there is the right and wrong way—remember the price of the wrong way is too great. Go to some big city where you will find opportunities. Don't let people mislead you. You must be a master—not a slave. Keep clean, be strong, defiant, and you will be a success."

Wingate suggested a scene in which the cobbler comes to New York to denounce

Lily's immorality. That wasn't practical, so Zanuck recut another scene, in which Lily receives a book from him as a Christmas present. In place of more Nietzschean advice, Zanuck added a note from the cobbler, who calls her a coward and advises her to change her ways.

The ending also had generated complaints. Even though Lily realizes too late that she has lost the one man she ever loved, she still has her jewels as consolation. With his stars unavailable, Zanuck concocted a hasty scene in which the bank's board of directors reveals that Brent has miraculously recovered. He and Lily have sold her jewels to save the bank and retired to a life of hard work and poverty in Pittsburgh. The film ends with a stock shot of steel mills but nary a glimpse of Stanwyck or Brent in their new life.

The new version of *Baby Face* got by the New York censors with only a few cuts but was banned outright in Ohio, Virginia, Quebec, Australia, and Geneva. Even with the changes, it seemed to be about as racy as a Hollywood movie could get. Nor was Hays pleased to read the film's review in *Liberty* magazine: "Three cheers for Sin! If you don't think it pays, get a load of Barbara Stanwyck as she sins her way to the top floor of Manhattan's swellest bank. . . . This is about the roughest story that has come to the screen, but done disarmingly well. . . . No embarrassing sin scenes; only the results are shown."[9]

Platinum-plated Sin

With films like *Baby Face*, Barbara Stanwyck added several large logs to the bonfire of the vanities that threatened to engulf Hollywood. When Jean Harlow rose to stardom, however, she threw in a couple of sticks of dynamite.

Sex had been Harlean Carpenter's stock in trade from the moment she signed on with Central Casting, using the professional name Jean Harlow. She created a minor sensation as a society woman who unknowingly loses the back of her dress in the 1929 Laurel and Hardy two-reeler *Double Whoopee*. In her first starring role, as a promiscuous English beauty in Howard Hughes's 1930 *Hell's Angels*, she scandalized audiences by asking her man of the hour "Would you be shocked if I put on something more comfortable?" Playing another two-timer in 1931's *Goldie*, she was the first woman in a talking picture to be referred to as a "tramp."

Despite her early notoriety, Harlow didn't really come into her own as a screen star until MGM cast her in an adaptation of Katharine Brush's novel *Red-Headed Woman*. The novel had been around the studio for a while as Irving J. Thalberg tried to come up with the right combination of writer and star to make the difficult story work. He got it when the studio signed Anita Loos to pen the script, and his assistant Paul Bern suggested Harlow for the role.

Harlow stars as Lil, a secretary who dreams of making it big in small-town society. To that end, she pursues her boss, banking executive Bill Legendre (Chester Morris), eventually winning him from his wife (Leila Hyams). When the town's upper crust refuses to accept her, she seduces an older and richer man, then follows him to New York, where she plans to divorce Bill and marry the older man while carrying on an affair with his chauffeur (Charles Boyer). After Bill reveals the affair, Lil tries to shoot him. The film ends with Lil in France, where she's found another rich patsy and is continuing her affair with Boyer.

Thalberg saw the film as a farce, a spoof of the sex-charged pictures that were already stirring up trouble. He had a hard time getting anybody else to see it that way, however. Lamar Trotti read the script for the MPPDA in April 1932 and took it very seriously, advising that the film would be impossible to get past the censors. Thalberg argued that the farcical treatment would make the picture palatable, but even the film's director, Jack Conway, didn't get the joke. Nor did the first preview audience. Thalberg had to change the opening to set a lighter tone, adding a scene in which Harlow shows off Morris's picture on her garter. Even today, however, the film's uneven tone is apparent, with scenes alternating between high farce and high melodrama. What holds it together are the glossy production values, a very strong cast, and the amazing rapport Harlow manages to build with her audience.

Red-Headed Woman drew varied responses within the MPPDA, depending on whether it was seen in a private preview or with an audience. According to Joy, audiences laughed at Lil and sided with the banker's wife, often applauding when she told Lil off.

The film was banned in England, though King George V kept a private copy to show guests at Buckingham Palace. Massachusetts cut every possible indication of Lil's affair with the chauffeur; Pennsylvania cut the final shot of Boyer driving Harlow's car; and Ohio cut the entire race-track sequence set in France, robbing the film of its comic ending. For all of this, however, *Red-Headed Woman* did quite well at the box office, and the critics raved about Harlow's skills as a comedienne. So, MGM set out to create another sex-charged vehicle for her—*Red Dust*.

Wilson Collison's play had been floating around Hollywood even longer than *Red-Headed Woman*. A reader's report from 1927 explains why. The original drama tells of a steamy romantic quadrangle on an Indochinese plantation. Lucien, the French overseer, is in love with Maurice, a recent widow, as is his half-mad assistant, Guidon.

Guidon has brought Vantene, a prostitute, from Saigon, but she falls for Lucien and parades around nearly naked, trying to seduce him. She also does her best to protect Maurice from Guidon. This leads to a scene in which Guidon whips Vantene, only to be whipped in turn by Lucien. Finally, Maurice kills Guidon when he tries to rape her. Lucien sends her back to Paris but stays on the plantation and falls for Vantene.

According to the reader's report, "its two illicit love stories seem to ban it from the screen." Another reader suggested that "if Vantene were made a moral woman, the story might be useful for the screen. It is too illicit now." In 1930, a reader questioned such plot elements as the whipping scene, Vantene's prostitution, and the ending in which Maurice escapes punishment for killing Guidon.

In 1931 MGM tried developing *Red Dust* as a vehicle for Greta Garbo, transforming Vantene into a chic kept woman in Saigon who falls for a young plantation overseer (Clark Gable). That adaptation ultimately went nowhere. A year later, the studio had moved back towards the original play to create a vehicle for Gable and Jean Harlow. Vantene's arrival at the plantation was expanded so she could have an affair with Gable (now named Dennis), and the widow (Mary Astor) was a widow no longer. Her husband was allowed to live, thus providing a barrier to her involvement with Gable.

Most of Joy's objections concerned the characterization of Vantene. Starting with the first script pages, submitted in July 1932, he urged Thalberg to tone down any references to her career as a prostitute. Instead of being hired by Gable's assistant to come to the plantation, she is merely his guest. And though there were some quips alluding to her profession (Gable: "Take a walk." Harlow: "I've had plenty of practice"), Gable's attempt to pay Harlow for her favors was softened, mainly because of complaints from the Ohio censors. In addition, writer John Lee Mahin restructured the plot to make Vantene more of a sarcastic bystander than an active participant. As Joy would write MGM executive William Orr, "Harlow's role, therefore, should be considered free from offense."

There were still cuts made by local censors, but nothing as devastating as those ordered for *Red-Headed Woman*. *Red Dust* was another hit, establishing both Gable and Harlow as major box-office stars at MGM. Though it was still raw enough to be part of the problem, it didn't create any significant new protests of its own. It didn't need to. A month after *Red Dust*'s October premiere, Paramount went into production on a film that would brand its star, justly or unjustly, as the woman who brought censorship to Hollywood.

Hollywood Goes West

For blazing into the censorship wars came Mae West. Her films carried sex to a level that made them a genre unto themselves, much as West, during her first years in Hollywood, was a law unto herself.

During a vaudeville career that reached back to the early years of the century, West had built up a repertoire of bawdy movements and line readings. She introduced the shimmy to Broadway in 1918. In 1925 she spent a week in jail after the police closed her play *SEX*. Her pioneering look at homosexuality, *The Drag*, was so inflammatory she couldn't even get a Broadway booking, and *Pleasure Man* was closed by the police after only two performances.

The hit of her life, however, was *Diamond Lil*, a tale of sex and crime in the Bowery during the Gay Nineties. The play opened on Broadway in April 1928 and ran nine months before West took it on a successful cross-country tour, including a stop in Los Angeles that generated interest in the film rights.

Universal ran the script through the Studio Relations Committee in January 1930, prior to the Production Code's adoption, and it was banned under the Formula. When the studio proposed hiring West as a writer, Hays marshalled all of his persuasive powers to change their minds. It would take two years for the actress to make it to Hollywood.

According to Mae West, Hollywood panted at her doorstep for years until Paramount finally snapped her up in 1932. The truth, according to West biographer Maurice Leonard, was a little less flattering. Although she had written a hit novel, *The Constant Sinner*, West had not been successful in creating a stage follow-up to *Diamond Lil*. When an adaptation of *The Constant Sinner* ran only eight weeks in 1931, the thirty-nine-year-old actress-writer began to wonder if she hadn't played out her image as the all-American vamp.

Two friends from earlier days came to the rescue: budding Paramount star George Raft and producer William Le Baron. Speakeasy queen Texas Guinan had turned down a glorified cameo in *Night After Night*. Since West had based her stage character partly on Guinan's rowdy nightclub patter, she seemed a logical second choice. When West arrived in Hollywood, she was appalled by the lackluster script and asked to write her own dialogue. She even offered to give her salary back to Paramount rather than do the role as written. Studio head Adolph Zukor finally agreed to give her a chance.

In her first scene, West hands her furs over to a nightclub hatcheck girl, revealing an impressive array of jewelry. "Goodness," says the girl, "what lovely diamonds!" "Goodness had nothing to do with it, dearie," quips Mae, sashaying up the nightclub stairs (a move Mae fought to keep in the film). Audiences around the nation roared at her good-natured irreverence. As Raft would later say, "Mae West stole everything but the cameras."[10]

Suddenly, theater owners were clamoring for more West films. Paramount, which would post a $21 million deficit in 1932, was not about to look a gift hit in the mouth. So they offered West a chance to star in her own film. Since she had made *Night After Night* on a one-picture contract, West held all the power and used it to get the studio to agree to a film version of *Diamond Lil*.

Paramount kept the arrangement secret until a month before production was due to start. When Hays found out, he reminded them sternly that the play had been banned and told them not even to bother resubmitting it with a different name. A day after receiving Hays's letter, Zukor told him they would drop the project, but two weeks later Dr. Wingate, who had just taken over the Studio Relations Committee, informed Hays that Paramount had signed Lowell Sherman to direct the film. As if West's infamous vehicle weren't trouble enough, the director had cohosted Fatty Arbuckle's notorious Labor Day party.

The argument went back and forth until Hays brought the matter before the MPPDA's New York board on November 28, 1932. Although Hays hoped the board, consisting mostly of East Coast moneymen rather than West Coast production heads, could be scared off by the threat of renewed protests, he had underestimated Zukor's persuasiveness. Invoking his studio's dire economic situation, Zukor won the board's permission to make a film using suitable materials from *Diamond Lil*, but under a different title. All Hays could do was insist that the play be mentioned nowhere on-screen or in the film's advertising and demand, with the new title, changes in the locale and the character names.

He didn't even get that much. While the film was retitled *She Done Him Wrong*, and Diamond Lil became Lady Lou, the locale remained the same. Paramount suggested moving the action to Rio, but Wingate felt that would rouse complaints from South America. A suggestion to set the film on San Francisco's Barbary Coast was considered, but that notorious red-light district was too controversial, so they returned to the original setting.

Wingate managed to cut down the many references to Lou's previous affairs, changed the hero from a detective posing as a Salvation Army officer to a detective posing as an unspecified mission worker, and even got West to change the last line. The play had ended with Lil, the infamous saloon singer, telling the hero, "I always knew you could be had," echoing an earlier line delivered when he spurned her advances. In the film, the detective (Cary Grant) jokingly scolds Lou, saying, "You bad girl." "You'll find out," Lou coos.

There were other elements Wingate couldn't get Paramount to remove, including a pair of gay lovers Lou calls "the Cherry Sisters." Wingate also lost the battle to remove some of the play's more suggestive lines, including West's reference to herself as "one of the finest women ever walked the streets"; her quip to a fallen woman, "When women go wrong, men go right after them"; and her famous invitation to Grant, "Why don't you come up some time, see me."

Even the removal of these lines would not have changed the film's impact. Although the melodramatic plotting seemed primitive even in 1933, West's characterization was a decided departure from the typical screen ingenue and even from Garbo's tragic shady ladies. Here was a woman who reveled in her sexuality and enjoyed everything it could bring her. As she explains to a jilted girl she saves from suicide, "Men's all alike—married or single—I happen to be smart enough to play it their way." The dream lover she sang about was "A Guy What Takes His Time" ("I'm a fast-movin' gal who likes 'em slow/Got no use for fancy drivin'/Want to see a guy arrivin' in low"). Even when she settles for settling down with Grant at the end, she gets the last word, promising him pleasures he would never get from the typical ingenue. West personified the sex film's dream of feminist self-determination, but without the final concession to the status quo.

The state censors weren't as easily controlled as Wingate, making major deletions in lines and songs. So many of them cut the middle verses of "A Guy What Takes His Time" that the studio finally removed them from all prints, leaving a jarring, expensive cut.

None of this could dim the audience's enthusiasm. *She Done Him Wrong* cost Paramount only two hundred thousand dollars to make but brought in two million dollars domestically and another million in international release. That may not have been enough to pull the studio into the black, but it helped.

It did little for Hollywood's public image, however, at least among the moralists. Martin Quigley called the Production Code a failure. Father Lord warned Hollywood not to risk the wrath of the Church Militant. In an editorial in *Picturegoer,* Malcolm D. Phillips admitted liking the film but questioned its appropriateness: "The most high-powered publicity campaign I can remember has been devoted to the glorification of Mae West—whose loudly sexy screen personality has become a symbol of the moral irrresponsibility, if not the decadence, of Hollywood today. . . . She should never have been invested with the glamour of a goddess or the importance of a prophet. She should never have been boosted to an eminence that sets a film character that is little more than a common courtesan up as an example and a model for the girlhood of the world."[11]

None of this could deter West or Paramount from creating another bawdy comedy as a follow-up to *She Done Him Wrong*. In *I'm No Angel*, she plays Tira, a lion tamer who takes high society by storm and even wins a proposal from sleek lawyer Cary Grant, only to almost lose everything when a beau from her past steps into the picture. It would appear from the MPPDA files that Wingate had no problem with the basic plot, but rather with the details. Once again he tried to cut lines that would rank among West's most famous, including "When I'm good, I'm good. But when I'm bad I'm better." The bulk of the correspondence, however, is devoted to songs. The MPPDA rejected the title "No One Does It Like That Dallas Man." The writers switched it to "There Is No One Like My Dallas Man," tried to revert to the original, then settled for "No One Loves Me Like That Dallas Man." Wingate also had problems with one of the lyrics:

Why, brother—he's a wild horse trainer
With a special whip—
Gals, you'll go insaner
When he gets you in his grip.

This was changed to:

Why, brother—he's a cowboy wooer,
Roamin' on the hills,
Just a big lassoer,
With a stirrup full of thrills.

Even with the changes, Wingate warned the studio to watch out for suggestive hand gestures accompanying "Roamin' on the hills."

Wingate had less luck with the title song. Two lines in particular struck him as too suggestive: "Love me, honey, love me till I just don't care" and "You're my ace in the hole." Again the writers sent him laundered versions—"Love me, honey, ask me if you think I care" and "You're my real man, I declare"—then switched back to the originals, this time for good. Since the song played only over the closing credits, cutting portions for local censors, as Paramount did in Pennsylvania, was less of a problem. When Wingate saw the final cut in September 1933, he was pleasantly surprised, wiring the New York office that it was "on the whole much better than we expected."

I'm No Angel duplicated West's earlier success with critics and at the box office. She was taken up by the intelligentsia and even posed as the Statue of Liberty on the cover of *Vanity Fair*. But the acclaim would soon be drowned out by shouts from another arena. With *I'm No Angel*, the moralists had had enough of Mae West. She may not have been the only reason for the uproar, but her films gave the protesters one of their loudest rallying cries.

The Final Outrage

Will Hays did what he could in the face of continued protests over the movies. He issued press release after press release proclaiming that the Production Code was truly cleaning up the screen. In 1933 he got the MPPDA board to vote its continued support of the Code. He set up a system whereby Wingate and the Studio Relations Committee could appeal decisions of the Hollywood Jury. He even got ten of the civic groups that screened films for the MPPDA to publish *The Green Sheet*, a compilation of film ratings designed to draw educators' and parents' attention to Hollywood's better product.

None of it was enough. For a while, the one defense Hays had was that nobody had proven a causal link between the movies and any social ills. That would change with the publication of *Our Movie Made Children* in 1933.

In 1929 the Motion Picture Research Council, a procensorship group, got a grant from the Payne Study and Experiment Fund to probe the influence of movies on behavior. Over the next three years, nineteen researchers conducted a series of studies on such topics as "Getting Ideas from the Movies," "Relationship of Motion Pictures to the Character and Attitudes of Children," and "Boys, Movies, and City Streets." Criminals, delinquent children, and prison wardens were quizzed about the influence of movies on crime. Test groups rated movie plots in relation to their concepts of contemporary moral standards. Researchers even tallied up the professions and marital status of film characters, reacting in horror when the statistics differed from national norms.

The first results of the Payne Fund studies appeared in the January 1933 issue of *McCall's* magazine. America was shocked, but the reformers were delighted. Suddenly there was cold scientific evidence that the movies were destroying a whole generation. The Motion Picture Research Council commissioned free-lance writer Henry James Forman to summarize the findings for the general public in *Our Movie Made Children*. The result was a surprise best-seller that helped generate public opinion against the movies. Forman lambasted Hollywood for leading children to delinquency, corrupting their values, and disrupting their sleep. Reporting on the claims of juvenile delinquents that the movies had led them astray, he marveled, "Fagin's school was child's play to this curriculum of crime." Following the story of a young man who seduced his girlfriend after watching movie love scenes and who eventually ended up serving time for rape, Forman stated, "The road to delinquency, in a few words, is heavily dotted with movie addicts, and obviously, it needs no crusaders or preachers or reformers to come to this conclusion."[12]

There was some question, however, as to whether the researchers themselves had reached these conclusions. Scientists involved in the Payne Fund studies complained that Forman's book misrepresented their findings to make a stronger case against the movies. Others raised serious questions about the methodology involved. Were juvenile delinquents the best judges of what led them into crime, or were they merely saying what they thought the researchers wanted to hear? Did the movies influence behavior and attitudes or merely reflect them? Was it the function of any art form to support traditional values, even when public behavior consistently deviated from them? The questions were raised most perceptively by Mortimer J. Adler in *Art and Prudence*, a massive consideration of the Payne Fund studies (most of which he found notably lacking in scientific objectivity) and the historical debate between artists and moralists. Adler's book had been suggested by Hays himself, who hoped it would settle the issue.

Whatever harm *Our Movie Made Children* did, however, was inflicted with the full cooperation of Hollywood, for the studios were willing to push the envelope as far as possible in a desperate drive to keep audiences coming back for more. According to Jack Vizzard, numerous Hollywood producers claimed the questionable honor of producing the film that brought stricter censorship to the screen. Tradition has given the nod to two 1933 films: Warner Bros.' *Convention City* and Paramount's *The Story of Temple Drake*.

Convention City fits into the Warners gold-digger tradition but takes a more jaundiced view than the Busby Berkeley films. It follows the businessmen (and one woman) at a sales convention in Atlantic City—"all about life, liberty, business and the pursuit of sex" as the studio synopsis puts it. An unhappily married salesman (Adolphe Menjou) considers a liaison with a female colleague (Mary Astor) but also tries to seduce the boss's daughter in hopes of landing a promotion. A henpecked husband (Guy Kibbee) ditches his wife so he can dally with a chorus girl (Joan Blondell), one of many borderline prostitutes working the convention.

The script posed numerous problems for Wingate, but he let a lot of it by because Warners production head Hal Wallis promised him that it would all be played for comedy. A major concern at the studio was keeping Blondell's ample bosom properly covered, no small task considering that the script (the film itself has been lost) has her spend almost half the film in her underwear as she tries to work a badger game on Kibbee. In a memo to Wallis, studio head Jack L. Warner urged: "We must put brassieres on Joan Blondell and make her cover up her breasts because, otherwise, we are going to have these pictures stopped in a lot of places. I believe in showing their forms but, for Lord's sake, don't let those bulbs stick out." Wallis passed his comments on, complaining that one evening gown left her "practically undressed and stripped to the waist. . . . We want to be able to show the pictures when we get through making them."

The high—or low—point of the film's rowdiness comes at the conclusion, as the still-drunken salesmen board the train for home. As they bid goodbye to the women who have kept them entertained all week, and the romantic couples pair off for the final fadeout, one group has to be stopped from bringing a goat on the train.

The Story of Temple Drake took a more serious approach and, in the opinion of many, took Hollywood as far as it could go without crossing the line into out-and-out obscenity. William Faulkner's attack on southern gentility, *Sanctuary*, had raised a furor on its publication in 1931. It told the tale of Temple Drake, a willful southern belle given to wild drinking sprees with college boys. When a minor car accident lands her at a bootlegger's shack, she's raped with a corncob by the degenerate, impotent Popeye, then forced to work in a brothel he owns. At the end, she even admits to having enjoyed this degradation.

Lamar Trotti reported on the novel in June 1931: "This is a sadistic story of horror—probably the most sickening novel ever written in this country. Important because of its brilliant style, it has had quite a large sale. . . . I did not read all of the book, it was too much for me." In Trotti's opinion, the story was "utterly unthinkable as a motion picture," but he felt the novel could be used as evidence of how much cleaner movies were than other media.

As unthinkable as the story was, however, Paramount picked up the rights in late 1932, just as the studio was going into production on *She Done Him Wrong*. They didn't even bother consulting Hays about the purchase, probably realizing in advance what his response would be. Hays tried to block the production, but his New York office registered the title and approved the treatment anyway.

The ball was now in Dr. Wingate's court. First, he demanded a title change and, as with other controversial stories, stipulated that no mention be made of the original in the film's credits or advertising. He made Paramount turn the brothel into a boarding-house, cutting a shot of hats on a hatrack and transforming a curtained doorway into an open arch in the process. Eventually, he even demanded that Paramount remove a shot of Jobyna Howland, as the madam, from the opening credits.

Wingate also questioned Temple Drake's (Miriam Hopkins) redemption after she murders Popeye (renamed Trigger to avoid any reference to the popular comic-strip character). As in the novel, she gives up her chance to keep her degradation quiet by taking the witness stand in defense of another bootlegger falsely accused of murder. After screening the film, Joe Breen complained that the defense attorney's comment to Temple's grandfather, "You ought to be proud of her," seemed to be justifying her fall from grace. In desperation, Wingate tried to get Paramount to add an epilogue showing Temple as a welfare worker in China.

Wingate's biggest problem with the film was the rape scene. So many people who hadn't even read the book knew about Temple's rape by corncob that Wingate insisted that any reference to corncobs be removed. He even cut a line in which Temple is sent to spend the night in the corn crib. When Hays heard a rumor that Trigger would pick up a corncob after the rape, he sent an outraged letter to Adolph Zukor: "If this report is true it indicates an attitude that makes impossible a compliance with the spirit of the Code by those who are party to it."

Reviews were mixed. *Film Daily* complained that the cleansing of the story left it hard to follow. *Variety* seconded that opinion while holding that nothing could remove the bad taste of the original. Even in his positive review, Aaronson of the *Motion Picture Herald* advised Paramount to focus advertising on the story and the acting rather than the source material. But the advertising campaign only added fuel to the fire, using such slogans as "Lust trapped me. Desire ruined me. I'm a shame-drenched sinner." The *Chicago Tribune* critic seemed to be leading an outraged nation when he wrote, "I've been investigating a sewer. Where's all the clean talk of Hays to women's clubs?"[13]

The Church Steps In

The year *Convention City* and *The Story of Temple Drake* came out, Hollywood fell victim to the Great Depression. Initially, the economic crisis had had no effect on the movie industry, largely because of the novelty of talking pictures. Hollywood finally hit a slump in 1933. Of all the majors, only MGM and Columbia showed a profit. This sudden change in fortunes made Hollywood more vulnerable than ever to outside pressure.

In addition, already in place was a warrior with the zeal and the vision to force Hollywood to conform to his personal dream of what the screen—and American life—could be. Joseph Ignatius Breen came to the film capital after holding diplomatic positions in Jamaica, Budapest, and Ireland, where he reportedly was sentenced to death for "fomenting sedition."[14] As a reporter in Philadelphia in 1925, he campaigned so vehemently against references to birth control in the novel *Seed* that Universal dropped the element from their film version.

The newspaperman moved into public relations in 1926 as press agent for the Catholic Church's Eucharistic Congress, then stayed on to perform similar duties for the Chicago World's Fair. His work caught the eye of Martin Quigley, who soon learned that the two shared both a devotion to the church and similar moral visions. In 1930, Quigley hired Breen to work on Code-related matters in his New York office. There, Breen met Will Hays, who was equally impressed. Hays arranged to borrow Breen on a half-time basis to work on MPPDA public relations, then signed him on full time.

With an eye to dealing more closely with the industry, Breen campaigned for a transfer to Hollywood, where he went in 1931 to handle the MPPDA's West Coast public relations. Once there, he became increasingly involved in the work of the Studio Relations Committee. Although Hays passed over Breen as a replacement for Colonel Joy, the contentious Irishman quickly gained a reputation as Dr. Wingate's chief enforcer. As matters got worse, Breen was named Hays's assistant in the fall of 1933, putting him over Wingate's head. Even with his new authority and his love of a good fight, however, Breen didn't always get his way. The Hollywood Jury voted against him repeatedly, allowing MGM to retain Garbo's bedroom scene in *Queen Christina* and a nude swim in *Tarzan and His Mate*.

According to Jack Vizzard, it was Breen, in conference with Quigley and members of the Catholic hierarchy, who came up with the idea of using the church to force studio heads to conform to the Production Code. Starting in the summer of 1933, church-influenced speakers upped their attacks on Hollywood. After conferring with Bishop John J. Cantwell of Los Angeles, Dr. A. H. Giannini, president of the Bank of America, exhorted the MPPDA's members to exercise more self-control. In a speech before the National Conference of Catholic Charities in New York, Archbishop A. G. Cicognani proclaimed, "What a massacre of innocent youth is taking place hour by hour! How shall the crimes that have their direct source in motion pictures be measured?"[15]

Finally, the Synod of Bishops, at their November 1933 meeting, formed a special committee to look into the situation. This led to the creation of the Legion of Decency in April 1934. Originally, the Legion was a loosely organized group of Catholics interested in fighting indecent pictures. During church services, members pledged to avoid such films:

> I wish to join the Legion of Decency, which condemns vile and
> unwholesome moving pictures. I unite with all who protest against
> them as a grave menace to youth, to home life, to country and to
> religion.
> I condemn absolutely those salacious motion pictures which, with

The adoption of stricter self-regulation in Hollywood marked the start of roughly two decades during which Joe Breen and the PCA reviewed 98 percent of the movies released in the United States. This virtual stranglehold on U.S. film distribution was possible because most of the major studios owned their own theaters.

MPPDA members controlled only 20 percent of American movie screens, but that included more than half of the first-run theaters in the country. In addition, the members used their booking policies to control the nation's independently owned first- and second-run houses. Twentieth Century-Fox's exhibition contracts stipulated that the studio's films could not be shown on double bills with pictures not bearing the PCA Seal of Approval. Other studios could refuse to deal with second-run theaters or chains that also showed films not bearing the Seal.

This still left a good number of theaters for films that did not or could not pass the PCA's approval process. The states'-rights circuit consisted of smaller distributors who booked films into a given state, usually to rural houses that wouldn't even qualify as second-run theaters. In addition, each major city also had its grind houses, theaters in the seedier downtown areas that rarely had a chance to book major-studio product.

What did these theaters show if they weren't booking Code-approved Hollywood pictures? Not porn. Pornographic movies of the time were limited to stag films, sexual shorts distributed privately for screenings at parties or in brothels, though some movie theaters did show them after hours and behind locked doors. Overseas product had only limited appeal at first, confined to art houses and smaller theaters in ethnic neighborhoods. To meet the continuing demand for film product, independent producers working outside the MPPDA's control—and frequently outside Hollywood—developed the exploitation picture. These films competed with the big-budget Hollywood film by offering something Hollywood couldn't—forbidden subjects.

Exploitation dates back to the earliest days of movies. Even the major studios dabbled in moralistic tales filled with titillating displays of the sins they vigorously condemned. The glory days of the exploitation film came in the thirties and forties, when strict Code enforcement drove such subjects underground.

Sex was the central focus of most exploitation films. Pseudodocumentaries like 1937's *Love Life of a Gorilla* gave the filmmaker a chance to parade topless native women before the camera while hinting at more perverse primitive pleasures. These would be replaced in the late forties by nudist-colony films, which depicted the joys of nudism as a way of life—although the camera rarely strayed below the waist.

More prolific were the cautionary tales. These usually involved a young innocent whose ignorance of the facts of life leaves her seduced and abandoned or a crusading reporter/educator/politician who takes aim at the depredations of ignorance and/or crime. There was never any real sexual action depicted on-screen. But at the very least there was always the opportunity to show a little more skin than Joe Breen would have allowed.

Along with sex came related topics such as venereal disease, childbirth, and birth control. In addition, the same plots could be used to expose the evils of drugs, though marijuana would appear to have been the only drug dealt with extensively. Exploitation king Kroger Babb tried a film on alcoholism, *One Too Many,* but it didn't sell well. Lesbianism turned up as the subject of only one film, 1937's *Children of Loneliness,* which purported to be an adaptation of Radclyffe Hall's *The Well of Loneliness.* Male homosexuality was never touched on.

The small group of producer/distributors working in the field came to be called "the forty thieves." Many of them learned showmanship on the carnival circuit and brought something of the carnival to their movie careers. Often their films were distributed as road shows, accompanied by a lecture on sex education and the sale of books on the topic. When the films were too hot to play in a city's theaters, the distributors set up tents outside city limits.

Most of these exploitation films were laughable even by contemporary standards, yet they served a purpose. Even though they were filled with misinformation, they fostered some degree of public awareness. Those that have survived provide a valuable look at popular attitudes on subjects Hollywood never touched. Some of the better-made, faster-moving ones even have a camp value, like 1938's *The Burning Question,* which decades later played the midnight-movie circuit as *Reefer Madness.*

More important, however, were the battles exploitation filmmakers had to fight simply to get their product before the public. The courts upheld bans on such early films as *The Road to Ruin* (1928), in which the erring heroine agrees to prostitute herself to finance an abortion, only to discover that her first customer is her father; *Tomorrow's Children* (1934), in which reformers fight to have the children of an alcoholic couple sterilized; and *The Birth of a Baby* (1938), one of the first films to include a "birth reel." But later pictures, like *Mom and Dad* (1948), a sex-education saga Babb distributed into the fifties, began winning their court battles after the Supreme Court issued its *Miracle* decision (see Chapter Seven).

The year after *Mom and Dad* was produced, Babb was involved with a drug film designed to capitalize on Robert Mitchum's arrest for smoking marijuana. *Wild Weed* (also known as *Devil's Weed* and *She Should'a Said No!*) starred one of Mitchum's codefendants, Lila Leeds, as a young innocent seduced into marijuana addiction. The picture was rejected twice by the Pennsylvania censorship board. The third time, the distributor took the board to court and won. In 1957, the Court of Common Pleas in Philadelphia struck down Pennsylvania's forty-six-year-old film censorship law. The nation's first state censorship board was history, and *Wild Weed* won a place in the annals of constitutional law. ✂

other degrading agencies, are corrupting public morals and promoting a sex mania in our land. . . .

I make this protest in a spirit of self-respect, and with the conviction that the American public does not demand filthy pictures, but clean entertainment and educational features.[16]

Soon, other organizations—including synagogues and Protestant churches—took up the pledge as well. Hollywood tried to look the other way during all this agitation, but once the boycotts started, they couldn't. The Detroit branch of the Legion of Decency issued a list of sixty-three condemned films in May 1934. Forty-three of them had been passed by the Studio Relations Committee, including *Convention City*, *Design for Living*, and *The Story of Temple Drake*. At about the same time, Father Lord started naming five condemned films a month in his magazine, *Queen's Work*, and the International Federation of Catholic Alumnae (IFCA), a Catholic women's group, created a listing of recommended films.

The first organized boycott hit Philadelphia. Cardinal Dougherty asked parishioners to stop going to the movies altogether, and box-office receipts fell 40 percent. The pain was particularly sharp for Warner Bros., which had major holdings in the city. The studio heads finally came together to settle the issue. As Breen would later describe it: "There was Harry Warner, standing up at the head of the table, shedding tears the size of horse turds, and pleading for someone to get him off the hook. And well he should, for you could fire a cannon down the center aisle of any theatre in Philadelphia, without danger of hitting anyone! And there was Barney Balaban [of Paramount], watching him in terror, wondering if he was going to be next in Chicago, and Nick Schenck [of MGM], wondering when he was going to be hit by a bucket of shit in New York."[17]

To make matters worse, the Federal Council of Churches of Christ in America was threatening not only to enlist its entire membership of twenty-two million in the Legion, but to campaign vigorously for federal censorship as well. Finally, the studio heads agreed to accept more rigid enforcement of the Production Code. Breen and Quigley took the news to a June 1934 bishops' meeting in Cincinnati and got the church's agreement to call off the boycott.

On July 1, 1934, the MPPDA's board made it official. The Studio Relations Committee became the Production Code Administration (PCA) under Breen's leadership. To give the Code teeth, the board created the Seal of Approval to be administered by the PCA. No film could have a Seal unless it adhered to the Code; no member could release, distribute, or exhibit a film without the Seal. Any member defying the new rule would be fined $25,000.[18]

In addition, the Hollywood Jury was abolished. Producers wishing to appeal Breen's decisions on their work would have to go to the New York board, which consisted not of filmmakers but of moneymen more concerned with avoiding another costly boycott than with fighting for artistic freedom.

By working with both Hollywood on the inside and the Legion of Decency on the outside, Breen had effected a revolution in film content. What would follow was a stream of film product promoting a consistent ethos. Hollywood would continue to supply dreams for the movie screens of the nation, but the chief dreammaker was now Joe Breen.

"Leave Us Alone and Let Us Make Our Living in Our Own Way! Or Is That Too Much to Ask?"

Chapter Five

When Bette Davis shouted the above at Humphrey Bogart in 1937's *Marked Woman*, she could have been speaking for all of Hollywood after Joe Breen's rise to power. In short order he saw to it that no crime went unpunished and no criminal became a hero. Drug addiction, nudity, and homosexuality were banished from the screen. And a borderline prostitute like Davis's character in *Marked Woman* was transformed into a nightclub hostess, selling drinks and food but not herself.

By the time he issued the first Seal of Approval—to John Ford's historical drama *The World Moves On*—Breen was already an old hand at evaluating scripts and films in moral terms from his years as Dr. Wingate's enforcer. In addition, much of the structure for evaluation was already in place when he took over. Every morning at ten, Breen conducted the "huddle," a meeting in which staff members discussed the scripts they had been assigned and worked out strategies for dealing with problems. The rest of the day they reviewed scripts, met with filmmakers, and prepared letters, all of which went out over Breen's name to give the PCA a consistent identity.

Each script was assigned to two members of the staff, some of whom specialized in particular types of films. Breen worked mostly on the problem scripts, but also settled disputes between staffers and backed them up when it came time to bring their recommendations to the studios. In addition, he spent hours on the phone helping writers and directors with last-minute problems.

Sin and sex after Joe Breen took over the Production Code Administration: The script for Marked Woman *(1937) identified Bette Davis's character as a nightclub hostess, but one look at her sequined gown and hip-swinging walk and most audience members knew what she really did for a living.*

Studios usually sent Breen source materials and story treatments, and after a while the PCA's input played a crucial role in the decision to purchase a property. Equally important was the Production Code letter on the script's suitability. Most of these letters consisted of two parts: a general statement of whether or not the subject and its treatment were acceptable under the Code and a specific list of lines and business that could raise problems. Although each letter cautioned that the final judgment would be based on the film itself, Breen's acceptance of the story was all that was necessary to secure financing for a picture.

Once a film was passed, the PCA continued to run interference with local censorship boards. This also meant facing a new entry into the censors' ranks—the Legion of Decency. During the Legion's initial campaign, Father Fitzgeorge Dineen of Chicago had circulated a list of condemned films compiled in Detroit and IFCA's list of recommended movies. In 1936, IFCA's New York office took over the job of condemning films. In addition, some local chapters issued their own condemned lists until IFCA became the central authority.

This new version of the Legion of Decency rated films in three categories: A, morally unobjectionable; B, morally objectionable in part for all; and C, condemned. All Legion members pledged to boycott films rated C, making the rating a serious economic threat to any film so labeled (it would be almost twenty years before any Hollywood studio dared issue a condemned film). Many Legion members also pledged to avoid B-rated films. As a result, Breen and his staff frequently had to help studios negotiate cuts to lower a picture's rating to A.

Under Breen, the PCA gradually developed a vision of morality reflected in the films they passed. Each script was analyzed in terms of its theme, which the PCA defined as the question put to the main character and the way he or she answers it. If the protagonist responded to the question in a manner consistent with traditional morality, the theme was labeled "moral." If the protagonist took the wrong steps to solve his or her problem, the error needed to be clearly identified as such.

This is where "compensating moral value" came in. The concept had developed through script evaluation letters written since the Code's adoption in 1930. As Olga Martin, Breen's secretary during the early thirties, put it, "Any theme must contain at least sufficient good in the story to compensate for, and to counteract, any evil which it relates."[1] Compensating moral value could be achieved through varying combinations of four elements:

1—The voice of morality supplied by a sympathetic character who condemns any immoral actions;

Censored Hollywood

2—Suffering by the wrongdoer for his or her actions;

3—Reform and regeneration of the wrongdoer who chooses to repent and change his or her life; and

4—Punishment of the wrongdoer and retribution for his or her sins.

As a result of this doctrine, Greta Garbo and Robert Taylor could dally in unsanctified bliss in 1937's *Camille*, as long as Lionel Barrymore, as Taylor's father, was given his chance to condemn the affair. Burgess Meredith could shoot Lon Chaney, Jr. to save him from lynching at the end of 1939's *Of Mice and Men*, but only if a scene was added in which Meredith was arrested for the crime.

It took a powerful load of compensating moral values to get W. Somerset Maugham's *The Moon and Sixpence* to the screen in 1942. The novel, loosely based on the life of Paul Gauguin, follows the sexual adventures of artist Charles Strickland as he steals his best friend's wife, deserts her to run off to the South Seas, and settles down with a Tahitian beauty. Although Maugham's narrative condemned Strickland's behavior and gave him a suitably severe punishment—death from leprosy—Hollywood insiders felt that it could not be translated to the screen.

The property had been kicking around Hollywood for two decades before it fell into the hands of independent producer David L. Loew and writer-director Albert Lewin. Previous treatments had failed because in translating the novel into dramatic form the adaptors lost the book's moral tone. Lewin supplied the appropriate compensating moral values by adding a narrator. In a thinly disguised portrayal of Maugham, Herbert Marshall could give voice to all of the original author's condemnations of Strickland (George Sanders) while the protagonist went his evil ways. To add an extra moral fillip to the tale, Lewin had the stolen wife commit suicide after Strickland deserts her.

Not only was the story acceptable under the Code (though it should be noted that the film was approved while Breen was temporarily out of service as Code administrator), but Lewin's ingenuity generated positive press coverage and reviews that helped make the picture a box-office winner. More sophisticated circles, however, saw the device as a clever means of getting around the censors without really changing anything. As Thornton Delehanty wrote in the *New York Herald Tribune*: "Anyone in the audience who would prefer to watch what is going on can close his ears to the admonitory intonements from Never, Never Land."[2] This pattern would be repeated throughout the Production Code years. Breen and his colleagues could clean up a story on screen, but many in the audience still knew what lay behind the veneer of purity.

For certain subjects, of course, no amount of moral value could compensate. Arson, the kidnapping of children, drug abuse, abortion, sexual perversion, and other topics were considered so subversive they could not even be implied. Where such topics existed in a film's source material or could reasonably be inferred from the action, Breen demanded that the writers establish some alternative intepretation.

Joan Bennett's sidewalk pickup of Walter Pidgeon in *Man Hunt* (1941) labeled her a prostitute even though the word was never spoken on-screen. So the film's set decorator was ordered to place a sewing machine prominently in her apartment to affirmatively establish that she was nothing more than a friendly seamstress. In the original script for 1949's *Beyond the Forest*, Doc Moline (Joseph Cotten) pulls his wife (Bette Davis) from a doctor's office where she has gone to end an unwanted pregnancy. Even though abortion was never mentioned in the screenplay, Breen made Warner Bros. change the doctor to a "psychological consultant" so nobody could guess what Davis was really after. Then the Legion of Decency did him one better by removing any medical implication; they threatened to condemn the film unless the scene was reshot in a lawyer's office.

Breen did not acquire all of his power instantly; he had to fight some pretty tough characters to prove that he meant business. On his first meeting with Harry Cohn (head of Columbia Pictures and reputed to be one of Hollywood's meanest men), Cohn looked over Breen's qualifications and said, "What's this shit?" "I take that as a compliment," Breen replied. "My friends inform me that if there's an expert in this town on shit—it's you. So if I have to be judged, I'm glad it's by professionals."[3]

Cohn got off easy. When director W. S. Van Dyke suggested that Breen was taking bribes to pass films, Breen slugged him. One studio actually did attempt to bribe Breen. He woke up one Christmas morning to find a new Cadillac parked in front of his home in Malibu. He immediately called the studio head and screamed for him to "Get that GODDAMN THING out of here—TODAY!"[4] Throughout his career, Breen separated himself from the Hollywood social scene, eschewing parties and premieres in favor of evenings at home with his wife and six children. His only film-colony friends were the "Irish Mafia," a group of drinking buddies including James Cagney, Spencer Tracy, and Pat O'Brien.

Breen got some support from the changing economy. By 1935, things were looking better for the nation and for Hollywood. Attendance rose 15 percent in 1934, and some studios posted a 100 percent increase in revenues. Though other factors were at work beyond the adoption of the Production Code, the combination of cleaner movies and busier box office worked in Breen's favor.

Also helpful was a cessation of hostilities with reformers and religious groups. Not only had the churches called off their boycotts, but Pope Pius XI issued an encyclical praising Hollywood's improved morality. Studio heads were also impressed when Hays used Code enforcement to dissuade Father Charles Coughlin of Detroit—one of the Catholic Church's most influential spokesmen—from making a speech blaming Hollywood's censorship problems on Jewish industry leaders.

Finally, with Breen eliminating objectionable material before it even reached the screen, the studios were having less trouble with local censors. In 1936, *Variety* headlined, "Picture Censors Jittery. *Joebreening* to K.O. their jobs."[5]

"Joebreening" could mean more than just cutting films, however. When Breen took an interest in a picture, he could be a powerful ally. He had a particular fondness for social-problem pictures and often helped filmmakers fight off complaints from pressure groups and business interests. Breen stood behind Warner Bros. when it made *Black Fury*, a 1935 Paul Muni vehicle depicting the effect of organized crime on labor relations in the Pennsylvania coal mines. When the National Coal Association objected to the film, Breen advised Hays that the picture gave a fair representation of both sides of the issue. Breen also defended the film against the New York censors, who had claimed that "the picture heroizes a man who wins a strike by dynamiting a mine." As a result of his intercession, the film was passed not just in New York but in Pennsylvania, the site of the strikes on which the film was based.

Breen also stood up for the film version of Sidney Kingsley's play *Dead End*, which showed how poverty and bad influences turn slum children into criminals. When RKO and Fox first submitted the script in 1935, he seemed unusually conciliatory. New York staffers, who routinely evaluated all Broadway shows, had listed seven major Code violations, including the depiction of a syphilitic prostitute and "the characterization of youths organized and trained for future gang leaders and gangsters." But Breen assured the studios that all of this could be adapted to meet the Code's requirements in the interest of capturing "an important document that could be treated for the screen." Ultimately, both studios passed on the property, but when Samuel Goldwyn filmed it in 1937, Breen was equally helpful, shepherding the picture past censors in New York, England, and Austria.

The Decline and Fall of Sex and Violence

Production Code enforcement had an almost instant effect on the industry. As soon as he came into power, Breen divided all films in release into three categories. Class III films posed no problems and were allowed to remain in distribution, though he could demand some reediting. Class II films posed more problems. Pictures like *I'm No Angel* and the MGM gangster film *Manhattan Melodrama* were allowed to complete their

One can gauge the Production Code's effect on American filmmaking by looking at remakes of films originally released before Code enforcement. Hollywood's penchant for retelling successful stories and the need to remake films that could no longer be released after 1934 have left a catalogue of stories reshaped for different times.

As daring as Gloria Swanson's *Sadie Thompson* must have seemed in 1928, the 1932 version went as far as the screen ever would with Maugham's story. The remake was made under the stage version's previously banned title, *Rain*. It used as much of the play's questionable dialogue as the producer could get away with, and Joan Crawford as Sadie was more of a tramp than Swanson ever could have been. But even in the freewheeling days of the early thirties, there was material in the play that could not be brought to the screen. Davidson was still just a reformer, and references to his sexless marriage remained cut.

Sadie finally fell victim to the Production Code in 1953, when Columbia picked up the rights for its top star, Rita Hayworth. Although Breen's opposition to low-cut dresses and sensuous dancing had been worn down over the years—Hayworth performed a heated dance number that was cut in some localities—his commitment to sending out a positive moral message had not wavered. Whereas previous Sadies had gone off to a life of marital bliss in Australia, Hayworth's Sadie returns to San Francisco to accept punishment for her earlier sins.

The Letter was another Maugham property produced before and after Production Code enforcement. The play first reached the screen in 1929 with Jeanne Eagels starring as Leslie Crosbie, a woman who murders her lover and gets away with it by lying on the witness stand. Leslie's punishment for her crime is a life of guilt, as she announces in the closing line: "With all my heart, I still love the man I killed!"[6]

That wasn't enough retribution for Joe Breen. When Warner Bros. approached him about a remake in 1938, he insisted that they come up with a more suitable punishment for Leslie. After two years, somebody got the idea that she would be killed by her ex-lover's Eurasian mistress. But that left another murderer running loose; so the killer was apprehended by a local policeman who just happened to be passing by as she left the scene of the crime.

The following year, Warners and Breen would do better by another oft-filmed story. Dashiell Hammett's *The Maltese Falcon* had provided Warners with one of the most sex-charged films of the early thirties and one of the biggest flops of the mid-thirties. In 1941, the story's third version would sail through the Breen Office to become a surprise hit, making Humphrey Bogart a star and John Huston one of Hollywood's hottest directors.

Warner Bros. bought the book in 1931 and tried to keep in all of the sexual elements that had helped make it a hit. Detective Sam Spade (Ricardo Cortez) is involved with both his partner's wife (Thelma Todd) and a new client, the duplicitous Miss Wonderly (Bebe Daniels). His search for the black bird brings him into contact with effeminate thief Joel Cairo (Otto Matieson), fat man Casper Gutman (Dudley Digges), and Gutman's bodyguard and possible lover, Wilmer (Dwight Frye).

Colonel Joy tried to tone down the film, with little success. In one sequence, Miss Wonderly spends the night in Sam's apartment. At Joy's insistence, the studio had Sam say, "You can sleep in the bedroom—I'll spend the night out here on the divan." The next morning, however, there is a clear indentation in the pillow next to her head. The woman is roused from her slumbers when Iva Archer, the widow of Sam's partner, comes to the door. "Why is that dame wearing my kimono?" Iva demands on spotting Miss Wonderly.

Later, Sam suspects Miss Wonderly of stealing a thousand-dollar bill and forces her to strip to prove she doesn't have it. Joy tried to cut the scene, but Darryl F. Zanuck refused, arguing that since her underwear was not seen flying off, the audience would not assume she was naked.

The homosexual element is more subtle. Spade's secretary introduces the unseen Cairo as a new client and a real looker, leading Sam to expect a beautiful woman. When Gutman agrees to let Wilmer take the rap for murder, he caresses the boy's cheek with reckless abandon.

Breen refused to approve *The Maltese Falcon* for reissue, so Warners remade the story in 1935 as *Satan Met a Lady* with Warren William as detective Ted Shayne and Bette Davis as his scheming client. Breen's main objections were to the shady side of Shayne's character and his womanizing. A scene in which he intimidates a wealthy older woman into paying him protection money was changed so that he simply scares her into hiring him as a bodyguard. The biggest change, however, was the transformation of Casper Gutman into criminal queen Madame Barabbas (Alison Skipworth), with Wilmer now her nephew Kenneth (Maynard Holmes). The sexual side of their relationship remained, however, in Skipworth's reading of the line "He's been more than a son to me."

John Huston was already experienced at writing under the Production Code when he started work on his adaptation of Hammett's novel in 1940. Although he stuck closer to the original than any of his predecessors, he managed to eliminate most of the objectionable materials before a script was submitted to the PCA. There were still some objections, but they were mostly cosmetic. Breen changed Iva from Sam's mistress to his pursuer. To get around the implication that Sam and Brigid Shaughnessy had had an affair, Breen cut her line "Not after what we've been to each other." In addition, he ordered the studio to tone down Joel Cairo's effeminacy, but made no notes about the relationship between Gutman and Wilmer. Yet none of this was totally removed from the story. Huston had written his adaptation so cleverly that Breen never even asked that Sam's chasteness or Gutman's heterosexuality be affirmatively established. Instead, the characters' transgressions and deviations were left to the audience's imagination, which was the greatest strength of writing under the Production Code anyway. ✄

current exhibition contracts, but no new contracts were to be signed. Pictures in Class I —including *Baby Face*, *Convention City*, and *The Story of Temple Drake*—were to be withdrawn immediately.

To get a film back into circulation, the studio had to resubmit it to the PCA and obtain a Seal of Approval. For many films this posed no problem. Others were sent back to the studios as hopeless cases. Breen blocked the reissue of *She Done Him Wrong* in 1935 and again in 1949. He kept *Little Caesar* and *The Public Enemy* out of theaters until 1953. On some stories, the studio could attempt remakes. When Breen rejected Warners' 1931 version of *The Maltese Falcon*, the studio repackaged the film in more acceptable form (to Breen, if not the critics) as 1935's *Satan Met a Lady*.

In other cases, getting a film back into distribution simply meant recutting it to meet the requirements of the Production Code, under which the film was supposed to have been made in the first place. For its 1938 reissue, *King Kong* (1933) lost some brief bits of sex and violence that would not be restored until three decades later. The same year, *All Quiet on the Western Front* (1930) lost a nude bathing scene and a sequence in which Lew Ayres and his friends spend the night with some French farm girls.

Breen's biggest reediting job, however, was probably the 1932 version of *A Farewell to Arms*. The film, adapted from Ernest Hemingway's controversial novel, had raised considerable protest on its initial release because of its seeming glorification of premarital sex, but it also had been a major box-office hit. Now, with leading man Gary Cooper one of Hollywood's top stars, the prospect of a reissue was too enticing to resist.

In January 1938, Paramount approached Francis Harmon of the MPPDA's New York office about cutting the film for reissue. Breen thought it was "a hopeless task" but gave Harmon permission to issue a Seal if he thought it had been suitably reedited. When Harmon was ready to pass an edited version of the film two months later, Breen stepped back in and tried to convince Paramount to withdraw the picture. Instead, the studio offered to make even more changes. They cut major chunks from the love scenes and other discussions of the illicit relationship between Cooper and leading lady Helen Hayes. They also married off the pair by inserting a shot in which a man's hand places a wedding ring on a woman's finger. The new version was moral enough to earn a Seal, but it didn't make a whole lot of sense, particularly since the wedding insert was followed by a scene in which Cooper and Hayes discuss their plans to get married.

In addition to classifying and recutting existing films, Breen went to work on the genres and stars that had caused so much trouble before. In 1935, Hays got the producers to amend the Code to add further restrictions on the gangster picture. Although they hailed it as an end to the cycle, all they actually did was ban or limit those elements that had roused the most protest, including the use of machine guns, the flaunting of any kind of weaponry, and the killing of police officers.

At the same time, Warner Bros. released a film that Hays and Breen could herald as a new kind of crime film. *G-Men* marked James Cagney's transition from crook to cop, following his rise through the ranks of the FBI. He was still a hardheaded tough guy, but his move to the right side of the law made him a bigger star than ever. In a February 1935 letter, Breen complimented Warner Bros. on sounding "a new note in the general category of crime stories." The critics were equally impressed, but were quick to note the limits of this new cycle: "*Little Caesar*, *Scarface* and *Public Enemy* were more than portrayals of gangster tactics; they were biographies of curious mentalities. . . . But in the new idea of glorifying the government gunners who wipe out the killers there is no chance for that kind of character development and build-up."[7]

Those objections proved correct, and it wasn't long before the stars moved back into gangster roles, though with increased supervision by Breen. The gangster film continued in sanitized form until World War II, when Hollywood had other villains to fight (and even produced some films in which American gangsters took on the Axis). This was no great hardship for the genre's major stars. Cagney, Edward G. Robinson, and Paul Muni had no trouble establishing their box-office value in other genres, while Humphrey Bogart actually got his start as a screen gangster after Breen started clamping down on the genre.

But they were all men, who, as a rule, have had an easier time surviving changes in film styles and audience tastes. For the women who had been making sex films up to 1934, there was more trouble. Actresses like Barbara Stanwyck and Loretta Young, who had made successful films in a variety of genres, had no trouble under the new Hays restrictions. Those who had specialized in sex films, however, had to adapt or face early retirement.

Jean Harlow's *The Girl from Missouri* was one of several films started before Production Code enforcement and completed under Breen's watchful eye. As a result, there are frequent jarring cuts in the picture, indicating hasty attempts to change the natures of some scenes in mid-course. Yet writers Anita Loos and John Emerson were so successful at exploiting Harlow's talents within the bounds of the Production Code that the picture could have been titled *The Red-Headed Woman Gets Morals*.

Once again, Harlow stars as a young woman trying to make it to the top of society. This time, however, she's determined to protect her virginity in the process. As she tells her best friend, "Nobody ever thinks I have ideals, but I have, and I'll show 'em I have."

Throughout the picture, she proves her point by steadfastly resisting all temptations to trade her virtue for a night of passion or a few years as a kept woman. The film's entertainment value derives from the contrast between her exuberant naiveté and the more jaded expectations of her social betters.

Of course, Harlow's new morality didn't mean showing less skin. Loos and Emerson took every opportunity to get her into revealing costumes, culminating with her revenge on future father-in-law Lionel Barrymore. Realizing that he had framed her to end her engagement to his son (Franchot Tone), she returns the favor, wearing only her underwear as she bursts in on her "daddy" during a press conference.

Everybody loved the new Jean Harlow. The *Brooklyn Eagle*'s review headlined "Jean Harlow Turns Up on the Screen at the Capitol Theatre Pure as the Driven Snow,"[8] while the *New York Daily Mirror* heralded "NEW HARLOW PICTURE HAS MORALS: 'Holdout for Matrimony' Advice to Girls in Capitol Film."[9] The picture's box-office success assured Harlow of more such moral vehicles. In later films, she even got to stop bleaching her hair, a weekly ritual she had come to dread.

Constance Bennett also had a film in production during the transition to more rigid Code enforcement, but the script proved far less adaptable to Hollywood's new standards. *Outcast Lady* was a remake of *A Woman of Affairs* and was planned as a more faithful adaptation of Michael Arlen's *The Green Hat*. Even before the Legion of Decency boycott, Breen managed to convince Louis B. Mayer to cut any reference to venereal disease. Instead, Bennett is handed an anonymous note on her wedding day warning her about some unspecified secret in her new husband's past. The note alone is enough to drive him to suicide, with the audience never learning the reason.

MGM fought harder to retain Bennett's illegitimate baby, keeping in scenes about the birth until just before the picture's August 1934 premiere. By then, however, Breen had come into full power and refused to pass the film without more cuts. The studio had to insert hasty retakes to cover plot points lost with the scissored scenes. Breen could praise the revised film as a tale of "two clean straight-forward characters" who "refrain from giving in to their passion for each other," but he was the only one impressed with it. Critics were quick to pounce on the many plot holes left by Breen's cutting. As *Variety*'s reviewer complained: "Forced to soft pedal because of current clean-up campaign, Metro has been put on the sacrificial block with this one."[10]

In all fairness, MGM didn't need Breen's help to botch *Outcast Lady*. The whole affair is leaden, burdened with overwritten scenes and performances that have more to do with wearing clothes well than with eliciting any honest emotional response. The film's box-office failure hastened Bennett's fall from stardom. Audiences had already begun to tire of her formulaic confessional melodramas. Although she enjoyed a brief comeback as a comedienne in 1937's *Topper*, her own shortcomings as an actress and competition from younger women soon ended her career as a star.

Mae West also suffered at Breen's hands, though, again, he can be given only partial blame for her late-thirties decline. Her vehicle for 1934 was originally titled *That St. Louis Woman*, then submitted to the Studio Relations Committee as *It Ain't No Sin*. The title had to go: Not only was it sacrilegious; it was ungrammatical. Paramount initially suggested changing it to *It Isn't a Sin*, but soon agreed to the less inflammatory *Belle of the Nineties*. One factor influencing their decision was another church protest. A group of priests in New York had picketed beneath promotional posters for *It Ain't No Sin* with signs proclaiming "It Is!"

Breen considered the original story a glorification of sin and crime. West stars as Ruby Carter, a St. Louis vaudeville star in love with a fast-rising young boxer, the Tiger Kid (Roger Pryor). Ruby has become a star because of her notorious past, as described in the synopsis's opening scene: "In police headquarters, three detectives are examining the records on Ruby Carter. Not only are they impressed with her picture, but, also, with her extraordinary luck in getting out of police scraps. Suspected of murder, she was not indicted for lack of evidence; arrested for possessing stolen bonds, the bank president refused to prosecute; when a millionaire disappeared from his yacht on which she was the sole guest—she inherited some of his money—and was acquitted."

The Tiger Kid dumps Ruby after his manager tricks him into thinking she's been unfaithful, so Ruby takes off for a singing job in New Orleans. There, she has an affair with a wealthy younger man (John Mack Brown) while fending off advances from the crooked club owner, Ace (John Miljan). When the Kid arrives in New Orleans for a boxing match, Ace uses his knowledge of the Kid's criminal past to blackmail him into stealing Ruby's jewels. Discovering that her masked robber was the Kid, Ruby dopes him during the championship match, plunging Ace, who had bet heavily on him, into serious financial difficulties.

Ruby steals back her diamonds, also taking most of Ace's cash. As Ace is preparing to burn the place down, the Tiger Kid shows up and accidentally kills him. Ruby finishes setting the fire, and she and the Kid take off on a riverboat. As the synopsis ends: "Tiger and Ruby are in a cabin of the upriver boat. 'Well,' he says, 'where do we go from here?' Ruby smiles. 'Didn't your mother tell you anything?'"

All of this was too much for Breen, who responded to the script with two separate letters: a five-page listing of lines and business that violated the Code and a statement of more general concerns. Initially, Paramount resisted Breen's efforts to clean up the script and even neglected to submit rewrites. The film's producer, Emmanuel Cohen, complained about the recently instituted practice of sending copies of all PCA correspondence to the studios' New York offices, but Breen held his ground, realizing that Cohen was just trying to keep the moneymen out of the argument.

The carbons to New York had their desired effect. Two days after his confrontation with Cohen, Breen wired studio head Adolph Zukor that he could not approve the film because of its "general low tone[,] immoral and criminal theme of story and its lack of sufficient compensating moral values." Two days after that, Cohen screened a revised version of the film for Breen. Five major cuts had been made, including all references to Ruby's criminal past, the indication that Ruby has stolen Ace's money, and the sexual side of Ruby's relationship with her wealthy young lover.

The studio also altered the ending. In his final confrontation with the Tiger Kid, Ace carries a gun, so the killing could be excused as self-defense. Ruby sets the fire accidentally. She then picks up a pillow with the intention of beating out the flames but is diverted by the cries of Ace's former mistress (Katherine De Mille), whom he had locked in a closet. By the time Ruby and the Kid rescue the woman, it's too late to put out the fire. Paramount also reset the final scene in a justice of the peace's office, where Ruby and the Kid are married.

West tried to cope with Breen's new power by throwing lines and scenes into her scripts that had no chance of getting past him. In so doing, she hoped to make him more amenable to the material she really wanted to film. Whether or not this worked, it was clear that her pictures were doomed to grow tamer, but she continued to protest. To make matters worse, her next film, *Going to Town*, showed a slight decline at the box office.

West may have been trying to tackle both sides of the problem at once when she started work on *Klondike Annie* in late 1935. The film was guaranteed to shock with her portrayal of a singer who kills her Chinese lover in self-defense, then masquerades as a mission worker in Alaska and revitalizes the religious community there. Yet the film also gave her a chance to play a character who is changed by religion. Early on, she notes that she's found something moving in a religious tract given her by Sister Annie (Helen Jerome Eddy), the shipmate whose death opens the door to West's impersonation. She gets the local dance-hall girls, drinkers, and gamblers into the mission and converts a few with lines like "Any time you take religion for a joke, the laugh's on you." At the film's end, a conscience-stricken West decides to turn herself in. On her way back to the boat, Sister Annie's religious tract saves her life. Just as an assassin throws a knife at her, West drops the book and bends over to pick it up. The moment may have been melodrama at its clunkiest, but it clearly represented her desire to give religion its due. Off-screen, West was a generous contributor to the Catholic Church, despite the fact that some of its members were trying to put her out of a job.

When Paramount submitted the synopsis to the PCA, Hays responded personally. "It is imperative," he wrote, "that you make clear throughout the script that Miss West is not in any sense masquerading as a preacher, revivalist or any other character known and accepted as a minister of religion, ordained or otherwise." Instead, she should be "a social service worker." He also demanded that the murder be clearly shown to be in self-defense and that there be no illicit sex.

The studio agreed to all of this, but then submitted a script that reflected none of Hays's suggestions. Breen sent back six and a half pages of changes to delete the religious flavor and any vulgarity. Paramount had to eliminate a scene with the ship's captain (Victor McLaglen) that indicated he and West had just finished an exhausting bout of lovemaking. They also changed the hymns planned for a revival meeting to popular songs like "A Hot Time in the Old Town Tonight" that could be given a religious connotation. Unfortunately, they also cut the scene in which West kills her lover (Harold Huber) in self-defense, thus eliminating an important plot point.

Breen passed the film on December 31, 1935, then had to call it back in February when he learned that Paramount was trying to distribute an uncut version. Even with the film recut, Hays insisted on having the dialogue transcribed by a stenographer just to be sure all unacceptable religious references had been excised.

The Legion of Decency surprised Breen, West, and just about everybody. After indicating that they would probably condemn the film in an effort to drive West off the screen, they rated it B. West's chief enemy this time out wasn't the church, however; it was William Randolph Hearst. Hearst's papers refused to advertise the film and launched an all-out campaign against *Klondike Annie* and West's continued on-screen presence. Hearst's editorial writers brought up her censorship problems on Broadway, including her brief time in jail, and wondered how Hollywood could consider her "a fit subject to introduce into the wholesome homes of the country and present to the young people of clean moral families."[11] They rehashed salacious details from *Klondike Annie*, then asked "What were Will Hays and his censorship organization doing when this deliberate catering to a lewd element came forth?"[12] They even urged the Legion of Decency to reconsider its B rating and condemn the film.

Although Hearst's campaign caused a few problems—the film was banned in Lincoln, Nebraska—its overall effect was to pique audience interest. *Klondike Annie* topped the average weekly grosses at most theaters by $2,500 to $8,500. Hearst also may have helped divert attention from the film's largely negative reviews. Frank S. Nugent of the *New York Times* summed up the critics' complaints: "Neither as healthily rowdy nor as vulgarly suggestive as many of her earlier pictures, [*Klondike Annie*] emerges on the Paramount's screen as a tiresome and rather stupid combination of lavender and old japes. . . . It is unfortunate that there can be no truce between Miss West and the censors. Under present restrictions, there is no place on the screen for her former Rabelaisian humor; but there is no place anywhere for the stupid substitute that Miss West now is trying to pass as comedy."[13]

Today, *Klondike Annie*'s bad reviews seem as undeserved as do the moral condemnations. Despite a truncated opening in the Chinatown scenes—marred as much by Breen's deletions as by the stereotyped treatment of the film's Oriental characters—the picture holds up remarkably well. West and costar Victor McLaglen make a solid comic-romantic team, and her scenes in the mission have the same kind of energy West captured in her earlier, earthier films.

West's next film, *Go West, Young Man*, was a box-office disappointment, with critics complaining again that the bawdy actress with whom they'd fallen in love was now a thing of the past. She followed that contemporary comedy with *Every Day's a Holiday*, a return to the Gay Nineties roots of *Diamond Lil*. The meandering script stars West as Peaches O'Day, a confidence artist who specializes in selling the Brooklyn Bridge to unsuspecting tourists. When the police run her out of town, she returns disguised as a French musical comedy star and takes Broadway by storm. She then helps the police detective she loves (Edmund Lowe) run for mayor on a reform ticket.

Breen rejected the first draft on the grounds that there were too many "offensively

---

You Heard It Here First

What Joe Breen and other censors cut from *Belle of the Nineties:*

CALLBOY: I always wondered just how far up you wore your garters.
WEST: Just as low as you got your mind.

WEST: There are no good girls gone wrong . . . just bad ones found out.
    (Cut by Joe Breen)

MOLLY: So you're Ruby Carter.
WEST: The only thing my mother ever told me. Everything else I found out for myself.

Censored Hollywood

suggestive, or double-meaning lines" and too much drinking. Among the bits he ordered cut was this exchange between the villain, Quinn (Lloyd Nolan), and Peaches in her disguise as Mademoiselle Fifi:

> QUINN: Well, now you might not believe this but I'm the type of feller that puts all women on a pedestal.
>
> PEACHES: Oo la la! Zat mus' be a vairy uncomfortable position.

With the cuts made, *Every Day's a Holiday* got past Breen without further difficulties and was scheduled for a January 1938 release. On December 18, 1937, West triggered another uproar when she promoted the film with an appearance on "The Chase and Sanborn Hour," a radio program hosted by ventriloquist Edgar Bergen. After trading quips with Bergen's dummy, Charlie McCarthy, West appeared in a comedy sketch as Eve opposite Don Ameche as Adam and McCarthy as the serpent. There was nothing shocking about Arch Oboler's script—it had already been presented with another cast— and West sailed through the rehearsals without incident. During the live performance, however, she added a few suggestive line readings and some comic zingers of her own. When she asked, "Would you, honey, like to try this apple sometime?"[14] it was too much. NBC stopped transmission in the middle of the sketch. West would later brag about the furor, but at the time there were serious repercussions. The Legion of Decency threatened to start monitoring and classifying radio transmissions. The Hollywood studios began exercising greater control over their stars' radio appearances. And NBC banned West from the air permanently—for twelve years.

Paramount considered postponing the release of *Every Day's a Holiday*, but then

WEST: Ah, the man that hesitates is last.
  (Cut in Ohio)

WEST: Why, if he was the last man on earth, I wouldn't—I wouldn't—
MAID: The last man?
WEST: Well—maybe I am takin' in a little too much territory.
  (Cut in Australia)

WEST: A man in the house is worth two in the street.
  (Cut in England)

realized that the controversy would probably improve ticket sales. They were right. Patrons in the big cities lined up around the block when the film first opened, particularly when West appeared in person. Then they stopped coming. *Every Day's a Holiday* made some money, but nothing like the profits on West's earlier pictures. With Paramount uninterested in her next idea, a comic epic based on the life of Catherine the Great, she exercised her option to cancel her contract. Her career as a major film star was over.

Although Breen's strict enforcement of the Production Code tamed West's films, he can hardly be cited as the sole cause of her decline. West steadfastly refused to change her style to meet changing audience tastes. After leaving Paramount, she turned down a bid from MGM to costar with Clark Gable in an Anita Loos script she thought strayed too far from her established image. The same thinking would keep her from accepting Billy Wilder's offer to star as Norma Desmond in *Sunset Boulevard*. Although that stubbornness eventually paid off, contributing to her near-legendary status in later years, in the thirties she simply wore out her welcome with film audiences.

Only one screen star could blame Joe Breen for the end of her career. But then, she never had the options available to mere flesh-and-blood actresses. Betty Boop was introduced as a background figure in "Dizzie Dishes," a 1930 cartoon from the Fleischer brothers, Max and Dave, who had been producing animated shorts since 1924. Originally, she was a grotesque figure, a dog with long feminine legs and spitcurls modeled on singer Helen Kane's. As the Fleischers developed her in a series of shorts, she became the ultimate jazz baby.

The early Betty engaged in a series of risqué adventures, dressed most of the time in a strapless gown so short it left her garters showing. A lecherous ringmaster fondled her breasts in 1932's "Boop-Oop-A-Doop" and told her she'd have to come across if she wanted to keep her job with the circus. In "The Old Man of the Mountain" (1933) she was so frightened she jumped out of her clothes, parading in her underwear for much of the short. She danced a hula wearing only a lei and a grass skirt in "Betty Boop's Bamboo Isle" (1932) and even flashed her breast in 1934's "Betty Boop's Rise to Fame."

Betty survived a lot in her earlier films; in addition to lechers, she was attacked by ghosts, witches, and a fire-breathing dragon. But she couldn't survive the censors. When Breen started enforcing the Production Code in 1934, he got to work changing her image. The short black dress acquired a collar, sleeves, and an apron. Betty traded in her old sidekicks—a romantic dog and a heroic clown—for an eccentric grandfather. Suddenly, she was a demure single woman keeping house and dealing with domestic crises.

The magic was gone. The Fleischers stopped making Betty Boop cartoons in 1939, and the last entry in the series didn't even feature her. When she'd been rescued from the lecherous ringmaster in "Boop-Oop-A-Doop," Betty had proudly proclaimed, "He couldn't take my boop-oop-a-doop away!" He didn't have to. Joe Breen did it for him.

Hollywood Adjusts to Censorship

As Breen established his power base as Production Code administrator, Hollywood adjusted. Writers learned how to present questionable materials with more circumspection and symbolism. A romantic clinch could indicate that a couple were about to get more involved, or it couldn't. In the horror cycles at Universal and RKO, gruesome killings were seen in shadow or heard from behind closed doors, leaving the audience with nightmare visions worse than anything that could have been put on screen. It was all up to the imagination. When Rick and Ilsa finally got together in *Casablanca* (1942), producer Hal Wallis kept Breen happy by replacing a suggestive fadeout with a dissolve. Subsequent shots of the Casablanca airport, with its phallic tower, and of Humphrey Bogart smoking a cigarette made it clear that he and Ingrid Bergman had been doing more than just talking about their problems.

When symbolism wasn't enough, writers learned how to get around Breen and his staff. Just as Mae West had done, they deliberately inserted material they knew would never be passed, then swapped those cuts for the lines and business they really wanted. Rarely did anybody put this tactic into writing, but a quick look at an earlier draft of one famous picture suggests how the system might have worked.

Joseph L. Mankiewicz didn't have much to worry about with his script for *All About Eve* (1950). During the first scene in Margo Channing's (Bette Davis) dressing room, her maid, Birdie (Thelma Ritter), has two lines that would have been deemed vulgar under the Code, a reference to a cold night as the "First time I ever saw a brassiere break like a piece of matzo" and her response to Eve's (Ann Baxter) life story, "Everything but the bloodhounds snappin' at her rear end."[15] The first line would hardly have been missed and probably wouldn't have gotten many laughs in the Protestant Midwest. The second line, however, was a sure laugh-getter. When representatives of the Breen office went into script meetings with Mankiewicz, they tried to get both lines removed. The writer-director gave them the matzo line, then probably used that concession to keep the more important wisecrack.

Occasionally, writers would insert bits just to tweak the Production Code censors. When staffer Charles Metzger struck the word "filmy" from a description of the leading lady's negligee in a western script, the writer got back at him by adding a direction at the end of a brutal fight scene: "From offstage we hear the scream of a naked woman."[16]

Although the Production Code Administration had been set up to regulate Hollywood films, the procedure was open to any film distributed in the United States. Usually, foreign films were confined to a small number of import houses—by 1938, there were two hundred in eighty-four cities—few of which fell under Breen's control. When a film demonstrated mass appeal, however, it could be submitted to the MPPDA's New York office or, if it posed special problems, to the Breen office. Not surprisingly, most international films submitted for review came from England. Hays even visited the country to advise its filmmakers on Production Code requirements and encouraged them to submit scripts to the New York office before beginning production.

Even George Bernard Shaw came before the MPPDA for approval when producer Gabriel Pascal submitted the shooting script for *Pygmalion* in 1938. Although the play already was a classic of the modern stage, Francis Harmon of the New York office could not deem it suitable for American film audiences without the deletion of references to Eliza as "baggage," the suggestion that she was illegitimate, and her father's offer to sell her to Professor Higgins for five pounds.

These cuts were minor compared to the changes made in one of the sexiest films of the thirties, *Ecstasy*. The 1933 erotic drama from Czechoslovakia starred Hedy Kiesler (later Hedy Lamarr) as a beautiful young woman married to an older, impotent man. She leaves her husband to return to her family's farm, where, after a nude swim, she meets a handsome young engineer. During a rainstorm, she runs to the engineer's cottage, where they make love, and she experiences sexual fulfillment for the first time. When she returns to the farm, her husband is waiting to take her home. He learns of the affair and kills himself, which drives the woman to desert her new lover.

Censorship problems were nothing new to the film's director, Gustav Machaty. When Mussolini waived Italy's censorship law to allow *Ecstasy* to be screened at the second Venice Film Festival, there was an uproar from the Vatican that may have robbed the well-received picture of first prize. Then, Kiesler's husband, munitions tycoon Fritz Mandl, spent $280,000 trying to buy up every available copy and production still.

When distributor Samuel Cummins tried to import the film in 1935, it was blocked by U.S. Customs, marking the first time the customs laws had been used to keep a film out of the country. The federal district court agreed that the film was obscene, but before Cummins could file an appeal, a federal marshal burned the film. Cummins then brought in a revised version, which passed Customs in 1936. The few critics who saw both versions were amazed at the changes. Kiesler's nude run was now partially obscured by bushes (purportedly an alternate version shot for the more severe German censors). Scenes of horses copulating were trimmed. Before Kiesler's nude bathing scene, Cummins added a shot of a typewriter, with a voice-over announcing that she had been granted a divorce. Shots of Kiesler with a baby were tacked on at the end to give the impression that she and the engineer were now happily married.

Although the film's new version made little sense, it did great business in the few theaters that could show it. After seventeen months in the U.S., Cummins applied for the MPPDA Seal of Approval. The matter was so important, Breen himself sent the rejection letter. When Cummins decided to appeal in December 1937, Breen and his colleagues marshalled their forces to make a convincing case in front of the New York board. They pointed to the film's advertising, which capitalized on its salacious content with such press quotes as "A sensational bit of celluloid . . . needs an asbestos screen!"[17] When Cummins asserted that the film had passed local censors, Francis Harmon could point to the New York censors' ban, upheld in the Court of Appeals on the grounds that "this picture continually emphasizes the carnal side of the sex relationship."[18]

After the arguments, the MPPDA's board of directors settled in to watch the film but were so bored they tried to leave after only two reels. Their decision was a foregone conclusion. With scenes of nudity and graphic sexuality, *Ecstasy* was impossible under the Code.

The story didn't end there. Machaty had settled in Hollywood, where he directed the locust attack in *The Good Earth*. Twice he submitted scripts for a remake of *Ecstasy*, and twice Breen rejected him. In 1948, Machaty proposed a major recutting of the film. Breen accepted the dialogue summary but insisted that the title be changed and no reference be made to the original. This caused problems with the Federal Trade Commission. They insisted that even with a new title the film's relationship to *Ecstasy* would have to be advertised, which ran counter to PCA procedures.[19] Finally, Machaty won permission to distribute a recut version under the title *My Life*. He even promised to police exhibitors and make sure the film was advertised accurately.

Two years later, Breen learned that some of the objectionable materials had been restored. By that time, however, there were more pressing issues than a few shots of Hedy Kiesler's naked bosom and a justification of adultery. The distributors of imported films were being joined by Hollywood's own producers in the fight to get hitherto unacceptable materials onto the screen, with or without the PCA's Seal of Approval. ✂

One of the areas in which the Production Code had the greatest influence was the acquisition of materials by the studios. Clifford Odets's pioneering drama of Depression life, *Awake and Sing*, was deemed unfilmable in 1935 because the plot hinged on illicit sex and an illegitimate pregnancy. Other works, like James M. Cain's novels, were kept off the screen for years while the studios tried to come up with acceptable story treatments (see Chapter Six).

Breen also played a major role in reshaping source materials to fit the Code. Lillian Hellman's *The Children's Hour* had been a hit on Broadway with its fact-inspired tale of two schoolteachers destroyed by an accusation of lesbianism. Despite its success, however, nobody in Hollywood would touch the play because of the Production Code's prohibition against "sexual perversion." So Hellman approached independent producer Samuel Goldwyn on her own and convinced him that the play was less about sex than about the power of a lie to destroy lives.

Hellman rearranged the play's romantic triangle so that both of the women were in love with the same man, and she changed the lie to an accusation that Martha (the repressed lesbian in the original) had spent the night with her best friend's fiancé. Clearly, Hellman had rendered the work acceptable under the Code, but Breen insisted on referring the whole matter to Hays. On July 31, 1935, Breen informed Goldwyn that Hays had approved the film on three conditions:

1. Not to use the title, *The Children's Hour*;
2. To make no reference, directly or indirectly, in either advertising or exploitation of the picture to be made under this treatment, to the stage play *The Children's Hour*;
3. To remove from your finished production all possible suggestion of Lesbianism and any other matter which is likely to prove objectionable.

This posed no problem for Goldwyn. His purchase of the play had generated reams of free publicity already. Half the world, it seemed, knew that he was bringing *The Children's Hour* to the screen.

The picture, retitled *These Three*, would prove one of Goldwyn's most prestigious hits. Hellman's adaptation only flags when Karen (Merle Oberon) rejects her fiancé, Joe (Joel McCrea). In the play, Karen gets Joe to admit that he harbors suspicions about her relationship with Martha (Miriam Hopkins in the film), then she breaks their engagement. For the first part of the scene on film, Hellman switches Joe's and Karen's lines so that Joe gets Karen to admit her doubts. Then the scene reverts to its original form, with Karen once more breaking the engagement, this time because she's unworthy of Joe—a much less plausible motivation.

None of the press seemed aware of any confusion in the writing, concentrating instead on the fine performances of the leads and of young Bonita Granville as the girl whose lies set the plot in motion. Most also praised Hellman and Goldwyn for improving on the original. The *Time* critic wrote: "In the screen version the rumor charges one of the teachers with normal rather than abnormal misbehavior. This trivial change strengthens rather than weakens the story, makes it entirely fit for the consumption of all cinemaddicts with the most rudimentary knowledge of the facts of life."[20]

The praise was even greater when Breen helped Warner Bros. clean up Henry Bellaman's scandalous 1940 novel *Kings Row*. After picking up the rights for thirty thousand dollars, Warners spent two years bringing the script in line with the Code and getting the troubled production to the screen.

The story of Parris Mitchell (Robert Cummings), who is inspired by small-town scandal to become a crusading psychiatrist during the early years of this century, was shorn of a number of sins, including homosexuality, sadism, a lynching, skinny-dipping, miscegenation, suicide, two instances of euthanisia, and several acts of illicit sex. The thorniest problem was Parris's relationship with Cassie (Betty Field), the daughter of his tutor, Dr. Tower (Claude Rains). Bellaman depicted Cassie as a nymphomaniac who draws the teenage Parris into an affair. Just before Parris leaves to study medicine in Vienna, Dr. Tower kills his daughter and himself, leaving his considerable estate to the young man. The doctor's diary reveals that he had committed incest with Cassie, motivated by a warped desire to study the psychological effects of such a relationship.

Breen demanded that Cassie's nymphomania be changed to some form of dementia and eliminated the more pointed lines about her behavior. The incest was out, so Dr. Tower killed Cassie and himself because of her insanity and the fact that the girl was pregnant. Finally, Breen allowed Cassie and Parris one "sex affair" (the term he always used for intercourse) on condition that Parris condemn his actions. Out of all these changes came a film that many critics found better than the original book. As Phil Koury noted in the *Kansas City Star*: "It is an example of motion picture artistry proving that honest, human drama is none the less honest, or dramatic, or moving for the absence of the baser elements that Bellaman has seen fit to crowd into his book. It is pretty much an indication, too, that there is a fine story in the novel without the pornography. . . ."[21]

Breen v. Tolstoy

With *Kings Row*, it took only one line of condemnation to balance the leading characters' sexual transgressions with compensating moral value. It took a lot more than that, however, to get *Anna Karenina* (1935) past Breen.

Greta Garbo had first filmed the story in 1927 under the title *Love*, with John Gilbert as her lover, Vronsky. In September 1934, producer David O. Selznick submitted the novel and its silent adaptation. Breen felt the earlier version provided sufficient compensating moral value for Anna's adulterous affair, but objected to the film's failure to punish Vronsky. In the script by Lorna Moon and Frances Marion, Anna's suicide makes it possible for Vronsky to stay with his regiment after he had been threatened with dismissal because of their affair.[22]

Although Selznick would later blame Breen for removing many of the novel's most touching episodes—including the birth of Anna and Vronsky's illegitimate child and a sickroom scene in which Anna's husband and lover are reconciled—those scenes had already been excised for the 1927 version. There was an attempt to bring back the ille-

Film, Lies, and Politics

In 1934, after twelve years as president of the MPPDA, Will Hays returned to his roots in politics. Whereas his last political assignment had been getting Warren G. Harding into the White House, however, his current charge was keeping novelist Upton Sinclair out of the California governor's mansion.

Sinclair's surprise victory in the Democratic primary and his amazing two-to-one lead in the polls had the film industry and the rest of California's business interests in an uproar. His End Poverty in California—or EPIC—movement advocated putting the unemployed to work in state-run factories. Unused land would be turned into "land colonies" where the poor and unemployed would work together for the common good. "Production for use," a form of barter, would replace the old form of production for pay. To finance all of this, Sinclair proposed raising inheritance taxes and taxes on banks and public utilities. He also proposed higher taxes on the film studios and the creation of state-run studios where unemployed film workers would produce their own movies.

As soon as Sinclair's campaign began, the studio heads, most of them strict Republicans, started threatening to relocate, either to Florida or back to the medium's roots in New York. It may have been a hollow threat—facilities were severely limited in New York, and taxes were just as bad, while a move to Florida would require the construction of all new studios. Over the next two months, however, the moguls would stretch reality as surely as they did in any of their movies.

In October 1934, Hays sent the MPPDA's general counsel, Charles Pettijohn, to Hollywood to coordinate the studios' efforts. He also offered his own expertise to Republican candidate Frank Merriam. The studios started out by creating radio playlets dramatizing the horrors of life in

gitimate child in October 1934, but that was ruled unacceptable before the writers could go much further with it. In later notes on the film, Selznick would say that the cut almost made him abandon the project.

Through the scripting process, Breen cautioned Selznick to keep physical contact between Anna and Vronsky to a minimum, presumably so that their passion would not serve as a justification for adultery. He cut Anna's romantic defense of the affair, "Am I ashamed of everything I've done? Wouldn't I do the same again tomorrow?" More acceptable was her doubt-filled declaration to Vronsky, "Who cares what people say as long as I love you and you—don't change?"

As MGM was readying its production, United Artists sent Breen the script for another proposed adaptation of *Anna Karenina*. In comparison with what Selznick was trying to achieve, the UA script was virtual propaganda for adultery. In early scenes, members

California following a Sinclair victory. They also produced short films on the issue, the most damaging of which were three "California Election News" shorts produced by Irving J. Thalberg at MGM.

The first two of these were simple man-in-the-street interviews, though some of the subjects would seem to have come from Central Casting. All of the sympathetic interviewees—little old ladies in gingham dresses, distinguished businessmen—were for Merriam. The Sinclair supporters were either muddled or downright scary. One gentleman proclaimed, "Upton St. Clair is the author of the Russian government. And it worked out very well there, and I think it should do so here." Another supporter spoke with a heavy European accent: "I have always been a Socialist, and I believe Sinclair will do best for working people."[23] The third short was even worse. It purported to be an exposé on the number of transients flocking to California in hopes of a free handout should Sinclair become governor. None of this was really happening—the footage had been either staged for the short or pulled from other movies. When responses to the shorts triggered fights in theaters, the studios blamed EPIC terrorists. When Sinclair complained that Pettijohn's involvement in the campaign violated the MPPDA's policy of political neutrality, Hays wired back that the lawyer was acting on his own.

In November, Merriam beat Sinclair by 200,000 votes—a small lead, but a major improvement over the polls just a few months earlier. Hays and the studios had lied their way through one of the dirtiest political campaigns in American history and had gotten away with it. If the story had been submitted to Joe Breen, he would have banned it from the screen. ✂

of the Russian court deride Anna and Vronsky for not dabbling in illicit sex like everybody else. Later, Anna revels in her status as a kept woman. The script also maintained one of the more unacceptable episodes from Tolstoy's novel, in which Vronsky's country estate becomes a haven for Anna's philandering friends and their lovers. Breen would not pass the script, and UA eventually dropped the project.

This alternate script should have made Breen appreciate Selznick's efforts all the more. Instead, on March 5, 1935, he sent Louis B. Mayer a three-page letter filled with concerns, many of them new. Vronsky still wasn't suffering enough and should be forced to resign his commission because of his affair with Anna. He should be barely tolerated by his fellow officers. Moreover, there should be no scenes depicting Anna and Vronsky living in sin. Selznick was justifiably outraged. According to the terms of Garbo's contract, he had to have the picture finished by May, which left little time for the extensive rewrites Breen was demanding. He fired back a five-page response hinting that the production might have to be cancelled. Selznick agreed to have Vronsky dismissed from the army: "even though it is in violation of Tolstoi; even though it surprised me that at this late date you should make additional criticisms; even though the writers of the script are violently opposed to it; and even though it is very harmful to the important story point of Vronsky's voluntary sacrifice for Anna." He refused, however, to show Vronsky being rejected by his friends. In addition, he could not cut the scenes of Anna and Vronsky's life together: "If we eliminate these and any such references, I must challenge anyone to demonstrate to me how the picture of Anna Karenina can be made at all. If anyone can do this, he is much more competent than am I."

From this point, Breen's letters concentrate mostly on minor details, though he continues to urge Selznick, in presenting the affair, "to avoid shooting these scenes in a manner which would tend to glorify Anna's sin, while at the same time, ridiculing whose who condemn her for it."

Anna Karenina was granted the Seal of Approval on June 27, 1935, and opened in July to generally favorable reviews. In September, however, it was condemned by the Chicago branch of the Legion of Decency. At that point, Breen went to work in support of the film. He arranged a special screening for a group of clergy, which included one of the medium's staunchest critics, John Cantwell of Los Angeles, now an archbishop. Their favorable opinion and a letter from Cantwell convinced the Chicago priests to reverse their decision.

The author of an undated report on "*Anna Karenina* Under the Code" acclaims the film for making Tolstoy's story morally acceptable. As the writer points out, Anna's adultery is neither justified nor glamorized: "The sin of Anna and Vronsky is not presented as attractive or alluring. As soon as the relationship with Vronsky has begun, there is not a single hour of unalloyed bliss for Anna, while trouble is brewing for Vronsky, too. Anna, in her most mirthful moment, is melancholy. When she says: 'I am happy!' we know that she is deceiving herself. . . ."

This analysis is borne out by the film. Despite Garbo's powerful presence on-screen, there is something cold about the production. In *Love*, the chemistry between Garbo and Gilbert balances the warmth and lightness Garbo brings to the scenes with her son. In *Anna Karenina*, although Garbo's attachment to her son (Freddie Bartholomew) remains powerful, her scenes with Fredric March, as Vronsky, are gloomy. The two lovers never really connect (they didn't connect off-screen, either, and never worked together again). The only real passion in the film is in Basil Rathbone's performance as Anna's husband, Karenin. Rather than go for stock melodramatic villainy in the role (as Brandon Hurst had done in the silent version), he creates a portrait of a man whose soul is bound by social convention and insecurity. Even at his most censorious, his readings betray Karenin's deep love for his wife and son. As a result, Anna's affair with Vronsky seems less some grand passion than a rejection of her husband's cold exterior, with no attempt to see what lies beneath it. Rathbone's performance provides all the compensating moral value the film needs. If it makes the picture one-sided—all condemnation, no temptation—part of the fault can be laid at Breen's feet. His vehement insistence that there be no rewards for Anna's adultery created a major shift in the work's meaning.

The Code's Fantasy World

As long as Hollywood idealized reality, Breen's suggestions could sometimes improve a picture. In 1937, Production Code restrictions helped make *Camille* one of the screen's great romances. Breen had blocked a proposed film version of Alexandre Dumas's play at RKO because he felt the story glorified adultery. When MGM submitted it, he made them cut any suggestion that "living as a mistress is a highly profitable enterprise." Gone were the jewels and other gifts Marguerite received from the Baron de Varville, along with other lines referring to the business elements of her life and her cold-bloodedness in "procuring a 'master.'" Such deletions might have hurt a more realistic portrayal of prostitution, but they made the world of *Camille* more romantic, placing Garbo and leading man Robert Taylor in a never-never land of lost love.

Breen had a similar effect on *Casablanca*. In the unproduced play *Everybody Comes to Rick's*, the romantic leads remember an affair in Paris during which Rick cheated on his wife while Lois cheated on her lover. This was too immoral for the screen, however, so Rick lost his wife and children, and Lois became Ilsa Lund Laszlo, who left Rick in

Paris to return to her Resistance-leader husband. She couldn't cheat on her husband, either, so the writers had her think he was dead, only to be reunited with him as she is about to marry Rick. It may have seemed contrived, but within the context of the film it simply made the doomed love of Rick and Ilsa even more poignant, setting up a dynamite finish as the leading characters try to decide who should be paired with whom.

When Hollywood tried to deal with the world more realistically, however, the Production Code was a stumbling block. Although most of the audience knew that *Marked Woman* was based on a real-life criminal case in which a group of prostitutes testified against gangster Lucky Luciano, Breen insisted that Bette Davis, Lola Lane, and Mayo Methot be reduced to nightclub hostesses. Even though one in twenty-two Americans had venereal disease in 1936, the sickly streetwalker played by Claire Trevor in *Dead End* was given a cough to affirmatively establish that she suffered from tuberculosis rather than syphilis, thus keeping the "silent epidemic" silent.

The Production Code also contributed to one of Hollywood's greatest lapses in the late thirties, the studios' failure to deal with the growing political unrest in Europe. In all fairness, the problem was more economic than anything else. Hollywood feared that films reflecting poorly on a particular country would lose international sales. Paramount had major diplomatic problems with China over that nation's portrayal in 1932's *Shanghai Express*, then went through even greater difficulties in Spain over the depiction of the Civil Guard in 1935's *The Devil Is a Woman*. As the political situation overseas heated up, the studios also risked domestic protests if they seemed to be taking sides. Walter Wanger's 1938 tale of the Spanish Civil War, *Blockade*, was shorn of almost all political material, yet there was still enough left for the Catholic Church to protest that the film sided with the anticlerical Republicans. During most of this, the PCA simply advised about national sensitivities, then tried to help studios that had gone too far deal with foreign censors. But Breen found himself more and more involved. Under his guidance, Universal cut most of the political commentary from *The Road Back*, a sequel to Erich Maria Remarque's *All Quiet on the Western Front*. The result was an incoherent mess.

While Breen was working on *The Road Back*, he received the first of many letters from Dr. G. Gyssling of the German consulate expressing concern over a proposed screen version of another Remarque novel, *Three Comrades*. The book follows three veterans through the turbulent years following World War I. One of the men, Erich, marries a woman with tuberculosis, and another is killed by Nazi demonstrators. When MGM submitted the first draft for *Three Comrades* in May 1937, Breen found only one speech he thought might offend the German government. After repeated communication from Gyssling, however, Breen tried to convince Louis B. Mayer to drop the project altogether, arguing that the story was "a serious indictment of the German nation and people and is certain to be violently resented by the present government in that country."

When Mayer refused to cancel the film, Breen responded with more changes. The action would be confined to a two-year period following the end of the war, thus predating the Nazi movement. The studio would cut all persecution of Jews and Catholics, a book-burning scene, and a reference to "democracy." But that still might not solve all of the diplomatic problems raised by the film's source: "You will have in mind that the author of the novel . . . Mr. Erich Maria Remarque, is among those literary men who are proscribed in present-day Germany, and whose books are forbidden circulation in that country. You will further have in mind that Mr. Remarque is now exiled from his native land."

One suggestion Breen made was forcefully rejected by producer Joseph L. Mankiewicz. To affirmatively establish that the political agitators in the film were not Nazis, Breen suggested making them Communists. Supposedly, Mayer, himself a staunch conservative, was willing to go along with this idea until Mankiewicz threatened to walk out on the production.

Three Comrades opened to generally favorable reviews, with relatively few critics noting the changes in the novel's political background. At the time, the film's poor performance at the box office was blamed on its gloomy ending. *Variety*'s review, however, suggests that Breen may have eliminated those very elements that might have sold the film to U.S. audiences: "In the light of events on the continent in the past five years, the background of 1921 in Germany seems like a century ago. There is developed in the film no relation between the historical events of that period and the Reich of today. The story is dated and lacks showmanship values of current European movements."[24] Yet *Three Comrades* had been so effectively neutered that it played uncut in Japan during World War II.

Before long, Breen would be unable to keep the truth about world politics off the screen. The outbreak of war in Europe would bring Hollywood more than just a renewed political consciousness. It also would mark a shift in attitudes among filmmakers and the public that ultimately would lead to the end of the Production Code. The battle would outlast World War II, but the first breach in Breen's moral barricade would take place as Hitler was invading Poland in 1939.

"I Want Kisses
That Come from Life"

Chapter Six

When Lana Turner said the above to John Garfield near the end of *The Postman Always Rings Twice* (1946), she was asking for a new start. She wanted to escape from the web of murder, adultery, and deceit the two had woven and find her way into the dream world of marital bliss promoted by Hollywood. For filmmakers in the forties, however, the same plea could have represented an escape from the world of dreams to a place where everything—from kisses to crime to social issues—came from life.

The dream world fostered by the Production Code exploded in 1939 when Hitler's armies marched into Poland. As the Axis chalked up victory after victory, the idea that good always won out must have seemed like a fairy tale. But even before the war's effects hit America, Hollywood's own censorship battles had begun heating up again.

After five years of strict Code enforcement, many in the film capital were fed up with having to avoid subjects that were perfectly acceptable in the worlds of publishing and the stage. A fight was brewing, and the first punch would be thrown when one of Breen's toughest sparring partners acquired the rights to the biggest best-seller of all time.

The creation of *Gone With the Wind* has become the stuff of legend. Producer David O. Selznick's battle to include the line "Frankly, my dear, I don't give a damn" is one of the best-known of Production Code stories, though contrary to legend he did not have to pay a five-thousand-dollar fine for including the forbidden word. The controversy even

Joe Breen kept the novel The Postman Always Rings Twice *off the screen for twelve years, but in 1946 MGM put enough "compensating moral value" into the story to satisfy the Production Code. John Garfield and Lana Turner's steamy embraces helped bring a new realism to Hollywood.*

inspired an amendment to the Code that allowed the limited use of profanity in quotes from history or the classics.[1] But that was not the most important change wrought by Selznick's epic. *Gone With the Wind* also presented sexual relationships with a frankness previously barred from the screen.

When Selznick submitted his first draft in October 1937, most of Breen's complaints were about sexuality. His initial letter voices three principle concerns: the sympathetic depiction of the prostitute Belle Watling, the emphasis on Melanie's difficult labor, and the marital relations between Rhett and Scarlett. The letter includes handwritten notations of everything Selznick agreed to. He okayed cuts in the childbirth scene, the

Black Americans and the Censors

Joe Breen's fight to keep the word "nigger" out of *Gone With the Wind* was a rare instance in which the censors tried to maintain the dignity of black Americans on screen. Despite the Chicago board's sensitivity to racially derogatory material, most local censors, particularly those south of the Mason-Dixon line, were more concerned with keeping positive images of blacks off local screens. Their justification, when they bothered to give one, was that such material would prove inflammatory, though one can hardly understand how a single musical number featuring Lena Horne could inspire racial unrest.

Warner Bros. took a big chance in 1942 with the depiction of black cook Hattie McDaniel and her son (Ernest Anderson) in *In This Our Life*. The picture was a turgid melodrama starring Bette Davis as a willful young woman who steals her sister's fiancé, drives him to suicide, then tries to steal another man from her sister. In contrast to Davis's tale of degradation, the film depicts Anderson's struggles to win acceptance in the community and work his way into law school.

Driving from one of her many heated emotional confrontations, a frantic Davis runs down a mother and child, then races from the scene of the accident. After pinning the crime on Anderson, Davis visits him in prison and tries to bribe him to take the rap for her. He tells her off in no uncertain terms, a scene that elicited cheers of delight from black audiences. It also triggered fights in military theaters and other establishments with racially mixed seating.

As a result, Warners cut the scene from prints to be shown in theaters patronized by blacks. In addition, that scene and one in which McDaniel laments "Colored boys don't have a chance anyhow!" were cut in many southern states. Justifying the action, Mrs. Alonzo Richardson, the censor for Atlanta, wrote to Breen: "The feeling against the Motion Picture Industry for constantly promoting the negro is certain. I hear it everywhere I go. At every meeting and with the increased impertinence of the negroes in spite of things done for their own good, it is not a good time to exploit them in the South." This could not stop some filmmakers' continuing efforts to deal

deletion of Rhett's rape of Scarlett and the elimination of several lines about Belle. The only suggestion he refused to follow (marked "in" on the letter) was to change Belle from a prostitute to "a loose character operating a drinking saloon or gambling joint." Ultimately, however, Selznick would ignore almost all of Breen's suggestions.

To appease Breen, the childbirth scene was shot largely in silhouette, so that viewers would not have to watch Melanie's pained reactions to labor. Breen had suggested changing her line "It began at daybreak" to the less pointed "I have known since daybreak," but Selznick refused. He also refused to cut Prissy's lines about childbirth, including "Put a knife under Miss Melly's bed and it cut the pain in two" and "I don't

sympathetically with black Americans. Although stereotyped portrayals remained, more and more films featured black characters like Dooley Wilson in *Casablanca* and Rex Ingram in *Sahara,* who were treated with respect and dignity.

After the war, the American social-problem picture began dealing with racial issues, though not without continued resistance from local censors. In 1949, the independent production *Lost Boundaries* dealt with a black family passing for white in a small New England town, while Twentieth Century-Fox tackled racial issues in *Pinky.* In both films, light-skinned blacks were played by white actors, primarily because of the fear of censorship action against films with black casts. This was particularly important in *Pinky,* in which the title character, played by Jeanne Crain, is in love with a white doctor.

Despite this concession to censorship fears, both films were frequently banned in the South. Atlanta censor Christine Smith kept *Lost Boundaries* out of the city on the grounds that it was "likely to have an adverse effect upon the peace, morals and good order of the city."[2] The lower courts upheld her decision, and the Supreme Court, still adhering to the *Mutual Film* precedent, refused to hear the case. *Pinky* faced a similar ban in Marshall, Texas, where censors said the film was "of such character as to be prejudicial to the best interest of the people of said City." By the time this case reached the Supreme Court, however, things had changed (see Chapter 7). *Mutual Film* had been overturned, replaced by a new precedent that recognized film as protected speech. Writing for the majority, Justice William O. Douglas stated: "If a board of censors can tell the American people what it is in their best interests to see or to read or to hear, then thought is regimented, authority substituted for liberty, and the great purpose of the First Amendment to keep uncontrolled the freedom of expression defeated."[3] It would take several more years before Hollywood started dealing more thoroughly with racial issues, but the groundwork had been laid.

know nothing 'bout birthing babies." Selznick was even less accommodating with Belle Watling, refusing to cut shots of Belle's girls leaning out of the windows above the saloon. Mrs. Meade's fervent inquiry about the nature of Belle's establishment remained, but her explanation, "This is my only chance to hear what a bad house looks like," was removed. Selznick also agreed to give no indication that Rhett ever spent the night with Belle.

But there were plenty of indications of Rhett's relationship with Scarlett. When Selznick submitted the second half of the final script in January 1939, Breen deemed it unacceptable because of the Code prohibition on depicting "the sacred intimacies of private life—either before marriage . . . or after marriage." Again, Selznick stood firm. He would not cut the scene in which Scarlett informs Rhett that she doesn't want any more babies, though he did soften two of Rhett's lines. "You realize, of course, I could divorce you for refusing me my rights" became "Do you know I could divorce you for this." "The world is full of beds, and the beds are full of women" was replaced by "The world is full of many things and many people, and I shan't be lonely. I'll find comfort elsewhere."

Breen and Selznick had their biggest squabble over Rhett's rape of Scarlett. On receiving the first draft in 1937, Breen had suggested changing the rape to a love scene: "It is our thought . . . that you merely have him take her in his arms, kiss her, and then gently start with her toward the bedroom. It is our thought that you should not go so far as to throw her on the bed." Breen reiterated his demands to cut the rape in January 1939. After a meeting with Selznick in February 1939, however, the rape was definitely in. Possibly Selznick and story editor Val Lewton had argued its importance to the plot, but another note in the memo about that meeting suggests a trade occurred.

One of Breen's other concerns about the script was the use of the word "nigger." In 1937 he had cautioned that only the black characters should use that word, while whites should use the comparatively less offensive "darkie." Breen had repeated his objections in January 1939, warning that "this word is highly offensive to negroes throughout the United States and will be quite forcefully resented by them." At the same February meeting in which Breen agreed to allow the rape, Selznick agreed to cut the word "nigger." Selznick had to have been aware of the black press's negative reaction to Margaret Mitchell's book and its proposed film version. Nor was he likely to have been ignorant of the effect the word "nigger" would have had on blacks as well as many whites. The loss of one word would hardly have hurt the film, but the loss of the rape scene would have. It's highly likely, then, that he put up a fight to keep "nigger" so he could trade it for something more important. Later Breen would suggest cutting the scene as Rhett starts up the stairs (the scene fades as he reaches the top) and eliminating Scarlett's satis-fied preening the morning after.

The production continued without major problems from Breen, though he tried to cut Scarlett's response after she kills the Union soldier, "Well, I've done murder," and the start of one of her most famous lines, "As God is my witness. . . ." The MPPDA also ran interference for Selznick, dealing with complaints from Negro organizations about the novel's treatment of blacks and from the Sons of Union Veterans of the Civil War about the characterization of the Union soldier who tries to rob Tara (Selznick made the soldier a deserter).

Gone With the Wind won its Seal of Approval on September 27, 1939, though Selznick didn't finish working on the film until December. After the smoke had cleared, he had gotten away with more than any other producer since 1934. He even got his film past the Legion of Decency, though the Catholic group noted, in giving the film a B rat-ing, "the attractive portrayal of the immoral character of a supporting role in the story," referring, of course, to Belle Watling. The only cuts made by American censors were two shots of Scarlett that showed too much bosom for Chicago. If Breen seemed out of step with American tastes, however, he was right in line with the British. When the film opened in Great Britain in April 1940, the British Board of Film Censors cut Melanie's labor pains and part of the scene in which Scarlett decides to have no more children.

Tussle Over Russell

Following his battles with David O. Selznick, Joe Breen probably deserved a good rest. Instead, he took on another of the toughest characters in town, Howard Hughes, as the two got into a tussle over Jane Russell.

After challenging censors around the nation with *Scarface* and coproducing MGM's 1933 Jean Harlow vehicle *Bombshell*, Hughes had retired from filmmaking. By 1940, he was ready to get back to the screen with an unconventional look at the legend of Billy the Kid. He registered the title *The Outlaw* on April 19, 1940, the same day his producer-director, Howard Hawks, met with Breen to discuss his desire to "get away from the formula ending of having to affirmatively punish 'Billy the Kid' for his criminal activities." Hughes had hoped that by focusing on romantic conflict rather than law-breaking, he could justify an ending in which Sheriff Pat Garrett would turn Billy loose "motivated solely by his desire to acquiesce in the request of Billy's sweetheart." Breen couldn't approve the story on a mere description, so he advised Hawks to get the thing written and then submit it for approval. That was the the last he would hear of the tale until the film was in production.

Meanwhile, Hughes set out to find a pair of unknowns to star as Billy the Kid and Rio, the Mexican girl he wins from Doc Holliday. The latter role particularly interested him, with his eye for beauty and preoccupation with women's breasts. Sifting through photos of would-be actresses, he discovered the young Jane Russell and told his assistant Noah Dietrich, "Today I saw the most beautiful pair of knockers I've ever seen in my life."[4] Russell was tested and signed. Newcomer Jack Beutel would play Billy, with veterans Walter Huston as Holliday and Thomas Mitchell as Garrett. In addition, Hughes signed public-relations wizard Russell Birdwell, the genius behind the *Gone With the Wind* campaign, to make his new stars household names by the time the picture was released.

On December 3, 1940, Breen wrote to Hawks, noting that since shooting had already started it might be appropriate for the producer-director to submit a script. By the end of the month, Breen had the script and a raft of objections to it. The plot developments he had discussed with Hawks months earlier were unacceptable. Billy was too clearly characterized as a criminal to be set free at the end. Even worse was the thread of sexuality running through the script. Billy first meets Rio when she ambushes him in a barn to avenge his killing of her brother. Billy disarms her, then rapes her. Later, Billy is wounded escaping from Garrett, and Holliday asks Rio to nurse him. When she can't get Billy warm enough to stop his chills, she strips and gets into bed with him. After Billy's recovery, the two make love, a breach of Doc's trust Billy justifies on the grounds that Holliday has taken his horse: "You borrow from me, I borrow from you." Later, Holliday refuses to take Rio back. "Cattle don't graze after sheep," he tells Billy.

After Breen sent his objections to Hawks, PCA staffer Geoffrey Shurlock met with writer Jules Furthman. Handling the criminal element was easy enough. Furthman simply cut references to Billy's past as an outlaw and made sure that any killing he did, past or present, was in self-defense. Furthman also agreed that the rape scene, which already had been shot, would be trimmed to omit "any suggestion of a sex affair." All they did, however, was have Billy pull Rio into the shadows. He warns her to stop struggling or she'll tear her dress. Then the material is heard ripping, leaving the audience to draw its own conclusions.

When Breen saw the finished film in March 1941, he rejected it because of the suggestion of Rio's illicit relationships with Doc and Billy and the way Jane Russell had been photographed. In shooting the film, Hughes, who had replaced Hawks as director, had focused the camera primarily on Russell's breasts and cleavage. As Breen wrote to Hays: "In my more than ten years of critical examination of motion pictures, I have never seen anything quite so unacceptable as the shots of the breasts of the character of Rio. This is the young girl, whom Mr. Hughes recently picked up and who has never before, according to my information, appeared on the motion picture screen. Throughout almost half the picture the girl's breasts, which are quite large and prominent, are shockingly emphasized and, in almost every instance, are very substantially uncovered. . . . Many of these breast shots cannot be eliminated without destroying completely the continuity of the story."

Hughes changed the horse-trading line to "Tit for tat" at Breen's suggestion but appealed to the MPPDA's New York board about the other cuts. The board sided with Breen, though they rejected "Tit for tat" and insisted on a return to the original line. In a memo Francis Harmon labeled the "Five Star Final," they listed six cuts, ranging from three feet of Rio simply sitting in a chair to sixteen feet and fourteen frames of breast shots as she bends in front of a mirror.

The Seal was granted on May 23, 1941. In June, Harmon caught Hughes trying to send out a print with just the board's cuts and none of those Breen had made earlier. The film was reedited again and shipped to local censors, who cut it so badly that Hughes decided to postpone its release for eighteen months.

By June 18, 1941, *The Outlaw* was no longer Breen's problem. Three months earlier, the battles over cleavage and punishment for crime had finally become too much for him, and he resigned his position as director of the Production Code Administration. As screenwriter Adela Rogers St. John suggested, after reviewing thirty-six thousand stories a year for five years, "He's plumb wore out."[5]

Breen had no immediate prospects when he handed in his resignation. Through the years, however, the studios had offered him executive positions, as much to get him out of the way as in recognition of his story sense and organizational abilities. Shortly after he announced his resignation he signed on as head of production for RKO Studios at $1,700 a week.

Meanwhile, Hays didn't seem to know what to do. Shurlock was put in charge of the PCA but was not named director. In fact, most official correspondence during Breen's absence was simply signed "Production Code Administration," giving the impression that nobody was in charge. This was more than borne out as producers started pushing the envelope again. *The Moon and Sixpence* was one of several properties banned under Breen that suddenly got approval. Low-cut gowns and risqué jokes multiplied until reformers and the Legion of Decency started complaining again. The situation reached a crisis point when the Legion condemned its first Hollywood film since the boycott of 1934.

Two-Faced Woman was another story Breen had rejected. In its original form, it told of the mismatched marriage of New York playwright Christopher Audley and Swedish outdoorswoman Diana. The two buy a ranch in California, but Christopher's increasingly lengthy business trips to New York leave Diana feeling neglected. Pretending to be her twin sister, Evelyn, Diana seduces Christopher. The two have an affair that leaves her pregnant, at which point she reveals the deception.

Breen rejected the story in 1940, but MGM kept their writers at work turning it into a follow-up to Greta Garbo's comic hit of 1939, *Ninotchka*. Under the title *The Twins*, the shooting script was submitted in June 1941. The day before he left for New York to finalize his RKO contract, Breen wrote to Mayer urging him "to lean backwards to avoid any objectionable details or lines that might emphasize the sex suggestive features of the finished picture."

Once Breen had departed, the writers went their own way. The characters were changed to magazine publisher Larry Blake (Melvyn Douglas) and skiing instructor Karin Borg. The pregnancy was out, but there was still a clear indication that Larry was seduced by his wife's twin, Katherine. In addition, Larry's ex-mistress, Griselda Vaughan (Constance Bennett), makes a shameless play for the married man, informing him, "No matter how much you get married, you and I are inevitable." Larry discovers his wife's masquerade after they spend the night together and he notices that Karen's toenails are painted, just as Katherine's were.

This got past the PCA in a flurry of confusion. Instead of submitting a complete rewrite, MGM sent the script in twenty-three separate installments. One particularly low-cut gown Garbo wore was passed because nobody at the PCA saw it until the lengthy and expensive nightclub scene had been filmed. *Two-Faced Woman* was granted the Production Code Seal on October 6, 1941.

Conservative forces within the Catholic Church were already alarmed at the increasing permissiveness of Hollywood films since Breen's departure. Possibly because it came from the film capital's leading studio, MGM, the Legion of Decency decided to make an example of *Two-Faced Woman*, condemning it on November 24, 1941. In their statement, they blasted the film's "immoral and un-Christian attitude toward marriage and its obligations; impudently suggestive scenes, dialogue and situations; suggestive costumes." The Legion's secretary, the Reverend John J. McClafferty, used the occasion to warn Hollywood "not to let the wartime trend 'away from God' creep into movies."[6]

Once again Hollywood was under attack. Archbishop Francis J. Spellman denounced the film in a letter to be read from the pulpits of all New York churches. New York congressman Martin J. Kennedy wrote to Hays labeling the film "an affront to the Congress of the United States" and demanding that it be withdrawn.

To appease the Legion of Decency, MGM had to cut suggestive lines (including Griselda's come-on to Larry) and as many shots as they could of Garbo's low-cut dress. Then, to keep the husband's behavior on the up-and-up, the studio called back Melvyn Douglas to shoot another scene in which he learns of his wife's disguise before succumbing to her "twin's" charms. None of his confusion in their later scenes together was changed, however, leaving the film making little sense but at least earning it a B rating from the Legion.

Two-Faced Woman was far from a hit and marked the end of Garbo's screen career. MGM would blame the picture's failure on the changes made to placate the Legion of Decency. In truth, the film was a misfire before any changes were made. Garbo's visit to New York is well played, and inventively staged by director George Cukor. But it's not enough to compensate for the basic flaw in the premise: Karin and Larry are so mismatched, their courtship so rushed and thoughtless, that the picture lacks any credibility. They remain a colossal mismatch, with none of their differences resolved in the end.

While the PCA was dealing with this and other crises, Breen was having problems of his own. He quickly learned that in his new position at RKO he was little more than a glorified administrator. RKO president George Schaefer maintained control of all major decisions, while Breen was expected simply to supervise the budgets and personnel. Within less than a year he wanted out and approached Hays to see if his former job was still available. After an amicable parting with RKO and a vacation in Mexico, Breen returned as Production Code director in May 1942.

WWII and the Code

Breen came back to a changing world. With the U.S.'s entry into World War II, an entire generation felt its moral code loosening. Juvenile delinquency became a major problem among young people whose fathers and older brothers were off at war. Women enjoyed increased mobility and freedom as they worked in factories to help the war effort and grasped for precious moments of happiness with husbands and boyfriends.

Hollywood did its best to hold the line against social change with a series of escapist films that were designed to show GIs overseas and their families at home what they were fighting for. MGM's Andy Hardy films, which had started in 1937, continued to extol small-town American values and the joys of family life. The Hardys were joined by other all-American families: the Smiths of *Meet Me in St. Louis* (1944), the Macauleys of *The Human Comedy* (1943), and the Jacobsons of *Our Vines Have Tender Grapes* (1945). Even families in other nations were presented in terms of American virtue in everything from *Mrs. Miniver* (1942) to *Song of Russia* (1943).

At the same time, however, realism was gaining a foothold in Hollywood. Documentaries and newsreels became an important means of keeping in touch with what was happening at the front. Many war films adopted a documentary style in their presentation of battle action, putting a human face on the headlines about Wake Island, Bataan, and Corregidor.

Although Breen continued to defend the movies' moral code, some things started slipping through in the name of the war effort. RKO's 1943 propaganda film *Hitler's Children* opened with a shot that probably would have been cut in any other context: a copy of the film's source, Gregor Zeimer's *Education for Death*, flies from a pile of burning books and bleeds profusely as the credits roll. The rest of the film lives up to that shock opening, delivering a rabble-rousing exposé of the Third Reich's youth programs. Dissident women are sterilized. A pregnant party member hopes to suffer greatly in childbirth for the glory of the Führer. To save his radical girlfriend (Bonita Granville) from punishment, a young Brownshirt (Tim Holt) offers to get her pregnant: "The most they demand is that you have a child for the State. They never inquire who the father is."

The MPPDA Goes to War

With the outbreak of World War II, Will Hays led the way for Hollywood as the film capital carved out an important role in the U.S. war effort. The MPPDA helped organize the National Co-ordinating Committee (later re-named the War Activities Committee, or WAC) to oversee the industry's work in this area. Hays even loaned WAC his East Coast associate Francis Harmon to run the organization with RKO president George Schaefer.

WAC helped coordinate the production of training and educational films to be shown to enlisted men and the production of newsreels and other informational films for audiences on the homefront. It also arranged for the shipment of entertainment films overseas, where soldiers saw some pictures as much as two years before their domestic releases. WAC even got Eastman and DuPont to contribute more than thirty-two million feet of 16-millimeter film with which to make military prints.

To raise money for the war effort, WAC arranged a series of "bond premieres" around the nation. On the day a film opened, theaters would waive ticket prices and admit only patrons buying war bonds. In 1944 alone there were fifteen thousand such premieres, raising more than $15 million.

Censorship was also a part of the war effort. While Breen advised producers of special government concerns in a variety of areas, WAC arranged government clearances. On-screen references

Censored Hollywood

The war hit Breen closer to home when Preston Sturges came out with *The Miracle of Morgan's Creek* in 1944—so close, in fact, that critic James Agee suggested "the Hays office has been either hypnotized into a liberality for which it should be thanked, or has been raped in its sleep."[7] Here were the adventures of Trudy Kockenlocker (Betty Hutton), a victory girl giving her all for Uncle Sam. After a wild party with servicemen from a nearby base, she returns home with vague recollections of having wed a "Private Ratzkiwatzki." Discovering she's pregnant, she enlists spurned suitor Norval Jones (Eddie Bracken) to impersonate the private and marry her, thus rendering her a bigamist but at least leaving her with a license and a ring. Norval is caught and sent to jail by an outraged populace. Then, a last-minute surprise makes Norval a national hero: Trudy gives birth to sextuplets on Christmas Eve.

One reason Breen let so much get by was the fact that nobody saw a completed script until the film was finished. Sturges went into production in the fall of 1942 with only ten pages written. When Breen finally saw the first part of the script in October, he ruled it unacceptable. Sturges got around Breen's decision by conceding minor points: the soldiers would not be presented as "immoral or sex-crazed"; instead of being drunk

to the war effort were checked to make sure they didn't give away any secrets. Even locations had to be preapproved, lest a filmmaker unwittingly provide the enemy with footage of strategic areas.

None of this was done without paybacks. To secure Hollywood's full cooperation and availability during the war, Hays got the Justice Department to call off its antitrust suits against the major studios, allowing them to keep their theatrical holdings for the duration. In addition, Hays arranged for filmmaking to be declared an "essential industry," guaranteeing that materials would be readily available to the studios and key personnel would not be drafted.

Not everything went as planned. Even though they were exempt from the draft, many studio employees, including such major stars as Clark Gable and James Stewart, volunteered for military service. The studios spent years after the war tracking down pirated military prints. And the Justice Department renewed its action against the studios almost as soon as the Armistice was signed.

The on-screen results were often inspiring, however, showing the armed services what they were fighting for and keeping audiences at home in touch with the war overseas. Hollywood would reap copious praise for its contribution to the war effort, with President Franklin Roosevelt commending the industry for serving the country "without the slightest resort to the totalitarian methods of our enemies."[8]

when she got married, Trudy would be suffering from a concussion; and there would be no slapstick business during the course of the wedding ceremony. But he got to keep the basic plot and such questionable lines as Norval's response to Trudy's pregnancy:

Monsieur Verdoux: Joe Breen's Smoking Gun

For all the protests over Joe Breen's administration of the Production Code, most of the concerns voiced in his letters to producers seem a little silly by contemporary standards. For the most part, the PCA letters seem concerned with inconsequentialities, presenting the censor as bean counter rather than any great threat to the marketplace of ideas. Even where Breen insists on compensating moral value and the proper punishment for all criminal and sexual transgressions, there is little sense that he is trying to control the filmmakers' way of thinking. He simply seems to be tying up the loose ends.

That was not the case, however, with Charles Chaplin's *Monsieur Verdoux*. In correspondence related to that 1947 feature, Breen is clearly trying to decide what ideas may and may not be expressed on screen.

Chaplin conceived *Monsieur Verdoux*, originally titled *A Comedy of Murders*, in the midst of World War II. He stars as an unemployed bank teller who supports his invalid wife and young son by marrying a series of rich, unhappy women and murdering them for their money. When he's finally caught, he justifies his crimes in court by comparing them to the horrors of modern warfare. "Numbers sanctify," he states from the witness stand.

After two years' work on the script, Chaplin sent it to the PCA for approval, only to be rejected. Some of Breen's objections were easily dealt with. To get rid of "the distasteful flavor of illicit sex," Chaplin changed one of the wives' lines from "Come to bed" to "Go to bed." At one point, Verdoux picks up a young streetwalker to test a new poison he's devised. After some conversation, he relents, gives her dinner, and lets her go. Years later he meets her again, this time as the well-kept mistress of a munitions manufacturer. To appease Breen, Chaplin cut some of the more pointed references to her profession and made her the businessman's fiancée.

Breen's major objections, however, were to the story's philosophical basis. Although he tried to avoid arguing Verdoux's moral viewpoint, initially stating that the problem lay solely in the character's attempts to justify his murders, Breen would later write: "I think it is pretty well established that mankind has agreed, down through the centuries, that to kill under certain circumstances—for lawful war—is not a violation of the moral or the human law. On the other hand, to murder, to kill unlawfully, is universally agreed to be a crime against both the moral and the human law."[9]

When Breen and an associate (possibly Jack Vizzard) met with Chaplin to discuss the problems, they also objected to Verdoux's blasphemous attitudes toward God, as expressed in a scene

"Some sort of fun lasts longer than others."

Sturges's sporadic submission of script pages certainly contributed to Breen's leniency, but there may have been another explanation. When Paramount requested

with a priest shortly before the execution. Chaplin had to fight for such inflammatory lines as "Who knows what sin is . . . who knows what mysterious destiny it serves?" and "What would you be doing without sin?" justifying them as expressions of Verdoux's bravado on the way to the gallows. As a compromise, he agreed to give the priest more lines with which to rebut Verdoux's statements.

To the associate's complaint that "you impugn society and the whole state," Chaplin replied, "Well, after all, the state and society are not simon-pure, and criticism of them is not inadmissable, surely?"[10] Chaplin also argued that, contrary to the Production Code's requirements, good and evil were not always clearly delineated: "*The Dialogues of Plato* have struggled with that question." "With such arguments," Vizzard would later write, "did Chaplin dig his grave as a would-be intellectual."[11]

Chaplin had a lot of unwanted help digging his grave on this one. Although Breen helped him get the film past the Legion of Decency, he couldn't control the critics, who decried *Monsieur Verdoux* as immoral and, worse for attendance, unfunny. He also couldn't control the American Legion, which denounced the film's creator as un-American.

Chaplin was subpoenaed by HUAC at the same time to discuss his alleged leftist leanings (he had been an early supporter of Upton Sinclair and several antifascist organizations of the thirties). Although HUAC decided not to hear his testimony, the *New York Daily News* labeled him a "fellow traveler." At the same time, a messy paternity suit, eventually decided in his favor, and ongoing complaints that he had grown rich in the U.S. without ever becoming an American citizen, led to picket lines at theaters showing *Monsieur Verdoux*.

The film did well during its first six weeks in New York, but then business started falling off. In addition, the American Legion sent letters to theater owners outside New York threatening a one-year boycott if they booked the film. *Monsieur Verdoux* barely broke even at a time when its distributor, United Artists, was undergoing financial difficulties of its own. As a result, Chaplin was forced to sell out his part ownership in the company he had helped found.

After its unsuccessful initial run, Chaplin withdrew *Monsieur Verdoux* from circulation for seventeen years. Within a few years, the U.S. government withdrew him from circulation as well, denying him permission to reenter the country in 1952. Where Breen had failed, the new modes of thought control developing in the U.S. helped end the career of one of the screen's greatest talents. ✂

permission to remake the film in 1955, Breen's replacement, Geoffrey Shurlock, suggested that Sturges's evocation of wartime hysteria had made the subject matter acceptable: "Without this background the sordid element could be even more apparent and objectionable. Preston Sturges directed the picture in a very frantic and slapstick manner, which helped cover up this fundamental unpleasantness. Told in a more leisurely fashion, the camouflage would probably turn out very thin."

This is borne out by the film's reception. Despite a few complaints and one patron who wanted to deliver his response to the PCA in person "and punctuate it with a swift kick in your posterior," *The Miracle of Morgan's Creek* played to SRO crowds. Some churchmen complained that "every laugh is a chuckle at license, lies or lust,"[12] but it got a B rating from the Legion of Decency and was passed uncut by every state but Kansas.

Even Andy Hardy ventured into the land of realism, though Breen didn't let him get very far. In 1941, MGM decided to let Andy (Mickey Rooney) grow up in *Life Begins for Andy Hardy*. Breen managed to keep the teenager's new maturity pristine, but there was one element the studio refused to cut—Judge Hardy's lecture on the birds and the bees. MGM had tried to insert a similar scene with Andy's sister in an earlier film but had bowed to pressure from the Breen office. This time they fought to keep lines like "Many a marriage has been ruined because all of its wonders are stale. Know what I mean?" The scene was delicately handled but still earned the film an "adults only" rating from the Legion of Decency. At the same time, some reviewers considered its inclusion a social boon: "The Hardy series have always been a godsend to parents throughout the country in helping them reason with their children. This picture, located at the most important period of a boy's life, and as such a touchy situation for parents to handle, will be of even greater benefit to both parents and youngsters at the moment of their big decision regarding their future life."[13]

The result of Hollywood's new fascination with realism would be a series of cracks in the Production Code that were hard to fill. No single film dealt the Code a decisive blow, but each concession inspired imitation and prompted filmmakers to push the envelope a little bit further.

Return of *The Outlaw*

As the U.S. went to war with the Axis, and producers went to war with Joe Breen, the movies were at war with the Justice Department. In 1938, the government had filed suit against Hollywood's major studios, charging that their ownership of production, distribution, and exhibition constituted an illegal trust. As a compromise, they signed a consent decree in 1940 under which the studios stopped acquiring new theaters and got rid of their more restrictive distribution policies. The truce would not last forever.

Under the advice of the MPPDA's lawyers, Hays engineered a major change in Production Code enforcement in March 1942. Exhibitors would now be allowed to show films that had not been granted the Seal of Approval. Only producers and distributors could be fined for violating the Code. Though this change would ultimately contribute to the Code's downfall, its immediate effect was to protect the MPPDA from lawsuits by disgruntled producers who had been denied the Seal of Approval, which is exactly what happened when Howard Hughes decided to put *The Outlaw* into release.

After casting about for a location where he could open the film without censorship problems, Hughes picked San Francisco. He plastered the city with provocative photos of Jane Russell over the caption "Sex has not been rationed,"[14] to which local troublemakers added indications of exactly which acts did not require coupon booklets. After numerous complaints—including one from Russell's aunt, who accused him of "selling my niece as though she were some cheap stripper"[15]—the posters were taken down.

Hughes had not bothered submitting *The Outlaw* to the Legion of Decency's New York office, so the group sent some of its San Francisco affiliates to view the film there. "Stupid," wrote one reviewer; "no changes could cure it." "Amateurish," noted another; "no reason why it should be shown." Beyond their aesthetic judgment, they were offended by the film's sexuality and slapped it with a condemned rating.

MPPDA executives suddenly had to defend the film, arguing that the Legion's San Francisco previewers had been less experienced than their New York counterparts and had been swayed by the advertising campaign. Hughes was happy to let the condemned rating stand, at least for now. *The Outlaw* was not getting good reviews, but audiences were lining up anyway because of the film's notoriety. The Legion of Decency rating simply added to its appeal.

After seven weeks in San Francisco, during which the film grossed $158,000 (equivalent to about $1 million in 1994), Hughes withdrew it from release. Some have suggested he wanted to build up curiosity about *The Outlaw*'s sexual content to counterbalance the bad reviews. In *The Dame in the Kimono*, Leonard Leff and Jerold Simmons theorize that Hughes simply lost interest in the project for a while. A third reason could have been the nature of wartime distribution. The main audience for *The Outlaw* was overseas and, thanks to Will Hays, could have seen the film for free had it gone into general release at the time (see "The MPPDA Goes to War," p. 122). Instead, Hughes let it sit on the shelf until the war was over, and returning GIs would have to pay full admission to see the picture stateside.

Hughes certainly didn't stop publicizing the film. During production, photographers had taken numerous provocative shots of the young Jane Russell, who was too inexperienced to realize what they were doing: "My boobs were bulging out over the top of my blouse. . . . But I didn't know it until I saw myself on the covers and centerfolds of practically every magazine on the newsstands. One weekend was all it took. Those pictures came out for the next five years."[16] "Those pictures" made Russell one of the most popular pinups of World War II. By the time the war was over, she was a major star, even though nobody outside of San Francisco and a few local censor boards had seen her in the movies.

By 1946, Hughes felt the nation was suitably primed for *The Outlaw*. Breen sent Shurlock to double-check the print and make sure it was the version approved by the MPPDA's board. This time, however, the problem wasn't with the film but with the advertising campaign. The Advertising Code Administration (ACA) rejected stills and other artwork, but Hughes refused to withdraw them. Slogans like "What are the two great reasons for Jane Russell's rise to stardom?" and "How would you like to tussle with Russell?" were put on billboards and in magazine ads over ACA objections. Another ad claimed, inaccurately, "Exactly as filmed—not a frame cut." The height of tastelessness was probably an aerial campaign in which a skywriting plane blazoned the film's title over Pasadena followed by two large circles with dots in them.

On April 9, 1946, the association formally charged Hughes with violating the Advertising Code and scheduled a hearing for April 23. The judgment went against Hughes, so he sued for $7.5 million, claiming that the association's operations violated antitrust laws: "The defendant and its co-conspirators have the power to bar from affiliated theatres by direct order, and from other theatres by the threat of boycott, a motion picture produced by an independent producer or distributed by an independent distributor and thus to exclude competitors from the industry." Although Hughes's contention in this was basically correct—the majors could indeed force independent exhibitors to refuse films without the Seal—Judge D. J. Bright ruled for the association on June 14, 1946, arguing that the voluntary nature of submission under the Production Code protected the organization from charges of unfair practices: "I know of no law which authorizes a party to accept the good in a contract and reject what he does not like. It [Hughes Tool Company] cannot have its cake and eat it too."[17]

After months of going back and forth, the Seal of Approval was withdrawn on September 6, 1946. The immediate effect of this was a rash of local bannings and cancelled bookings. When the major first-run circuit in Dallas refused to show the film, Hughes booked *The Outlaw* into twenty-two of the city's fifty-one neighborhood houses. The film took in almost forty thousand dollars in just two days (the city's weekly record for film receipts was twenty-six thousand dollars), attracting seventy-seven thousand patrons—21 percent of the Dallas population.

Although the New York State board had passed *The Outlaw*, New York City's license commissioner threatened to close any theater showing the film. In addition, state boards in Massachusetts, Ohio, and Maryland banned it. Hughes took most of these cases to court, losing almost every time. In upholding Maryland's ban, Judge E. Paul Mason noted that Jane Russell's "breasts hung like a thunderstorm over a summer landscape. . . . They are prominent and vigorously threaten to burst forth at any moment."[18]

The film continued to do record business, however, eventually grossing over $3 million domestically and $1.5 million overseas. In 1949 *The Outlaw* was edited yet again to win back its Seal of Approval. In addition, the new version was submitted to the Legion of Decency and rated B. The cut version also got past the local censors, though it would take until 1954 for Ohio to overturn the final ban on the film.

A Tale of Two Trollops

In her autobiography, Russell says of the bosom mania triggered by *The Outlaw*: "I honestly feel sorry if *The Outlaw* publicity campaign was responsible for the young girls who decided that the only way to make it in show business was to shove out their bosom or take their clothes off altogether."[19] Although the excesses she describes didn't really begin in earnest until the late sixties, she could just as easily have been discussing two other sex sagas that shook up the Breen office in the wake of *The Outlaw*: *Duel in the Sun* (1946) and *Forever Amber* (1947).

Duel in the Sun told the story of Pearl Chavez, a half-breed whose presence brings to the surface conflicts among the McCanlesses, a powerful ranching family. Pearl is courted by simple, honest Jesse McCanles, but prefers his wild-living brother Lewt, even though he constantly abuses her. Finally, she kills Lewt in a shootout to protect Jesse from him.

Selznick saw the picture as a means of achieving two ends. The story could be realized on an epic scale, thus giving him the chance to top his earlier success with *Gone With the Wind*. The role of Pearl would also give him the chance to prove his protégée Jennifer Jones's versatility as a dramatic actress and make her one of Hollywood's leading sexpots. The latter impetus would prove the source of numerous censorship problems.

Breen rejected *Duel in the Sun* when it was first submitted in 1944, complaining about the glorification of Pearl and Lewt's illicit love. He insisted that instead of becoming

Lewt's lover after he rapes her, Pearl should demand that he marry her, with his refusal triggering much of their animosity. At Breen's insistence, Selznick eventually softened the whorelike characterization of Pearl's mother; changed the Sin-killer, a religious hypocrite out to purify Pearl, from a minister to a lay preacher; and eliminated a scene in which Pearl and Lewt are aroused by the sight of two horses breeding.

Selznick made several other cuts in the film to please Breen, but there was one issue on which he would not back down—the film's ending. In Niven Busch's novel, Pearl kills Lewt so she can go off to a happy life with Jesse. Selznick thought this sacrificed a potentially powerful climax and changed it so that the two shoot each other, then share one last, passionate embrace before dying. Breen complained that the ending glorified the characters' illicit relationship, but Selznick kept to his original concept.

The film's chaotic production may have helped the producer get past Breen's objections. Director King Vidor had walked off the picture after months of location work in Arizona, leaving Selznick to finish production with the assistance of William Dieterle and any other director he could get to help. The script was rewritten daily on the set, often with the cast and crew waiting around while Selznick finished the day's pages. The PCA received the script in forty-three installments, some no longer than a page or two, between March 1, 1945, and August 20, 1946. By the time Breen got to see the film, it was too late to make some of the changes he wanted. *Duel in the Sun* was awarded the Seal of Approval on December 11, 1946, so it could have an early release in Los Angeles to qualify for the Academy Awards.

The film's hurried production schedule also led to problems with the Legion of Decency. Because of a strike at the Technicolor labs, Selznick had only one good print as the film's Los Angeles premiere neared. Rather than ship the print to the Legion's New York offices, he opened it without obtaining a rating. Archbishop John Cantwell of Los Angeles told Catholics to stay away until it was rated. Selznick complained publicly about the ruling but privately could console himself that attendance had risen after the pronouncement. When the Legion of Decency finally got hold of the film, they threatened to condemn it.

Breen and Selznick brought in Martin Quigley to help them negotiate cuts with the Legion (a task Quigley would take on repeatedly through the years). In all, six minutes were cut to win the film a B rating, including a seductive dance Jones had learned in two different versions; Breen already had rejected the first.

Eventually, the furor over *Duel in the Sun* made it into the Congressional Record. In support of a House resolution banning the film from the District of Columbia, Representative John D. Rankin read a letter from Memphis censor Lloyd Binford, who had banned the film outright: "This production contains all the impurities of the foulest human dross. It is sadism at its deepest level. It is the fleshpots of Pharaoh, modernized and filled to overflowing. It is a barbaric symphony of passion and hatred, spilling from a blood-tinted screen."[20] Although the bill died in committee, the publicity was a goldmine.

Selznick had spent one million dollars selling *Duel in the Sun* to a war-weary public. Instead of opening the film in just one first-run house in each of the major cities, he became the first major producer to open a film "wide," playing it in more than two hundred theaters around the nation at once. As a result, he took in over $10 million at the box office.

Just as fiery was the controversy over Twentieth Century-Fox's *Forever Amber*, which almost inspired a repeat of the Legion of Decency's 1934 boycott. While the book was still in galleys, Hollywood took an interest in Kathleen Winsor's steamy tale of Amber St. Clare, a Restoration beauty who sleeps her way to the top of the English court. Before it even hit the stores in 1944, Hays had gotten the major studios to agree not to pick up the rights. News of that agreement may have contributed to the novel's first-week sale of one hundred thousand copies. *Forever Amber* was the biggest debut novel since *Gone With the Wind*, and no gentlemen's agreement could stand up to a success like that. The book was banned in Boston, but that ban eventually was overturned—the first such decision in this century—when the court decided that "while conducive to sleep, it is not conducive to the desire to sleep with a member of the opposite sex."[21]

In November 1944, Fox optioned the story, wisely making the final purchase contingent upon its ability to produce a screen treatment that would pass the Code. This would be quite an accomplishment considering the book's contents. Citing a Bennett Cerf column, Colonel Joy notified Breen that the original novel contained:

70 references to sexual intercourse

39 illegitimate pregnancies

7 abortions

10 descriptions of women dressing, undressing, or bathing in the presence of men

5 references to incest

10 references to the badger game

13 ridiculing marriage

49 "miscellaneous objectionable passages"

It took Fox a year, but by November 1945 they finally had a script that Breen could pass. They reduced Amber's thirty lovers to six, changed her early affair with Bruce Carlton to a one-night fling that leaves her pregnant, and turned an older character, Lord Almsbury, into the voice of morality. Instead of acting out of erotic abandon, Amber sleeps her way to wealth and power in a misguided effort to win back Bruce, her one true love. And rather than run off with Bruce at the end, she loses him to an American woman. Amber even gives Bruce her other great love, their illegitimate child.

Forever Amber went through a troubled production process. After thirty-nine days of shooting, studio head Darryl F. Zanuck scrapped the production, dissatisfied with Hollywood newcomer Peggy Cummins's performance in the title role. She was replaced by studio star Linda Darnell, with Otto Preminger taking over from John Stahl as director. The budget eventually shot from $3 million to $6 million.

When the picture finally turned up at the PCA offices, it was significantly different from the last script approved. Amber's night with Bruce had become an affair; Almsbury's moralizing lines had been cut; and the ending gave the impression that Amber would continue in her life of luxury as a royal courtesan. Zanuck admitted that the film had been rewritten twice since winning Breen's approval. In the rush to complete the mammoth production, nobody had bothered to submit the new drafts. So he went back to the editing room and recut the film to meet PCA demands. The film was granted the Seal on June 20, 1947, and scheduled for an October 22 release.

On the day *Forever Amber* opened at New York's Roxy Theatre, the Legion of Decency condemned the film as a "glorification of immorality and licentiousness." Initially, the Condemned rating was a box-office boon; the film grossed a record $328,000 in its first two weeks at the Roxy. But as Zanuck and the Legion went around about cuts, the uncut film started generating more attacks. Archbishop John T. McNicholas of Cincinnati suggested that Catholics should boycott all movies for a week to show Hollywood they meant business. His statements may have contributed to a 50 percent drop in *Forever Amber*'s receipts during its second week in Cincinnati. In Philadelphia, Cardinal Dougherty ordered parishioners to boycott all theaters showing the film for one year and threatened to extend the ban to any theaters showing Fox films.

Forever Amber was not the sole cause of these complaints. *The Outlaw* also was igniting controversy wherever it played. Many blamed Hollywood for the continuing problems with juvenile delinquency. When Breen approved the script for 1945's *Dillinger*, after a ten-year MPPDA ban on film representations of the notorious bank robber, teen criminals were caught imitating the Dillinger gang's on-screen crimes. A Production Code amendment that allowed films about police efforts to stop narcotics smuggling (but not depictions of addiction or the actual traffic in illegal drugs) had triggered more protests. *Forever Amber* simply became the focus for the church's wrath.

With exhibitors hounding him to recut the film, Zanuck finally came up with a set of changes the Legion of Decency would accept. References to Amber's life of luxury were cut wherever possible, along with any shots of illicit passion that could be eliminated. The picture would now end as Amber watched her son go off with Bruce. In addition, Cornel Wilde, who played Bruce, dubbed in two new lines that would play in the final scene over reaction shots of Darnell: "In Heaven's name, Amber, haven't we caused enough unhappiness?" and "May God have mercy on us both for our sins." Finally, Zanuck added a written prologue:

> This is the tragic story of Amber St. Clare . . .
> . . . slave to ambition . . .
> . . . stranger to virtue . . .
> . . . fated to find the wealth and power she ruthlessly gained wither to ashes in the
> fires lit by passion and fed by defiance of the eternal command . . .
> . . . the wages of sin is death.

On December 9, 1947, the Legion of Decency rerated *Forever Amber* B, but with a stern warning that "the film still lacks the adequate morally compensating values which should be present in a story of this kind." The critics had already taken their own potshots at the production. As *Life* headlined, "Deprived of beds, the famous trull seems merely dull."[22] Like Selznick and Hughes before him, Zanuck had played the controversy for all it was worth, but the film's $8 million domestic take was barely enough to offset its impressive price tag.

Hollywood Raises Cain

While Breen was trying to clean up Hollywood's three great sex epics of the forties, another trio of films—all adapted from novels by James M. Cain—stretched the Code further. Cain's sordid stories of crime and passion had begun attracting public and critical attention in the thirties, starting with *The Postman Always Rings Twice*. Breen had kept Cain's books off the screen for almost a decade, but in 1944 Paramount and writer-director Billy Wilder got by the PCA with an adaptation of *Double Indemnity*.

The story of Phyllis Dietrichson—who murders her husband with the help of her lover, Walter Neff—had first reached Hollywood in 1935 and was so hot that five studios bid on the rights, driving the price up to $25,000. The bidding war halted abruptly when Breen decided that the story could not possibly fit the Production Code.

As originally written, *Double Indemnity* ended with Neff confessing to the insurance investigators to clear the victim's daughter, with whom he had fallen in love. To save face, the insurance company withholds information from the authorities. The killers leave the country and eventually commit suicide. According to Breen, this violated the Code on several counts: by showing the killers escaping justice; by dealing "improperly with an illicit and adulterous sex relationship"; and by presenting the details of a crime. In addition, Neff's confession to save the woman he loves made him too heroic. Breen warned the studios that such a story would lead to "the hardening of audiences, especially those who are young and impressionable, to the thought and fact of crime."

Double Indemnity was a hit when it was published in *Liberty* magazine and later in book form, but Hollywood avoided the property until 1943. Then producer Joseph Sistrom suggested it to Billy Wilder. Wilder was intrigued but had a hard time getting anyone else interested. His writing partner at the time, Charles Brackett, refused to have anything to do with the project, so Wilder wound up cowriting it with novelist Raymond Chandler. His first two choices to star—Barbara Stanwyck and Fred MacMurray—had to be talked into playing totally unsympathetic characters. Even Paramount, Wilder's home studio, was certain that Breen would never approve the script.

But approve it he did. Wilder had made several important changes to the story. Instead of falling in love with his victim's daughter and trying to clear her, Neff simply dates the girl to distract her from her suspicions of Phyllis. Discovering that Phyllis is planning his own death, Walter confronts her, and the two shoot each other. As originally filmed, Neff was to have gone to the gas chamber for his crimes, but the scene was considered too grim, so he died after telling all to an associate (Edward G. Robinson).

Wilder's changes had made the story moral enough for Breen, though the PCA director did change some details. He cautioned about some of Stanwyck's costumes (though he missed a very tight sweater she wore in some scenes) and removed Neff's advice about wearing gloves so as not to leave fingerprints.

The result was a major hit. Critics hailed the film for its groundbreaking depiction of a murder from the killers' viewpoint. Even the Catholic newspaper *The Tidings* praised Wilder's efforts to prove that "there is 'no perfect crime' . . . those of criminal tendencies who might have been tempted to try out the formula for murder which this plot propounds, now may reflect what happened to the characters who perpetrated this."[23]

The success of *Double Indemnity* opened the door for other screen adaptations of Cain's work. *Mildred Pierce* had been turned down by Breen when David O. Selznick submitted it in 1941, the year the novel became a best-seller. It told of a working-class woman who throws out her husband because she suspects him of an affair with a neighbor. She then sleeps with his best friend, Wally, and with Monty, a dissolute playboy, to secure money for her spoiled daughter, Veda. After building a successful restaurant chain, Mildred marries Monty to earn Veda an entrée into society, not realizing that Monty also has an eye on the girl. When the affair is revealed, Veda and Monty run off to New York, leaving Mildred to pick up the pieces.

Breen objected to the story because of Mildred's sex affairs, her husband's infidelity, and Monty's "legal incest" with Veda. Selznick wasn't all that hot on the story anyway and let it drop. But another producer, Warner Bros.' Jerry Wald, had taken an interest in the property, adding it to his list of promising stories with adaptation problems. Wald started tinkering with *Mildred Pierce* in the summer of 1943. Feeling that the ending was anticlimactic, he came up with the idea of starting with a murder and telling the story in flashback. When he originally submitted it to Breen in February 1944, Mildred murdered Veda on discovering her affair with Monty. Breen rejected the story because of its "sordid and repellent elements," including the fact that Monty was "making love to both mother and daughter at the same time."

Wald met with Breen and worked out ways to make the story more acceptable. Wally would no longer be "on the make" for Mildred but would be more romantically interested. Mildred's early affair with Monty would be cut, as would his marrying her to get closer to Veda. "It was also agreed that a very definite effort would be made to raise the general all-over tone of the picture, and thus add to its general overall acceptability." Three days after the meeting Warners approved the purchase of the rights for $15,000.

Through rewrites, Wald made the story even more palatable. At Breen's insistence, Mildred's husband fervently denied any affair with the neighbor. In addition, he behaved himself after the separation, clearing the way for a romantic reunion for the two at the film's end. When Monty's affair with Veda is discovered, he breaks off with her, and she kills him. This intensifies Mildred's misguided nobility as she tries to take the blame for the crime, while making it possible to punish Veda for her sins. Yet there were enough sordid elements remaining—Veda's annulled marriage and fake pregnancy, her affair with Monty—to maintain at least some of the story's sizzle.

With these changes, *Mildred Pierce* became one of the screen's classic soap operas. Although Howard Barnes of the *New York Herald Tribune* reported that New York audiences were laughing at the dramatic high points, less sophisticated patrons around the country made it one of the top hits of 1945. Even though most of the steamier elements had been shorn from the novel, Warners' publicity department trumpeted the film with such slogans as "In their kind of affair somebody always gets hurt, and Mildred Pierce was the kind of girl who couldn't be hurt anymore" and "She's the kind of woman men want . . . but *shouldn't have*!"

Things got steamier still when MGM filmed *The Postman Always Rings Twice* with Lana Turner and John Garfield in 1946. The novel tells of Frank, a derelict who takes a job at a roadside café, where he falls in love with the owner's young wife, Cora. As the two engage in a torrid affair, they plan to kill her husband. They get away with the crime thanks to the illicit manipulations of their defense lawyer and the insurance investigators, but their happiness is cut short when Cora is killed in a car accident. Frank is convicted on circumstantial evidence and goes to the chair.

When the story was in galleys under the title *Bar-B-Q* in 1933, both RKO and Columbia submitted it to Breen, but he persuaded them to drop their plans. Then MGM picked up the rights for $25,000 without consulting him. In March 1934, Breen wrote to Louis B. Mayer rejecting the story. Using the current uproar about indecent movies and objections from the legal profession about their depiction on screen, he convinced MGM to drop the production. Gustav Machaty, the director of *Ecstasy*, came up with an acceptable treatment in 1940, eliminating the adulterous sex and making the husband's death accidental, but nothing came of it. Three years later, Paramount considered picking up the property but gave up on it because of Breen's objections.

Finally, in 1945, MGM writer-producer Carey Wilson came up with a suitable adaptation. He cut the affair back to the merest indication and, at Breen's suggestion, minimized physical contact between Frank and Cora while her husband was still alive. The defense attorney was less venal, while the crooked insurance investigator became a private detective. In addition, Cora's husband, Nick, was made more sympathetic at the start (helped greatly by the casting of character actor Cecil Kellaway, who gave one of his best performances in the role). Only when he decides to sell the café and move to Canada, where Cora will have to nurse his invalid sister, do the lovers decide to kill him.

When the film went into production, Wilson came up with another idea for playing against the story's sexuality. Turner would wear white throughout the picture. As director Tay Garnett recalled: "We figured that dressing Lana in white somehow made everything she did seem less sensuous. It was also attractive as hell. And it somehow took a little of the stigma off everything that she did."[24]

During filming, MGM's publicity department triggered a minor controversy by releasing stills of Turner and Garfield's sizzling beach scene. Breen had to deal with complaints from the Federal Council of Churches of Christ in America, copies of which he sent to Wilson with the admonition to avoid "the wrong kind of publicity in an enterprise of this kind . . . . From the type of publicity which your studio has been handing out, these people will get the impression that there is some dirty work at the crossroads!"

The Postman Always Rings Twice was the third successful Cain adaptation in a row. Although the author would complain years later that nobody at MGM seemed to have decided whether Frank and Cora became lovers before or after her husband's death, at the time he praised the film lavishly. Critics lauded it for satisfying both the demands of the original novel and Production Code requirements, but critic Bosley Crowther also took the opportunity to chide the PCA: "The guardians of the Production Code, who held up the story for so long, can make highly unfortunate mistakes. (They can also rectify them, as the release of *The Postman* testifies.) More tolerance in the Code's administration, with respectable producers, at least, seems the hope, under present circumstances, for a few more truthful, adult films."[25]

Trouble at the Top

Getting "a few more truthful, adult films" on screen would not be an easy matter. For every critic lauding the new realism of *The Postman Always Rings Twice* and other Hollywood films, there were a dozen reformers screaming that Hollywood was polluting American life. With reformers on one side and critics and film artists on the other, Breen was truly caught in the middle as he fought to defend the Production Code in the turbulent years following World War II.

Even without outside pressure, things were pretty turbulent at the MPPDA. In 1945, Will Hays announced his retirement. Although he would stay on with the association as an advisor for five more years, this was clearly the end of an era. The board chose as his replacement Eric Johnston, a businessman and manufacturer with an impressive record as president of the U.S. Chamber of Commerce, where he had dealt with two problems that would prove increasingly important to Hollywood in the postwar years: Communist infiltration of the United States and foreign trade disputes.

Johnston was not at all suited to the Hollywood side of the job. The moguls were too rough for his taste, so he left relations with the studios to Breen and concentrated on governmental relations, using his connections and negotiating skills to free up film money being held in Europe and to carry on Hays's lobbying efforts in Washington. In recognition of the increasing importance of the medium's national and international connections, the MPPDA changed its name to the Motion Picture Association of America (MPAA).

As Johnston established himself at the MPAA, Hollywood was facing a series of economic and political threats. With the end of the war, the Justice Department renewed its antitrust suits against the major studios, now demanding that they divest themselves of their theatrical holdings. Increasingly, actors who finished their seven-year contracts at the studios that had made them stars were refusing to re-sign, going independent in the hope of making more money and exercising more control over their careers. These problems were coupled with a serious decline at the box office. Servicemen returning from the war settled down with their new families, preferring quiet evenings in the sub-urbs to a trip into the city to see a movie. When television became more readily available in the early fifties, it would cut weekly film attendance in half.

According to historian Robert Sklar in *Movie-Made America*, the studios made a major tactical error in the face of declining receipts. Although studies at the time indi-cated that the majority of the film audience was upscale and well-educated, the studios met the box-office decline by placing greater emphasis on projects with "mass appeal," ultimately alienating their largest audience.

Contributing to the problem were the chilling effects of the House Un-American Activities Committee's investigations into alleged Communist infiltration of the film industry. The attack had started in 1940, partly fueled by the rise of unionism in the film capital, but the approaching war had shifted the focus to more pressing matters. The issue was revived in 1947. After a series of violent labor disputes, HUAC called a group of "friendly" witnesses—including Jack Warner, Walt Disney, and Gary Cooper—to laud the industry's patriotism and denounce communism.

Next up were a group of "unfriendly" witnesses—writers, producers, and directors with suspected ties to the Communist Party. When the first ten of these, the "Hollywood Ten," refused to testify, citing constitutional safeguards on freedom of thought, they were sentenced to prison terms for contempt of Congress. (One even served time with former HUAC chairman Martin Dies, who had been cited for fraud.)

Johnston tried to put a halt to the hysteria, announcing that "as long as I live I will never be party to anything as un-American as a blacklist."[26] When he tried to hold fast to that position, the studio heads threatened to dissolve the MPAA if necessary to pro-tect Hollywood from governmental reprisals. On November 24, 1947, the same day Congress cited the Hollywood Ten, Johnston issued an official industry statement fol-lowing a meeting at the Waldorf-Astoria Hotel in New York. The Ten were suspended from their contracts, and the studios promised that they would not knowingly hire any fellow travelers.

While Johnston was dealing with threats from Washington, he also had problems closer to home. After another five years of fighting to uphold the Code, Breen was ready to retire. Johnston refused to accept his resignation on several occasions but also consulted Quigley about a possible replacement. The result was the brief, unhappy censorship career of Stephen Jackson, chief magistrate of the New York City Court of Domestic Relations. In 1947, Jackson went to Hollywood to learn from the master and, eventually, stand in for Breen while the director took an extended vacation in Jamaica.

That vacation would prove to be Jackson's undoing. Lacking Breen's instinct for when to fight and when to retreat, he alienated the studios with seemingly capricious demands. In *Johnny Belinda* (1948) he tried to clean up the scene in which the deaf-mute heroine (Jane Wyman) gets her first look at a girdle and brassiere on a store mannequin. After repeated demands that the garments be changed to something less titillating, he gave in, damaging his credibility with Warner Bros. A scene in *Tap Roots* (1948) implied that the southern-belle heroine (Susan Hayward) had spent the night with a Union officer. The writers tried to affirmatively establish that nothing had happened by showing the officer waking up on the sofa in full uniform. That wasn't enough for Jackson. His insistence that the man be shown asleep sitting up and holding a cup of coffee became a joke at the PCA. As a result of Jackson's gaffes, the studio heads got together and told Johnston that they couldn't work with the man. So Jackson went back to court, and Breen stayed in office a few years longer.

Joe Breen Against the World

One of the strongest challenges to the Production Code in the late forties came from the increasing popularity of foreign-made films in America. Working in a different world from Hollywood, a world recently torn apart by war, European filmmakers were developing a strong commitment to presenting life exactly as it was lived. Their work put them on a collision course with Breen, while the critical favor they were winning in major U.S. cities guaranteed that any conflict would reflect poorly on the Code.

The first major challenge had come early in the war years with the U.S. release of *In Which We Serve* in 1942. Noël Coward's story of the birth and death of a British destroyer did a great deal to generate U.S. sympathies for his homeland. It also pioneered in capturing the off-color language of men at sea.

When United Artists submitted the film to the PCA, Breen demanded seventeen cuts for language: ten "damn"s, two "hell"s, two "God"s, two "bastard"s, and one "lousy." UA appealed to the MPPDA board, the first such appeal since 1937, arguing that the film's importance as a "great patriotic document" should exempt it from the Code's restrictions on language. Although Breen argued that the film's strengths would survive with or without the vulgarity, the board struck a compromise. Since most of the cast was occupied with other films or military duty, it was impossible to loop the offending lines; UA also argued that making all seventeen cuts would leave a choppy soundtrack that could hurt the film commercially. So the board settled for twelve cuts. When UA noted that four of the cuts had not been mentioned in Breen's earlier letters, the MPPDA backed off on those as well.

Still, the English were furious over this desecration. British information minister Brendan Bracken denounced the PCA in the House of Commons for their "squeamishness and old maiden aunt-like apprehensions,"[27] but declined to repeat the words that had been cut. A *New York Herald Tribune* editorial marveled at the "inexplicable morality of Hollywood": "Apparently we may be permitted to see nonsensical films suggesting infidelity, seduction and lust, interspersed with gun waving, shooting and assorted brutalities, just so the language is moderately proper and virtue finally triumphs. . . . Would they know immorality if it walked up and bit them?"[28]

After the war, the number of foreign-made films on U.S. screens increased. French romanticism flowered in Marcel Carné's 1945 *Children of Paradise* and Jean Cocteau's 1946 *Beauty and the Beast*. The British imitated Hollywood's bosom mania so effectively in *The Wicked Lady* (1945) that some close-ups of star Margaret Lockwood had to be optically enlarged to remove her ample cleavage from the bottom of each frame. Particularly challenging to the censors was the new school of realism developed in Italy by Roberto Rossellini's *Open City* (1945) and Vittorio De Sica's *Shoeshine* (1946).

Usually, these films opened in import houses without obtaining the PCA Seal. If a film proved particularly popular, the distributors applied for a Seal in order to play second-run chains. In most cases, they went through the MPAA's New York offices and had to make only minor cuts. *Open City* lost a shot of a child on a chamber pot, while *Shoeshine*'s subtitles were stripped of a few profanities.

France's *Devil in the Flesh* required major surgery, however, and threatened to spark an international incident. Raymond Radiguet's novel about a French schoolboy's affair with the wife of a soldier during World War I was so controversial it was kept off the screen for twenty-five years. When Claude Autant-Lara filmed it in 1946, it triggered a protest from French veterans. The picture was banned in Canada and was threatened with prosecution by U.S. Customs until a screening committee judged it to be "of the highest order."[29]

Producer Paul Graetz approached the PCA about obtaining a Seal for *Devil in the Flesh* in 1947, before the film's U.S. premiere, but it took him until late 1948 to submit a copy for screening. Over the next fifteen months, Breen and his staff viewed the film repeatedly in an effort to come up with a set of cuts that would render the story acceptable. Each time, the film seemed hopeless. Cutting all the details of the affair would render the picture virtually incomprehensible but would still leave a film that seemed to glorify adultery.

Throughout negotiations, Graetz used all of his persuasive powers to convince Breen to bend the rules. He got the French embassy to look into the matter, hinting that the refusal of a Seal could change the country's policy on importing U.S. films. He also subtly accused the PCA of using the Seal to keep foreign product out of most American theaters—an easily refuted charge considering the number of international films Breen had passed.

Breen stood firm, but his position cost him prestige in the press. Writing of the case in the *Hollywood Citizen News*, Lowell E. Redelings joined a growing list of critics and filmmakers calling for a revision of the Production Code: "There is a crying need in Hollywood films for true situations taken from life as it is lived, not as studio executive heads THINK it is lived. If Production Code revisions will tend to encourage more realism in the industry's product, then a movement should be launched toward this end."[30]

The protests against the Code got even louder when Breen denied the Seal to one of the masterpieces of postwar film, *The Bicycle Thief*. Vittorio De Sica's tale of a workingman's desperate fight to recover the stolen bicycle he needs to keep his job had opened in New York on December 12, 1949, to critical acclaim, winning the New York Film Critics Award for Best Foreign Film and the National Board of Review Award for Best Picture. It was also doing record business, outgrossing such earlier art-house hits as *Open City* and *Paisan*.

U.S. distributors Arthur Mayer and Joseph Burstyn applied to the PCA for a Seal of Approval, hoping to book the film on the second-run circuit. In a letter dated January 31, 1950, Breen made approval contingent upon the deletion of two scenes. During a frantic day of searching the streets for the bicycle, the man's young son tries to relieve himself against a wall, only to be forced to zip his pants back up when his father calls for him. Later, the father, Antonio, finds the thief and chases him into a bordello, from which both men are forcibly ejected. Neither scene was handled exploitatively, but they clearly violated Code restrictions.

Burstyn and Mayer could not cut the film without the director's approval, which De Sica refused to give, protesting that the picture had played uncut everywhere else. In a wire, he advised Burstyn and Mayer to "wait decision tribunal public opinion."

That decision was swift in arriving, with most of the press coming down against the Code, particularly after the board upheld Breen's decision. There were some members of the press who sided with Breen. Eileen Creelman of the *New York World-Telegram and Sun* complained about "this business of deliberate vulgarity in foreign films,"[31] which she said was driving moviegoers away from art houses. The *Motion Picture Herald*, which earlier had labeled the film Communist propaganda, considered the two scenes hardly worth fighting for and hinted that the producers were merely exploiting the situation for box-office reasons.

Others were quick to defend the picture. William Tusher of ABC Radio insisted that "there is not a lewd or suggestive frame in the entire film." Several critics warned that the controversy could mark the end of the Production Code. Others, like Bosley Crowther, wondered "whether the Code has not here been used to support some parochial resentment toward aliens and adult artistry."[32]

Mayer and Burstyn were quick to turn the controversy to their advantage. After the board denied their appeal, they changed their advertising campaign to incorporate an image of the boy from *The Bicycle Thief* with captions reading : "Please, come and see me before they cut me out of *Bicycle Thief*!" When Warner Bros. cancelled a booking at their Princess Theatre in Philadelphia because the film had failed to win the Seal, Burstyn and Mayer triggered more headlines by threatening to sue.

As a result, attendance for the film continued to grow. In October 1950, *The Bicycle Thief* became the first film without a Production Code Seal to be booked into the independent Skouras circuit in the New York territory. The earlier change in Code enforcement, exempting exhibitors from the fine for showing unapproved pictures, had finally borne fruit. Two other independent chains were quick to pick up the picture as well.

The Bicycle Thief dealt Breen and the Code a swell black eye. Although Breen claimed at the film's appeal that he had never been asked to approve a joke about urination before, Crowther could point to a similar scene he had passed in the Fox film *Cheaper by the Dozen* (1950): Father Clifton Webb stops his car in the middle of a country road, turns to the children in the backseat, and says, "Anyone who wants to see Mrs. Murphy better do it now," at which point all of the boys run into the woods. Similarly, Universal's *Buccaneer Girl* (1950) features a scene unmistakably set in a brothel, with Elsa Lanchester clearly playing the madam.

Contrary to what some critics suggested, these inconsistencies probably weren't motivated by any desire to protect American product. Although many of the studio heads resented the new popularity of foreign films, the PCA had been more than accommodating to other European pictures. And few would have argued that Hollywood product was in danger of being supplanted at the box office by films like *The Bicycle Thief*.

The cause for Breen's rejection of the film may have been more ideological. The *Motion Picture Herald*'s charge that the film was Communist propaganda was ill founded; the Communist Party was one of the many social institutions that failed Antonio. But so was the church. When he chases a witness into a church mission, he's thrown out by do-gooders with no real interest in his problems. In another scene, while Antonio huddles for shelter from a sudden rainstorm, he's surrounded by priests, all speaking German, a metaphor for a church removed from its members' real human problems. This pessimistic, anticlerical attitude may have predisposed Breen to take a firm stand on the technicalities of the Code that, today, seems mean-spirited.

Neorealism Hollywood Style

The war and the influx of Italian films following it sparked a new realism in Hollywood, too, as America's leading filmmakers started trying to deal with major social issues, often in spite of Joe Breen and the Production Code. The new American realism was given a major boost by the success of *The Best Years of Our Lives* in 1946. Producer Sam Goldwyn and director William Wyler set out to tell the true story of America's World War II veterans, but Breen tried to block them on some of the most important details. Goldwyn and Wyler wanted to suggest in the film that men returning home for the first time in years might actually want to make love to their wives. When Breen tried to cut any indication of this, suggesting that a dissolve at the end of a scene between bank president Fredric March and his wife (Myrna Loy) would offend viewers, Goldwyn's story editor, Pat Duggan, wrote back that "the dissolve in this scene will not 'prove extremely offensive.' We are not showing the consummation scene. The dramatic implications, as written, are very important to us and we ask you to let the scene remain as it is."

Another plot dealt with a lieutenant (Dana Andrews) who returns to discover that the woman he'd married in haste is a stranger to him. Initially, Breen objected to the lieutenant's admission that he had committed "sex sins while he was overseas," so the writers reduced that to a single, inexplicit exchange between Andrews and wife Virginia Mayo. As the writers moved the two towards divorce, Breen tried to stop them, or at least excise any "condonation of this tragedy." At one point, March and Loy's daughter (Teresa Wright), who has fallen for Andrews, vows to break up his marriage. At Breen's insistance, her parents vigorously condemned her attitude. But he couldn't get Goldwyn to change the final scene, in which Wright and Andrews seem to be headed for a future together.

The Best Years of Our Lives was one of the most acclaimed films of the forties. It also became the biggest moneymaker of the decade. Far from offending people with its frank treatment of marital relations, the film was hailed on the floor of Congress as "a credit to the United States" and "required seeing for every American."[33]

The following year, RKO moved into social realism with *Crossfire*, a film depicting an anti-Semitic murder. The film was based on *The Brick Foxhole*, a novel by future director Richard Brooks in which the victim was a homosexual. Executives at RKO knew this would have to be changed, but they submitted the book to Breen to get his overall opinion of the story's objectionable elements. As was to be expected, he informed them in July 1945 that "the story is thoroughly and completely unacceptable, on a dozen or more counts." Even after the studio changed the victim to a Jewish businessman named Samuels and gave Robert Ryan, as the killer, several vehemently anti-Semitic speeches, Breen ordered that "there will be no suggestion of a 'pansy' character about Samuels or his relationship with the soldiers." Breen also insisted that police detective Robert Young's speeches about bigotry be broadened to include "all forms of racial and religious intolerance" so that the story would not be "open to the charge of being a special pleading against anti-Semitism."

Breen had no such problem with the year's other major treatment of anti-Semitism, *Gentlemen's Agreement*. Instead, he objected to the characterization of the leading lady (Dorothy McGuire) as a divorcée, since her sympathetic presentation "carries the flavor of acceptance and a tacit justification of divorce."[34]

Sexual realism hit the screen in 1950 when director-writer Ida Lupino filmed *Outrage*. Lupino had entered film production in 1949 with the intention of creating realistic treatments of women's issues. For her maiden effort, she produced and cowrote *Not Wanted*, which dealt with the problems facing an unwed mother. She made her directorial debut in 1950 with *Never Fear*, a story about the effects of polio on a young woman's marriage.

For her third production, Lupino decided to create the first Hollywood film focusing on rape, *Outrage*. Rape had been a plot point before but had hardly been dealt with realistically. In *Gone With the Wind*, Scarlett woke up smiling after Rhett forced himself on her. Rio in *The Outlaw* fell in love with Billy the Kid after he raped her. Breen had objected to the frantic coupling of Harold Roark (Gary Cooper) and Dominique Francon (Patricia Neal) in *The Fountainhead* (1949), so the writers changed their one-night stand to a rape. Like her cinematic sisters, Dominique, too, fell in love with her rapist. Only in *Johnny Belinda*, in which Stephen McNally violates deaf-mute Jane Wyman and then tries to steal their illegitimate child, was the crime presented as a crime rather than a manly variation of foreplay. *Outrage* would treat the matter more extensively, with most of the picture devoted to young innocent Mala Powers's recovery from her rape by a psychopathic stranger.

The PCA objected to the identity of the rapist. According to staff members Geoffrey Shurlock and Eugene Dougherty, the rapist's being a stranger added an unacceptable element of sexual perversion to the story. After much arguing, Lupino's husband, producer Collier Young, agreed to change the script. He also agreed that the word "rape" would never be used. Throughout the film, the act is referred to as a "criminal assault" or a "criminal attack," two euphemisms for rape commonly used by the press.

Ironically, creating a connection between Powers and her assailant, though running against statistics about rape, added another pioneering element to the film. As rewritten, the rapist works at a lunch counter outside the woman's office building. In the film's first scene, he comes on to her rather crudely, thus making *Outrage* one of the first films to present a realistic depiction of sexual harassment and link it to sexual violence.

Outrage was not a major success. Lupino was praised for her sensitive treatment of the subject, but most reviewers considered the film too downbeat to attract audiences. Although the picture seems primitive today, the sequence involving Powers's pursuit and assault is still powerful. Another Code restriction prevented the depiction of the woman's struggles to fight off her rapist. As a result, Lupino shot the scene as an extended chase through a nightmarish cityscape. When Powers is finally cornered, the camera pulls upwards so that the actual attack is blocked by the corner of a building, creating a chilling sense of the heroine's isolation.

This dreamlike assault scene provides an unconscious comment on the Hollywood in which Lupino made *Outrage*. As Powers tries to elude her pursuer, she makes one mistake after another, running into deserted and confined areas where she has little chance of escape. To contemporary, street-wise audiences her behavior seems unrealistic. Yet it fits the world of the film. Although the film in no way blames the victim, and treats her own condemnation of herself as a mistake, it is clear that the almost idyllic small town in which she has grown up has done little to prepare her for the realities of life—much as the dream world of moral order fostered by the Production Code had little relation to the real world audiences entered when they left the theater.

With changing times, the fight to maintain Hollywood's veneer of purity was destined for defeat. As the fifties began, two court cases would force the screen further down the road to freedom, landing a pair of crippling blows to the Code and its defenders.

"Here We Go,
Down and Dirty!"

Chapter Seven

Frank Sinatra captured the spirit of the fifties when he kicked off his illegal poker game in *The Man with the Golden Arm* with the above line. Through the decade, changes in the industry, the legal system and the PCA itself ushered in a new era of permissiveness as previously "illegal" topics became acceptable screen fare. The continuing success of foreign films on American screens and increasing competition from television created a new market for "adults only" fare, a market Hollywood was desperate to tap.

Society itself was loosening up. Although Eisenhower conformity ruled on the surface, there were indications of a darker side to American life. Drugs and juvenile delinquency were becoming major problems, while racial tensions grew around the nation. *The Kinsey Report*, although vehemently contested in some arenas, suggested that Americans weren't practicing the rigid morality they had been preaching. Writers from Tennessee Williams to James Jones to Grace Metalious tapped this sexual current, often to great acclaim and impressive profits, while the Beat Generation captured the growing malaise among younger people.

Two legal decisions—one in 1948, another in 1952—changed the nature of film censorship in America. The first seemed only tangentially related to the subject. In 1948, the Justice Department's first antitrust suit against the Hollywood majors reached the Supreme Court, which sided with the government in *U. S. v. Paramount*, ordering the studio to divest itself of its theatrical holdings.

Censored Hollywood

Vivien Leigh's on-screen suffering as Blanche Dubois in A Streetcar Named Desire *(1951) was matched by the off-screen trials director Elia Kazan faced in trying to get Tennessee Williams's unique vision past the Production Code Administration and the Legion of Decency.*

Over the next eleven years, the other major studios would be dismantled, climaxing with the divorcement of MGM and Loew's Theatres in 1959. As a result, the studios—and the Production Code Administration—lost control of the major first-run houses and chains. Not only did this cripple Hollywood economically by robbing the studios of their guaranteed market, but it made Code enforcement increasingly difficult. Independent producers who chose to bypass the Code now had access to the country's best theaters.

The Supreme Court's *Paramount* decision hinted at even greater changes to come. Writing for the majority, Justice William O. Douglas, one of the Court's most ardent civil libertarians, tried to make it clear that the antitrust decision was not intended to limit the artistic rights of filmmakers: "We have no doubt that moving pictures, like newspapers and radio, are included in the press whose freedom is guaranteed by the First Amendment."[1]

It would take the Court four years to make such First Amendment protections official. Meanwhile, they refused to hear cases involving Atlanta's ban on *Lost Boundaries* and the Memphis ban on *Curley*, two films dealing with racial issues. Court historians have suggested that there was not enough of a consensus on the bench to make either of these a precedent-setting case. When Joseph Burstyn brought Roberto Rossellini's forty-one-minute film *The Miracle* to New York, however, the Court had the case it needed to take a new position on film censorship.

It's easy to understand how *The Miracle* could raise objections. It deals with the plight of a simpleminded peasant (Anna Magnani) who fancies that a passing stranger (Frederico Fellini) is St. Joseph. When the man plies her with wine and seduces her, leaving her pregnant, she decides her unborn child is the Son of God. Although the older women in her village humor her, the young people mock her, eventually driving her into the wilderness. When her time comes, she gives birth in a deserted church rather than return to the village. She seems transformed as she takes the new baby in her arms, saying, "My son! My love! My flesh!" Were it not for Rossellini's serious tone and Magnani's powerful performance, the story elements could easily have made it a satire of Christ's birth—which is exactly what religious conservatives saw in the film.

Criticism ranged from the accusation that it was intended as a mockery of Christian doctrine to charges of more calculated subversion. An editorial in Martin Quigley's *Motion Picture Herald* blasted the film as Communist propaganda: "It would be difficult to conceive of a subject matter or story treatment more offensive to traditional religious beliefs. It is impossible to know what was Rossellini's motive in making it. However, it is to be noted, it was produced several years ago in the days when he was flirting with the extreme Left and Anna Magnani and others of his associates were active Leftists."[2]

On the opposite side were those who defended the film as a sincere, thoughtful statement of religious faith. The motion picture critic for *Il Popolo*, the official newspaper of Italy's pro-Catholic Christian Democratic Party, called it "a beautiful thing, humanly felt, alive, true and without religious profanation."[3] For his part, Rossellini claimed he had been trying to denounce the seemingly faithful and not the faith they professed: "In *The Miracle*, men are still without pity because they still have not gone back to God. But God is already present in the faith, however confused, of the poor, persecuted woman. . . . *The Miracle* occurs when, with the birth of the child, the poor demented woman regains sanity in her maternal love."[4]

The Miracle had already been the subject of controversy in Italy, where it was condemned by more conservative church factions, including the Vatican and the Italian Legion of Decency, but defended by more progressive churchmen. No legal action was taken against the film, but it grossed only $30,000, roughly half its cost. The picture got through U.S. Customs with no problem and actually passed the New York Board of Censors twice, first on its own, then when Burstyn coupled it with Jean Renoir's *A Day in the Country* and Marcel Pagnol's *Jofroi* in the omnibus film *Ways of Love*. When it opened at New York's Paris Theatre on December 12, 1950, however, accounts of its plot in newspaper reviews raised the ire of more than a few church members. On Christmas Eve, the Legion of Decency condemned *Ways of Love*, though the judgment appears to have been based solely on their reaction to *The Miracle*.

The first legal action against *Ways of Love* had taken place the day before, when the city's license commissioner, Edward T. McCaffrey, a former state commander of the Catholic War Veterans, tried to ban the picture. This tactic had worked in the past to keep films passed by the state board out of New York City, but this time it failed. Burstyn contested the judgment in court and won on January 5, 1951. Two days later, Cardinal Spellman issued a statement blasting the film as both "a subversion to the very inspired word of God" and "a vicious insult to Italian womanhood." He even suggested the film's title be changed to "'Woman Further Defamed' by Roberto Rossellini,"[5] referring to the director's notorious liaison with actress Ingrid Bergman.

Starting on the day Spellman released his statement, the Paris Theatre in New York was surrounded by pickets, few of whom had seen *The Miracle*. In addition to carrying signs decrying the film, they shouted such slogans as "Don't look at that filth!" and "This is a Communist picture!" at ticket buyers. Some even cried "Buy American!" In addition, two performances were disrupted by bomb threats. After the second such threat, the fire lieutenant cited the theater's manager for allowing patrons to stand in the rear of the sold-out house. The protests did not have their desired effect. As the film's notoriety grew, so did attendance, and *Ways of Love* seemed poised to set a new box-office record for foreign films. Then the pressure reached the New York Board of Regents, which supervised the state censorship board. Usually, the regents reviewed censorship decisions only when a producer protested cuts or a threatened ban on his film. In this case, however, they decided to review the censors' passage of *The Miracle*.

The pressure went beyond the film and its theater. When New York Film Critics chose *Ways of Love* as the Best Foreign Film of 1950, Martin Quigley phoned the manager of Radio City Music Hall, where the awards were to be presented, to warn him about a possible boycott. The critics moved their ceremonies to a private party, where Burstyn apologized to the other winners for all the trouble he had caused them. He would later apologize to the directors of the two other films included in *Ways of Love*, because of the furor raised by Rossellini's portion of the bill.

On February 15, 1951, the regents revoked the film's license on the grounds that it was sacrilegious and violated the religious freedom of Christians. The management of the Paris Theatre replaced *The Miracle* with a cartoon, and Burstyn launched a thirty-month legal battle. The New York State Supreme Court upheld the ban, referring to the *Mutual Film* precedent and defending the regents' use of sacrilege as a standard.

Throughout the controversy, the MPAA remained silent. According to one member of the group's board, the reason for its silence was fear of reprisals from the Catholic Church. The motivation may have been more innocent, however. Although the MPAA frequently filed friend-of-the-court briefs in censorship cases, it was not compelled to do so, particularly when the film being censored had not been submitted for the Seal of Approval. In addition, *The Miracle* probably would not have qualified for a Seal anyway, because of the Production Code ban on films offending religious groups.

In February 1952, the U.S. Supreme Court agreed to hear Burstyn's appeal. Briefs were filed early in April, with the Court hearing oral arguments April 24 and handing down its judgment a month later, a surprisingly speedy process. "The *Miracle* Happens," *New York Times* critic Bosley Crowther headlined in reporting the decision. "The motion picture medium was acknowledged of legal age last week when the United States Supreme Court handed down its decision in the *Miracle* case."[6] Writing for a unanimous court, Justice Tom Clark overturned the *Mutual Film* precedent point by point. On the earlier court's dismissal of film as mere entertainment, he said:

> It cannot be doubted that motion pictures are a significant medium for
> the communication of ideas. They may affect public attitudes and behavior
> in a variety of ways, ranging from direct espousal of a political or social doc-

trine to the subtle shaping of thought which characterizes all artistic expression. The importance of motion pictures as an organ of public opinion is not lessened by the fact that they are designed to entertain as well as to inform.[7]

Nor should film be subject to censorship because it is an industry conducted for profit, as such a category would also include the press. Finally, the medium's supposed capacity for evil, if it existed at all, was not sufficient justification for "substantially unbridled censorship such as we have here.[8]

As amazing as this new precedent was, the Court actually handed down a narrow ruling in the *Miracle* case, stating only that the New York statute enjoining sacrilege was too broad to satisfy the Fourteenth Amendment. Nor was it "the business of government in our nation to suppress real or imagined attacks upon a particular religious doctrine."[9] Yet the Court upheld the basic idea of film censorship, allowing that there might be specific rules for governing freedom of the screen that would not be appropriate to other media.

The immediate upshot of the *Miracle* decision was a series of cases in which the Supreme Court overturned local censors and further limited the grounds on which a film could be banned. New York's ban of *La Ronde* was overturned in 1954 because the terms "immoral" or "tending to corrupt morals" were too broad. The same happened with the Gilling, Texas ban of *Pinky* as "prejudicial to the best interests of the people of said City" and Ohio's ban of the 1959 version of *Native Son* as "'harmful' or 'conducive [to] immorality [or] crime.'"[10]

In all of those cases, however, the Court handed down its verdicts without comment, simply referring to *Burstyn* v. *Wilson* as a precedent, possibly because there was not a sufficient consensus on the reasons underlying these reversals. As a result, the lower courts were confused as to the extent to which the *Miracle* precedent applied. Some allowed censors' bans to stand, letting the Supreme Court make the final determination. Others decided that the new precedent outlawed all prior restraint. The latter assumption led to the voiding of state censorship laws in Ohio (1954), Massachusetts (1955), and Pennsylvania (1956).

With the Production Code still in place, it would take several years for the *Miracle* decision to have an effect on Hollywood. Through the fifties, however, as film attendance continued to decline in the face of competition from television, the studios would turn more and more to adult material as a means of bringing audiences back into theaters.

A Hollywood Miracle: Movies for Adults

Even before the *Miracle* decision, Hollywood's producers had been straining under the Production Code, and it took all of Breen's energies to gain even token changes. He won numerous concessions on sexual materials in John Huston's *The Asphalt Jungle* (1950)—Doll (Jean Hagen) was not characterized as a prostitute; Doc's (Sam Jaffe) fascination with young girls was presented as nostalgia rather than perversion—but the film still presented the most detailed depiction yet of a crime's commission. Not all of the story's sexual implications were wiped out, either. Though a crooked judge (Louis Calhern) who fences stolen property introduces a scantily dressed companion (Marilyn Monroe) as his "niece," few in the audience missed the fact that she was his mistress.

When George Stevens decided to film Theodore Dreiser's *An American Tragedy* as *A Place in the Sun* in 1951, Breen lost point after point in his efforts to clean up the story. He wanted the scene in which George (Montgomery Clift) first spends the night with a factory worker named Alice (Shelley Winters) to be less explicit, but Paramount maintained all the objectionable details. George sneaks into her room, where the two dance to music from a radio by the window. As the camera stays with the radio, George and Alice move into the darkness, where her voice is heard whispering his name. The lighting changes to indicate morning, and George leaves.

The studio cut a few lines from the scene in which Alice reveals that she is pregnant, but kept one exchange that Breen had thought too pointed:

> ALICE: Remember the first night you came here? Remember you said if there was any trouble, you'd stand by me?
> GEORGE: Yeah?
> ALICE: Well, it's happened—oh, I'm so afraid.

Breen also objected to a scene in which Alice visits a doctor to try to get an abortion, even though the Code contained no specific injunction against the subject. The studio cut the more pointed lines, but they refused to insert a speech Breen wanted in which the doctor would speak of his obligation to see her through the pregnancy, and the impression that she wanted an illegal operation remained nonetheless.

Abortion was also an issue in *Detective Story* (1951). In Sidney Kingsley's play, morally rigid police detective Jim McLeod arrests an abortionist, then learns that Mrs. McLeod had used the man's services years earlier. This revelation devastates him to the point that he sacrifices his life to stop a psychopathic gunman. He begs his wife's forgiveness with his dying breath.

Breen informed Paramount early on that the story had two major Code problems that prevented him from passing it. In addition to the abortion references, McLeod's death violated a restriction against cop killing that had been added to the Code to curtail the flow of gangster films in 1938. Breen suggested making the abortionist the operator of a baby farm where unwed mothers gave up their newborns for illegal adoptions. Mary McLeod would have given birth to an illegitimate child under his treatment. Although Wyler agreed to consider the issue, he also tried to convince the studio to file an appeal.

Aware of the situation, Breen wrote to Johnston defending his ban on abortions. The subject was consistently cut out by state censors, he argued, and had been easily removed from such Hollywood productions as *Rebecca* and *Kitty Foyle*. More recently, *Beyond the Forest* and *The Doctor and the Girl* had undergone major cuts to delete any suggestion of abortion, the former under threat of a Condemned rating from the Legion of Decency. Even though Wyler had argued that abortion was soundly condemned in *Detective Story*, "the evil of the abortion type of murder is so heinous in its very nature, that we best serve our audiences, especially the young and the adolescent, by making certain not to call it to their attention." Finally, Breen warned that however restrained Wyler's approach to the topic might be, it would trigger complaints from audience members and abuses from other filmmakers.

Wyler ultimately agreed to a compromise. He would cut the references to abortion and insert a line referring to the doctor's baby farm as his chief illegal activity. He also cut Mary's statement that the doctor's quackery had left her incapable of bearing children. In a more conciliatory mood, Breen facilitated the picture's approval, recommending—and winning—Code revisions allowing cop killing when necessary to the plot and suicide when properly condemned within the context of the film. Even with the changes, however, most patrons assumed that the doctor's illegal activities included abortion.

Breen's opposition to abortion as a subject was based on the assumption that films were still a form of family entertainment. He specifically questioned the suitability of such subject matter for younger audiences. This, in fact, had been one of the basic assumptions underlying the Production Code—that even the most mature films must be presented in a way that would not corrupt children. This assumption would be challenged with two major cases involving films clearly targeted for adult audiences: *A Streetcar Named Desire* (1951) and *From Here to Eternity* (1953).

Both Tennessee Williams's play and James Jones's novel had challenged the limits of what was permissible in their respective media. *Streetcar*—with its references to homosexuality, nymphomania, and rape—had created a sensation on Broadway. When agent Charles K. Feldman acquired the screen rights in 1950, the controversy threatened to reach the screen, but only if Breen would let it. *Streetcar* marked a turning point for the PCA. According to Geoffrey Shurlock: "For the first time we were confronted with a picture that was obviously not family entertainment. . . . Now we know that a good deal of what we decide in censoring movies is not morality but taste. It began with *Streetcar*."[11]

Breen had three objections to the script, which were outlined in an April 28, 1950 meeting. Blanche's sexual behavior was too close to nymphomania. According to an unsigned memo, "Her peculiar and neurotic attitude towards sex and particularly to a sex attraction for young boys has about it an erotic flavor that seems to verge on perversion of a sort." He also objected to the characterization of Blanche's deceased husband, Allan Grey, as a homosexual and to Stanley's rape of Blanche, which Breen claimed was "justified" and unpunished.

Blanche's nymphomania was the easiest problem to get around. The filmmakers changed a few words here and there. Her sexual panic, which drove her to hunt for protection "in the most—unlikely places—even, at last, in a seventeen-year-old-boy" became a panic that drove her "to a seventeen-year-old boy." They also agreed to make it clear that Blanche is looking for love rather than sex, though Williams and director Elia Kazan ignored Breen's suggestion that she call each of the men she approaches "Allan," as though she were trying to right the wrongs done to her late husband.

Blanche's husband caused more trouble. In the play, she states that she caught Allan with an older man. After pretending nothing had happened, she finally said to him, "I saw! I know! You disgust me,"[12] a statement that drove the boy to suicide. Breen insisted that the filmmakers affirmatively establish that Allan was *not* homosexual, but nobody could decide exactly how they should do that. Warner Bros. story editor Finlay McDermid suggested that if Allan was homosexual, he might have married a woman in search of a mother substitute. Since the sixteen-year-old Blanche would hardly have been emotionally equipped for such a role, maybe Allan would have turned to an older woman for comfort. In that way, the writers could keep Allan gay without ever saying he was.

After numerous revisions that Breen rejected, Williams finally cut all overt references to Allan's homosexuality. In the film, he is simply weak and ineffectual. As Blanche recalls their relationship: "I didn't understand why this boy that wrote poetry didn't seem to be able to do anything else. Lost every job. He came to me for help. I didn't know that. I didn't know anything except that I loved him unendurably. And that I had failed him in some mysterious way. We were very young. Oh! And his poems—they all came back—little white cards saying 'sorry.' He became silent with me. At night I pretended to sleep and I heard him crying. Crying—the way a lost child cries." There was no sudden discovery of Allan in the arms of another. Instead, Blanche triggered his suicide by saying, "You're weak. I've lost respect for you. I can't pretend that I haven't." Admittedly, the change weakened the story; but as with cuts Breen had made in other films, most audiences understood perfectly well what Blanche was talking about.

The rape was the thorniest issue of all, an issue revealing not just Breen's curiously selective judgment but the industry's inability to understand *Streetcar* at all. How could Breen say this, or any rape, was justified? The answer lies in Hollywood's interpretation of *Streetcar*. Where Tennessee Williams had written a great, messy, poetic, and very moral work of art, communicating more through images and indirection than through any overt statement, Hollywood was more used to simple melodrama, with moral issues painted in black and white. As a result, many studio heads failed to understand the contradictory natures of Williams's characters, the fact that Blanche could maintain sympathy while doing foolish, immoral, self-destructive things. When Louis B. Mayer saw the play out of town before its Broadway premiere (his daughter Irene Mayer Selznick was the producer), he responded to it as the tale of an "awful woman" who tried to break up a "fine young couple's happy home."[13] McDermid thought the film would depict "not only the story of the tragedy of Blanche but of the devastating effect upon a married couple of an attempt to care for a psychotic they cannot possibly understand and who can only succeed in ruining their relationship." With Blanche cast as the villainess, it's easier to understand how some could view Stanley's rape of her as an attempt to protect his home.

There were numerous suggestions of how to cut the rape. Breen suggested that Stanley should merely slap Blanche and then leave. The rape would be a figment of her imagination, and Stanley would disprove her charges. Feldman thought it would be more "honest" if Stanley were about to rape Blanche, then realized she was insane and stopped. But Kazan was adamant; the rape was essential as the final intrusion of reality on Blanche's fantasy world. He would withdraw from the production if it was cut.

Throughout filming, Breen sent letters complaining that the rape had not been removed from any of the revised scripts. Kazan assured him that he had worked out a solution but wanted to try filming it first, a cagey maneuver to get the rape on film and make it more difficult for Breen to cut. Jack Vizzard warned them that whatever they shot must affirmatively establish that there had been no rape; but again, Kazan did the scene his own way.

All he really cut from the original play was the stage direction in which Stanley carries Blanche into the bedroom. For the film, the scene would be handled "by suggestion and delicacy," as indicated in script pages dated October 7, 1950. As in the play, Blanche tries to defend herself with a broken beer bottle:

> STANLEY: Oh! You want some rough house! All right, let's have some rough house!
> *They have advanced so that we are now able to see the action in a large mirror only.*
>
> Tiger—Tiger!
> *He is feigning—Suddenly he leaps in and seizes her arm—then he has her—*
>
> Drop that bottle-top. Drop it!
> *He has managed to wrest the bottle top from her—He throws it . . . It smashes into the mirror and the glass shatters. . . .*
>
> We've had this date with each other from the beginning!
> *And on the broken glass we dissolve.*

In another script addition, dated November 2, Williams gave Stella a new final line: "We're not going back in there. Not this time. We're never going back. Never, never back, never back again." Although few audience members believed her, the line gave the illusion that Stanley would have to pay for raping Blanche, an act that could seem justifiable only in the eyes of a Hollywood producer—or a censor.

After numerous battles and compromises, *A Streetcar Named Desire* finished filming and won the Production Code Seal. Athough Williams had complained of the "great concessions we made which we felt were dangerous, to attitudes which we thought were narrow," Breen had passed more objectionable material than ever before. Not only was the rape present, but little had been done to affirmatively establish that Blanche was anything but sexually perverse or that her husband was anything but a homosexual. In addition, Kazan maintained an overall feeling of sensuality in almost every frame of the film.

During previews, Kazan made several cuts to tighten the film and make certain scenes more powerful (Preview audiences had laughed at reaction shots of the newsboy Blanche tries to seduce.). Feldman wanted more cuts, but Jack Warner promised that the version Kazan had edited was the version that would be released. Accepting his assurance on the matter, Kazan went off to work on his next project, *Viva Zapata.*

Then Kazan got word that the film's premiere had been canceled because of trouble with the Legion of Decency. As soon as he returned from location shooting in Mexico, he tried to find out what was happening, but couldn't get a straight answer from anyone. Hearing that the film's editor, David Weisbart, had flown to New York, Kazan tracked him down. All Weisbart said was that he was not in New York on any business connected with *Streetcar*, but that "it might develop into that."

Now seriously concerned over the fate of what he considered his best film, Kazan left the final cutting of *Viva Zapata* in the hands of Twentieth Century-Fox studio head Darryl F. Zanuck and flew to New York. There he learned that *Streetcar* had been condemned by the Legion of Decency, whose representatives felt "the entire tone of the picture is 'desire,'" with "no mitigating circumstances whatsoever." In their opinion, the picture was totally unredeemable.

The PCA sent Jack Vizzard to deal with the matter, while Warners hired Martin Quigley to negotiate cuts. Neither was the best possible choice from Kazan's perspective. Vizzard, who originally had trained for the priesthood, had earlier expressed his judgment of the picture as "sordid and morbid."[14] Quigley, the coauthor of the Production Code, had expressed a similar opinion. After screening the film, he had said to Vizzard, "I tell you, this fellow Kazan is the type who will one day blow his brains out."[15]

Quigley suggested twelve cuts, amounting to between three and four minutes of screen time. Blanche's line to the newsboy "I would like to kiss you softly and sweetly on the mouth" lost its last three words. Quigley cut Stanley's line "You know, you might not be bad to interfere with" immediately prior to the rape, curiously deleting the implication that Stanley had not regarded Blanche sexually until that moment. The biggest change occurred in the scene depicting Stella's return to Stanley after he's struck her during an argument. In place of the sensual close-ups in which Stella fought between attraction and revulsion, the studio substituted a long shot of the action. In addition, Alex North's scoring, which built on the scene's sexual tension, was replaced with a less provocative cue.

Kazan made one last effort to save his version of *A Streetcar Named Desire*. He asked Warners to try releasing the film in both his and the Legion's versions, with each clearly marked so audience members could choose for themselves. At the very least, he suggested they should allow the original cut to be screened at the Venice Film Festival. Neither was possible. The Legion mandated that only their approved version could be released, on threat of reinstating the Condemned rating. Kazan's version would remain unavailable until Warners restored the film in 1993.

The Legion—and Hollywood—did not emerge unscathed from the *Streetcar* controversy. Against the advice of Feldman, Kazan wrote an article on his experiences for the *New York Times*, giving the press another club with which to attack censorship. Although the film still shocked many patrons, it did surprisingly well at the box office, opening the doors further for the PCA's acceptance of more adult Hollywood films.

Among the pictures that might not have been passed without *Streetcar*'s influence was an adaptation of one of the literary world's most shocking first novels, *From Here to Eternity*. James Jones's 861-page novel had raised a considerable controversy when it first appeared in 1951. Its tale of an enlisted man, Robert E. Lee Prewitt, subjected to mistreatment and brutality because he refuses to box on the company team was considered an affront to the U.S. Army. The novel detailed two sexual affairs and the operation of a brothel in Hawaii just before the outbreak of World War II. In addition, Jones captured the language of military men in all its colorful detail.

The novel's length and wealth of objectionable materials led many to wonder if it ever could be adapted to the screen, but Columbia Pictures head Harry Cohn picked up the rights for $82,000 without ever reading it. It took more than a year to develop a suitable screenplay. Jones attempted a treatment, but Cohn thought it strayed too far from the original. After rejecting other adaptations because they softened the novel too much, he assigned the screenplay to Daniel Taradash, who finally came up with a method for licking this tough property. Taradash realized that much of the story's brutality would be better communicated through suggestion, so instead of sending Prewitt to the military stockade run by the sadistic "Fatso" Judson, he sent Prewitt's friend Maggio. This left Prewitt alive for a more heroic ending: After killing Judson to avenge Maggio's death, he tries to return to duty after the Pearl Harbor attack, only to be shot by guards.

Before facing Joe Breen with their screenplay, Taradash and producer Buddy Adler had an equally imposing group of censors to please—the U.S. Army. They would need military permission to do location shooting at Schofield Barracks, and that meant the Army had to accept their script. Some staffers wanted the title changed, fearing that *From Here to Eternity* was already firmly associated with antimilitary sentiments, but Adler refused to budge on that matter. He and Taradash agreed to two major changes, however. The captain who orders Prewitt's mistreatment had been promoted in Jones's book; in the film, he's cashiered, and his superiors soundly condemn his actions. In addition, Judson and Maggio were given a longstanding animosity, so that Judson's torture of the soldier wouldn't seem like standard procedure.

With Army approval secured, Adler submitted his script to Breen, who proved surprisingly conciliatory. Taradash already had cleaned up the film's language, so Breen was left with only three major objections. The New Congress Club was changed from a brothel to a "social club," or, as Taradash described it in the screenplay, "a sort of primitive USO, a place of well-worn merriment. It is not a house of prostitution." The women working there were characterized as B-girls, selling drinks and snacks rather than themselves. Yet when one of the girls describes the "privileges" accorded members—"dancing, snack bar, soft drink bar and gentlemanly relaxation with the opposite gender as long as they are gentlemen, and no liquor is permitted. Get it?"— Montgomery Clift's reading of Prewitt's reply, "I get it,"[16] makes it clear that there may be a lot more going on.

Line reading was important in getting around another of Breen's objections. He felt that some of Prewitt's dialogue with the girl he meets at the New Congress Club, Alma (Donna Reed), gave too pointed an indication that they were sexually involved and even made light of the relationship. Cohn and Adler insisted that lines like "This is just like bein' married, ain't it?" and "We can even get married" would be played without any suggestiveness.

Breen's third major sticking point was the adulterous relationship between Army sergeant Burt Lancaster and his captain's wife, Deborah Kerr. Not only were the two unpunished, but their love scenes almost glorified illicit sex. Breen tried to make the two wear robes throughout their famous surfside love scene, but lost on that one. His major victory was getting Taradash to push back the start of their sexual relationship. Instead of their kissing at the end of their first scene, the romance was held until the beach scene, so that they seemed to have become involved more out of affection for each other than out of lust.

Breen still insisted, however, that the two be punished for their affair. By building up the husband's less pleasant characteristics, including his unfaithfulness, Taradash got by with one line of condemnation spoken by Kerr when she and Lancaster end their relationship, the first time on-screen adulterers had ever gotten off so lightly.

On the whole, the film got off pretty lightly, too. It was rated B by the Legion of Decency because it "reflects the acceptability of divorce; tends to condone immoral actions; suggestive situations," but praised loudly by critics for bringing Jones's difficult novel to the screen. Even Martin Quigley came out in favor of the adaptation, praising Cohn and his studio for "preserving the dramatic impact of this powerful novel, meanwhile dispensing with much shocking incident and language which in a motion picture would only have aroused public resentment and limited its audience."[17]

From Here to Eternity went on to gross $19 million on its initial release, ranking second at the box office for its year. In many ways, it marked the pinnacle of Breen's later years with the PCA, showing how a story that many had considered offensive could maintain its strength on-screen (in the opinions of some, it actually gained in the translation) despite changes to accommodate the Code. If anything, Breen's approval of the film demonstrates his ability to adapt to the times, albeit within strict limits.

But Joe Breen was growing tired again. A lung operation and recurring back problems added to the exhaustion created by two decades of fighting producers. Two films in this period would mark his last stand as the keeper of Hollywood's morals.

Breen's Last Stand

The Moon Is Blue was little more than a minor sex farce when it opened on Broadway in 1951. It showed how Patty O'Neill, a young woman determined to retain her virginity until she's married, resists the advances of David Slater, an aging roué, and wins the heart of Donald Gresham, a young architect with more liberal attitudes. The original production did well, while the touring company crisscrossed the country with little incident. But there was something about the piece that put it on a collision course with Joe Breen.

Part of the problem was language. Playwright F. Hugh Herbert had peppered the

Locking Up the Truth

In many ways, censorship, no matter how seemingly insignificant its targets, is an inherently political act. The censor uses his or her power to suppress ideas. Even when Joe Breen demanded more coverage for Jane Russell's breasts, he was trying to keep from the screen the idea that sex was fun or that sexual arousal was a desirable state (just as later activists would protest pornography's inherent message that women are sex objects). With Warner Bros.' 1950 *Caged,* the film that set the conventions for the women's-prison picture, the political side of censorship would become more overt, dredging up memories of the days when the Mob could use political influence to keep such films as *The Racket* and *Alibi* out of Chicago.

Producer Jerry Wald wanted *Caged* to be "a true picture of what a woman's prison life is like, and how it affects the woman subjected to it." To that end he sent cowriter Virginia Kellogg to masquerade as a convict in four state pens. She visited each for two weeks, taking two weeks off in between to recover her wits. As a prisoner, she witnessed crime syndicate representatives recruiting within prison walls and matrons who exploited their power by mistreating prisoners and selling liquor and dope. Both of these elements would turn up in the script.

Wald used the story of Kellogg's prison research to generate valuable publicity for *Caged,* but in some areas it backfired. In Ohio, one of the states Kellogg had visited on her prison tour, the

script with references to virginity, seduction, and pregnancy. Since most of the time those words were put into the mouth of the play's virginal heroine, many found the language refreshing. Breen considered it merely vulgar.

But the problem went deeper than that. In making light of its heroine's moral stance, the play was in violation of Code restrictions on the use of seduction or illicit sex as a source of comedy. Further, at one point in the play Gresham tells Patty off, calling her a "professional virgin." Accusing her of advertising her virginity, he tells her that "those who advertise usually have something to sell."[18] Even though Gresham turns out to be as much interested in guarding Patty's virginity as she, his attack, in Breen's eyes, robbed the play of any compensating moral value. As a result, he felt the work implied that "low forms of sex relationship are the accepted or common thing"—another violation of the Code.

The script was first submitted in 1951, with Breen discouraging Paramount and Warners from acquiring the rights. A year later, Otto Preminger, who had directed the stage version, decided to make it the inaugural production of an independent company he had formed with Herbert. According to later reports, Preminger, Herbert, and their leading man, William Holden, wanted to make *The Moon Is Blue* a test case, refusing to

censors feared audiences would think such conditions still existed in the Buckeye State. As a result, they threatened to ban the picture until Warners added a prologue assuring audiences that the story was fictional and "that in most states . . . every effort is made to rehabilitate inmates so that, upon release, they may be restored to society."

Although Kellogg had confined her research to the U.S., one board in Canada was equally concerned about how the film would reflect on their province. To appease Saskatchewan's censors, Warners added an even lengthier prologue, indicating that "every malpractice depicted in this film exists in this country's prison system today" but praising Saskatchewan for its own prison reforms.

No concessions, however, could get the film passed in Worcester, Massachusetts. Officially, the Worcester Board of Motion Pictures and Theatre Review rejected the film because it taught younger viewers how to commit crimes and then buy their way out of prison. Unofficially, one of the censors informed the studio's legal department that the film had been banned because of a scandal at Sherbourne Women's Reformatory in nearby Framingham. The incident had involved the state's lieutenant governor and his brother-in-law, who just happened to be a major figure in Worcester politics. Warners canceled its distribution plans there in return for the censors' more favorable treatment of other releases. ✄

submit it to the PCA. A script got to Breen anyway, and he renewed his objections in a letter dated January 2, 1953. Preminger made only one concession to Breen; he agreed to insert a few lines condemning "Slater's immoral philosophy of life." But he wouldn't budge on anything else.

On April 10, 1953, Breen informed Preminger that the finished film could not be granted the Seal of Approval. He rejected it officially on April 21. Preminger filed an appeal and tried to weight matters in his favor by submitting the film successfully to the New York censor board, but his appeal was denied in May. To make matters worse, the Legion of Decency slapped the film with a Condemned rating, though Jack Vizzard has suggested that they condemned the film merely as a show of support for the PCA.

United Artists decided to distribute *The Moon Is Blue* anyway, quitting the MPAA in protest and thus escaping the $25,000 fine. Initially, the picture seemed headed for trouble when the Fox West Coast chain decided to cancel its bookings. But the Supreme Court's divestiture decisions worked out in UA's favor. Freed from studio control, two other chains, United Paramount and Stanley Warner, picked the film up.

The MPAA ban and the Legion's condemnation actually helped the picture at the box office, where it quickly moved into the profit column. Even local bans on the film turned out for the best. When Lloyd Binford kept *The Moon Is Blue* out of Memphis, it played to SRO business thirty miles away in Holly Springs, Mississippi.

A good deal of the controversy about *The Moon Is Blue* rebounded onto the censors themselves. When Birmingham, Alabama censors tried to cut a scene and restrict attendance to those over twenty-one, the city's clubwomen protested that the film provided "a good moral lesson to teenagers."[19] In Hollywood, Preminger and others started calling for a new system that would allow some films to be rated adults only. Even conservative trade columnist W. R. Wilkerson picked up the cry: "Anyone seeing *Moon Is Blue* can easily understand the Breen and Legion slaps. Still, the zip in the picture is carried on with such comedy there will be little objection on the part of adult audiences. And it's a good picture. However, if we had a theatre and booked the picture, we would restrict its showing to 'adults only,' relieving our conscience—and jumping our ticket sales."[20]

The Moon Is Blue's success demonstrated the need for Hollywood to generate more adult-oriented product in order to compete with television and helped inspire a more liberal approach to the Code. By 1961, the film even had won the Seal of Approval, opening the door for a reissue and television sales. For Breen, the film would become an embarrassment. Most reports on the picture claimed that he had banned it solely on the grounds of language, which trivialized his objections. When asked about *The Moon Is*

Blue later, he would simply shrug and say, "Well, we're entitled to one mistake every few years, aren't we?"[21]

Breen may have felt more justified in his objections to *The French Line*, an RKO musical marking the return to the censorship wars of producer Howard Hughes and star Jane Russell. But many saw the film as another indication that the Production Code had outlived its usefulness.

Hughes made *The French Line* to capitalize on Russell's success in *Gentlemen Prefer Blondes*. He engaged Mary Loos, niece of *Blondes* writer Anita Loos, to pen the screenplay, which, like the other film's, revolved around an ocean journey to Paris. This time, Russell was a Texas oil heiress who masquerades as a fashion model to see if she can find a man who won't be threatened by her wealth. Just to do *Blondes* one better, Hughes decided to shoot the film in 3-D, a fad that already was running its course.

If Breen's March 1953 letter on the screenplay serves as any indication, it would appear that the writers forgot about the Production Code altogether. The leading man, Pierre (Gilbert Roland), characterizes himself as a "professor of love" about to embark on a world tour to see how many women he can seduce. The heroine's best friend is Firelle, a gay fashion designer. And the script was filled with vulgar references to Russell's breasts, despite the fact that her performance in *Gentlemen Prefer Blondes* had more than proven her abilities as comedienne and musical star.

Breen won out on the first two points. Pierre's role as an international seducer was softened, while Firelle became Madame Firelli. He objected to the breast jokes throughout filming, but most of them stayed, overshadowed by another pressing problem that developed during production.

As he had on *The Outlaw*, Hughes seemed determined to exploit Russell's breasts and cleavage as fully as possible. Early on, Breen cautioned that a number during which Russell shed her clothes and took a bubble bath should not be treated as a striptease. Although the star was carefully masked by furniture and soap bubbles, the tease remained. At one point, a mirrored closet door behind Russell seems about to expose her bare buttocks as she undresses. The maid opens the door at a key moment, thus cutting off the audience's view.

In July, Hughes's RKO Studios submitted the lyrics to a number that would eventually cause even more problems. "Looking for Trouble" and a patter insert were passed on paper without problems, but things changed in production. As originally staged, Russell was to have become one of the first U.S. actresses to wear a bikini on screen. No longer the naive beginner who had allowed herself to be photographed in compromising poses for *The Outlaw*, however, Russell refused to wear the costume, dubbing it "a jeweled G-string."[22] When Hughes persisted in ordering her to wear it, she walked off the set for a week.

Finally, costumer Michael Woulfe came up with an acceptable compromise—a one-piece black satin swimsuit with strategic leaf-shaped cutouts surrounding a jewel placed over Russell's navel. But though the costume was less revealing than many others worn on-screen at the time, it was photographed from a variety of intrusive angles. In addition, the number's staging underlined the suggestiveness of lines like "I'll melt all the snow in Alaska/Till it steams like the tropical Amazon/I'm gonna pop all the corn in Nebraska. . . ."

When Breen and his staff screened the film, Jack Vizzard noted thirteen costumes or scenes that were too suggestive to pass the Code, including Russell's "Looking for Trouble" number. They even tried to warn Hughes that the number could get the film closed on obscenity charges, but to no avail.

In all, the PCA looked at the film five times, futilely trying to reach a compromise. Without obtaining a Production Code Seal, Hughes went ahead preparing for a December 29, 1953 premiere in St. Louis. Ads that had not been run through the Advertising Code Administration invited audiences to come see "Jane Russell in 3-D. It'll knock both your eyes out!"

Breen sent Vizzard to St. Louis to handle the situation. There, Vizzard got Archbishop Joseph E. Ritter to condemn the film from the pulpit, forbidding all Catholics to see the film under pain of mortal sin. Russell was so angered by Hughes's actions that she issued her own condemnation of the film and canceled plans to attend the premiere. On opening day, with patrons lining up around the block, the St. Louis police stood in the rear of the Fox Theatre to determine if the film should be closed on morals charges, then decided it wasn't all that bad.

But although attendance was strong at the start, word of mouth and bad reviews killed the picture. The independent chains decided it wasn't worth booking *The French Line*, particularly after the Legion of Decency condemned it. So by February 1954, RKO started negotiating with the PCA to get the film passed.

Since the Pennsylvania and New York censors had concentrated their efforts on the "Looking for Trouble" number, Hughes agreed to cut the patter section, during which Russell reclined seductively on a couch while dreaming of the man who could make "my own private chemical reaction start to work." He also substituted a long shot of the number for the many suggestive camera angles Breen had objected to originally.

After a year of negotiations, the PCA awarded its Seal of Approval in March 1955. Although censors like those in Ohio immediately passed the approved version, it did little to help the film at the box office. Yet Hughes had one triumph in court. A 1954 suit he had brought against the Ohio censors over proposed cuts in *The French Line* and *Son of Sinbad* resulted in the Ohio Supreme Court declaring that state's censorship law unconstitutional.

Little could diminish criticism of the Production Code or Breen's strict enforcement of it, however. Independent producer Samuel Goldwyn used the controversy over *The French Line* to renew his call for a revised code, warning that "we must realize that in the almost quarter of a century since the Code's adoption, the world has moved on. But the Code has stood still. Today there is a far greater maturity among audiences."[23]

Just as the language issue had trivialized Breen's objections to *The Moon Is Blue*, so the censors' seeming obsession with Russell's breasts made the battle over *The French Line* seem petty. Nor did the forgettable musical's lack of quality reflect credit on either side of the issue. If anything, Breen's efforts seemed to have helped Hughes sell more tickets than the picture deserved. The most cogent critique of the situation came from within the PCA itself. In his memoirs, Jack Vizzard looked back on the whole brouhaha with amazement: "That the eternal fate of a human being should have to be connected to Jane Russell's mammaries, no matter how heroic, was a bit much."[24]

That Breen was out of step with changing times was also demonstrated by his treatment of the trailblazing biker drama *The Wild One* (1954). Initially, he deemed the script unacceptable because of the bad example set by the motorcycle gang's antisocial behavior: "The callousness of the young hoodlums in upsetting the normal tenor of life in a small town, the manner in which they panic the citizens, the ineffectiveness of law and order for the majority of the script, the brawling, drunkenness, vandalism and irresponsibility of the young men are, in our opinion, all very dangerous elements. They cannot help but suggest to younger members of the audience, it seems to us, the possibilities that lie in their power to get away with hoodlumism, if only they organize into bands."

Although Breen got some of the violence cut during meetings with producer Stanley Kramer, he allowed a good deal of it to stand in return for a cautionary prologue, a few statements to indicate that star Marlon Brando and his gang were not typical bikers, an indication that the gang would have to pay for the damage they had committed, and a stronger sense that Brando was reformed by his contact with the local citizens. In addition, Kramer added a stinging condemnation of Brando and his type, delivered by the county sheriff (Jay C. Flippen) who ends the mayhem: "I don't get you. I don't get your act at all. And I don't think you do, either. I don't think you know what you're trying to do or how to go about it. I think you're stupid, real stupid, and real lucky. Last night you scraped by—just barely. But a man's dead on account of something you let get started, even though you didn't start it. I don't know if there's any good in you. I don't know if there's anything in you."

But the film's moralizing, even when delivered by as solid a performer as Flippen, cannot stand up in the long run against Brando's electric performance as the rebel biker or the visceral impact of the scenes of gang violence. Although the four remaining state censorship boards passed *The Wild One* uncut, it was banned in Montreal after an outburst of gang violence there was blamed (some say unjustly) on the film. The British Board of Film Censors kept the picture out of release there for eighteen years for fear of its effect on young people. Clearly, Breen's preoccupation with sex and his tolerance for violence were beginning to lag behind the shifting tides of morality.

The Old Order Changes

By 1954, the fate of human souls was no longer Joe Breen's concern. The feisty Irishman was sixty-four and had earned the right to remove himself from the battle. In February, he announced his retirement. A month later, he stepped onto the stage of the RKO Pantages Theatre in Hollywood to accept a special Oscar voted him by the filmmakers he had spent the last two decades fighting. By this point, the end of the Production Code may already have seemed inevitable to some, but Breen's retirement surely hastened it.

The end was still several years away, however. With the Legion of Decency and the state boards still powerful, the major studios continued to depend on the Production Code to defend them from outside censorship, even as they fought to get around the Code whenever possible.

This paradoxical attitude was embodied in the man named as Breen's successor on October 15, 1954—Geoffrey Shurlock. Shurlock was a decided contrast to Breen. The short, soft-spoken man was steeped in culture. He was a student of drama, fluent in French and Spanish, and an acknowledged expert on Japanese art and history.

He actually had joined the MPPDA's Hollywood office a year before Breen, signing on with Dr. Wingate in 1932. With the creation of the Production Code Administration in 1934, Shurlock had become Breen's chief assistant. The two were alike in maintaining their distance from the Hollywood social scene but decidedly different in their approaches to the job. Although Breen was perfectly capable of compromise when he felt it necessary, he possessed the Irishman's love of a good brawl. Viewing the world in terms of moral absolutes, he frequently stood fast against script elements he considered in blatant violation of the Production Code and the moral order. Shurlock took a different perspective. "There is no hard-and-fast rule about any script," he told reporter

Murray Schumach. "Each story has to be judged individually on the basis of morality and reasonable decency."[25]

With questionable materials, Breen's practice had been to come out swinging, damning objectionable elements from the start and trying to discourage the production of stories that violated the Code. Shurlock, however, viewed his role more as "expanding a script than cutting something out."[26] Generally, he encouraged screenwriters to forget about the Code and work freely. Then, he and his staff would step in to clean things up. Where no compromise could be reached and the material was not in flagrant violation of the Code, Shurlock would frequently give in just to gauge the reaction of other censors and the public. As a result, during Shurlock's fourteen years as Production Code director, the association gradually expanded the boundaries of what was permissible on screen. Jack Vizzard dubbed this unconventional approach to film censorship "a study in reverse English."[27]

Shurlock was hardly a pushover, however; he simply had a different take from Breen's on when to stand fast and when to bend. With the biography of singer Ruth Etting, *Love Me or Leave Me* (1955), he insisted that Ruth (Doris Day) and her gangster sponsor, Marty "the Gimp" Snyder (James Cagney), be married rather than just engage in an affair. He eliminated any sexual relations between Hal and Madge (William Holden and Kim Novak) in *Picnic* (1955). And he kept a close watch over MGM's political drama *Trial* (1955) to weed out any Communist propaganda.[28] Changes like that created little controversy. In the case of *Picnic*, the film may actually have benefited from Shurlock's strictness.

In at least one case, however, Shurlock's hard line proved to be a major mistake, though his position was almost unavoidable given the restrictions of the Production Code.

Nelson Algren's novel about drug addiction, *The Man with the Golden Arm*, had been kicking around Hollywood since 1950 but had been consistently rejected by Breen. The increase in drug addiction after World War II provided a good argument for revising the Code, but Breen and Johnston also had to consider how the Legion of Decency and the Treasury Department's Bureau of Narcotics might react to the subject.

In 1955, still preening over the success he'd had defying the Code with *The Moon Is Blue*, Otto Preminger set out to film the story, with Frank Sinatra as Frankie Machine, who survives a drug treatment program only to be drawn back into addiction as he's trying to forge a new career as a jazz drummer. Shurlock cautioned that the basic subject was forbidden by the Code but also agreed to evaluate the film as if the drug story were acceptable. In September 1955, he warned Preminger about a number of other trouble spots, including Frankie's brutal beating after he tries to cheat in an illegal poker game, the depiction of a local club as a strip joint, and the climax, in which Frankie's wife (Eleanor Parker) commits suicide to avoid arrest for murder.

Preminger tried to work around these other problems, but it was clear by the time he submitted the film in December that it could not be given a Code Seal. Even had the MPAA board been receptive to an appeal or a change in the Code, they were under external pressure from narcotics commissioner Harry Anslinger, who felt the film's "happy" ending, in which Frankie is cured and goes off to a new life with the woman he loves (Kim Novak), would glamorize addiction.

Once again, Preminger's distributor, United Artists, backed him and went ahead with plans to distribute the film without the Seal. Then Preminger was given an unexpected assist from the Legion of Decency. Rather than side with Shurlock and the PCA, the organization gave the film a B rating. With the favorable Legion rating, United Artists secured bookings in major theaters around the country, where *The Man with the Golden Arm* did strong business. The theater owners dealt another blow to the Production Code by telling the press that they weren't really concerned with the Seal of Approval anymore; they had their own standards. Although some in the press agreed with Commissioner Anslinger that the film glamorized addiction, others were quick to hail it as an important social statement that demanded to be seen: "After much torment Sinatra walks away believing he again is cured, but it is obvious that his future is uncertain. It makes for a powerful condemnation of the use of narcotics, merciless in its display of the cruelties of the habit. This is the kind of message that should be spread, not suppressed."[29]

With the success of *The Man with the Golden Arm*, Shurlock and Johnston finally agreed to update the Production Code. In 1956, the board approved changes that would allow the responsible depiction of drug addiction, prostitution, and miscegenation. They also loosened restrictions on the words "hell" and "damn," along with a variety of archaic expressions. United Artists resubmitted the film and won the Seal of Approval in 1961. They then reissued it on a double bill with *The Moon Is Blue*.

Whether he was reacting in embarrassment over his ban of *The Man with the Golden Arm* or relapsing into the same leniency he'd shown as acting PCA director in 1941, Shurlock started lowering the barriers against questionable material in the late fifties. Instead of viewing the Code as a series of absolute restrictions on film content, he dealt with questionable materials in context. Often he passed films because of the manner in which a scene was played, its place within the film as a whole, or even the reputation of the filmmaker. At times, these breaches in the Code went unnoticed; at other times, they triggered protests from religious leaders.

Humphrey Bogart had tried to film *The Sweet Smell of Success* in 1949, but Breen had kept Ernest Lehman's original short story, "Tell Me About It Tomorrow," from the screen. The plot revolved around J. J. Hunsecker, a powerful gossip columnist with a near-incestuous attachment to his sister. When the girl becomes engaged to a young jazz musician, Hunsecker gets an unscrupulous press agent, Sidney Falco, to break up the affair by planting some marijuana on the musician and turning him over to a sadistic police officer. Suspecting Falco, the sister fakes a suicide attempt to get him into a compromising position. Hunsecker discovers the two and kills Falco. Breen rejected the story because of the suggestion of incest, the use of marijuana, and the sister's getting away with murder.

Seven years later, producing partners Burt Lancaster and Harold Hecht got hold of the material and got it past Shurlock. Instead of killing Falco (Tony Curtis) for supposedly trying to rape his sister, Hunsecker (Lancaster) merely turns him over to the sadistic police officer. Writer Clifford Odets even made sure that there were some more honorable officers around to condemn their colleague's behavior. But they got to keep Hunsecker's incestuous yen for his sister and the references to marijuana. They also got by with a steamy scene in which Falco sets up his sometime girlfriend, Rita (Barbara Nichols), with another columnist to plant a derogatory item about the young musician. The solution to that scene was in the playing; at Shurlock's insistence, "Rita must be played as a crushed woman"—something Nichols pulled off quite effectively.

Effective playing and casting was also an important factor in getting *Gigi* on-screen after years of negotiation with the Breen Office. Colette's novel focused on a turn-of-the-century French girl raised to be a high-class courtesan only to win a marriage proposal from her first sponsor. It had first crossed Breen's desk in 1950 when the American distributors of a French film version starring Danielle Delorme applied for the Production Code Seal. Breen turned them down on the grounds that the story treated as acceptable what was essentially a form of prostitution.

MGM producer Arthur Freed first professed an interest in the property in 1951 but could not get support from studio head Dore Schary. In 1953, Audrey Hepburn starred in a hit Broadway adaptation written by Anita Loos, and Freed asked MGM's PCA liaison, Robert Vogel, to discuss a possible musical version with Shurlock.

Freed tempered the plot's suggestiveness by focusing on Gigi's girlish innocence. In the film, she falls deeply in love with Gaston and only goes to him as his mistress for fear that he will not have her any other way. But when Gaston sees Gigi as a sophisticated woman of the world, he realizes he truly loves her and asks for her hand in marriage. With Leslie Caron in the title role and director Vincente Minnelli achieving a

The art-house market continued to grow through the fifties as audiences turned to international product in a search for artistic visions and frank sensuality not found in Hollywood's offerings. Towards the end of the decade, three French films brought discriminating viewers an added bonus. Their popularity paved the way for more films dealing with human sexuality on an adult level while also winning victories in the courts.

Of the three, Roger Vadim's *And God Created Woman* (1957) was more important at the box office than in the courtroom. Although Kingsley Distributors fought its share of legal battles to get the film before audiences, the picture's main claim to fame was its impressive commercial performance, which made Brigitte Bardot the world's first international sex star.

Vadim had set out to showcase his young protégée in a steamy tale of a young woman who marries one man (Jean-Louis Trintignant) while casting her nets for his older brother (Christian Marquand) and a wealthy yachtsman (Curt Jurgens). *And God Created Woman* opened in the U.S. in December 1957 and immediately generated capacity crowds. The inexpensive French film brought in more than $4 million at the box office, thus paving the way for more sex-oriented imports.

Compared to *And God Created Woman, Lady Chatterley's Lover* (1957) seemed like Saturday-matinee fare. D. H. Lawrence's controversial novel had been banned by the U.S. Postal Department for over thirty years, a ban finally overturned by the Supreme Court in 1960. Despite the book's notoriety, Hollywood had been pursuing the property for almost as long. Nicholas Schenck tried to register the title in 1932, but Hays personally blocked it. David O. Selznick submitted the story to Breen in 1950, but he rejected it.

Eventually, the rights were picked up by French writer-director Marc Allegret, who maintained the story's justification of adultery but kept the love scenes relatively chaste. The crippled, impotent Sir Clifford Chatterley (Leo Genn) urges his wife (Danielle Darrieux) to take a lover and give him an heir.

When the New York censor board demanded that three scenes be cut from the film, its distributors appealed to the board of regents, which governed the censors' operations. The regents, however, banned the film completely on the grounds that its "whole theme . . . is the presentation of adultery as a desirable, acceptable and proper pattern of behavior."[30]

In 1959, *Kingsley International Pictures* v. *Regents of the University of the State of New York* reached the U.S. Supreme Court, which unanimously struck down the ban. The regents had branded the film "immoral" simply for telling a story that justified adultery. This, according to Justice Potter Stewart's majority opinion, was a violation of the First Amendment. No matter how unpopular or unconventional an idea was, it could not be censored.

Most in the legal and artistic communities felt that the Court had thrown out all criteria for censorship except out-and-out obscenity, which film critic Bosley Crowther optimistically predicted could never find a market. Others took a negative view of the Court's actions. Senator James O. Eastland of Mississippi even tried to float a constitutional amendment giving each state the right "to decide on the basis of its own public policy questions of decency and morality."[31]

The Court would carry its restrictions on censorship even further when it decided on the obscenity of Louis Malle's *The Lovers* (1958). Like *Lady Chatterley*, *The Lovers* presented a romanticized view of adultery. Jeanne Moreau stars as an upper-middle-class wife and mother bored with her inattentive husband and her cultured Argentine lover. When her car breaks down, she meets a young archaeologist (Jean-Marc Bory) with radical ideas. He spends the night at her estate, where the two make love. The next morning, they run off together, with the woman insisting tearfully that "I shall never regret it."

The Lovers was as much a social commentary as an exercise in eroticism, thus making the story doubly shocking. In addition, the lush black-and-white photography by Henri Decae and a score based on Brahms's Sextet No. 1 in B-flat combined to make the film intensely sensual, particularly during a twenty-minute sequence in which Moreau and Bory share their love in a drifting rowboat, her bed, and a bathtub. Although nudity was kept to a minimum, the film's distributors, Zenith International Film, had to fight censorship battles in Chicago; Boston; Dayton, Ohio; Providence, Rhode Island; Portland, Oregon; Memphis, Tennessee; and the states of New York, Virginia, and Maryland. It was a suit against Nico Jacobellis, the manager of the Ohio Art Theatre in Cleveland Heights, however, that brought the film to the Supreme Court.

Although as an employee of the small chain that owned the Ohio Art Theatre, Jacobellis could not have refused to show *The Lovers* without losing his job, he was arrested in November 1959. Jacobellis's employer, Louis Sher, and the film's distributor picked up his legal costs and took the case to the Supreme Court after lower courts upheld the conviction. The Court ruled that the film was not obscene, with Justice William Brennan writing in his majority opinion that, "material dealing with sex in a manner that advocates ideas, or that has literary or scientific or artistic value or any other form of social importance, may not be branded obscenity."[32] Concurring, Justice Stewart confirmed what most lawyers had suspected after the *Lady Chatterley* case. From now on, the Court would uphold censorship only in the case of hard-core pornography, though he declined to define the term, stating simply that "I know it when I see it."[33]

Justice Stewart's statement would become one of the most famous in the history of censorship litigation, partly because it predicted the uncertainty of the years to come. For as the film industry moved into the sixties, the new freedom fostered by the Supreme Court would soon leave censors, audiences, filmmakers, and even the nation's highest court increasingly confused and frustrated. ✄

delicate balance between Parisian sophistication and girlish romanticism, MGM pulled off the deception. Few critics found anything to complain about in the story, and it sailed through the four remaining state censorship boards uncut.

David O. Selznick would be less fortunate with his 1957 adaptation of *A Farewell to Arms*, but he really had nobody but himself to blame. As he had done with *A Duel in the Sun* a decade earlier, he bludgeoned his way through the PCA, determined to get as much on screen as possible.

Shurlock made most of the same objections that had greeted the film's 1932 version: the story went into copious detail about the sexual relationship between Frederick Henry (Rock Hudson) and Catherine Barkley (Selznick's wife, Jennifer Jones), who seemed to glory in their unwed status. Selznick made as few concessions as possible. He put in some lines condemning the affair, including Frederick's ludicrous reflection after Catherine and their illegitimate baby die, "Poor kid! Maybe this is the price you pay for sleeping together." But he refused to cut Catherine's refusal to marry Frederick because, as she says, "I couldn't feel more married." When Shurlock tried to stand up to him, Selznick whipped off a lengthy telegram: RULES ARE MADE FOR ME THAT HAVE NOT APPLIED TO MANY OF SHODDY PICTURES PRESENTLY ON MARKET, OR TO PRODUCERS OR DIRECTORS WHO HAVE NOTHING LIKE REPUTATIONS FOR DISTINGUISHED AND RESPECTABLE WORK.

At one point, Frederick and Catherine check into a hotel and are given a mirrored room the proprietor describes as "one of our most popular." The hitherto innocent Catherine quips, "I never felt like a whore before." Shurlock tried to get Selznick to substitute "harlot" or "prostitute," but again the producer would not budge, making his wife the first actor to speak the word "whore" on-screen in more than two decades.

After almost two years of fighting over *A Farewell to Arms*, Shurlock granted the film a Seal of Approval in September 1957, but that didn't stop the censorship problems. Critics blasted the film as a new low in bad taste: "This smutty version of Ernest Hemingway's novel will set thousands of stomachs to turning. It left this reviewer stunned and embarrassed. . . . Producer David O. Selznick should change the screen into the shape of a keyhole."[34] The Legion of Decency stuck the film with a B rating, complaining that "in the guise of dramatic realism, this film presents material in such a sensational and excessive manner that it is judged to be morally unacceptable for entertainment motion picture purposes."

A Farewell to Arms also inspired strong protests from other producers, who felt that Selznick had been allowed to get away with too much. In February 1958, Hal Wallis sent Shurlock an enraged letter: "The bars were certainly let down on this one and it makes me doubly resentful over the efforts made from time to time to get me to delete inconsequential things from my scripts. . . . I have made pictures over a long period of time and have always taken pride in the fact that they are made with good taste. I ask that you tell your staff to take this into account and to take into account *A Farewell to Arms* when writing me about any future productions of mine."

The Troubled Boy and the Girl in the Crib

As was to be expected, Shurlock's growing leniency generated mixed responses. Opposition to Hollywood among religious groups was growing again, though many church leaders were more concerned with an issue that hit closer to home, television. The critics, despite complaints about the excesses of a misfire like *A Farewell to Arms*, were quick to praise the PCA when a particularly difficult work survived the process intact. With two 1956 films, *Tea and Sympathy* and *Baby Doll*, Shurlock and the PCA ran the gamut from praise to condemnation.

Tea and Sympathy opened on Broadway on September 30, 1953, and was too big a hit for Hollywood to ignore, despite its questionable subject matter. It focused on Tom Lee, a sensitive prep-school boy whose classmates suspect him of homosexuality because of his interests in sewing and classical music. When Tom is caught skinny-dipping with a male teacher, the other boys begin persecuting him in earnest, egged on by Tom's macho housemaster, Bill Reynolds. To prove his manhood, Tom tries to score with the town whore, but when he can't perform, he attempts suicide. Bill's wife, Laura, has been drawn to the young man and has tried to get her husband to ease up on him. Feeling rejected by Bill, who prefers to spend time with "his boys," Laura saves Tom from a life of doubt and self-loathing by offering herself to him. As the lights dim, she unbuttons her blouse and speaks one of the American stage's most famous curtain lines: "Years from now . . . when you talk about this . . . and you will . . . be kind."[35]

Within a month of its premiere, Martin Quigley wrote to warn Breen that this play could become a major problem. In the present climate, Quigley wondered if producers would be willing to tone it down to pass the Code. Nor did he think that would be the best course to take: "None, I think it, but a vandal would lay profane hand upon it." Breen concurred with Quigley's judgment: "If the basic element of the story is changed, and the ending rewritten, then, I fear, they will have no story."

These reactions point up an interesting dichotomy in the thinking of Breen, Quigley, and Shurlock. None of them were personally offended by all of the materials they tried to keep out of the movies, as long as they were confined to other media. On screen, however, such materials were available to a larger, less sophisticated audience and could inspire a backlash against the industry. Hollywood's censors consistently sacrificed their own tastes in the interest of protecting audiences and even Hollywood itself.

Over the next year, six different studios or producers approached Breen about filming the play. At MGM's request, he sent Jack Vizzard and Geoffrey Shurlock to see it in October 1953. While there, they ran into Sam Goldwyn, who also was scouting the property. The three scheduled a meeting with playwright Robert Anderson and the play's director, Elia Kazan, at which Anderson stated his "minimum requirements as to what any screenplay based on this stage play should contain":

1) It was a "sine qua non" that the leading lady solve the boy's problem by giving herself to him sexually. It would be unacceptable to the author that she merely offer him her love.

2) It was essential that the boy's problem spring from the malicious charge of his homosexuality against him . . . .

3) The proper telling of the story, according to the author, requires the sequence in which the boy, egged on by a companion who wishes to help him out of his dilemma, pays a visit to . . ."the town whore."

These three requirements would make it impossible for the PCA to pass the story. Initially, Anderson spoke of having the film produced independently and released without the Seal of Approval. Milton Sperling at Warner Bros. had the studio's permission to produce the film in just this manner, but Jack Vizzard managed to convince them that such a move would damage the industry.[36]

In September 1954, MGM offered Anderson a very generous deal for the screen rights. They would pay him $100,000 simply to option the property. He would keep that fee, along with any script drafts, treatments and other notes, in the event that the PCA refused to pass the script. Should the film be made, Anderson would be paid an additional $300,000.

In March 1955, MGM submitted a screenplay that Shurlock could work with. There were still problems, but they had made considerable progress in toning down the play. Tom's problem was now effeminacy, complicated by a strong crush on Laura that set him off from the other boys. Rather than being encouraged by his sympathetic roommate to visit the town whore, he does so on his own after hearing the other boys talk about her. And Laura would give herself to Tom for fear that he was going to attempt suicide again.

This latter element still needed some work. Shurlock felt that it did not diminish the play's original justification of adultery; if anything, it almost glorified what he considered her sin. Anderson solved the problem by telling the story in a flashback triggered by the adult Tom's return to the school. At the end of the film, Bill, now a tired old man, gives him a letter Laura had left that not only condemns her behavior but deems it unneccessary:

> As you must know, I couldn't go back to Bill after that afternoon with you and pretend that nothing had happened. And my not going back ruined his life. . . . both of you, in a sense, were crying out to be saved from what you thought you wanted. In answering your cry, I took the easier way, and unhappily, the wrong way. . . .
>
> These are terrible things to write to you, Tom, about sin and guilt, but you are old enough now to know that when you drop a pebble in the water, there are ever-widening circles of ripples—ripples that may carry afar a burden of good or of evil.
>
> Anyway, Tom, I have come to realize that I showed a lack of faith in you, in your ability to meet a crisis by youself and come through it manfully alone.

These changes were met with praise by the press, as were the performances of Deborah Kerr and John Kerr, both holdovers from the Broadway production. Although Edwin Schallert of the *Los Angeles Times* feared that those who had seen the original would find the film a letdown and considered the plot's watered-down motivation flimsy at best, Bosley Crowther saw the film as a major step forward for the PCA: "That long-time formidable obstruction to morally controversial material in American films—we speak of the operation of the industry's own Production Code—is slowly and quietly being loosened to accord with what is obviously a change in social attitudes. And the industry is much better for it, as is certainly the medium of films."[37]

The only people unhappy with *Tea and Sympathy* were Martin Quigley and Robert Anderson. The former tried to get the Legion of Decency to condemn the film, but they passed it with a B rating. In later years, Anderson would claim to have been pressured into changing his script more than he wanted: "You become convinced you're saving the story, but you're not."[38] Most, however, would have agreed that the film successfully negotiated the Production Code without losing its power—as long as audiences left before the tacked-on final scene.

Within a month, however, any praise Shurlock had won evaporated as the industry faced one of the strongest religious protests ever directed at a single film. As Shurlock and his associates were struggling to make *Tea and Sympathy* acceptable for mass audiences, Elia Kazan and Tennessee Williams came calling with another assault on the Code, *Baby Doll*.

Kazan had learned a great deal since his experience with *A Streetcar Named Desire*. When he signed with Warner Bros. to produce and direct an expanded version of Williams's one-act play *Twenty-seven Wagons Full of Cotton*, he agreed to make whatever changes were necessary to receive the PCA Seal of Approval. But he also had the final cut, thus allowing him to refuse to make any other changes. In addition, Kazan had joined the growing ranks of directors and stars producing their own work. These new hyphenates got numerous tax breaks by working for themselves while maintaining more control of their films—a situation weakening both studio influence and PCA authority.

Like many of the most controversial properties passed by Shurlock, *Baby Doll* had started out under Breen's supervision. When the material was submitted to him under the slightly altered title *Twenty-seven Wagon Loads of Cotton*, in August 1952, Breen did not ban it outright but expressed concern over a variety of issues.

The story was set in rural Mississippi and concentrated on three characters, none of whom could be regarded as heroic. Archie Lee Meighan is suffering on two fronts. He has promised to allow his wife, Baby Doll, to remain a virgin until she turns twenty— she even sleeps in a crib rather than share his bed—but as the birthday nears, his frustration has reached almost unendurable levels. In addition, his run-down cotton gin is losing business to a more modern operation belonging to recent arrival Silva Vacarro. When Archie Lee burns down Silva's gin, his rival investigates, first questioning, then seducing Baby Doll.

Breen's first concern was the "low and sordid tone of the story as a whole. As far as the three principals are concerned, this story seems mainly interested in crime, sex, murder and revenge." To supply some compensating moral value for the picture, Breen urged Williams to build up one of the area's black residents, Charlie, as the voice of morality.

In conferences, Williams and Kazan had explained their vision of the story as the inexorable progression to evil. In their view, the ill treatment Silva received in the rural community and his inability to get justice through legal means had set him on the road to vengeance. Breen thought this would be acceptable if the role of the town constable could be built up to indicate that he wants to help Silva but has no evidence to go on. In addition, it would be necessary to show that any sexual relations between Silva and Baby Doll had occurred spontaneously and were not part of his revenge plot against Archie Lee.

With these objections, Breen voiced an overriding confusion about the script. Once again Williams had produced a story that was more complex morally than the typical Hollywood picture. According to Breen: "One of the problems which concerns us most has to do with the question of whom we are 'cheering' for in this story. It is difficult in the present version to know where the sympathies of the audience are supposed to lie." In truth, it was never Williams's intention to place audience sympathies squarely with one character or another. He had created an objective portrait of three characters who could be either sympathetic or unsympathetic, depending on the situation. In his mind, the audience would watch these people with the same detachment he had used in creating them.

Williams did little to bring the script within Production Code standards at this point. Earlier, he had considered having a cyclone kill off some of the characters as punishment for their sins. He later experimented with having Archie Lee kill Silva, then go off to jail, but that didn't really solve the problems. The process dragged on for three years as Williams took time off to work on other projects. At one point, Warners story editor Finlay McDermid even wondered if Williams was the writer "who would ultimately bring the picture into focus."

By 1955, however, Williams had come up with a workable script. McDermid praised the piece for its resemblance to "some of the best French ironic comedies, the ones that didn't win Code seals in this country." But Shurlock still had two major reservations about the picture: "The first of these was the justified adultery that the script seemed to indicate. The second was the element of the unconsummated marriage between Baby Doll and Archie."

Kazan dealt with the former by cutting any overt implication that Silva and Baby Doll engaged in sexual relations. Though the long scene in which he gets her to sign a statement charging her husband with arson remained highly sexual, she ends by putting him to bed in her crib, a move that Kazan argued would make sexual intercourse impossible. Later, Silva assures Archie Lee that no seduction took place. The script called for an "angry and hurt" reaction from Baby Doll, but Kazan cut it to remove the implication that Silva was lying. Kazan also assured Shurlock that the film would end with Silva rejecting Baby Doll (the ending is actually more ambiguous, with Silva leaving but saying he'll be back the next day to use Archie Lee's cotton gin).

Kazan was much less conciliatory in dealing with Archie Lee's relations with Baby Doll. Shurlock wanted the element of his frustration removed altogether, arguing that the scenes in which he spied on her and came on to her and the scene in which he complains to his doctor would have to be cut. Writing from the film's location in Mississippi, Kazan refused to make the changes: "This film is about one thing and only one thing. It's about a middle aged man who is held at arm's length by his young wife. . . . Tell the boys that the hero of this film, for me, is Archie Lee. He is a pathetic misguided, confused, desperate man. Sin and violence and so forth come out of fear and desperation. Archie Lee should be pathetic. And will be. And amusingly so!"

One thing working to Kazan's benefit was the fact that the film's location was far from the reach of both the studio and the PCA. When he brought *Baby Doll* back to Hollywood in 1956, it was pretty much a fait accompli. Shurlock was happy to discover that the adultery had indeed been eliminated and that Archie Lee's sexual frustration had been dealt with in good taste.

Their major concern now was the swing scene, in which Silva gets the truth out of Baby Doll. In a memo, Jack Vizzard stated: "There was no one on the entire staff which reviewed the picture who did not think that this scene clearly intimated that Silva was agitating the girl, and in a manner, seducing her (by prolonged stroking and caressing of her skin, by pressing himself intimately on her, and by purring words of tenderness at her) up to the point of suggestion that the girl is having physical reactions which are orgiastic [sic]." Kazan insisted that nothing of the sort had happened. He took Vizzard and Eugene Dougherty through the film frame by frame until they gave in. *Baby Doll* won its Seal of Approval on September 14, 1956.

The Legion of Decency was less accommodating, however. In late November, they condemned the film in a statement attacking both *Baby Doll* and the MPAA: "The subject matter of the film indicates an open disregard of the Code by its administrators. . . . It dwells almost without variation or relief upon carnal suggestiveness in action, dialogue and costuming. Its unmitigated emphasis on lust and the various scenes of cruelty are degrading and corruptive. As such, it is grievously offensive to Christian and traditional standards of morality and decency."[39]

Under the terms of his contract, Kazan was not required to cut the film to obtain a satisfactory rating from the Legion. For a while, it even seemed that the C rating would not hurt the film, as several independent theater chains rushed to sign exhibition contracts.

The Legion's vehement attack may have been based on three factors in addition to the film's sensuality. Warners had launched an all-out advertising blitz designed to capitalize on the film's sexual elements, featuring star Carroll Baker in a crib sucking her thumb. In addition, as Jack Vizzard points out in his memoirs, the Legion of Decency was coming at the film cold, where the PCA had viewed it in the context of earlier, racier versions. When members of the MPAA's New York board finally saw the film, they too questioned the PCA's passage of it. Further, although the film eschews overt political content, it makes some pretty strong political statements nonetheless. Without ever referring to racial issues, *Baby Doll*, in Vizzard's words, "lays naked the arrogance by which trashy whites try to sustain the status quo economically, and the cruelty to which they will go to keep it intact."[40] And Baby Doll, though hardly a feminist heroine, makes a surprising stab at self-determination when she decides that she would rather give up her virginity to Silva than to her husband. This underlying political subtext may have added to the vehemence with which the film was attacked.

Early in December, New York's Cardinal Spellman returned from a tour of overseas military bases to find *Baby Doll* posters adorning the land. On strong urging from the Legion and Martin Quigley, he took to the pulpit for the first time in seven years. In 1949, he had attacked the Communists for imprisoning Hungary's Cardinal Jozsef Mindszenty. Now, without having seen the film, he was attacking Warner Bros. for releasing what he called "a contemptuous defiance of the natural law, the observance of which has been the source of strength in our national life." He called on not just Catholics but "every loyal citizen" to boycott the film.[41]

Spellman's pronouncement generated immediate responses in defense of the film. Kazan extolled the work's "honesty and charity," while Tennessee Williams wondered, "I cannot believe that an ancient and august branch of the Christian faith is not larger in heart and mind. . . ."[42] The clergy jumped into the battle, too. A week after Spellman's sermon, Dr. James A. Pike, dean of the Protestant Episcopal Cathedral of St. John the Divine, devoted a sermon to a defense of the film: "I don't think that I sinned in seeing it. Those who do not want the sexual aspect of life included in the portrayal of a real-life situation had better burn their Bibles, as well as abstain from the movies."[43] He also condemned the Catholic Church's endorsement of Cecil B. DeMille's recent *The Ten Commandments*, which he claimed featured sequences much more carnal than anything in *Baby Doll*.

European Catholics also took a more lenient view of the film. The Archdiocese of Paris passed the film with an adults-only rating, while the Reverand John A. Burke, head of the United Kingdom's version of the Legion of Decency, hailed the film as "a brilliant piece of work on a decadent subject . . . obviously not the sort of thing for thoughtless people."[44] Not everyone overseas must have viewed the film in that light, however. Burke's defense of the film cost him his job.

As pressure against *Baby Doll* increased, bookings fell off. Some local bishops threatened theaters with six-month boycotts for showing the film. In other areas, priests stood in theater lobbies to take down the names of parishioners attending in defiance of the Legion's condemnation. Although the film opened to strong business almost everywhere, receipts dropped significantly within a week. By the end of its initial release, the film had barely broken even. Kazan claims never to have seen any profits from the picture he helped finance.

Why did *Baby Doll* fail where *The Moon Is Blue* had succeeded? The Legion had condemned *The Moon Is Blue* only to support Breen's refusal to grant the film a Seal of Approval. As a result, the church hierarchy did not attack it as vehemently as they did *Baby Doll*. Also, as revolutionary as some of *The Moon Is Blue*'s language and attitudes may have been, the picture was fundamentally little different from the popular romantic comedies Hollywood had been turning out for years. By contrast, *Baby Doll* was a difficult, challenging work confronting its viewers with the uglier side of human character and offering no real solution to the problems it raised. The difference between the two films boiled down to two thousand bookings: six thousand theaters showed *The Moon Is Blue*; only four thousand booked *Baby Doll*.

In essence, Kazan had made a European art film, albeit on U.S. soil and with the backing of one of Hollywood's major studios. Early on, Warner Bros. executives claimed that the Legion's condemned rating would help them at the box office. They may have been right. Without that condemnation to draw the curious, this difficult, if extremely well-made film might not have broken even.

Dragging the Legion into the Present

The Legion itself was in the throes of change during the late fifties. Quigley's conservative influence was waning as a new generation of prelates rebelled against the suggestion that he was the real power behind the organization.

In 1956, the Legion added a new classification to deal with *Storm Center*, a drama about book burning starring Bette Davis. Although the film focused on conservative objections to a book about communism, the parallels to the church's own use of censorship was clear and probably would have brought the picture a Condemned rating in earlier years. Instead, the Legion created a "Separate Classification," which henceforth would be used for "certain films which, while not morally offensive, require some analysis and explanation as a protection to the uninformed against wrong interpretations and false conclusions."[45]

In 1957, the Legion expanded its A rating into A-I, "morally unobjectionable for general patronage"; A-II, "morally unobjectionable for adults and adolescents;" and "A-III, morally unobjectionable for adults."[46] By creating a system of classification based on audience maturity, the Legion relaxed its standards to make more films acceptable. At the same time, they changed the overall approach to their ratings, urging that filmgoers' individual responsibility was more important than blind obedience to the Legion.

They could still take a hard line, of course. The Legion almost condemned Billy Wilder's *Some Like It Hot* in 1959, rating it B with a stern notice that "this film, though it purports to be a comedy, contains screen material elements that are judged to be seriously offensive to Christian and traditional standards of morality and decency." In a letter to Shurlock, the Legion's secretary, Monsignor Thomas Little, decried the PCA's passage of the film: "In the present atmosphere of our society, which seems to be calling for censorship and controls, this picture will only add fuel to the fire."

But times were clearly changing, as the Legion, the PCA, and many conservative Americans were dragged unwillingly into the sixties. As young people clamored for social change, film grew in stature as an art form, and European product made even greater inroads on American screens, the nation's two major censorship organizations would have to choose between changing with the times or becoming anachronistic jokes.

Fun and Games
with George and Martha

Chapter Eight

For the liberal side of the cultural wars, the sixties represented an extended playtime as more and more restrictions on expression fell to an increasingly activist court system. A new generation came into power in the U.S. with the election of John F. Kennedy, the nation's second-youngest president. As "Camelot" was installed in the White House, many saw the dawn of a new cultural era. And though that euphoria would soon be diminished by the realities of a changing world, a great thaw had set in, melting away the last vestiges of fifties conformity.

The new administration brought with it a renewed interest in social issues. Television dealt with such realities as birth control, race relations, and drug abuse in trend-setting dramatic series like "The Defenders," "The Nurses," and "East Side, West Side." International films pushed the envelope with their unflinching, often nonjudgmental treatment of what was still considered the "seamier" side of life.

As the sixties dawned, two European hits set the pace for American filmmakers. *Room at the Top* (1959) depicted the sexual entanglements of a working-class Englishman (Laurence Harvey) trying to better his lot, much as *A Place in the Sun* had told a similar story in 1951. This time, however, the protagonist got everything he wanted, with only a little angst as punishment for his misdeeds. *Never on Sunday* (1960) made a Greek prostitute (Melina Mercouri) its heroine as she fights to live her life her own way despite a puritanical American (Jules Dassin) out to reform her. Both films did impressive business, despite limited distribution and a strict adults-only policy. Both also

George and Martha (Richard Burton and Elizabeth Taylor) finally call it a night in Who's Afraid of Virginia Woolf? *(1966). By the time director Mike Nichols was finished with his screen version of Edward Albee's controversial play, he had helped put the Production Code in its grave.*

cracked the Academy Awards, with *Room* capturing Best Actress (Simone Signoret) and Best Screenplay, while *Sunday* took honors for its chart-topping title song. And both ran into censorship problems in the same city, Atlanta.

Atlanta's censor, Mrs. Christine Smith Gilliam, was far from the most popular woman in town. The city's growing sophistication was threatened by a woman who, since the end of World War II, had routinely barred films for racially inflammatory content, sexual license, or vulgar language. When she decided that *Never on Sunday* and *Room at the Top* represented "unacceptable ideas," however, she ran up against the new restrictions set down by the Supreme Court in the *Lady Chatterley's Lover* case.

Never on Sunday was the first suit to reach the courts. It would have spelled the end of film censorship in Atlanta had not the state's supreme court overturned Lopert Pictures' appeal on procedural grounds. When the same distributor sued to overturn Smith's ban on *Room at the Top*, the courts used the case to rule Atlanta's film censorship ordinance unconstitutional.

None of this escaped notice in Hollywood, where increased sexuality was viewed as a practical solution to competition not just from foreign films but from the more heavily censored television medium. In addition, the emergence of the director as a serious artist during the sixties meant that more and more, Shurlock and his associates were arguing not with businessmen out to generate profits but with artists out to protect their integrity.

The PCA Seal was still important in securing bookings and getting by local censors. But the changing nature of Hollywood production had placed even more importance on the initial letter from Shurlock approving a script. With few exceptions, no director could obtain production money without that letter. Rather than use the situation to clamp down on rebellious filmmakers, however, the gentlemanly PCA director became more accommodating than ever, tentatively approving plot lines that would come back to haunt him when it was time to screen the finished picture.

Through the decade, Production Code barriers continued to fall, until it seemed that an "anything goes" philosophy had taken over. Restrictions on illicit sex had started loosening in 1959, when Shurlock passed Warner Bros.' *A Summer Place*, in which an adulterous affair leads to no greater punishment than the realization that the perpetrators' children (Troy Donahue and Sandra Dee) have followed their elders' example so well they are now unwed parents-to-be.

The same year, Shurlock tried to deny the Code Seal to *Happy Anniversary*, a comedy about the disastrous effects that follow when longtime couple David Niven and Mitzi Gaynor reveal they were sexually involved with each other before marriage. The MPAA had recently changed its review board, adding exhibitors and independent producers, and United Artists was so confident of their more liberal viewpoint that the studio opened the picture without a Seal while the appeal was pending. Their faith was borne out when the board agreed to pass the film with the addition of one line dubbed over a rear shot of Niven: "I was wrong. I never should have taken Alice to that hotel room before we were married. What could I have been thinking of?"

Splendor in the Grass (1961) treated illicit sex more seriously but was no less revolutionary for that. William Inge's tale of a corn-belt Romeo and Juliet in the twenties went beyond such similar films as *A Summer Place* and *Blue Denim*, which depicted teen sex as a sad mistake. *Splendor in the Grass* dealt not with youthful lovers who pay the price of indiscretion but with two young people who pay the price of denying their natural impulses. The idea actually ran counter to the Code, but Shurlock let it pass, merely cautioning producer-director Elia Kazan to exercise restraint in shooting the love scenes.

Gradually, sleeping around became a staple plot element. By the time United Artists imported Tony Richardson's *Tom Jones* in 1963, things had loosened up so much that they submitted the film to the Legion of Decency first, using that group's B rating as a lever to secure PCA approval, despite the fact that the film's bed-hopping hero at one point discovers that the woman who has just seduced him may be his long-lost mother. The picture went on to become the top-grossing foreign film released in America to that time and the year's Oscar winner for Best Picture.

The British invasion continued with the James Bond films, starting with *Dr. No* in 1963. Shurlock passed that and the second Bond film, *From Russia with Love* (1964), with no compunction. When friends complained about the films' rampant sexuality, he shrugged and said, "It's only a little fucking. What's all the shouting about?"[1]

With the third Bond film, 1965's *Goldfinger*, Shurlock questioned the name of Honor Blackman's character, Pussy Galore, then passed it when producer Albert "Cubby" Broccoli said it had played in England without complaints. Shurlock also had problems with the opening scene. Pulled out of bed by a call from headquarters, Bond (Sean Connery) looks at the beautiful woman beside him and says he can't talk now because "something big has just come up." When Broccoli said the joke didn't bother him, Shurlock let it by.

Language was another barrier that fell early in the decade, precipitated by the success of Otto Preminger's *Anatomy of a Murder* in 1959. The film was based on the trial of a man who had killed his wife's rapist. In novelizing the case, Michigan Supreme Court Justice John Voelker (writing under the name Robert Traver) had transcribed the clinical language used in evidence, and Preminger wanted to present the film with the same kind of realism.

When Shurlock first received the script in December 1958, he objected to the inclusion of such words and phrases as "sperm," "sexual climax," and "penetration" as well as the frequent repetition of "rape" and "panties." Preminger agreed to cut down on some references and changed others, but refused to cut "penetration." Justice Voelker, who was serving as a consultant on the film, felt the word necessary because it was the only legally accepted condition for rape in Michigan. Shurlock argued back that hearing those words "over the loud speaker of a public theater" was "not quite the same thing as laying down a judgment in a restricted court of law," but ended up passing the film with few changes.

The rough language used in *Anatomy of a Murder* was essential to its courtroom setting. Shurlock could use that distinction to keep those words out of other films, but not for long. The courts were also easing up in this area. In a 1962 decision, the New York Court of Appeals overturned the state's ban on Shirley Clarke's *The Connection*, a cinéma verité treatment of drug addiction in which the word "shit" was used repeatedly as slang for heroin. The regents had considered the repetition of the word obscene, but the courts overruled them, arguing that it had to be considered in context.

One of Hollywood's longest-standing restrictions fell in 1961 when the MPAA board amended the Production Code to allow the depiction of homosexuality. *A Streetcar Named Desire* had hardly been the last film to raise the issue, but even as homosexuality was turning up as the subject of plays and novels, the PCA had insisted on eliminating or at least clouding any film references to what was still considered sexual perversion.

On Broadway, the plot of Tennessee Williams's *Cat on a Hot Tin Roof* had hinged on the suspicion that the male lead, Brick, had been sexually involved with his best friend, Skipper. In the play, Brick's wife, Maggie, had seduced Skipper to keep anything from happening between the two men. When MGM filmed the story in 1958, Shurlock insisted that any such implications be cut. Instead, Skipper was described as a weakling and a user who seduced Maggie while Brick was sidelined with a football injury.

With *Spartacus*, director Stanley Kubrick tried to keep in a seduction scene between Roman general Laurence Olivier and Greek slave Tony Curtis. The scene had been written so indirectly that Kubrick may have hoped for some dispensation: Olivier questions Curtis about whether he prefers snails or oysters and the slave only gradually catches the drift of the conversation. But Shurlock's readers caught on much sooner than Curtis's character. They began questioning the scene with the first script submission in August 1958. The PCA's objections continued through revisions and production, but the scene was shot and included in the film. Only when both Shurlock and the Legion of Decency objected did Universal cut the seduction. It would be returned to the film for its 1991 restoration, but by that time the soundtrack had been lost and the dialogue had to be redubbed by Curtis and Anthony Hopkins, the latter imitating the late Olivier.

Other late-fifties films had gotten away with subtle implications of homosexuality. In Gerd Oswald's low-budget thriller *Screaming Mimi* (1958), nobody ever states that the nightclub owner played by Gypsy Rose Lee is a lesbian, but the implication is strong nonetheless. Throughout the film she's in the company of a young woman who appears to be her protégée. When the film's reporter-hero (Phil Carey) interrupts a dance lesson Lee is giving the girl, the hitherto friendly hostess is decidedly cold to him. After a few futile attempts to get information out of her, Carey leaves, dropping a cryptic comment on the way out: "I'm sorry, girls, I didn't realize it was just tea for two."

The comment may not have been all that cryptic. It was one of several lesbian elements the PCA tried to eliminate from the script. That it remained may have been the result of creative bargaining. Earlier scripts had suggested that Lee also was involved with her club's star dancer (Anita Ekberg). Although the film's producer argued that Shurlock was reading things into the relationship, he toned down the references while still keeping Lee's scenes with the younger dancer.

Even more overt were the references to homosexuality in another Williams adaptation, *Suddenly Last Summer* (1959). The one-act play detailed the tragic fate of Sebastian Venable, a failed poet killed under mysterious circumstances during a vacation trip with his cousin Catherine. Sebastian's mother wants Catherine lobotomized to stop her ravings about the trip, but under examination the girl reveals that Sebastian had been a predatory homosexual who used first his mother, then Catherine to lure young men into his clutches during their vacations. While staying at a Spanish coastal resort, he was attacked and cannibalized by the young boys with whom he had been having sex.

As soon as independent producer Sam Spiegel submitted Gore Vidal's adapted script, Shurlock objected on the grounds that the references to homosexuality were a direct violation of the Code. He found the cannibalism "so revolting, that we did not feel justified in giving the Code seal," and he felt Sebastian and his mother's comments about God bordered on blasphemy.

Spiegel met with Shurlock on May 25, 1959, and defended the property. In his opinion, the homosexuality was acceptable because it was punished. The cannibalism could be deleted by cutting one line (though the impression remains in the film), while the depiction of mother and son as psychopaths would temper any criticism of their religious views. In an unusual move, Spiegel said he did not need the PCA letter approving the story but would prefer to let director Joseph L. Mankiewicz finish making the film his own way.

When the film was completed, there were no overt references to Sebastian's sexual behavior, nor did the audience ever see more of him than a fleeting glimpse of his back. What's more, the psychiatrist (Montgomery Clift) treating Catherine (Elizabeth Taylor) seemed incapable of understanding what she was talking about. His continued demands for her to explain her story may have been intended to create the impression that Sebastian's fate was still some great mystery.[2]

Shurlock didn't want to pass the film, so Spiegel went to the Review Board. Without filing a formal appeal, he won the Seal by making two deletions: a scene in the Spanish town showing Sebastian with two boys and a line using the word "procurement." Spiegel then went to the Legion of Decency, which granted the film a Separate Classification, noting that "the Production Code, in giving its Seal to the film and thereby indicating its approval of it for general patronage, violates a particular application of its general principles, namely, that 'sex-perversion or any inference of it is forbidden.' "

What may have moved both the MPAA and the Legion to pass the film was its implicit condemnation of homosexuality, with Sebastian killed by his former sexual partners and his mother (Katharine Hepburn) going mad in the final reel. Reviews were mixed, but all noted the film's groundbreaking subject matter, with *Daily Variety* calling it "the most bizarre motion picture ever made by a major American company."[3]

The walls would tumble for good with Hollywood's next major attempt to deal with homosexuality. After the amazing success of *Ben-Hur* (1959), William Wyler probably could have filmed anything he wanted. He chose to bring Lillian Hellman's 1934 play *The Children's Hour* to the screen. Although he had directed the heavily altered 1936 film version, *These Three* (see Chapter 5), he refused to call the new project a remake. "This time," he said, "I have actually filmed Lillian Hellman's play, which we were not able to do twenty-five years ago."[4]

But he still had to face the same organization that had bowdlerized the play a quarter of a century earlier. Shurlock's first letter on the script, dated May 3, 1961, labeled the story unsuitable because it hinged on a false accusation of lesbianism, though the PCA director also noted that that was the only objectionable element in the script.

At this point, the film's distributor stepped in. Arthur Krim of United Artists wrote to Eric Johnston on May 10 to inform him that the company had three projects in preparation that touched on homosexuality: *The Children's Hour*, *Advise and Consent* (which eventually went to Columbia), and *The Best Man*. He assured Johnston that there would be no "acts or suggestions of acts of homosexuality itself," while also threatening to release the pictures without the Code Seal if necessary.

Although Johnston and Shurlock would deny any influence on Krim's part, the Code was amended on October 3: "In keeping with the culture, the mores and the values of our time, homosexuality and other sexual aberrations may now be treated with care, discretion and restraint."[5] *The Children's Hour* received the Code Seal on November 27, 1961. Even the Legion of Decency fell in line on this one, rating the film A-III, adults only.

But Code approval did not help the film, artistically or financially. Hellman, who had been unavailable to write the screenplay, complained that Wyler had stuck too close to the original and should have changed it to fit the times. Most of the critics agreed with that assessment. Noting that even in 1934 Hellman's play had been "behind the sophistication of the times," Bosley Crowther labeled the film seriously dated: "The hint [of lesbianism] is intruded with such astonishment and it is made to seem such a shattering thing (even without evidence to support it) that it becomes socially absurd. It is incredible that educated people living in an urban American community today would react as violently and cruelly to a questionable innuendo as they are made to do in this film."[6]

Therein lay the crux of the problem. Audiences that would have attended a film dealing with lesbianism found the play out of date. Those who could accept the shocked reaction to such an accusation would not have gone to the film anyway.

Opponents of the Production Code amendment predicted that it would open the floodgates to gay-oriented material, but that hardly happened. The British film *Oscar Wilde* (1960), which starred Robert Morley in an adaptation of his own play, had been denied the Code Seal in 1960. Now Shurlock passed the film with the deletion of only one line, Alfred Douglas's accusation that his father had "paid more attention to your horses, hounds, and whores" than he had to his sons. Nor were most of Hollywood's early depictions of homosexuality all that sympathetic.[7] In *Walk on the Wild Side* (1962), Barbara Stanwyck played one of the screen's most predatory lesbians, a ruthless madam who keeps some of her girls virtual prisoners in her bordello. In *Advise and Consent* (1962), Otto Preminger took audiences into the screen's first gay bar, filled with preening, effeminate stereotypes.

Advise and Consent also helped popularize the stereotype of homosexuality as a dirty little secret destructive enough to drive even the strongest character over the edge. Just as Martha Dobie (Shirley MacLaine) in *The Children's Hour* had hanged herself after realizing that she was a lesbian, so the strong-willed Senator Brig Anderson (Don Murray) in Preminger's film cut his throat rather than face blackmail by political opponents who had unearthed a homosexual liaison in his past. Although the subplot was allegedly based on a true incident in which a senator killed himself over his son's homosexuality, more than one critic complained that the suicide was out of character.

The most favorable depiction of a gay character during these years came not from Hollywood but from England. In *The L-Shaped Room* (1963), Leslie Caron plays a young woman who moves into a boardinghouse after becoming pregnant out of wedlock. Her landlady (Cicely Courtneidge) is a retired vaudevillian who speaks fondly of the one great love of her life, then shows Caron a picture of her ladyfriend, saying, "It takes all kinds, dearie." Shurlock tried to have the character removed from the film, claiming that her homosexuality was not necessary to the plot, but writer-director Bryan Forbes refused.

It was not until the late sixties that Hollywood began to produce any films in which homosexuality was the central issue. And it would take longer than that for the subject to be dealt with in a positive light. With the exception of a few low-budget, independent American releases and the occasional import, most films were made on the assumption that audiences were not ready to accept gay characters as anything other than jokes or villains.

Nymphettes and Hookers

The gradual relaxation of Production Code standards is most clearly reflected in three films from the first half of the sixties: *Lolita* (1961), *Kiss Me, Stupid* (1964), and *The Pawnbroker* (1965). The first of these helped weaken the Code's stand against sexual perversion. The second demonstrated Shurlock's inability to ride herd on Hollywood's increasingly independent production community. The third toppled the Code's last major taboo, nudity.

Vladimir Nabokov's satirical novel had been the surprise hit of 1955, particularly to those who had considered it unprintable. One British publisher had been so shocked at the story of a mature man in love with a twelve-year-old girl that he tore up his copy of the manuscript. In America, one publisher advised Nabokov to burn all copies of the book, while another suggested that the story might not be so objectionable if Lolita were a boy. Even after the book became a best-seller, it was a source of controversy. Both France and Argentina banned it. The Cincinnati Public Library refused to place it on its shelves. And the town of Lolita, Texas, considered changing its name to Jackson.

Hollywood was strongly divided about the book. None of the major studios wanted to tackle the controversy, but at the same time they could hardly ignore a novel that stayed on the *New York Times* best-seller list for fifty-six weeks and sold out in England the day it hit the stands.

Independent producer James B. Harris and director Stanley Kubrick contacted

Shurlock about their interest in picking up film rights to *Lolita* in September 1958. Shurlock informed them that the story as written would probably be denied the Seal on the grounds that the affair between the narrator, Humbert Humbert, and Lolita constituted sexual perversion. When Harris and Kubrick suggested having the two get married in a state with a low age of consent, Shurlock agreed that that might solve the problem.

Harris and Kubrick picked up the rights shortly afterwards for $150,000 against a percentage of the gross, but few in Hollywood believed that they could film the story. Cary Grant announced that he had turned down the leading role on moral grounds, though the producers claimed it never had been offered him. Former swashbuckler Errol Flynn lobbied to secure the leading roles for himself and his own teenage protégée, Beverly Aadland.

In March 1959, Shurlock met with Harris, Kubrick, and representatives of Warner Bros., which was considering backing the film. At this time, they came up with the idea of raising Lolita's age to fifteen to make the story more palatable. But Shurlock continued arguing against making the film altogether, warning them that "the novel itself seems to have aroused so much resentment and revulsion, in so many quarters on account of its depravity, we felt there was a danger that no matter how well the re-write was handled, a great deal of damage might be done to the industry and to the Code even before the picture was released."

As negotiations with Shurlock dragged on, Harris and Kubrick found it increasingly difficult to get studio backing without giving up creative control of the picture. But if they made the film on their own, the Code letter authorizing the script would become even more important. To help them deal with Shurlock they asked the British Board of Film Censors to review their first draft in 1960 and point out problem areas, but that group's secretary, John Trevelyan, was equally unhelpful. He suggested that the film would only work "if it had the mood of Greek tragedy, if it showed the tragedy of a man who through an obsession brought ruin and disaster to himself and to those around him, but it seems to us fantastic to play it for cheap laughs."

When they submitted the script to Shurlock, he rejected it. In desperation, they turned to Martin Quigley to help them shepherd the script through the Production Code process. Quigley did a solid job as intercessor and unofficial censor. When he sent the second draft to Shurlock in January 1961, Quigley advised him that the principal problem with the first script had been the descriptive notes written by Nabokov. In Quigley's opinion, they had "tended to create a most distasteful odor about the whole screenplay."

Whether it was Quigley's carefully planted suggestion or the revisions themselves, Shurlock accepted the second draft. By this point, excitement was building over

Nabokov's "hot" screenplay and the casting of James Mason as Humbert; Peter Sellers as his rival, Clare Quilty; and Shelley Winters as Lolita's mother. As a result, there was a lot more interest in backing the film. With Shurlock's favorable letter in hand, Harris and Kubrick easily secured financing from a consortium of Canadian bankers.

Of course, it would not have been a Production Code letter without some requests for changes. Shurlock wanted to cut an exchange in which Winters informs Sellers that her daughter is "having a cavity filled by your uncle," to which Sellers responds, "I know, he's a wicked old man." Harris argued that he'd shot the scene with Winters pointing to her teeth on the cavity line to make it clear they were talking about dentistry. He kept the scene, but it played just as suggestively, getting big laughs from most audiences.

Another exchange Shurlock tried to cut involved Winters and Mason. "You just touch me, and I go limp as a noodle," the former confesses. "Yes," says Mason, "I know the feeling." In a letter to Quigley dated January 30, 1961, Harris refused to make the deletion. He reminded Quigley that they already had changed Mason's response from "Yes, you do the same thing to me"—a change he thought would ensure that "the audience will not detect the dirty joke that may have been in the original conversation." Next to that part of the letter, somebody has scribbled the pertinent question "Then why use it?" But the exchange remained.

Shurlock's two principal problems with the script concerned Lolita's age and her seduction of Humbert. Nabokov's script contained no direct indications that Lolita was fifteen, but Harris argued that the nature of her high-school activities and the apparent age of her schoolmates made it clear that she was no longer a twelve-year-old. On the seduction scene, Shurlock advised that "the seduction must be done by suggestion, without any pointed dialogue, and certainly not on a bed." "It is difficult to imagine how in the hotel room there can be any other place for a seduction to take place except on the bed," Harris countered. "Wouldn't it be more offensive if we implied that such a thing happened on the floor or some other place?" When pushed to identify more offensive details about the seduction, Shurlock suggested that the most objectionable parts came towards the scene's end. Originally, Lolita was to taunt Humbert with hints about her relationship with a boy at summer camp. She then would whisper in his ear and lead him off to bed. Shurlock found the hints and the whispering offensive, but Harris cut only the former.

When the finished film was screened for the PCA, Shurlock requested only four cuts: the end of the seduction scene after Lolita whispers in Humbert's ear; the "limp noodle" exchange between Humbert and Charlotte; Charlotte's attempt to rent a room to

Humbert with the line "Where could you get more peace?"; and some grunting noises Humbert makes after he locks himself in the bathroom to escape Charlotte's amorous advances. After some discussion, Harris cut the first and last of these, receiving the Seal on August 31, 1961. With the Seal granted, *Lolita* became the object of a heated bidding war for distribution rights, which eventually went to MGM.

The PCA's approval may have helped the film with the Legion of Decency, which gave it a Separate Classification and asked only that the ads carry the recommendation "For persons over 18 only"[8] and an indication that the movie had been approved by the MPAA. The MPAA refused to go along with the latter, but the Legion passed the film nonetheless. Ironically, its rating meant that *Lolita*'s female lead, Sue Lyon, a fourteen-year-old actress-model Kubrick had spotted on television, could have been barred from seeing her own performance.

For all the cutting, *Lolita* remained a naughty delight, filled with double entendres and sexual situations. If anything, the raising of Lolita's age benefited the film, making Humbert less a child molester than a doomed romantic. It also emphasized the disparity between the sophisticated intellectual's idealization of youth and the object of his desires, a callous, sexually savvy teenager barely beyond the comic-book-and-bubble-gum stage. This impression was helped greatly by Lyon's natural, intelligent performance.

The critics were strongly divided over the film. Hollis Alpert praised the change in Lolita's age for saving it from "what might have been unpleasantness" and for making possible "the most accomplished piece of American filmmaking seen in some time. . . . For all the sometimes sly, sometimes savage humor, there is an understanding of Humbert's moral disease at its heart, and this makes it more moral, actually, than a good many of Hollywood's so-called 'clean' pictures."[9] Others thought the film had sacrificed the novel's pungency by raising Lolita's age. *Time* magazine led its unfavorable review with "Wind up the Lolita doll and it goes to Hollywood and commits nymphanticide."[10] But Harris's determination not to name Lolita's age paid off with at least one critic. In responding to claims that Sue Lyon had been made to look too old for the role, Pauline Kael wondered, "Have the reviewers looked at the schoolgirls of America lately? The classmates of my fourteen-year-old daughter are not merely nubile: some of them look badly used."[11]

The film's reputation was a great help at the box office: It grossed $4.5 million on a $2 million investment. Moreover, the tastefully risqué script Shurlock had passed provided solid evidence that the time had come to lift the Code's prohibition on films depicting sexual perversion.

Where tasteful naughtiness had made *Lolita* a box-office winner, the tasteless variety banished Billy Wilder's *Kiss Me, Stupid* to box-office purgatory. Many in the industry marveled that Wilder had gotten his sex farce past Shurlock with next to no changes. The plot, adapted from the Italian comedy *L'ora della fantasia*, dealt with Orville J. Spooner (Ray Walston), a small-town piano teacher who dreams of selling his songs to international star Dino (Dean Martin). When Dino is stranded in Orville's home town, Climax, Nevada, the songwriter hopes to use the opportunity to peddle his work, but fears that the notorious womanizer will seduce Mrs. Spooner (Felicia Farr). Orville picks a fight with his wife, who takes off for the local roadhouse. Then he hires part-time prostitute Polly the Pistol (Kim Novak) to impersonate his wife and succumb to Dino. Polly plays her part so well, however, that Orville can't tolerate Dino's advances towards her. He throws the singer out and takes Polly to bed, telling her, "Tonight, *you* are Mrs. Orville J. Spooner." Dino ends up at the roadhouse, where he spends the night with a drunken Mrs. Spooner in Polly's trailer. Weeks later, the Spooners hear Dino sing one of Orville's songs on national television. Orville wonders how Dino got hold of the song, but all Mrs. Spooner says is "Kiss me, stupid."

Wilder got all of this by Shurlock through one simple expedient: He didn't submit anything to the PCA until the film was finished. He had stopped submitting scripts to Shurlock in the mid-fifties, after the Production Code director had turned down his adaptation of *The Bad Seed*, the play and novel about an eight-year-old murderess. When the PCA approved producer-director Mervyn LeRoy's treatment of the material a few months later, Wilder swore never to let Shurlock look at another of his films until it was finished. As a result, he had gotten away with his treatment of cross-dressing, homosexuality, and seduction in *Some Like It Hot* (1959), illicit sex in *The Apartment* (1960), and prostitution in *Irma La Douce* (1963).

Of course, Shurlock still didn't have to pass *Kiss Me, Stupid*, but after the film was screened for the PCA, he startled his colleagues by saying he would. "If dogs want to return to their vomit," he said, "I'm not going to stop them."[12]

There was more to his decision than that, however. By the time *Kiss Me, Stupid* came along, Hollywood's new permissiveness was in full swing. Though Wilder's film treated its vulgarity with an in-your-face brashness few other directors would have attempted, it really was no worse than other pictures Shurlock had felt compelled to pass.

He would later admit that he was fed up with the situation. Studios invested millions in risqué films, then expected him to clean them up to pass the Legion of Decency and local censors. Compounding the problem was the fact that Eric Johnston had died a year earlier, and the MPAA's board had yet to name his successor. Without a strong leader at the helm, Shurlock could do little to either amend the Code or strengthen its enforcement. With *Kiss Me, Stupid* he had hoped to "precipitate a crisis"[13] and make the studio heads take decisive action.

The controversy over *Kiss Me, Stupid* more than lived up to Shurlock's expectations. Even with the Seal in hand, Wilder gave in to his backers, the Walter Mirisch Corporation, and reshot the trailer scene between Martin and Farr to make it less obvious that the two had made love. In the new version of the scene, Martin falls asleep while Farr is giving him a back rub. The next morning, Farr appears to be naked beneath the covers until she sits up, revealing that the top of her dress had simply slipped down to leave her shoulders bare.

But that wasn't enough for the Legion of Decency. They demanded more changes in the scenes between Novak and Martin. At one point Martin tries to get Novak into the backyard alone on the pretext of seeing her herb garden. The Legion objected to the line "She can show me her parsley." "What do they want?" Wilder asked. "Broccoli?"[14] Despite his sneering at the Legion's literalness, however, the real reason Wilder didn't reshoot the scene was the fact that Novak had left to make a film in England and was unavailable. With no way to change the film, Wilder accepted a Condemned rating, the first given to an American film since *Baby Doll*.

In announcing the rating, the Legion took a slap at the PCA's greater permissiveness of late: "It is difficult to understand how such approval is not the final betrayal of the trust which has been placed by so many in the organized industry's self-regulation."[15] As a result, United Artists decided to distribute the film through a subsidiary, Lopert Pictures, which previously had handled only imports, including the Legion-condemned *Never on Sunday*.

Some argued that *Kiss Me, Stupid* did not deserve such fervent condemnation and had only been singled out by the Legion in an effort to make an example. Members of the Catholic hierarchy had been appalled by the industry's record in 1964, when only 19 percent of films reviewed had been classified A-I, suitable for all audiences. The same year, sixteen films, or just over 5 percent, were condemned, a new high for the Legion.

The Legion's condemnation of *Kiss Me, Stupid* had mixed results. Coupled with bad reviews, it brought the film a quick fade at the box office. Even without a state censorship board, first-run theaters in Columbus, Ohio, refused to book the picture after a letter-writing campaign by local churchwomen. Other localities were considering new censorship or age-classification ordinances. Texas congressman Walter Rogers was even calling for a government investigation of what he considered immoral films.

But the furor quickly passed with precious little result. Even some of the critics who considered *Kiss Me, Stupid* an artistic misfire questioned the criticism directed at it. As

Bosley Crowther wrote, the film was "as moral as a preacher's Sunday sermon. It shows that the all-consuming greed of certain cheap little people for fame and money can lead to shame and unhappiness."[16] The critics were also quick to deride the Legion's other judgments, particularly the awarding of its A-I rating to such cinematic milestones as *Godzilla vs. the Thing* and *Gladiators 7*. By contrast, films condemned by the Legion in recent years had included such provocative and thoughtful European pictures as *L'avventura*, *Breathless*, and *Jules and Jim*.

The Code's growing liberality and the Legion's continued conservatism would come into conflict even more dramatically over *The Pawnbroker*. This time, however, there would be little dissension among the critics. The MPAA's accommodation to changing times and tastes won praise, while the Legion was soundly rebuked for condemning this moral, artistically ambitious film simply for two brief glimpses of women's breasts.

The Pawnbroker was hardly the first Hollywood film to try to get past the Code's and the Legion's opposition to nudity. As early as 1959, actress Linda Cristal had filmed a nude bed scene in the juvenile-crime drama *Cry Tough*. The scene could not be shown in America but, as would happen with more and more films in the sixties, remained in European prints. Elia Kazan had shot a brief nude scene with Natalie Wood for *Splendor in the Grass*. There was nothing titillating about the scene. Wood was discreetly shown taking a bath while arguing with her mother; as her anger rose, she jumped from the tub and ran to her room, with her buttocks revealed in a brief long shot. But again, the scene had to be cut before Shurlock would grant the Code Seal. Rear nudity was also attempted by Elizabeth Taylor in *Cleopatra* (1963), Kim Novak in *Of Human Bondage* (1964), and other actresses, but never made it to American screens.

Beyond the PCA's reach, however, nudity had become a major selling point in the exploitation market. In the fifties, films about primitive tribes, nudist colonies, and burlesque houses had challenged the censors, who often lost in the courts when judges decided that nudity in and of itself was not obscene.

Then cheesecake photographer Russ Meyer created a revolution. In 1959, he raised $24,000 and shot *The Immoral Mr. Teas*, a cheerfully loony tale of a man who can't seem to avoid large-breasted women in low-cut tops, then acquires the power to see them without their clothes. *The Immoral Mr. Teas* was a breakthrough for the genre. There are no paunchy men in masks, no tired hookers with glazed looks on their faces. All of the women are attractive and seem more than just young; they actually seem to be enjoying themselves. The film is well shot and even has a sense of humor. The nonstop narration apes the scientific ramblings of many a pseudodocumentary. When three nude sunbathers take off in a rowboat, the narrator extols the importance of naval travel.

When one of them gets into a swing made from an old automobile tire, the narrator relates the history of rubber.

The film performed impressively at the box office, returning a $1 million profit on its initial release. More important, however, it broke out of the grind houses to play in legitimate theaters, many of which found it so profitable that they converted to all-adult entertainment. The result was a new exploitation genre, the "nudie-cutie," and unparalleled growth for the exploitation film industry. Within three years, *The Immoral Mr. Teas* had inspired 150 imitations.

But that only made it more difficult to get nude scenes past the censors. The "nudie-cuties" ghettoized screen nudity, characterizing it in the public's mind as just so much cheap exploitation.

That was the kind of prejudice independent producer Ely Landau and director Sidney Lumet faced when they first presented Shurlock with their adaptation of Edward Lewis Wallant's novel *The Pawnbroker* in December 1964. The PCA director informed them that there were two scenes in the film that made it impossible for him to issue a Seal. The less objectionable of the two showed the pawnbroker's assistant (Jaime Sanchez) in bed with his girlfriend, a black prostitute played by Thelma Oliver. More difficult was a scene in which Oliver goes to the pawnbroker (Rod Steiger) to raise money so that Sanchez won't return to his former life of crime. At one point, the desperate woman bares her breasts, offering herself to Steiger in return for more money. This triggers his bitter memories of seeing his wife nude in a concentration-camp brothel.

Landau defended the scenes as integral parts of a serious, highly moral story, but Shurlock had to stand behind the Code. After the debacle of *Kiss Me, Stupid*, the presidents of the major film companies had demanded that he crack down on filmmakers. In addition, Shurlock felt there was a growing public outcry against screen permissiveness that could mushroom if he passed *The Pawnbroker*'s two nude scenes.

On March 23, 1965, the MPAA's Review Board met to consider Landau's appeal. After screening the film and debating its merits for three hours, the board exercised its power to grant a special exception from the terms of the Production Code on the condition that the nude scenes be shortened. They left it to Shurlock to decide if such cuts were sufficient.

There were several factors beyond *The Pawnbroker*'s obvious merits that may have influenced the board in this case. For one thing, with changes in Hollywood production practice since the forties, many directors had become independent producers in their own rights, and these could now be represented on the Review Board. In fact, Joseph L. Mankiewicz had argued eloquently in the film's defense during the board's lengthy discussions. In addition, Landau had already stated that he would release *The Pawnbroker* without a Seal if necessary. His distributor, Allied Artists, had even revived its art-film subsidiary, Stratford Pictures, just in case the Seal was denied. Finally, Shurlock's own record as PCA director made the Board's decision almost unavoidable. As Landau was quick to point out in interviews, how could they refuse the Seal to a serious artistic effort like *The Pawnbroker* while granting it to such self-consciously tawdry pictures as *The Carpetbaggers* and *Kiss Me, Stupid*?

The board may have hoped to forestall criticism of its decision by leaving the final judgment in Shurlock's lap, but he wasn't about to play hero or villain in this case. He suggested that Landau simply cut Oliver's nude scene with Steiger after the actress started walking. Landau wasn't willing to cut that much but agreed to scissor a few frames, which was enough to make Shurlock happy.

But it didn't appease the Legion of Decency. The group delayed handing down its decision until after the film had opened, indicating strong division among their reviewers. Some of them had suggested waiting until the first ads were placed to see if Landau would try to exploit the controversy. But the ads were simply and tastefully done, and the Legion finally had to make its decision. They announced their condemnation in May, issuing one of the mildest statements ever made about a condemned film: "An acceptable classification is denied this film for the sole reason that nudity has been used in its treatment. Although nudity is not in itself obscenity and it might even have an artistic function in a film of quality, it is never a necessary or indispensable means to achieve dramatic effect. The present film is no exception because the director could have accomplished his artistic objectives by the less literal and more demanding method of indirection."[17]

The Legion's ambivalance is understandable. Like many of the forbidden details in sixties films, the nude scenes in *The Pawnbroker* raise an interesting paradox. The film as a whole is so strong that it could easily survive without them, yet they add to the emotional context, particularly the shots of Steiger's wife in the concentration camp, in a way that separates the powerful from the nearly unbearable.

In condemning *The Pawnbroker* on the basis of nudity, the Legion left itself more vulnerable to criticism than ever before. Episcopal bishop James A. Pike, who had blasted the church's stand on *Baby Doll* a decade earlier, hailed *The Pawnbroker* as "one of the truly significant religious (because it deals with ultimate matters) films of our time." He even singled out the nude scenes for praise, saying, "I find this motion picture important, not despite its realism, but because of it."[18] Other critics were quick to point out excesses in other films passed by the Legion.

As another sign of the Legion's weakening power, *The Pawnbroker* was the first condemned film to play in a major theater in heavily Catholic Albany, New York, since *Baby Doll*, and did so with notably little church protest. After taking in $3 million at the box office during its initial release, the film changed distributors when American International Pictures (AIP) bought out portions of Allied Artists. AIP used frame blow-ups to eliminate the nude scenes, which had amounted to only two feet of film, and resubmitted the picture. It was re-classified A-III, adults only, marking the first time a Legion rating had been changed after a film's initial run.

In many ways *The Pawnbroker* was the Legion's last stand. The criticism heaped upon their decision to condemn the film helped inspire a gradual liberalization of the organization's ratings. By 1965, the International Federation of Catholic Alumnae were no longer solely responsible for screening films. They had been joined by a diverse group of priests, teachers, businessmen, and even students, who would give their judgments a more liberal slant. To reflect that alteration, in 1966 the group's name was changed to the National Catholic Office of Motion Pictures (NCOMP). That acronym would be thrown back at them several times in the coming years.

The Man from Texas

Times were changing for the MPAA, too. Eric Johnston's death in 1963 had left the organization adrift for two years, forestalling any Code revisions or the increasingly heated urgings that the PCA adopt a system of age classification. Johnston's executive secretary, Ralph Hetzel, kept the organization going as interim president, and many thought he would have made a solid replacement, but there was little he could do without the board's backing. The board's members, most of them studio presidents, wanted somebody from outside the organization with solid government and international connections. They considered some of the late President Kennedy's advisors, then started pursuing lawyer Louis Nizer. The courtship of Nizer went on for so long that *Variety* even announced his imminent appointment. Then, Lew Wasserman, president of Universal-International, decided the matter required more thought.

A prominent member of the Democratic Party, Wasserman looked over President Lyndon Johnson's staff for a possible successor and found one in forty-five-year-old businessman Jack Valenti. Valenti had been heading an advertising and public relations firm in Houston when called upon to serve as special advisor to President Johnson. He was almost notorious for his hard work and dedication and, in addition, had strong relationships with the governments of the United States and other countries. Along with all that, he possessed an air of sophistication and a polished presence as a speaker that would make him an ideal figurehead for the organization.

Valenti hesitated at first, not wanting to desert his President. It also was rumored that Johnson did not want to lose one of his most valued aides. But Wasserman was very persuasive, as was the offer of a salary estimated at more than $170,000 a year, plus perks. In May 1966, Valenti was named president of the MPAA (with Nizer appointed as special counsel) and went to Hollywood to make his presence known.

Some of the PCA's old guard were not thrilled with the appointment. The liberal Valenti was a marked change from the more conservative Johnston. In addition, where Johnston had stayed away from Hollywood as much as possible, leaving Shurlock and his staff pretty much alone, Valenti had no problem dealing directly with filmmakers. Moreover, he made it clear from the beginning that he was there to make changes. In his first speech in Hollywood, he pronounced, "I did not take the job of president of the Motion Picture Association in order to preside over a feckless Code!"[19]

Rumors at the time suggested that Valenti was there to accomplish one of two things. Some thought he would spearhead a revision of the Production Code to bring it more in line with contemporary mores. Others thought he would finally usher in a conversion to age classification.

By 1966, morals in the U.S. had loosened to the extent that couples were beginning to live together openly without benefit of marriage, teen pregnancy was on the rise, and the younger generation was not only experimenting with such drugs as marijuana and LSD, but flaunting it. Racial minorities were fighting for equal rights and greater public visibility, while homosexuals were just beginning their move into the public eye. Moreover, the arts were exercising greater freedom than ever before, with nudity working its way into theatrical productions and such experimental forms as the happening. With the Production Code firmly in place, however, much of this was kept off the nation's movie screens. Even some television dramas were proving more liberal in their choice of subject matter than Hollywood's movies.

The obvious path for Hollywood to take would have been the scrapping of the Production Code altogether in favor of a system of age classification similar to those used in other countries. In fact, the first arguments for age classification in the U.S. date back as far as the thirties. In the fifties, the rise of the art-house theaters, many with strict adults-only admission policies, made age classification seem more attractive. Moreover, such imported hits as *Never on Sunday* and *Room at the Top* made impressive profits despite their limitation to art houses and adult audiences. Each film had cost in the neighborhood of $300,000, but had grossed $3 million in the U.S. alone. Why couldn't Hollywood do just as well with the limited release of low-budget adult films? some wondered.

Even the Catholic Church was lobbying for some kind of ratings system. The Legion of Decency already had started classifying films according to their suitability for viewing by children, adolescents, and adults. Monsignor Little was hinting that they might liberalize their classifications if Hollywood adopted a voluntary ratings system.

For the time, however, most studios did not want to take a chance on age classification. Since the arrival of television in the fifties, teenagers had become an important part of the movie audience. Not only had their patronage contributed to the rise in drive-in screens, but there were even some film studios devoted almost entirely to films with teen appeal. Many studio heads feared that a system of age classification would deprive them of this increasingly important audience.

So, for the time being, Valenti was simply charged with enforcing the Code and, if necessary, revising it. He would meet his first great challenge within a month of his appointment, when Warner Bros. invited moviegoers around the nation "to George and Martha's for an Evening of Fun and Games."

Who's Afraid of Virginia Woolf? had been one of the most eagerly anticipated Broadway plays in years. Its author, Edward Albee, had shown tremendous promise with a series of one-act plays (including *The Zoo Story* and *The American Dream*) produced off-Broadway. Making his Broadway debut with his first full-length play, he was the great hope for an American playwright to take the place of the late Eugene O'Neill and such fifties giants as Tennessee Williams, Arthur Miller, and William Inge, who had fallen out of favor with more recent works.

The play seriously divided the theater community. While some hailed it as the greatest American drama in a decade, others were appalled at its vulgar language. The tale of two university professors and their wives tearing away at one another during an all-night drinking party was so shocking the Pulitzer Prize board denied it the drama award, even though the drama committee had voted overwhelmingly in Albee's favor.

Who's Afraid of Virginia Woolf? was the hit of the 1962–63 dramatic season. Even with no certainty that an adaptation could win the Production Code Seal, Jack Warner snapped up the rights for half a million dollars.

When Warner first approached Shurlock about the play in March 1963, Shurlock informed him that the play's "profanity and very blunt sexual dialogue" would make PCA approval impossible. In a five-page letter, Shurlock detailed every unacceptable line and phrase, including nineteen variations on "Jesus Christ," seventeen "goddamn"s, ten "sons of a bitch"s, eight "bastard"s and "bugger"s, and seven references to a power game called "Hump the Hostess."

First-time film director Mike Nichols and screenwriter Ernest Lehman tried to substitute euphemisms for some of Albee's riper terminology but thought the results ludicrous. According to Nichols: "Disguising profanity with clean but suggestive phrases is really dirtier. . . . People do certain things in bed that we all know they do, and people say certain things to each other that we all have heard. The whole point of the sexual revolution that's happening today is to let those things take their place and then go back into proportion. We feel the language in *Woolf* is essential to the fabric; it reveals who the people are and how they lived."[20] Instead, they simply softened the language, reducing the frequency of certain profanities and changing some of the "Jesus Christ"s to "Oh, my God"s.

The new script, submitted in October 1965, was still impossible under the Code, but Shurlock issued a Seal provisionally so the studio could prepare a title card. When the film was submitted in May 1966, however, Shurlock was compelled to reject it, "due to the presence of a good deal of profanity, blunt sexual references, and coarse and sometimes vulgar language."

Valenti was in a very difficult position with *Who's Afraid of Virginia Woolf?* According to Jack Vizzard, he was personally shocked by the film and initially contemplated taking a firm stand on it. But he gradually came to appreciate both the picture's quality and its relationship to other films that had been passed by the PCA. He stood behind Shurlock's refusal to grant the Seal, but also made it clear that the final judgment would be made by the Review Board.

Warner Bros. was in a very delicate position as well. The studio did not own a subsidiary distribution organization, nor was Jack Warner interested in pulling out of the MPAA to release the film without a Seal. They had already announced that the picture would premiere with a charity benefit in New York on June 23. If the Board backed Shurlock, Warner would, in all likelihood, cut the picture hastily to protect the studio's $7.5 million investment.

When the Review Board met to discuss *Who's Afraid of Virginia Woolf?* in June, there were two factors working in Warner Bros.' favor. First, they had decided to limit attendance to people eighteen and over (unless accompanied by an adult) and write that limit into all exhibition contracts. Second, the NCOMP was leaning toward passing the film, partly because of the studio's decision to restrict attendance. The Catholic organization had screened *Who's Afraid of Virginia Woolf?* for all eighty-one of its reviewers, a rare occurrence. The majority of these had judged the film's language and sexuality in context. "There is something being said here which is quite valid and, in its own terms, very moral," said one reviewer. "I can see little moral harm that will come from the use of vulgar language," said another. "Shock and disgust are not moral evils in themselves."[21]

The reviewers voted the film a Separate Classification, or A-IV rating, "morally unobjectionable for adults, with reservations." Those who wanted to condemn the picture came in a distant second. Even the normally conservative Monsignor Little backed their decision: "I've never heard those words on a screen before, but I've heard them at Coney Island. It is all right to use erotic elements when everything jells in artistic integrity."[22]

The NCOMP would not make an official pronouncement on the film until August. Meanwhile, the MPAA's Review Board decided to grant its second Special Exemption in two years. Warner was asked to make two cuts: the word "frigging" was deleted from one line, and star Elizabeth Taylor's "Screw you," shouted as husband Richard Burton opens the door on their guests, was redubbed "Damn you." All other vulgarity was approved. The board explained its decision in a press release dated June 10, 1966:

1. The film is not designed to be prurient. This film document, dealing with a tragic realism of life, is largely a reproduction of the Edward Albee play which won the New York Drama Critics Award in 1963 and has played throughout the country.

2. Warner Bros. has taken the position that no person under 18 will be admitted unless accompanied by a parent.

3. This Exemption means exactly that—approval of material in a specific, important film which would not be approved for a film of lesser quality, or a film determined to exploit language for language's sake. This Exemption means precisely the opposite. We desire to allow excellence to be displayed, and we insist that films, under whatever guise, which go beyond rational measures of community standards will not bear a Seal of Approval.

Both the MPAA and the NCOMP met with strong criticism for passing *Who's Afraid of Virginia Woolf?* In a *Motion Picture Herald* editorial, Martin Quigley, Jr., who had inherited the trade paper from his father, pronounced the Production Code dead at the hands of the MPAA's directors, producers who wanted to be daring, and audience members who accepted "'adult' ('dirty') material in imported films and in domestic publications in constantly increasing scope and depth."[23] In La Jolla, California, a group of outraged Catholics petitioned the church hierarchy to get rid of the "N.C.O.M. Petants."[24]

But there were even more critics who praised the film and its approval by the nation's two chief censorship bodies. Moreover, several industry commentators were quick to point out that Warners' imposition of an age restriction on the film, with full approval of the MPAA, had ushered in a classification system. When the studio reported its success in enforcing the film's age limit, not to mention the picture's impressive box-office performance, the transition from film cutting to film rating seemed inevitable.

Scarcely had the dust settled from the *Virginia Woolf* battles than the Review Board issued another Special Exemption, this time for Paramount's British import *Alfie* (1966). The film starred Michael Caine as an unrestrained womanizer. During a brief hospital stay, he befriends a married man, then seduces his lonely wife (Vivien Merchant). When the woman becomes pregnant, Alfie arranges an illegal abortion. The sight of the aborted fetus causes him to reevaluate his life and try to find a more lasting relationship. As moral as the story's ultimate effect was, however, Shurlock could not approve the film because of the abortion scene. Nor would the plot have made any sense without it. Shurlock advised Paramount to file an appeal.

The Review Board met on August 2, 1966, with even more producer-directors in attendance than when they had reviewed *The Pawnbroker*. In addition to Joseph L. Mankiewicz, the board now included Alan J. Pakula and *Pawnbroker* director Sidney Lumet. Again they issued an exception, on condition that the film be advertised with the line "Suggested for Mature Audiences."

Despite the Legion of Decency's longstanding tradition of banning anything that smacked of abortion, NCOMP passed *Alfie* with an A-IV rating, issuing a very positive review of the film: "In spite of light treatment of immoral situations develops theme that individual must accept responsibility of his actions." This was a very telling decision by the NCOMP. In the eyes of many, it indicated that the Catholic reviewers might be willing to accept changes in even the Production Code's most basic restrictions.

The NCOMP's surprising decision on *Alfie*, coupled with the Review Board's issuance of two Special Exceptions within six weeks, made it clear that a major revision of the Production Code was in order. On September 20, 1966, the board of directors announced the adoption of a new Code, a short document replacing most of the old prohibitions with loosely worded admonitions open to highly subjective application:

> The basic dignity and value of human life shall be respected and upheld. Restraint shall be exercised in portraying the taking of life.
>
> Evil, sin, crime and wrong-doing shall not be justified.
>
> Special restraint shall be exercised in portraying criminal or anti-social activities in which minors participate or are involved.
>
> Detailed and protracted acts of brutality, cruelty, physical violence, torture and abuse, shall not be presented.
>
> Indecent or undue exposure of the human body shall not be presented.
>
> Illicit sex relationships shall not be justified. Intimate sex scenes violating common standards of decency shall not be portrayed. Restraint and care shall be exercised

in presentations dealing with sex aberrations.

Obscene speech, gestures or movements shall not be presented. Undue profanity shall not be presented.

Religion shall not be demeaned.

Words or symbols comtemptuous of racial, religious or national groups, shall not be used so as to incite bigotry or hatred.

Excessive cruelty to animals shall not be portrayed, and animals shall not be treated inhumanely.[25]

Questionable materials were to be judged not in and of themselves but in relation to their importance to the film's plot. The PCA also could pass borderline films by adding the "Suggested for Mature Audiences," tag, though Valenti urged them to exercise restraint in that area.

The revised Code won praise for its accommodation to changing times, but some at the PCA doubted that it could do much to stem the tide of screen permissiveness. Within a few months, they would be proven right as the Code met and failed its first great challenge, Michelangelo Antonioni's *Blow-Up*.

Impressed with the success of foreign films with U.S. audiences, many American studios turned to Europe's top directors in the hopes of making quality pictures that could break out of the art-house circuit. It didn't always work. Critics thought François Truffaut's *Fahrenheit 451*, partially backed by Universal, was his worst film, while René Clément's *Joy House*, made for MGM, was an even bigger flop. But when MGM signed the master of Eurotrash ennui, Michelangelo Antonioni, they got one of the most important films of the decade, *Blow-Up*.

Like the protagonists of other Antonioni films, the photographer (David Hemmings) in *Blow-Up* is emotionally dessicated. He moves through a world of sensual excess, underlined by Carlo di Palma's exquisite color photography, that has left him incapable of feeling. While examining some candid shots he took in a park, he discovers what might be a murder. Suddenly, he finds some sense of purpose, as he enlarges the image again and again to reveal a shadowy gunman lurking in the bushes. Then the film and all the prints are stolen. Shaken, he joins a group of students miming a tennis game, no longer sure where reality leaves off and illusion begins.

When the film previewed in Hollywood, many of those in attendance were outraged, partially by its sexual excesses, but primarily by Antonioni's almost deliberate obscurity. MGM had little hope for the picture, planning to release it to art houses and theaters in college towns.

But they hadn't reckoned with the power of Antonioni's artistic vision and the controversy the film would raise. The first treatment for *Blow-Up* was submitted to Shurlock under the old Production Code in March 1966. At the time, Shurlock cautioned MGM's PCA liaison, Robert Vogel, about the script's indications of nudity. He also questioned two scenes. At one point, the photographer takes time off from his investigation for a sexual romp with a pair of teenage girls trying to break into modeling. In another scene, he visits a female friend to find her making love to her husband. The woman seems uninvolved until she glimpses the photographer watching, which arouses her passion. Both scenes would be in violation of the Code, and Shurlock thought the latter could also be judged pornographic.

In early November, MGM asked Shurlock and Vizzard to travel to New York, at the studio's expense, to screen the picture. At the same time, executives inquired about other studios that had released foreign films without the Production Code Seal. Already, MGM's leadership feared that the film would not pass the Code. Nor could they make any changes without the director's permission. Antonioni's contract guaranteed him full control and stipulated that the film could only be cut for government censors.

Dueling Freedoms: The Strange Case of *Titticut Follies*

In the early sixties, U.S. filmmakers turned to a new type of documentary as a vehicle for examining and indirectly commenting on society. Inspired by the work of French documentarians, they embraced cinéma verité, in which the camera simply records events as they happen. Narration was dropped in favor of creative editing that often went beyond mere words to comment on the action. With their often liberal take on society and its institutions, America's documentary filmmakers were on a collision course with censorship. The crash finally occurred when law professor Frederick Wiseman made his first film in 1967.

Wiseman had been interested in the power of film as a social document since his days in law school. After seeing Shirley Clarke's *The Connection* (1961), he offered to produce her next film, *The Cool Ones* (1963), a look at youth in Harlem. Merely producing wasn't enough for Wiseman, however. In 1967, he took a camera and spent twenty-nine days filming treatment methods at the Bridgewater (Massachusetts) State Hospital for the Criminally Insane. The resultant documentary, *Titticut Follies*, was strong medicine by any measure.

The film is framed by a musical show in which inmates and staff members entertain each other. In between routines, Wiseman presents a candid picture of life at Bridgewater. A sex offender is questioned by a staff member, who passes stern negative judgments on the young man's frequent masturbation. One inmate complains that his mental condition is actually deteriorating because of the primitive facilities and poor treatment. Others are stripped in demeaning "skin searches." In

Shurlock and Vizzard screened the film with Antonioni, though only a black-and-white "mud print" was available. Even in black-and-white, however, the film cast a powerful sensual spell. The two scenes Shurlock had objected to were, if anything, worse on screen. He and Vizzard even thought they had glimpsed some pubic hair during the sequence involving the two teenagers.

They tried to explain their objections to Antonioni, but he argued that both scenes were essential to the film. The scene with the teenagers was not sexual in his opinion but rather "a frolic, like young goats, like young animals." The lovemaking scene was designed to show "the girl's inability to be moved, even in the middle of sex. She is saturated with life, so she can't enjoy it. She is using the sight of the photographer to bring herself to climax. But he is so bored that he is unmoved. He ignores her. It is very important."[26]

Essential or not, Shurlock and Vizzard felt both scenes went so far beyond the boundaries of good taste that they could not be approved. Eventually, MGM snuck a few cuts into the latter sequence without telling Antonioni, primarily because of

the most telling sequence, shots of an inmate being force-fed are intercut with footage in which he is embalmed and buried.

When Wiseman tried to release his film, the public's right to know came into direct conflict with the privacy of the patients he had filmed. In a suit brought on the inmates' behalf, the film was banned outright and damned as "a nightmare of ghoulish obscenities."[27] An appeals court softened the ban to allow the picture to be shown to professionals, students, and organizations dealing with mental illness and its treatment, but it was still barred from public exhibition.

Wiseman, however, felt that there was another motivation for the ban. When officials at Bridgewater had filed suit two years earlier, they had charged that the film defamed them and invaded their privacy. In Wiseman's opinion, the Massachusetts ban was really aimed at protecting the staff, not the inmates. Although the federal district court in New York had denied the earlier suit, the Massachusetts ban would hold.

As Wiseman established himself as one of America's leading documentarians with acclaimed films like *High School* (1969), *Law and Order* (1970), and *Hospital* (1971), he continued to fight for *Titticut Follies*. In 1991, after twenty-five years, he won the right to distribute the film. It made its television debut on PBS two years later. Even with the ban, however, *Titticut Follies* inspired reforms at Bridgewater, proving that sometimes a film doesn't have to be seen to make its presence known. ✂

Shurlock's warnings that the scene could be labeled pornographic. Shurlock offered to grant the Seal to that revised version, but MGM backed out at the last minute, possibly for fear of attracting Antonioni's attention to the cuts.

Instead, MGM released the film through a subsidiary, Premier Films, marking the first time it had used this ploy to put out a film not passed by the PCA. The NCOMP added to the fire by condemning the film and MGM's release of it. In the opinion of NCOMP secretary Father Patrick Sullivan, the subsidiary arrangement was nothing but a "legal fiction"[28] that would lead to more violations of the Code.

The dual condemnation almost immediately created a backlash. Not only was the film hailed as a highly moral work by many critics, but more liberal members of the clergy also took it up. The Reverend William E. Wimer, director of the United Church of Christ's Audio-Visual Office, requested a screening for the United Church Assembly. A Presbyterian minister in Brooklyn even held Sunday service at a neighborhood theater so he could present the film in lieu of his sermon.

Along with the controversy it generated, *Blow-Up* demonstrated clearly that the economic power of the PCA and the NCOMP had been greatly diminished. Where MGM had expected only a limited payoff for the film, it became one of the year's box-office winners, making almost $7 million in six months on an initial cost of $1.6 million.

In *Blow-Up*'s wake, the PCA made a series of concessions that stretched the limits of the revised Code. *Torn Curtain* (1966), *Hurry Sundown* (1967), and *Bonnie and Clyde* (1967) all got away with intimations of oral sex, while nudity was approved in *Bedazzled* (1967) and *Barbarella* (1968). The Suggested for Mature Audiences tag became more and more commonplace, eventually being applied to 60 percent of all releases. When Shurlock stood firm against oral sex scenes in *Charlie Bubbles* (1968) and *I'll Never Forget What's-His-Name* (1968), the films' distributor, Universal, simply released them through a subsidiary without the Seal of Approval. Warner Bros. did the same with *The Fox* (1968), a D. H. Lawrence adaptation featuring both masturbation and a lesbian love scene. The film grossed $25 million on a $1 million investment.

Moreover, as restrictions on sexuality loosened, negative attitudes toward violence were growing. As a result, the PCA drew flak in the press for approving a series of violent movies, some of them not even bearing the Suggested for Mature Audiences tag. The cycle of brutal westerns from Italy, particularly those directed by Sergio Leone and starring Clint Eastwood, inspired protests. Two domestic releases in 1967—*Bonnie and Clyde* and *The Dirty Dozen*—also got the PCA in trouble.

To be fair, Shurlock had not seen a script for *Bonnie and Clyde* until the film was almost ready to begin shooting. Along with complaints about the picture's sexual elements, particularly the implication of nudity in the opening scene, he had tried to soften two scenes of brutality, including the famous scene in which a bank teller is shot in the face when he jumps on the running board of the Barrow Gang's getaway car.

On *The Dirty Dozen*, however, Shurlock and the PCA continued to demonstrate their preoccupation with sex. The story of twelve convicted criminals released from an army stockade to undertake a mission behind enemy lines during World War II first crossed Shurlock's desk in 1964. Overlooking the potential for violence in the story, he simply complained about too much profanity. He would succeed in toning down that and some ethnic slurs, as well as eliminating sex scenes involving Lee Marvin's character and a woman named Tessie.

When the film was released, it ignited a fierce critical controversy over violence on screen. While the picture's champions hailed it as a stirring antiwar indictment, others wondered if the message wasn't drowned out by the "rat-a-tat of small arms fire."[29] The *New York Times*'s Bosley Crowther predicted that movies like *The Dirty Dozen* would "deaden [the public's] sensitivities and make slaughter seem a meaningless cliché."[30] One critic even suggested that the film had helped spark the Detroit race riots. After the assassinations of Robert Kennedy and Martin Luther King, Jr. in 1968, the outcry against violent entertainment would grow even stronger.

Valenti made one final appeal to the studio heads, but by this point the nature of the business had changed almost entirely. Gone were the old-time movie moguls who had built the industry and felt at least a measure of responsibility for what they released. In their place were business conglomerates, which had begun taking over the studios in the mid-sixties. When a film like *Blow-Up* or *The Graduate* became a surprise hit, they looked not at the picture's artistic quality but at its subject matter, and set out to produce still more sexually explicit youth-oriented films.

After two and a half years of fighting to protect the Production Code, Valenti finally admitted that its day had passed. That meant either a complete end to Hollywood's self-regulation, which would have been a public relations disaster, or a transition to film classification. By including the Suggested for Mature Audiences tag in the revised Code, Valenti had paved the way for film ratings. Two court decisions in the mid-sixties would help him win over Hollywood's last holdouts.

"Yes, Little Friend, Freedom Is Hard to Take"

Chapter Nine

T he last official barriers against freedom of the screen fell in 1968, when Jack Valenti dismantled the Production Code and replaced it with the ratings system. Suddenly, filmmakers could put anything they wanted on screen—if they could get it by pressure groups and local prosecutors and were willing to accept certain age restrictions on their potential audience. In truth, with the fall of the Production Code, the seeds were sown from which new barriers would grow. Like the heroine of 1968's *I Am Curious (Yellow)*, who pays for her commitment to free love with shattered relationships and a case of scabies, filmmakers would soon learn that freedom can often be hard to take.

Valenti's arguments in favor of a ratings system were bolstered by two Supreme Court decisions in 1968. In *Ginsberg* v. *New York*, the Court upheld the conviction of a shop owner who had sold a soft-core magazine to a sixteen-year-old. Arguing that a "child—like someone in a captive audience—is not possessed of that full capacity for individual choice which is the presupposition of First Amendment guarantees,"[1] the Court established the doctrine of "variable obscenity." What was legal for distribution to adults could be considered obscene in the hands of children. State legislatures, frustrated at legal bars on their ability to prosecute adult materials, rushed to put *Ginsberg* on the books with a series of laws protecting young people from pornography. Nor could Hollywood ignore the decision. With increasing on-screen permissiveness, it might not be long before one of the major studios was prosecuted on similar charges.

Censored Hollywood

The screen's new freedom was almost as restrictive as Lena Nyman's approach to human relations in this dream sequence from I Am Curious (Yellow) *(1968), one of the most notorious and profitable sexual dramas released after the birth of the ratings system.*

The same month as the *Ginsberg* decision, the Court handed down another important ruling, *Interstate Circuit* v. *Dallas*. In response to changes in screen morality, the Dallas City Council had set up a ratings board to dictate what could be shown to those under sixteen. The Dallas Film Board met its first challenge when its members decided that Louis Malle's *Viva Maria* (1965), a rollicking tale of traveling theatrical performers drawn into a Latin American revolution, was too sexual and politically volatile for young audiences. Although the Supreme Court overturned Dallas's law, calling its criteria for barring younger audiences unconstitutionally vague, it also affirmed the basic constitutionality of such ordinances. Dallas rewrote its age-classification law; other localities considered similar measures, and Valenti set out to beat them to it.

Arguing that the industry had better act quickly to institute a ratings system before the government did it for them, he got the MPAA's members to agree to a change. The Supreme Court decisions had been announced in March 1968. Between June and September, Valenti worked with the nine member companies, the National Association of Theatre Owners (NATO) and the International Film Importers and Distributors of America (IFIDA). On October 7, 1968, he announced the industry's new ratings system, which would go into effect on November 1. Valenti had moved so quickly that not a single locality had a chance to pass its own age-classification law.

Like the Production Code that had preceded it, the brochure explaining the ratings system opened with a general statement of principle:

> This Code is designed to keep in close harmony with the mores, culture, the moral sense and change in our society.
>
> The objectives of the Code are:
> 1. To encourage artistic expression by expanding creative freedom.
> 2. To assure that the freedom which encourages the artist remains responsible and sensitive to the standards of the larger society.[2]

This was followed by a description of the MPAA's new voluntary ratings system:

(G) SUGGESTED FOR GENERAL AUDIENCES

(M) SUGGESTED FOR MATURE AUDIENCES—ADULTS & MATURE YOUNG PEOPLE

(R) RESTRICTED—PERSONS UNDER 16 NOT ADMITTED UNLESS ACCOMPANIED BY PARENT OR ADULT GUARDIAN

(X) PERSONS UNDER 16 NOT ADMITTED

Initially, Valenti had not wanted to go beyond the R rating, arguing that the system's primary goal was, as he told this writer, "to offer some advanced cautionary warnings to parents, so that they could make their own judgments about what movies their children should and should not see." The NATO members, however, insisted on some legal protection from local prosecutors, so the more restrictive rating was added. The studios went along with them, hoping that the X rating would distinguish their films from less respectable independent productions playing in adults-only houses.

But Valenti and the MPAA made one error that would bring more criticism on the ratings system than anything else. Whereas they copyrighted the three other ratings, they did not do so with the X. As the system was initially planned, any filmmaker who felt there was no point in submitting his or her picture for classification, or who wanted to generate a little extra controversy, could self-impose the X rating. This would create a major problem with the rating's public perception for years to come.

First Valenti had to organize a system for screening and classifying films. The Production Code Administration was transformed into the Code and Ratings Administration (CARA). Staff members would review scripts and advise on probable ratings. When a film was screened, they would make copious notes on objectionable materials and vote on a rating. A producer unhappy with his or her rating could appeal to the Review Board, request an additional screening, or cut the film and resubmit it. On resubmissions, the staff would either watch the entire film again or screen just those segments to which they had objected previously.

Response to the new system was mixed. Some critics complained that it went too far, allowing anything on screen. Others said it didn't go far enough. CARA's judgments were still based on the 1966 version of the Production Code, which was incorporated within the new system under the heading "Standards for Production." In addition, the old Production Code Seal was awarded to all films rated R or below.

Yet the ratings clearly served their purpose, driving the other national classification system, the NCOMP, out of business by 1980. In addition, no local classification or censorship ordinances were passed after the MPAA introduced the ratings, and the few remaining local boards gradually faded away. The last state board, Maryland's, was disbanded in 1981.

Some localities passed legislation based on the ratings sytem. The sheriff of Rutherford County, North Carolina, tried to limit area theaters to G-rated films, but lost in the courts when he arrested an exhibitor for showing the Clint Eastwood-Richard Burton adventure *Where Eagles Dare* in 1970. Kenosha, Wisconsin, passed an ordinance barring anyone under eighteen from attending R-rated films, but it failed to hold up in the courts when some parents sued for the right to take their children to the 1970 rock documentary *Woodstock*.

Despite these legal triumphs, however, the adoption of the ratings system was far from smooth. There were procedural problems almost from the start. Reviewing scripts had been practical when the Production Code was introduced in 1930. Through the sixties, however, unstable studio managements and the emergence of the director as auteur had made the practice less effective. There were simply too many factors that could change a film's focus between script approval and the final edit. Frequently, films that seemed perfectly suitable for family audiences on the page became significantly more adult on screen, leading to heated criticism from producers who felt they had been misled.

The screening and rescreening process also proved troublesome. Rarely does the CARA staff indicate more than the fact that a specific scene raises problems. Film-

All the President's Censors

With the rising availability of pornographic films, books, and magazines in the sixties, President Lyndon B. Johnson launched the President's Commission on Pornography, a twenty-million-dollar study of the issue, in 1967. To head the committee, Johnson chose William Lockhart, one of the nation's leading authorities on obscenity law. During their first meeting, at the Kinsey Institute in 1968, commissioners viewed classic stag films and more recent adult movies.

The commission's two-year study became a little more complicated when Richard Nixon was elected President. To replace a commissioner who had resigned, he chose Charles H. Keating, Jr., founder of Citizens for Decent Literature. Keating set the tone for his participation by boycotting all public meetings of the commission, charging that the sessions simply gave pornography free publicity.

In 1970, the commission released its findings. They recommended the repeal of all state and local obscenity laws on the grounds that there was no evidence to support the theory that pornography led to "social or individual harms, such as crime, delinquency, sexual or nonsexual deviancy, or severe emotional disturbances."[3] In their opinion, the only feasible antiporn legislation would bar the distribution of such materials to minors or to adults who did not wish to see them. The commission also presented the results of a national survey indicating that 60 percent of all adults shared their views.

Neither Keating, Nixon, nor the U.S. Senate were among that 60 percent, however. Joining with conservative commissioners Father Morton Hill, head of Morality in Media, and Tennessee minister Winfrey Link, Keating issued a vehement minority report, labeling the commission's work "a Magna Carta for the pornographer"[4] and charging Lockhart with bias because he was a member of the American Civil Liberties Union. President Nixon condemned the report before he even

makers often have to to reedit their work several times to get the right combination of cuts with which to achieve the desired rating. Industry observers have complained that the repeated rescreenings sometimes do little to change the film, but wear down the reviewers until they give in. AIP cut and rescreened *Count Yorga, Vampire* (1970) five times to avoid an R rating. Even though many staff members still had problems with the picture, they voted for the less restrictive rating simply because of the studio's five expensive reediting jobs.

These problems were compounded by instability at the top during the early years. Geoffrey Shurlock had retired with the institution of the ratings system, though he would stay on as an advisor for several years. His logical successor, Jack Vizzard, was

read it, stating that "American morality is not to be trifled with."[5] The Senate voted 60–5 to reject the commission's findings. Supreme Court Chief Justice Warren Burger would even cite Keating's minority report in decisions upholding obscenity laws.

After Ronald Reagan's re-election in 1984, he set up another government commission to investigate the issue under Attorney General Edwin Meese. Its findings, often referred to as the Meese Report, were issued in 1986. This time, the federal commission ruled that there was indeed a link between pornography and crime, both in the organization of the porn industry and in the psychological effects of obscene materials. They found current laws adequate but too little enforced. The only legislation they would add would be laws to make possession of child pornography a crime. In addition, they advocated such grassroots efforts as picketing, boycotts, and complaints to television advertisers.

These findings were far from unanimous. Two members of the commission issued a dissenting statement pointing out that the hearings had neglected mainstream pornography to concentrate on violent and degrading materials. Both the dissenters and some of the researchers also suggested that the report skewed the data to create more of a case for the correlation between pornography and violent crime than actually existed. The commissioners had also ignored a recent study from the Surgeon General indicating that no such link could be proven.

The Meese Report led to the creation of a National Obscenity Enforcement Unit within the Justice Department. The unit conducts training programs for law-enforcement officials and provides assistance to local governments seeking to stamp out pornography. According to Marjorie Heins, the unit's work has been condemned by three different federal courts as "bad-faith attempts to suppress First Amendment rights."[6] ✂

not a Valenti fan and had pretty much burned out. He retired at the same time as Shurlock, devoting his remaining years to writing. To maintain some continuity with the old PCA, Valenti promoted Eugene Dougherty, who had been Breen's personal secretary at RKO in 1941, then had moved to the PCA on Breen's return.

During Dougherty's three years as CARA director, he established a pattern that would dominate criticism of the Code for years. Habitually, he would give in to the major studios' requests for more favorable ratings while standing fast against smaller, independent producers. He also established CARA's reputation for conservatism, routinely awarding restrictive ratings to films like *Woodstock* and *Alice's Restaurant* (1970) simply on the basis of strong language or drug use. When Dougherty fell seriously ill in 1971, Valenti saw the opportunity to bring CARA more in line with contemporary mores and appointed psychiatrist Dr. Aaron Stern as director.

Stern had first become involved with the MPAA when Arthur Krim, president of United Artists, consulted him for advice on how to rate *Midnight Cowboy* in 1969. Although Dougherty was prepared to give the film an R, Krim was more comfortable placing it in the X category. On Stern's advice, he went with the self-imposed X. *Midnight Cowboy* was widely praised by critics and became the only X-rated film to win the Oscar for Best Picture. As a result of his input on the picture, Stern was invited to join the MPAA as a consultant.[7]

Stern's reasons for advising Krim to self-impose an X on *Midnight Cowboy* would suggest his initial approach to dealing with the ratings system. As he explained to a radio interviewer in 1971, he feared that children seeing the film might have their views of heterosexuality warped: "If you're a thirteen or fourteen year old, and you've never had intercourse with a woman that is gentle, tender, communicative, sensitive, and if the way in which it's depicted by [director] John Schlesinger in the film is your only criterion for evaluating intercourse . . . to a kid in the audience who's never known more meaningful interaction, he could completely distort this and be stripped away of his opportunity for meaningful choice."[8] Even allowing for Stern's outdated opinion about the origins of homosexuality and his ignorance of complaints that the film took a dim view of all forms of sexuality, the statement offers the surprising suggestion that the film should have been restricted simply because of the ideas it presents.

Before appointing Stern to replace Dougherty, Valenti had charged him with outlining stronger standards for the individual ratings. The standards Stern proposed reflected his background in psychiatry, particularly his interest in the effects film could have on young people. Overall, he felt that children needed to grow up in an atmosphere that reinforced the status quo. Anything that was too critical or questioning would upset them. In the depiction of sexuality, he felt that the G rating should be reserved for nonexplicit films in which sex was treated only "within the context of a loving relationship." In the GP (which had replaced the M in 1971), sex outside of such a relationship could be referred to but not shown explicitly. Either type of relationship would be allowed in the R category as long as the sex was not "gratuitous, excessive, or unrelated to the communicative needs of the film."[9]

Violence followed the same progression. For the G rating, it would be depicted as a tool of law and order but never as a means of solving problems. Those restrictions would not apply to the other ratings.

Most telling, however, was his classification of good and evil. In G-rated films, "there is a clear, both implicit and explicit, definition of right and wrong. In this regard, the broadly practiced social mores are not challenged."[10] Those mores are not "significantly" challenged in the GP category, while an R-rated film could deviate significantly from accepted moral standards.

Stern presented his new Code definitions in the summer of 1970, but they were not immediately approved. Any future move in that direction was forestalled when word got out. Valenti had created a CARA internship program in order to bring younger viewpoints into the ratings process. His first two interns, Stephen Farber and Estelle Changas, wrote an article for the *Los Angeles Times* revealing Stern's plans and calling them into question.

Stern's work also came to the attention of AIP head Samuel Z. Arkoff. Addressing a convention of the Theatre Owners of New England in August, Arkoff warned them about the ratings' potential use as "thought control": "[Stern] has told me that he feels any film that questions the validity of the existing social structure should not be seen by young people under seventeen except in the company of their parents. . . . To me this is an absolutely terrifying concept, alien to America. . . ."[11]

Stern's proposed ratings system was never adopted. Nonetheless, early applications of the ratings reflected an attempt to control not just adult elements in films but the attitudes toward them. Generally speaking, films presenting sexual license or drug use in a condemnatory context were granted more favorable ratings than those that seemed to be advocating greater freedom.

MGM's *The Magic Garden of Stanley Sweetheart* (1970) featured extensive nudity, lovemaking, and drug use during the course of a rather vapid coming-of-age tale. In the last reel, however, leading man Don Johnson rejects that lifestyle after his guru (Michael Greer) commits suicide. With a few snips, Dougherty granted the film an R rating. For his film version of Frank Marcus's play *The Killing of Sister George* (1968), Robert

Aldrich built on the story of a lesbian love triangle to depict London's homosexual sub-culture and add a graphic love scene between Susannah York and Coral Browne. Even when Aldrich offered to cut the sex scene, Dougherty told him the film would have to be rated X. For all the characters' suffering, it would seem the depiction of an entire lesbian underground came too close to condoning homosexuality.

Yet neither rating truly reflects the overall impression created by either film. Only the most literal mind would consider *The Magic Garden of Stanley Sweetheart* a compelling condemnation of the drug culture. Prior to Johnson's hasty reformation in the last scene, the audience is treated to glamorous sexual encounters and drug parties during which the leading players indulge themselves with few ill effects. By contrast, the lesbian subculture depicted in *The Killing of Sister George* is populated by self-loathing, romantically frustrated women to whom happiness seems an almost alien concept—hardly a recruiting program for the gay lifestyle.

For all the complaints about his approach to the ratings system, Stern's tenure as CARA director was marked by growing administrative stability. When he resigned his position in 1973 to accept a post as head of special projects at Columbia Pictures, many in the industry expressed genuine regret over his departure. At the same time, however, Valenti took advantage of the leadership change to make what he felt were much-needed changes in CARA's structure. First, he put an end to script reviews, which he considered ineffective. Second, he changed the nature of the reviewers. As he describes it, he abandoned the idea of professional reviewers, even those with psychological training "because we don't know what is damaging or injurious to children. That is something for courts to decide or medical research to decide. I thought that what we wanted was what the average parent in America would find to be an accurate rating."

Gradually, the professional reviewers were replaced by concerned parents, each serving for a two- or three-year term. At present, films are screened by a panel of eleven reviewers, all of them parents with some degree of education. Most often, only seven panelists will screen a single film. With controversial cases, however, all eleven are called into play. To head the new group, Valenti chose Richard Heffner, a professor of communications and public policy at Rutgers University, who remained with CARA until June 1994, working out of the MPAA's New York office.

Parental Guidance or General Confusion?

One complaint that has dogged the ratings since their inception is their lack of consistency. The problem, of course, is inherent to the system. Attempts to quantify subjective responses to any art form can lead to little more than confusion. In the early years,

Dougherty and Stern tried to use specific elements to place films into one rating or another, but the results were far from satisfactory. Under this initial system, any depiction of sexual intercourse drew an automatic X. Nudity outside the realm of intercourse guaranteed at least an R, as did certain types of profanity.

As a result, the 1972 coming-of-age film *Journey Through Rosebud* drew an X because of ten seconds of soft-focus lovemaking. With the scene removed, the film was too tame for even an R rating. Other pictures were threatened with Xs and Rs because of love scenes showing nothing more graphic than the participants' naked shoulders. These rules were relaxed within a few years, particularly after the major studios started contesting more restrictive ratings.

Other critics have complained that the ratings' chief inconsistency is their tendency to favor big-budget studio films. Although Valenti vigorously denies any favoritism, the system itself appears weighted towards the major studios, which have more money to spend on reediting films and appealing ratings than do the smaller, independent producers.

This charge was first made in earnest after MGM successfully appealed the R rating for *Ryan's Daughter* (1970). The film dealt with the romantic yearnings of a young Irish girl (Sarah Miles), who pursues and marries the local schoolteacher (Robert Mitchum), then leaves him for an affair with a British army officer (Christopher Jones). In addition to the adult theme, the film drew an R for a first-night scene between Miles and Mitchum and Miles's nude tryst with Jones. In appealing the rating, MGM executives stated that the studio's future depended on the film's success and even threatened to release it unrated. As a result, the Review Board lowered the rating.

But *Ryan's Daughter* was just one of several films, including independent productions, rerated by the Review Board in 1970. Jack Nicholson's *Drive, He Said* dropped from X to R despite male nudity, strong language, and an implication of sodomy. Nicholas Roeg's *Walkabout* had been rated R for two nude swimming scenes. Voting unanimously for the first time, the board lowered the rating.

The charges of favoritism have remained, however, bolstered by critics who don't always agree with CARA's criteria for issuing ratings. When Franklin J. Schaffner's *Papillon* (1973) escaped an R rating and William Friedkin's *The Exorcist* (1973) avoided an X, critics complained that both films should have been issued more restrictive ratings on the grounds of graphic violence. Although CARA and the Review Board were more lenient about violence at that time, the perception created was that these two major studio releases had been given special treatment.

All of these complaints reflect the central problem that has dogged the ratings system since its inception—uncertainty and disagreement over what each rating truly stands for. Don Siegel's *Dirty Harry* (1971) lost some punches and a little blood to drop from X to R, but the film's overall impression was little changed. Neither was the sensuality in the 1971 James Bond film *Diamonds Are Forever*, which lost a few breast shots to avoid an R.

The first rating to draw fire was the G. When films with adult language and sensuality like *Popi*, *If It's Tuesday This Must Be Belgium*, and *Darling Lili* drew G ratings, parents wrote in to complain. As a result, the G rating was tightened, with fewer films qualifying. Ironically, this made the rating less attractive to many teens and young adults, who accounted for an increasingly important portion of the potential audience. Although certain G-rated films, particularly animated features from the Disney studios, still performed impressively at the box office, other filmmakers would insert a few mild profanities into an otherwise pristine feature to move it to a higher rating. Between 1973 and 1983, the percentage of films rated G dropped from fifteen to three.

The rating just above G also created problems initially. Thinking the M rating meant mature audiences, parents kept their children away. So in 1971, Valenti had the label changed to GP, which meant "general patronage—parental guidance suggested." This, too, generated complaints when parents confused it with the G rating. As a stopgap, CARA began adding the tag "contains material which may be unsuitable for pre-teenagers" on more mature GP films. Finally, the tag was incorporated within a new rating, PG, "parental guidance suggested," in January 1972.

All this quibbling over the G and PG ratings quickly faded in the face of what would become the system's most controversial element—the X rating. Although the X had been created to protect exhibitors from obscenity prosecution, the rating was hardly confined to pornographic films. In fact, it was initially hailed as the ticket to greater screen freedom.

During the early years of the ratings system, Hollywood produced several respectable adult films that were categorized informally as "quality X"s. Aldrich's *The Killing of Sister George* in 1968 was the first X-rated film to feature established actors working for a major director. The same year, Brian De Palma made his feature-directing debut with the X-rated *Greetings*, an antiestablishment satire featuring the young Robert De Niro.[12] *Midnight Cowboy* won the Oscar for Best Picture despite its self-imposed X, while Stanley Kubrick's X-rated *A Clockwork Orange* picked up the New York Film Critics Award for Best Picture of 1970.[13]

At the same time, however, other X-rated films were generating vehement condemnation among audiences, critics, and even prosecutors. Some were misguided studio productions like 20th Century-Fox's *Myra Breckenridge* (1970), which turned Gore

Vidal's wicked satire of sexual mores and Hollywood camp into an overheated mess that not only lost a bundle at the box office but ranked high on most critics' ten-worst lists. Others were independent productions that despite nobler artistic intentions, gave moralists reason to howl. *Futz* and *End of the Road* introduced bestiality to the screen in 1970, while an adaptation of Henry Miller's *Quiet Days in Clichy* the same year broke through the last language barriers while featuring numerous scenes of uncensored sexual activity.

The height of the independent assault on viewers' sensitivities occurred when Grove Press, a pioneer in fighting literary censorship battles, decided to get into film distribution. Their first effort was the Swedish film *I Am Curious (Yellow)*, a multilayered social satire directed by Vilgot Sjöman.[14]

Scenes depicting Sjöman's crumbling relationship with leading lady Lena Nyman framed a tale of a young revolutionary (Nyman) pursuing a relationship with a bourgeois automobile salesman (Borje Alstedt). In between segments featuring her revolutionary pursuits are sequences in which she and Alstedt make love in a variety of locations (including a tree and a balcony at the Royal Palace). After a separation, she happily greets her naked lover by kissing his penis. During an extended nude scene, they alternate between arguing and lovemaking, with the two activities feeding into each other. The film's complex structure and its unevenness (some of the political scenes go on forever; much of the sexuality is shockingly effective) made it particularly vulnerable to the censors, who could argue that the boring segments only focused more attention on the sexual elements.

Customs officials felt the film's unbridled sensuality rendered it obscene and brought it to trial. A jury agreed with them, but their ruling was overturned on appeal in 1968. Because *I Am Curious (Yellow)* went further than any other film passed by the courts, many legal scholars argued that the ruling marked the end of government censorship.

It was only a measured victory, however. By refusing to pursue the case, Customs kept it from reaching the Supreme Court, where a precedent might have been set. As the film went into circulation, however, it attracted the attention of other censors. When Maryland's board ruled the film obscene, the appeal finally reached the nation's highest court.

A Supreme Court decision would have settled the issue once and for all, but two things made that impossible. Two of the Court's staunchest civil libertarians, Abe Fortas and Chief Justice Earl Warren, had retired, to be replaced by more conservative justices appointed by Richard Nixon. In addition, another free-speech advocate, Justice William O. Douglas, had to disqualify himself because he had accepted an honorarium from Grove Press when they reprinted excerpts from his book *Points of Rebellion*. The Court split 4–4 on the Maryland case, leaving the state's ban on the film intact and the rest of the country in a state of confusion.

One thing about which conservatives were not confused, however, was their reaction to the screen's new freedom. In their opinion, films like *I Am Curious (Yellow)* had gone entirely too far and were leading the country to damnation. Pornographic movies were increasingly visible in the years following the transition to film classification. Porn producers simply slapped a self-imposed X on their films; sometimes they would heat up their advertising with false claims that the film was rated double- or even triple-X.

Many filmmakers got around the courts by injecting "redeeming social value" into their pictures. In Russ Meyer's *Vixen*, the 1969 film that became the first big soft-core hit, most of the the political discussion occurs during the film's last ten minutes, in a scene set on an airplane after the final sexual number. According to Roger Ebert, when word of this got around in Chicago, audiences started leaving as soon as the characters got into the plane. Another 1969 film, *The Language of Love*, interspersed sex scenes with a panel discussion of sexuality.

The growing outrage over screen permissiveness in some circles put a powerful stigma on the X rating. The ground had been laid with the very choice of the letter X, long associated with poison and other harmful elements. Nor did public statements by Valenti and CARA's reviewers help matters. Although Valenti often decreed that "an X rating simply means unsuitable for viewing by children," he also referred to X-rated films as "trash and garbage, made by people out to exploit,"[15] a statement that triggered a lawsuit from one distributor. Dr. Jacqueline Bouhoutsos, a child psychologist working with CARA, went even further when she characterized such films as "garbage, pictures that shouldn't have been made for anybody, films without any kind of artistic merit, poor taste, disgusting, repulsive."[16]

Despite strong box office for adult pictures, many theaters refused to book X-rated films. Others bowed to community pressure to program only family fare. In addition, many newspapers refused to review or carry advertising for adult films. Their right to do so was bolstered by the courts' dismissal of a suit brought by Robert Aldrich to stop the *Los Angeles Times* from censoring ads for *The Killing of Sister George*. By 1972, thirty urban papers refused advertising for X-rated films, while 47 percent of exhibitors would not show such pictures.

As a result of this resistance, the only X-rated films capable of generating profits were low-budget sex films, particularly such widely heralded and heavily prosecuted pictures as *Deep Throat* (1972) and *The Devil in Miss Jones* (1973). For a major studio release, however, an X could mean the loss of 50 percent of its potential receipts. More and more, producers cut films or appealed to escape the poison of an X. In an era dominated by independent productions, the studios began writing distribution contracts requiring the delivery of films rated R or lower.

Valenti and the MPAA tried to help out by raising the age restriction on R and X films from sixteen to seventeen in 1970. As a result, movies like *M*A*S*H*, *Women in Love*, *Fellini Satyricon*, *Zabriskie Point*, and *The Boys in the Band* avoided the X category. But the move may have backfired when the NCOMP not only condemned several pictures CARA had passed but withdrew its support of the ratings system in 1971.

Dougherty had expressed the hope that the broadened R category would discourage filmmakers from pushing the limits any further, but some major studio productions still went too far for him. CARA reviewers tried to impose an X on *The Last Picture Show* in 1971 because of the scene in which local teens take a mentally retarded friend to visit the town whore and the sound of bedsprings creaking when high-school student Timothy Bottoms makes love to a married woman (Cloris Leachman). Director Peter Bogdanovich was loath to make any changes—and didn't have to when Columbia's appeal won the film an R rating.

Sam Peckinpah was less fortunate with *Straw Dogs* the same year. His liberal adaptation of Gordon M. Williams's *The Siege of Trencher's Farm* pitted meek mathematician Dustin Hoffman against a small English town filled with thugs and half-wits. At the film's climax, Hoffman, who has withstood months of harassment quietly, finally breaks out in an orgy of violence as he defends his home against a concerted attack.

Some of this brutality was cut to appease the MPAA, with the most damaging change occurring in a rape scene involving Hoffman's wife (Susan George). The sequence starts with George assaulted by a former boyfriend, an attack she ends up enjoying. Then, another of the local thugs enters and brutally sodomizes her. The scene is important in setting the limits for George's character, a woman torn between the small-town meanness with which she was raised and her aspirations to a better life she barely understands. All CARA's reviewers could see, however, was the anal rape, which would virtually guarantee the film an X rating. They insisted on cutting any indication of sodomy. Despite the charges of some critics at the time, the sequence still makes its point, but the cut diminishes the build to Hoffman's violence in the final reel.

Peckinpah was far from the only director forced to cut his work to win a more favorable rating. Stephen Farber estimates that one third of all films reviewed by CARA in 1969 were cut. Many critics complained that the stigma of the X—and in some cases the R—was responsible for more censorship than had existed under the Production Code.

With the rise in feminism in the late sixties and early seventies came a new type of censor. Concerned about the representation of women in pornography, several leading feminists created their own procensorship movement. Their argument was that violent and degrading images of women in pornography, even the exploitation of the naked female image in such magazines as *Playboy*, encouraged discrimination and violence against women.

Not all feminists who view pornography as degrading to women are procensorship. Ellen Willis has decried the misogynistic subtext of *Deep Throat* while criticizing the women-against-pornography movement. Robin Morgan, whose "Pornography is the theory; rape is the practice"[17] became the rallying cry for procensorship feminists, later joined the battle against them.

Although early feminists decried the depiction of women as sex objects in almost all of the media, the movement against pornography first gained focus and direction in 1975, when rumors spread through New York about the latest in perversity, snuff films. These were hard-core features that allegedly combined sex scenes with actual footage in which women were murdered. The following year, producer Alan Shackleton of Monarch Releasing Corporation took advantage of the rumors to turn some shelved footage shot in South America into *Snuff*. The original film depicted a series of Manson-like murders in gory detail. In an epilogue added by Shackleton, the camera pulls back to reveal a movie crew at work. The director takes the script girl into another room, where he kills and disembowels her. Rumors flew that the actress really had been killed.

Although the violence in *Snuff* was obviously faked, the rumors drew crowds. Moreover, it shocked feminists into action. According to Beverly LaBelle: "*Snuff* . . . marked the turning point in our consciousness about the meaning behind the countless movies and magazines devoted to the naked female body. *Snuff* forced us to stop turning the other way each time we passed an X-rated movie house. . . . [It] finally made the misogyny of pornography a major feminist concern."[18]

In 1976, two organizations—Women Against Violence Against Women and Women Against Violence and Pornography in the Media—were created. Women Against Pornography joined the ranks in 1979. These groups set up women's tours of the pornography districts in major cities, educating other women and the media about the extent to which the sex industry dehumanized women.

The movement played a valuable role in making people aware of the pervasiveness of misogynistic attitudes and images in U.S. culture. By campaigning for stronger antipornography laws, some feminists formed what Ellen Willis would categorize as "unholy alliances"[19] with religious conservatives. The most notable of these alliances occurred in 1983, when feminists Andrea Dworkin and Catharine MacKinnon wrote the Dworkin-MacKinnon Bills, antipornography legislation created for the cities of Minneapolis and Indianapolis. In Indianapolis, the two even collaborated with anti-ERA conservative Beulah Coughenour to draft and push through the bill.

The Dworkin-MacKinnon Bills treat pornography not in terms of decency but as a civil-rights issue, alleging that pornography promotes bigotry and discrimination against women. In the Minneapolis version of the bill, pornography is defined as "the sexually explicit subordination of women, graphically depicted whether in pictures or in words." Such subordination would include the presentation of women as "dehumanized sexual objects, things or commodities"; the depiction of women enjoying pain, humiliation, or rape; and the representation of women as "sexual objects tied up or cut up or mutilated or bruised or physically hurt."[20] The bill also would allow women who had been the victims of rape and other violence to sue the creators of pornographic works that had inspired their attackers.

The legislation was met with strong criticism. Opponents argued that the bills' criteria were so broad that they could be used to suppress everything from William Faulkner's *Sanctuary* to Alfred Hitchcock's *Psycho* to textbooks on gynecology to the Bible. Some even suggested that they could be used to censor such examples of feminist writing as Anaïs Nin's diaries, Rita Mae Brown's *Rubyfruit Jungle,* and Dworkin's own graphic descriptions of pornography.

Still others questioned the basic assumptions underlying the bill. The causal link between pornography and violent crime had not been conclusively proven, they argued. Even if it were, many wondered if the blanket suppression of such materials would end the problem. Finally, some feminists accused the women-against-pornography movement of fostering the image of women as victims who could not deal with misogynistic attitudes on their own. In their opinion, MacKinnon and Dworkin were fostering the very kind of thinking they were trying to stop.

The bill was first passed by the Minneapolis City Council, but the city's mayor vetoed it twice, arguing that it was unconstitutional. That constitutionality was put to the test when Indianapolis's mayor signed the ordinance. A court challenge followed immediately, with ten other cities awaiting the outcome to determine whether or not to pass similar legislation.

In November 1984, Judge Sarah Evans Barker declared the Dworkin-MacKinnon Bill unconstitutional. Her decision was upheld on appeal the following year, with Judge Frank Easterbrook calling the bill "thought control": "It establishes an 'approved' view of women, of how they may react to sexual encounters, of how the sexes may relate to each other. Those who espouse the approved view may use sexual images; those who do not, may not."[21]

Even though the Supreme Court refused to hear the case, efforts to pass similar legislation have not stopped. The citizens of Bellingham, Washington, approved the bill by a three-to-one margin in 1988, but it fell in the courts there, too. MacKinnon and Dworkin continue their efforts, confident that someday their vision will prevail. But they face powerful opposition in the war to legislate the erotic dreams of a nation. ✂

In the system's defense, Valenti would point to its voluntary nature; nobody had to submit a film.[22] Some producers even found a way to work the system to their advantage by premiering a film with a restrictive rating, then, after the picture's initial run and sixty days out of circulation (as per MPAA requirements), reediting it to win a lower classification.

As the procedures for rating films settled in, CARA developed a lower profile. Despite occasional complaints from producers forced to cut films to achieve more favorable ratings, audiences and critics grew accustomed to the situation. There were still complaints about on-screen permissiveness, but most of these were directed at the growing number of pornographic films with self-imposed Xs. Instead of ratings battles, the trade press was filled with court battles as a new wave of conservatism spread through the nation.

Confusion in the Courts

National reaction against the decline of censorship was inevitable. Although much of this was triggered by the glut of X-rated films following the institution of the ratings system, the reaction actually began with a Supreme Court decision issued a year before the MPAA abandoned the Production Code.

In 1966, Robert Redrup, a Times Square news dealer, was arrested for selling a dozen books and magazines to a plainclothesman. The case, *Redrup* v. *New York*, reached the Supreme Court in 1967. After viewing the materials, the Court overturned the conviction on the grounds that none of them "was of a character described as obscene in the constitutional sense."[23] Redrup's lawyers then suggested that if these materials weren't obscene, nothing was. As a result, the Court overturned thirty pending obscenity cases, viewing the materials and releasing them with a brief reference to the *Redrup* decision. The practice of viewing allegedly obscene materials and ruling them not obscene was even jokingly referred to as "Redruping." Only the conservatives weren't laughing.

The backlash hit when President Lyndon B. Johnson nominated Justice Abe Fortas to replace retiring Chief Justice Earl Warren in 1968. A representative of the Citizens for Decent Literature attacked Fortas's voting record on obscenity cases, wondering, "How much longer are the parents, the Christian people, the wholesome people, the right-thinking people going to put up with this kind of thing?"[24] Senator Strom Thurmond even showed the Senate Judiciary Committee some of the films the Court had deemed not obscene.

The attack on Fortas's voting record was not the primary reason he lost the nomination, but it certainly gave warning that a battle was brewing. With the election of Richard Nixon the same year, the stage was set for a major change in the court's make-up. Within a few years, Nixon named three new justices to join a Court now presided over by conservative Chief Justice Warren E. Burger. Their presence marked a shift to the right first felt in two 1973 opinions.

The Paris Theatre in Atlanta had been cited for showing two allegedly obscene films, *Magic Mirror* and *It All Comes Out in the End*. The Court's liberal faction wanted to use a 1969 ruling (*Stanley* v. *Georgia*) that affirmed the individual's right to private owner-ship of obscene materials to end the censorship of all films presented to adult audiences. Instead, however, a conservative majority led by Burger denied such freedom, stating that *Stanley* did not guarantee the public sale or presentation of obscene materials. In Burger's opinion, the State had a right to protect itself from material that "has a tenden-cy to injure the community as a whole, to endanger the public safety, or to jeopardize . . . the States' right to maintain a decent society." The theater's adults-only policy was irrelevant: "One of the earmarks of a decent society . . . resides in the prerogative of government to prevent consenting adults from engaging in degrading conduct."[25]

Burger's majority opinion hinted at the need for a new federal standard for obscenity that would make it tougher for pornographers to reach the Supreme Court, much less get convictions overturned there (for previous standards, see 'Dateline,' pp. 266 and 271). The same day as their decision on the *Magic Mirror* case, the Court issued another judgment that accomplished just that. California publisher Marvin Miller had been arrested for mailing brochures featuring adult materials to randomly chosen customers. The Court upheld his conviction on the grounds that the mailings had been unsolicited, but Burger also took the opportunity to change the Court's three-pronged definition of obscenity.

First, he made it clear that obscenity should be judged on community rather than national standards, setting the stage for chaos on the lower court level but, as he may have hoped, cutting down the number of such cases that would reach the Supreme Court. Second, instead of allowing the presence of any "redeeming social value" what-soever to contravene obscenity charges, Burger ruled that such "serious literary, artistic, political or scientific value"[26] must be weighed against the overall effect of the work. Finally, he attempted to define the types of materials that could be regulated:

1. Patently offensive representations of descriptions of ultimate sexual acts, normal or perverted, actual or simulated.
2. Patently offensive representations of descriptions of masturbation, excretory functions, and lewd exhibition of the genitals.[27]

Moralists cheered Burger's two decisions, hailing them as the long-awaited end to the pornography explosion. The American Library Association and the Association of American Publishers tried to get the Court to reconsider its findings but were turned down. Hollywood wasn't certain what to make of it. Some, like Jack Valenti, felt that the new standards wouldn't pose any problems for "responsible" film makers. Then a court in Albany, Georgia, slapped an obscenity charge on *Carnal Knowledge*, a major release from Avco Embassy directed by Mike Nichols and written by Jules Feiffer.

Feiffer's script presented an unstinting view of male sexual hypocrisy, following two college roommates through more than two decades of thwarted love affairs and shattered marriages. There was explicit dialogue and some nudity, but no explicit sex acts on screen, although the final scene showed the more cynical of the two, Jonathan (Jack Nicholson), preparing to receive a blow job from a prostitute (Rita Moreno).

The Supreme Court overturned the film's obscenity conviction unanimously but was divided in its reasoning. Writing for the majority, Justice William Rehnquist ruled that the film simply was not obscene. Closing up a loophole left by Burger's *Miller* ruling, he declared that only the depiction of hard-core sex acts could be prosecuted. Brennan, in a concurring opinion, argued that *Miller* had been seriously in error. Since the fifties he had changed his views on pornography. In place of the carefully worded three-part definition of obscenity he had concocted in the *Fanny Hill* case, he now felt that the state had no grounds for censoring any material, however offensive, "in the absence of distribution to juveniles or obtrusive exposure to unconsenting adults."[28]

The Court's ruling in this case simply added to the confusion raised by the *Miller* decision. Authorities were still to judge films by local community standards but were also to apply strict national rules set down by the Supreme Court. The Hollywood studios ordered producers and directors to make protection footage of any scenes that might be questioned by local authorities. According to director John Frankenheimer, the studios also canceled plans for film versions of two controversial novels, Gerald Walker's *Cruising* and Hubert Selby Jr.'s *Last Exit to Brooklyn*. Both projects would be revived years later—in 1980 and 1989, respectively—with the former arousing considerable protest from the emerging gay-rights movement because of its graphic depiction of a sadistic serial killer stalking gay leather bars.

The MPAA responded to *Miller* by drafting sample obscenity legislation of its own. Valenti's goal in this was to supply localities with a way of discriminating between hard-core pornography and serious adult films. Once word of the MPAA's plans got out, however, Valenti discovered opposition within the filmmaking community and eventually dropped the matter.

Through all of this, censorship activities in the courts continued to overshadow

Censored Hollywood

CARA's relatively tamer efforts. *Deep Throat* did for hard-core in 1972 what *Vixen* had done for soft-core in 1969. With its satirical tale of a young woman (Linda Lovelace) who can't enjoy sexual intercourse until her doctor (Harry Reems) discovers that her organs of pleasure are located in her throat, the film had a stronger plot and more humor than was typical of most porn films. It also had solid production values and, in Lovelace, porn's first true superstar.[29]

The film's backers, Phil Parisi and Lou Perry, had shot it in Miami for $24,000 and hadn't expected to make more than half a million dollars or so. Instead, it became a cause célèbre. Critics for major papers wrote often glowing reviews, even though the *New York Daily News* refused to accept the film's advertising. United Nations officials and Broadway performers were spotted in the audience at New York's New World Theatre. There were also numerous couples in attendance; *Deep Throat* was becoming a major date picture.

The film's success hardly went unnoticed by the authorities. Even before the *Miller* decision tightened the screws on obscenity, there were attempts to shutter *Deep Throat* and wildly different rulings by judges in various jurisdictions. After hearing expert testimony from both sides, the New York City judge decided that the film was "a feast of carrion and squalor . . . a Sodom and Gomorrah gone wild before the fire"[30] and fined the theater $3 million, twice its expected take on the picture. As attempts to censor *Deep Throat* grew, however, so did its audience.

None of this escaped the notice of the federal government. The *Miller* decision had suggested one way the federal government could attack pornographers—by prosecuting the distribution of their work in more conservative jurisdictions whose community standards would almost guarantee a conviction. So Assistant United States Attorney Larry Parrish, a workaholic with strong religious convictions about stamping out pornography, filed conspiracy charges against the film in Memphis, Tennessee.

The conspiracy charge was also a clever federal ploy. It allowed Parrish to prosecute anyone he wanted who was associated in some way with the creation and distribution of *Deep Throat*. In all, he filed charges against five corporations and twelve individuals, including actor Harry Reems. Reems had spent one day working on the film in January 1972, for which he had been paid one hundred dollars. Two and a half years later he was awakened in the middle of the night by FBI agents who had come to arrest him.

Reems's status as the first performer prosecuted on a national level for his work (comedian Lenny Bruce had only been tried on local charges) made him the First Amendment poster child as the case went to trial in 1976. With little money to pay his legal fees, he appealed to the entertainment industry, winning support from playwright Edward Albee, director Mike Nichols, singer-songwriter Rod McKuen, and actors Ruth Gordon, Warren Beatty, and Gregory Peck, among many others.

After Judge Harry W. Wellford instructed the jury to disregard the First Amendment and simply view the film as they felt the average Memphis citizen would, all of the defendants, including Reems, were found guilty. Most of the convictions were overturned on appeal, on the grounds that the film had been made prior to the *Miller* decision but judged in terms of the Court's new definition of obscenity. Parrish did not reinstitute his case against Reems. In all, the attempt to prosecute the actor and his "conspirators" cost U.S. taxpayers $5 million.

Deep Throat would be the only film attacked by the federal government on such a grand scale. A similar federal case against *The Devil in Miss Jones* (1973), a hard-core film hailed by many critics for bridging the gap between sex film and art film, was dropped in 1979 because many of the defendants had already been convicted for their involvement in *Deep Throat*. Chief U.S. Attorney Mike Code felt that another trial would constitute double jeopardy. Charges against *Devil* star Georgina Spelvin were also dropped.

Hard-core films weren't the only ones feeling the heat during this period. Bernardo Bertolucci's 1973 *Last Tango in Paris* had been hailed by some as the picture that bridged the gap between sex and art. The last great "quality X" starred Marlon Brando as an American expatriate in Paris working through his emotional problems during a series of trysts with a young Parisian woman (Maria Schneider). Their couplings range from gleeful sex play to more brutal practices, including sodomy. At first, their meetings are strictly anonymous, confined to an apartment they rent together. When Brando tries to carry the relationship outside the apartment, the girl panics and shoots him.

Most local attempts to ban the picture failed, with the courts overturning obscenity statutes in Montgomery, Alabama, and the state of Louisiana. Because of its X rating, however, UA had problems advertising the picture. The *Los Angeles Times* relegated all ads for X-rated films to the same section. Not wanting *Last Tango* lumped in with the growing number of hard-core features, the distributor had to place a full-page *Times* ad to separate the film from other adult fare.

Ironically, the biggest legal problems encountered by *Last Tango in Paris* were in Bertolucci's native Italy. In 1972, federal authorities there filed obscenity charges against the director, producer, and distributor as well as stars Brando and Schneider. All five were acquitted the following year, but continued legal problems led to an all-out ban in 1976 that would not be dropped until 1987. Despite the ban, however, *Last Tango* would become the second-highest-grossing film in Italian history, taking in more than $28 million at local box offices.

Even though the Supreme Court's *Miller* decision and the Meese Commission's report on pornography (see "All the President's Censors," p. 214) seemed to open the door for increased prosecution of questionable films, legal action declined. Rising crime rates kept many local prosecutors and law enforcers too busy dealing with murder, rape, and robbery to be bothered about what was showing at the local grind house. In addition, the development of the home-video market gradually put most adult theaters out of business as pornography became a more private concern.

The last major court battle over sex in film involved the maiden effort from *Penthouse* publisher Bob Guccione, *Caligula*. The 1980 epic was controversial before its release. Noted author Gore Vidal had written a screenplay dramatizing the life of Rome's infamous mad emperor, then sued to take his name off the production after the addition of graphic sex scenes. Customs officials tried to block the Italian-made film, but members of the Justice Department's Criminal Division declined to prosecute.

When the film opened in New York, Morality in Media filed a class-action suit in the name of three thousand Catholic priests, charging that the Justice Department had been derelict in not prosecuting the film. After both trial and appeals courts threw out the suit, Morality in Media organized local action against the film, leading to prosecution in Boston. The Boston judge cleared it on the testimony of a political science professor who argued that it constituted a serious indictment of unbridled political power.

Caligula's reputation led to a threat of prosecution in Atlanta. The distributor requested a federal court declaration ruling the film not obscene and enjoining any prosecution. Not only did both judge and jury agree with the assessment of the film's political value, but they issued a surprising opinion of the film's prurient appeal: The graphic depiction of sexual activities—including torture, necrophilia, and bestiality—would actually tend to inhibit sexual desire.

Caligula had already played in over one hundred cities in the North and the West. The Georgia decision opened the door for the film to play throughout the South without threat of prosecution. As a result, *Caligula* would become the U.S.'s highest-grossing independent production.

The *Caligula* decision was important for another reason. It made it clear that the courts could provide little assistance for the growing ranks of would-be censors. With neither the courts nor the industry itself to turn to, those who were not happy with the increasing permissiveness within the entertainment media took the battle, quite literally, to the streets.

Censorship: The Holy War

In 1980, the nation took a turn to the right that made the Nixon years seem tame by comparison. After four years under the moderate leadership of President Jimmy Carter, the nation voted Ronald Reagan into office. Reagan affected major economic changes, lowering taxes for those in upper income brackets, cutting off or limiting a variety of domestic programs, and raising defense spending. His election also brought into the open the growing cultural war between liberals and conservatives.

Among the new President's most fervent supporters were members of the religious right, particularly Jerry Falwell's recently formed Moral Majority. His and other conservative Christian groups were demanding a return to what they considered traditional morality. At their most extreme, they advocated the legislation of biblical morality, with some even proposing the death penalty or prison terms for homosexuals and adulterers. More moderate forces simply wanted to see the culture, including the entertainment media, brought more into line with their vision of right and wrong.

The major focus of their attacks on the media was television. Through letter-writing campaigns and threats of sponsor boycotts they worked concertedly to keep from the airwaves material they felt promoted such sins as abortion, promiscuity, and homosexuality. Their methods were nothing new—they had been used to protest "bad" films in the thirties. But rarely had they been more effective.

Through the 1980s, cable, home video, and video games siphoned off viewers from the major networks, leaving them particularly vulnerable to pressure groups. After protests against the depictions of abortion in the comedy series "Buffalo Bill," the short-lived dramatic series "TV 101," and the acclaimed telemovie *Roe vs. Wade,* few producers would touch the topic. Complaints about a lesbian nurse played sympathetically by Gail Strickland in "Heartbeat" were rumored to have influenced ABC's decision to cancel the series. After ABC lost sponsors for an episode of "thirtysomething" in which two gay men were shown in bed together, the episode became one of the few not repeated during the summer rerun season. Years later the network tried to pull a "Roseanne" episode in which star Roseanne Arnold kissed a lesbian played by Mariel Hemingway.

When Universal announced plans to release *The Last Temptation of Christ* in 1988, the Christian right, with a hearty assist from other religious groups, set out to take on Hollywood. This was hardly the first film to rouse religious groups' ire with its treatment of Gospel figures. Twenty years after the Supreme Court overturned New York's ban of *The Miracle,* clergy had complained about *Jesus Christ Superstar* (1972) because it depicted Christ as filled with doubts at Gethsemane, Mary Magdalene as possessing a carnal love for her Savior, and Judas as a sympathetic, almost tragic figure. In addition, Jewish groups had objected to what they considered anti-Semitic stereotyping of Herod and the Pharisees. More recently, the Catholic Church had protested Jean-Luc Godard's *Hail Mary* (1985), a contemporary retelling of the nativity with Mary as a student, basketball player, and part-time gas-station attendant.

The Last Temptation of Christ had been a subject of controversy since Nikos Kazantzakis's novel first appeared in 1948. The Greek Orthodox writer tried to deal with the conflicts between Christ's divine and human natures, and many readers felt the book had put them more closely in touch with their own struggles to lead Christian lives. Appalled at the book's concentration on Christ's human side, however, the Greek Orthodox Church rewarded Kazantzakis with a threat of excommunication and, years later, denied him the Christian funeral rite. When an English translation appeared in 1960, pressure groups tried to get U.S. libraries to ban the book.

In 1983, director Martin Scorsese announced plans to film *The Last Temptation of Christ* and release it through Paramount. The studio was met with floods of protest from religious fundamentalists. Although Paramount had held a series of symposia with theologians and found that most moderate religious leaders saw nothing wrong with the novel, they decided to scrap a project that even under the best of circumstances would have seemed decidedly uncommercial. The protests were so vehement that nobody else in Hollywood would touch the film, either. An attempt to mount the production with funding from various European backers had to be postponed because of Scorsese's busy schedule. In addition, an announcement that the French Ministry of Culture would contribute $300,000 met with protests from the Catholic Church.

Finally, Universal agreed to back the project, which reached the screen for an amazingly low $6.5 million in 1988. Initially, they engaged Christian marketing consultant Tim Penland to help them build a bridge to concerned religious groups. Within a few months, though, Penland resigned, charging that he was being used. After reading the final script and questioning several elements, he felt that the studio had not been interested in his objections. Instead, he joined with others trying to prevent the film's release.

As the volume of calls and letters reaching the studio increased, Universal set up a rough-cut screening for religious leaders in July. Although some of the Catholic representatives found the film offensive and hinted that their church might come out against it, moderate Protestant clergy praised the film's expression of faith and soft-pedaled any objectionable elements. The Reverend William Fore of the National Council of Churches even suggested that "the film will help people understand their own commitment to Jesus."[31] But many of the fundamentalist leaders refused to attend. The

Reverend Donald Wildmon, leader of the Mississippi-based American Family Association, would later state that he had declined the invitation because the screening had been repeatedly pushed back. He offered to withhold any protest until after seeing the film if Universal would delay the premiere to allow him more time should he still wish to campaign against the picture. When they refused, he decided to go ahead with his campaign without seeing the film .

Meanwhile, the demonstrations were increasing in fervor. Dr. R. L. Hymers Jr., pastor of Los Angeles's Fundamentalist Baptist Tabernacle, led many of his 250 parishioners in a July march from Universal Studios to the home of Lew Wasserman, chairman of parent company MCA. Included in the parade was an actor dressed as Christ, who was mistreated and nailed to a cross by another actor, in a business suit, who represented Wasserman.

Hymers's protests added a note of anti-Semitism to the campaign. Pickets carried signs saying "Wasserman Endangers Israel," while an airplane trailed a banner reading "Wasserman Fans Jew Hatred With *Temptation.*"[32] Wildmon also picked up on Hymers's theme by repeatedly pointing out that Universal was "a company whose decision-making body is dominated by non-Christians."[33] These remarks stirred up protests from Jewish leaders and filmmakers—even from the growing number protesting the film.

Bill Bright, president of the Campus Crusade for Christ, offered Universal $10 million to destroy the picture. The studio turned down his offer in a full-page ad placed in the *New York Times*, the *Los Angeles Times*, the *Washington Post*, and the *Atlanta Constitution*:

> . . . While we understand the deep feelings and convictions which
> have prompted this offer, we believe that to accept it would threaten
> the fundamental freedoms of religion and expression promised to all
> Americans under our Constitution. . . .
>
> As Thomas Jefferson noted, "Torrents of blood have been spilt in
> the old world in consequence of vain attempts to extinguish religious
> discord by proscribing all differences in religious opinion." The
> Twentieth Century has provided us with further evidence of the abuses
> which occur when monolithic authorities regulate artistic expression
> and religious beliefs. Though those in power may justify the burning
> of books at the time, the witness of history teaches the importance of
> standing up for freedom of conscience even when the view being
> expressed may be unpopular.

Through the first stages of the protest, Scorsese was too busy finishing the film to issue more than a few brief statements in his defense. He managed two television interviews at the end of July, in which he expressed his desire that the film would "make Jesus more accessible to ordinary people." He also explained that the picture was not based on the Gospel but on a novel, and defended his concentration on Christ's human side: "If he's God, when he had temptation brought in front of him, it was easy—he was God, it was easy to reject it. But if he has the human foibles, if he has all the parts of human nature that we have, then it was just as tough for him as it is for us."[34]

When Scorsese finally delivered the film, Universal decided to move the premiere date up a month to cut short the protests. The film would be "platformed," released to single screens in major cities before being put into wider release. Not only did the studio keep the names of theaters secret until the last minute, but they decided to omit three southern cities—Atlanta, Houston, and Dallas—normally included in such a release pattern. Executives feared that the religious right was too strong in those areas.

The week before the film's opening, the protests increased. Estimates of attendance at an August 11 demonstration in front of Universal ranged from 7,500 to 25,000. In addition to representatives of a variety of Christian faiths, speakers included a rabbi appalled at the film's depiction of Christianity and at least one Christian representative of the film industry. Traffic in Los Angeles was tied up for hours, but officials at Universal noted no vandalism and no effect on attendance at the Universal Studio Tour. In addition, the studio's parking lot made about $4,500 from the protesters.

The night before the opening, vandals defaced the front of the Los Angeles theater at which the film would appear. The next day, a group of Hollywood directors held a press conference to express their support for Scorsese. "Christianity survived for two thousand years. It will survive Martin Scorsese's $6.5 million movie," said Sydney Pollack. Clint Eastwood sent a simple message: "Freedom of expression is the American way."[35]

Spurred by the protests, audiences flocked to the film's opening. In New York, patrons began lining up at 10:30 A.M. for a first screening starting at 1:00 P.M. But this also created problems. Ticket buyers exchanged words with protesters. Police in some areas searched handbags and other personal belongings before admitting patrons to the theaters. Some theaters even made women surrender their bags after exhibitors received bomb threats.

The notoriety gave *The Last Temptation of Christ* one of the top per-screen averages of the week, $44,579. But mixed reviews and word of mouth did some damage. By the second week, the average had dropped to $26,459 per screen. In addition, several major theater chains, including General Cinema, refused to book the film. Fearing demonstrations and vandalism, Blockbuster, the nation's largest chain of video stores, declined to stock *The Last Temptation of Christ*. Because of the film's low budget, this did not constitute a major loss. Yet the film's problems gave Wildmon and his colleagues a chance to boast that they had kept Hollywood's new experiment in sacrilege from paying off.

What was it about *The Last Temptation of Christ* that generated such vehement protests? The more cursory news reports and statements from some of the less informed protesters would suggest that the sole problem was a brief scene in which Christ has sexual relations with Mary Magdalene. But that scene is easily enough explained in context. It occurs as part of Satan's last temptation; as Jesus is dying on the cross, he has a vision of his future as a normal man if he will only give up his divine purpose. Of course, Scorsese could have depicted this without the brief sex scene, but, as he explained to Ted Koppel on ABC's "Nightline": "I think it was important to show Him go through all the steps of the normal life. The last temptation is not to have sex with Mary Magdalene, but rather to live out an ordinary life, to be married, to make love to His wife for the purpose of having children, and to live out His life as an ordinary person."[36]

Other events taken out of context—including the depiction of Christ's early career as a carpenter building crosses for the Romans and his watching as childhood friend Mary Magdalene sells herself to a series of men—further inflamed the protesters' ire. But the complaints went deeper than that. For many the very notion of a Christ filled with doubts was anathema. At one point, Willem Dafoe, as Jesus, says "I lied. I am afraid. Lucifer is inside me." Throughout the film, until He resists the final temptation and accepts His death on the cross, Dafoe's Jesus is never sure whether He is working for God or the devil. This was an assault on the sensibilities of many born-again Christians, who view Christ as both their personal Savior and their dearest personal friend. For them, such statements and scenes leaped out of any artistic context to assume the status of blasphemy. According to Wildmon, these elements went against centuries of Christian tradition to depict a Christ more man than God. As Wildmon said on "Nightline," any depiction of the life of Christ is, in essence, a sermon, and "any sermon on Christ ought to be as truthful as it can be." When Scorsese suggested that he had used Christ's life as a metaphor to deepen understanding of His preachings, Wildmon countered with "I don't think God is the person that we can use as a metaphor."[37]

Attacks on *The Last Temptation of Christ* also generated a backlash among more moderate and liberal thinkers, who had some ideas of their own about the source of the protests. Film critic Roger Ebert suggested that leaders of the religious right were afraid the film might encourage people to think for themselves. Looking back on the situation, Marjorie Heins, director of the ACLU's Art Censorship Project, pointed to the money made from attacking the film: both Bright and Jerry Falwell sold videos based on the controversy, while Wildmon used the situation to solicit donations to his American Family Association. Others have suggested that the protests were designed to divert attention from recent scandals involving televangelists Jim Bakker and Jimmy Swaggart and to win back supporters who had strayed.

For conservative critic Michael Medved, the protest was the culmination of years of resentment at the entertainment media for ignoring and even deriding traditional moral values. The protesters were merely trying to exercise their constitutional right to express their opposition to a film they felt attacked their faith. Wildmon echoed this position in his "Nightline" appearance: "The bottom line is this. Mr. Scorsese has every right to do the film, Universal has every right to release the film, but those of us who are Christians, who are offended by . . . what has been done to our Lord, have every right to protest this film."[38]

The protests against *The Last Temptation of Christ* fall into a thorny ethical area in which the exercise of one group's free speech could limit the speech of others. For all Wildmon's protestations, his actions and those of the protesters seemed clearly aimed at keeping Scorsese's metaphorical depiction of Christ's life out of the marketplace of ideas.

If that was one of their goals, however, the protests failed miserably. Many critics, even those who praised the film, felt *The Last Temptation of Christ* was too serious and too long to appeal to the majority of filmgoers. The protests, in their opinion, gave the film more publicity than it might have garnered under normal circumstances, thus helping to raise its box-office appeal. Far from suppressing Scorsese's ideas, the demonstrations may actually have helped him reach a wider audience.

Shaking Up the Alphabet

The ratings system maintained a relatively low profile through the eighties. The major complaints during this period involved the depiction of violence on screen. Popular views of sex and violence had shifted as a result of the social turmoil of the sixties and seventies. The sexual revolution had liberalized attitudes in that area, leading many to deride the restrictive ratings CARA continued to issue on the grounds of nudity or sexual activity. At the same time, rising crime rates, television coverage of the Vietnam War, and the string of political assassinations in the sixties contributed to a growing backlash against violent entertainment and CARA's seeming leniency on the issue. These were bolstered by the U.S. Surgeon General's 1969 report linking such entertainment to violent behavior.

The first film under the ratings system to arouse protests was Sam Peckinpah's *The Wild Bunch* in 1969. Although some critics praised it as a breakthrough western, with its adult look at the decline of the old West, others complained about the film's high body count and the graphic bloodletting, often in slow motion. The producers only had to cut a few minutes of mayhem to escape an X rating, but then cut another thirty-five minutes after preview audiences fled a Kansas City screening in disgust. The theater was picketed the next day.

Yet Peckinpah's avowed purpose in making the film was not to exploit violence but to confront the prevalence of violence in American life. He even told the press that he found the film unbearable: "I don't think I'll be able to see it again for five years."[39] The NCOMP agreed with the director. In announcing the film's A-IV rating, the Catholic organization suggested that the film "could help thoughtful viewers to understand who we are and where we have come from in a way that, considering the history of the western genre, is singularly healthy."[40]

Many critics suggested that for all its bloodshed, *The Wild Bunch* was not as objectionable as the action films that seemed to glorify violence. Critics were appalled at audiences' cheers when Charles Bronson blew away muggers in *Death Wish* (1974). So was Brian Garfield, author of the original novel, who complained that a story he had intended as an attack on violence had been turned into a glorification of its protagonist's vigilantism.

Meanwhile, more sophisticated audiences were turning against violence. Critic Pauline Kael reported that moviegoers were hissing the blood in films like *Eyes of Laura Mars* and *The Fury* (both 1978). Despite its strong reviews and the Grand Prix at Cannes, Martin Scorsese's 1976 *Taxi Driver* was derided for depicting a would-be political assassin. When John Hinckley's fascination with the film and Jodie Foster's performance in it as a teenage prostitute led him to attempt to assassinate President Ronald Reagan in 1981, many considered his actions proof of the infective nature of film violence.

Equally damning was the violence at theaters where Walter Hill's *The Warriors* played in 1979. Young people flocked to the film's opening weekend, drawn in by a poster depicting a vast gathering of teen-gang types under the tag line "These are the Armies of the Night. They are 100,000 strong. They outnumber the cops five to one. They could run New York City. Tonight they're all out to get the Warriors."[41] Fights broke out at several venues. Two teenagers were killed in California theaters, another while returning from a screening in Boston. Although the violence clearly was a result of the masses of young people attracted by the film's advertising campaign, many attacked

The Warriors for inspiring them. The NCOMP even condemned the picture, while the French Ministry of Culture slapped it with an X rating, calling its violence pornographic. Yet the picture had passed CARA with an R rating. Later, it would be passed by the British Board of Film Censors uncut.

Finally, a spate of violent horror films inspired by John Carpenter's 1978 *Halloween* had many thinking that screen violence had gone about as far as it could go. The profitable series launched by Sean Cunningham's 1980 *Friday the 13th* presented little more than a string of grisly murders, some of them horrifyingly realistic, others laughably implausible.

Most of these films had been rated R and were restricted to older audiences. When the violence began creeping into PG pictures, however, parents complained vehemently. Among the first such films to draw protests were the Steven Spielberg-directed *Raiders of the Lost Ark* and the Spielberg-produced *Poltergeist,* both released in 1981.[42] The controversy over those two films quickly died, but when Spielberg directed the *Raiders* sequel, *Indiana Jones and the Temple of Doom*, and produced *Gremlins*, both in 1984, things heated up again. Parents did not appreciate having their children witness scenes in which a mad Hindu priest rips the heart from a human sacrifice in *Indiana Jones* or a woman churns up one evil gremlin in a blender and explodes another in the microwave.

Anticipating the problem, *Indiana Jones*'s distributor, Paramount, added a notation to its ads that "this film may be too intense for younger children." But that wasn't enough. Complaints poured in from parents, and the National Coalition on Television Violence issued a formal protest. Many suggested that the ratings system needed to be more specific about age restrictions. Paramount's chairman, Barry Diller, suggested that the time was ripe for a new rating between the PG and the R, suggesting an R-13 to ban children under 13. Even Spielberg thought the film was too intense. He told the press that he would feel uncomfortable allowing a ten-year-old to witness certain scenes and suggested the creation of a PG-2 to bar preteens.

On July 1, 1984, Valenti announced the creation of the PG-13 rating, bearing the legend "Parents strongly cautioned. Some material may be inappropriate for children under 13." Although the rating was an advisory rather than an out-and-out ban, some filmmakers still chose to cut their work to keep it in the PG category.

By the end of the eighties all other ratings business was overshadowed by renewed debate over the X. Since the inception of the ratings system, the number of X-rated films had declined dramatically, with few studios wanting to risk an estimated loss of one half to two thirds of their potential box office. Between November 1982 and October 1983, no studio released a film with an X rating. The few Xs that were released were low-budget independent productions or imports like Marco Bellochio's *Devil in the Flesh* (1986). Distributors not wanting the stigma of an X could release films without any rating at all, though there were still some theaters that would not book such pictures and newspapers that would not accept their advertising.

Because CARA's film raters had begun issuing more restrictive ratings on the basis of violence and horror, Empire Pictures chose to release Stuart Gordon's debut feature, *Re-Animator* (1985), without a rating. The half-horror, half-camp H. P. Lovecraft adaptation had been a major hit at the Cannes Film Festival, where it sold out two midnight screenings, and was the first horror film invited to the London Film Festival. When some newspapers and television stations refused their advertising, Empire put its money into radio spots. With the help of strong reviews and word of mouth, the film did solid business.

Vestron Video picked up the home-video rights in 1986 and requested an R-rated version for distribution to video stores and chains that would not carry X-rated films. Gordon supervised the cut himself and actually added material, so that the cut version ran nine minutes longer than the unrated one. When CARA issued the rating, Empire was forced to withdraw the unrated version from movie theaters. With the film's continued popularity, however, they finally surrendered the R rating and made only the unrated version available. Helping greatly in this decision was the fact that some video chains, like Blockbuster, will not carry X-rated films but will carry unrated ones.

Re-Animator wasn't the only film afloat in a sea of alphabet soup as the ratings system adapted to the growth of home video. Director Ken Russell's *Crimes of Passion* (1985) went before CARA five times before he could earn the R rating required by its distributor, New World Pictures. To bring into line this tale of a fashion designer (Kathleen Turner) who moonlights as a prostitute, Russell cut fifteen minutes, softening much of the language, shortening a scene in which Turner and leading man John Laughlin's lovemaking is depicted via shadows on her bedroom wall, and eliminating a scene in which Turner sodomizes a policeman with his own night stick.

For home video, New World released the picture in two versions: the R-rated one, which still was the only one allowed to be shown theatrically, and a longer version screened in Europe. As confusing as the situation may have been for some audience members, it was well received by reviewers like Andrew Sarris. Although he found the added scenes in the X version "somewhat loathsome," he was "grateful for the opportunity to see and judge for myself. I remain unalterably opposed to all censorship, even when it yields aesthetic dividends."[43]

Valenti continued to defend the X on the grounds that the system was totally voluntary. No filmmaker had to submit his work to CARA. If theater owners did not want to book X-rated films, that was their choice. As he told this writer: "If filmmakers have a right to tell a story, and no one can force them to censor that work, then exhibitors have a concomitant right to be able to choose what material they want to exhibit in their theaters. . . . Some theater owners are in a shopping mall, they're in a neighborhood. There are certain kinds of pictures they don't want to play."

For his part, Richard Heffner blamed a lot of the X's stigma on the press. At the time of the *Crimes of Passion* controversy, he told the *Los Angeles Times* that newspapers and other media had distorted the rating by refusing advertising for X-rated and unrated films. The X merely meant that parents would probably not want their children to see a given film, he explained, not that it was universally unsuitable: "A lot of damage is done to the chances of serious filmmakers tackling strong subjects by this seeming ban."[44]

With the mixed to very bad reviews for *Crimes of Passion*, the controversy soon died down. In 1990, however, when CARA issued X ratings for four films that many critics hailed as serious artistic works, the battle was renewed.

Peter Greenaway had been dazzling and confusing audiences for years with his highly personal, feverish vision in films like *The Draughtsman's Contract* (1983) and *The Belly of an Architect* (1987). His 1989 British-Dutch coproduction, *The Cook, the Thief, His Wife and Her Lover*, proved too much for CARA. The tale of four characters interacting in a posh London restaurant was probably as strange a mixture of sex, brutality, nudity, scatology, and cannibalism as the reviewers had ever seen. Despite impeccable production values and strong performances, particularly from Michael Gambon as the thief and Helen Mirren as his abused wife, it was hit with an X rating.

There was really nothing that could be cut to change the rating. The reviewers felt that it was the film's overall effect that would make parents loath to expose their children to the picture. Nor was Greenaway willing to make any changes. The film's U.S. distributor, Miramax, appealed the rating to no avail and even considered legal action. Instead, however, they decided to make the most of the rating, releasing the film unrated but advertising it as "X for Xtraordinary." Although some theaters canceled bookings and several newspapers refused ads, the film performed well. Valenti would later suggest to this writer that the entire brouhaha had been designed to capitalize on their problems with CARA: "They raised all kinds of Hell about censorship, then they had their people on 'Good Morning, America,' 'Nightline,' 'The Today Show,' everywhere else. They got a million dollars worth of free publicity, and they knew all along what they were doing."

Free publicity for *The Cook, the Thief, His Wife and Her Lover* turned into negative publicity for the MPAA. Critics who praised the film damned the rating, complaining that films much less suitable to younger audiences had received Rs. The artists involved in the film also commented on the situation in press interviews. According to Mirren: "There's unbelievable hypocrisy in Hollywood. I think *Pretty Woman* ought to have an 'X' rating. Why? Look at what it says to impressionable young girls. Go to Hollywood and be a hooker, and you'll end up with lots of money and a millionaire who looks like Richard Gere. You believe what the movies tell you at that age. You think that's what life is going to be like. That, to me, is a really immoral film."[45]

While *The Cook, the Thief, His Wife and Her Lover* was going through difficulties with CARA, first-time director James McNaughton faced similar problems with *Henry: Portrait of a Serial Killer* (1990). The former advertising man had been hired to make a low-budget horror film for MPI Home Video in 1985. Inspired by a television interview with mass murderer Henry Lee Lucas, he created a stark film shot in Chicago over a four-week period at a cost of a hundred thousand dollars. The picture's quality so impressed executives at MPI that they decided to try for a theatrical release. After a successful screening at the Chicago Film Festival in 1986, Atlantic Releasing picked up the film. Then CARA stepped in.

The only truly graphic murders represented on-screen occur on a fuzzy home video made by Henry (Michael Rooker) and his partner (Tom Towles). The effect is horrifying, but decidedly more aural than visual. Most of the other crimes are shown after the fact, with the camera panning slowly over dead bodies. But the film's overall impact was too strong for CARA, and they rated it X. As a result, Atlantic dropped the film.

That did not deter McNaughton or MPI, however. They found a small distributor in Las Vegas, Filmcat, and set out once again to release the picture. They also tried to change its rating, but McNaughton could see no way to cut his work. "Often a film is like a house of cards," he said, "pull out one and the house collapses."[46] Instead, they tried to challenge the MPAA's copyright of the R rating, charging that the organization was not applying its ratings in a uniform manner.

MPI's lawsuits were unsuccessful, but the film proved surprisingly popular in theaters and on home video. In addition, it was one of the first Xs from this period to be sold to cable television. Ironically, McNaughton permitted his house of cards to be toppled in Australia, cutting the film to satisfy that country's Film Censorship Board. Still, another blow had been struck against CARA's application of the X, with critics pointing to the greater incidence of violence in many an R-rated, big-studio action film.

As MPI's lawsuits were reaching the courts, Miramax came back into the picture, this time launching a legal battle of its own over the proposed X rating for Pedro

Almodóvar's *Tie Me Up! Tie Me Down!* Almodóvar's eagerly awaited follow-up to his U.S. breakthrough with *Women on the Verge of a Nervous Breakdown* dealt with a soft-porn star (Victoria Abril) kidnapped by an adoring fan (Antonio Banderas). Though she resists his initial attempts to win her love, she finally gives in when he gets beaten up trying to buy illegal drugs for her.

CARA based its X on two scenes: the actress's sexual use of an automated bathtub toy and a lovemaking scene with the kidnapper. When Almodóvar refused to make any cuts, and their appeal failed, Miramax opened the film without a rating. They took the MPAA to court in New York under a state law barring private organizations from acting in an "arbitrary and capricious" manner.[47] Miramax also tried to get the judge to require the MPAA to create an "A" rating to identify serious films that were not suitable for children. As evidence, their attorney, William Kunstler, submitted a tape with scenes from *Blue Velvet*, *The Accused*, *Fatal Attraction*, *9 1/2 Weeks*, and the 1981 remake of *The Postman Always Rings Twice* as examples of R-rated films with stronger sex scenes than anything in *Tie Me Up! Tie Me Down!*

On July 19, 1990, New York Supreme Court judge Charles E. Ramos ruled in the MPAA's favor, stating that Miramax had failed to prove discriminatory behavior. In addition, the film's ads seemed designed to capitalize on the controversy, leading him to suggest that Miramax had brought suit only as a publicity stunt.

Judge Ramos was just as tough on the MPAA, however. He charged that the economic necessity of cutting films to achieve more favorable ratings was a thinly veiled form of censorship. He also questioned the application of ratings by a panel of parents rather than those trained to determine what would and would not harm children. In his opinion, CARA's reliance on what he called the "Average American Parent (AAP)" for ratings determinations results in a standard that *"by definition*, restricts material not because it is harmful, but because it is not average fare."[48] Finally, he suggested that CARA did not adequately meet the needs of children because it concentrated more on sexual materials than on violence. Valenti disagreed with the judge's finding, stating that 74 percent of parents polled supported the current system. He also repeated his arguments that the ratings were designed solely for parental guidance.

But opposition to the X was mounting. Miramax's call for a rating to distinguish serious adult films from pornography was being echoed by film critics around the nation. It also was picked up in a petition signed by such major film directors as Francis Ford Coppola, Jonathan Demme, Spike Lee, Penny Marshall, Rob Reiner, John Sayles, and John Schlesinger. Valenti continued to reject that proposal, arguing that CARA had never taken on the role of film critic and would not do so now.

Until this point, the films that had been threatened by the X rating had been distributed independently. None of the directors was contractually bound to deliver films rated R or lower. Neither were the distributors prohibited from releasing unrated films. That restriction applied only to the MPAA's nine member companies. With the next challenge to the X, all that would change.

Philip Kaufman's *Henry and June* was far from kiddie fare, both sexually and intellectually. But it was hardly pornography, either. Kaufman had set out to detail the sexual awakening of writer Anaïs Nin (Maria de Madeiros), concentrating on her affair with Henry Miller (Fred Ward) and her fascination with his wife, June (Uma Thurman). In 1988, Kaufman had scored a hit with his R-rated adaptation of Milan Kundera's novel *The Unbearable Lightness of Being.* Using that film as his guide, he set out to make *Henry and June* a serious study of sexuality that would still fit within the R rating. What he didn't know, however, was how close his earlier film had come to an X. Although CARA director Richard Heffner was a great admirer of Kaufman's work, he would later admit that *The Unbearable Lightness of Being* had escaped an X only because he had not been there to vote on it.

When Kaufman screened a rough cut of *Henry and June* for CARA in July 1990, they issued an X rating, complaining about five scenes dealing with lesbianism and an erotic Japanese postcard portraying a woman with an octopus. The lesbian scenes were, of course, an integral part of the film. As to the postcard, Kaufman noted that "that drawing is a hundred years old and in all the art books. I can't imagine who it's going to excite unless there's a seventeen-year-old octopus in the audience."[49] For his part, Heffner advised against changing the film, urging Kaufman to release it with an X: "I think *Henry and June* is an absolutely beautiful, splendid film. But we believe most parents would consider this out of bounds for children. All we're saying with an X rating is that this is an adult film. We are not saying it's pornographic."[50] Because of his contract with Universal, however, Kaufman had to cut *Henry and June* to avoid an X or lose control of the film. Nor could Universal, as a member of the MPAA, release the film unrated.

Critics pointed to other pictures, including *Personal Best* and *Desert Hearts*, that had received R ratings despite more graphic treatments of lesbianism than appeared in Kaufman's film. Others complained about R-rated films like *Wild at Heart* and *Total Recall* that mixed sex and violence in a way they thought much more dangerous to children. Kaufman noted that *Henry and June*, which had no frontal nudity, was, if anything, less sexual than his R-rated *The Unbearable Lightness of Being.* The MPAA even received complaints from gay groups who charged that the film's X rating reflected a deep-seated prejudice against homosexuality.

As cries went up again for an alternative to the X rating, Kaufman engaged attorney Alan Dershowitz to help prepare an appeal to the Review Board. They filed a strongly worded brief, charging the MPAA with censorship and threatening antitrust action.

Valenti finally made the first major change to the ratings system since its inception in 1968. On September 27, 1990, he announced the death of the X.[51] In its place, CARA would now issue the NC-17. The rating bore the same legend, "No Children Under 17 Admitted," but could be copyrighted. This meant that the producers of pornography would no longer be able to self-impose CARA's highest rating, nor would they be likely to pay CARA to impose the new rating for them. "I think it would be hard to attract the raincoat crowd with a rating called NC-17. Don't you?"[52] Valenti said.

This was as far as Valenti could go to distinguish serious adult films from pornography. The MPAA's laywers had ruled out simply adding an A rating, advising him that distinguishing between a "good X" and a "bad X" would open the organization up to suits from dissatisfied producers.

With the new rating in place, *Henry and June* became the first film classified NC-17. Since Kaufman's contract with Universal only barred his delivering an X-rated film, the studio had nothing to complain about. Theaters, newspapers, and video stores that could or would not do business with X-rated films were in the clear, too. *Henry and June* was released in the director's cut, and all was well.

Or was it?

"I Feel Like I'm on the Edge of the World"

Chapter Ten

If filmmakers felt any euphoria over the replacement of the X rating by the NC-17, it faded just as quickly as did Edward Rochester's enchantment with his new home and bride in the film version of Jean Rhys's *Wide Sargasso Sea* (1993), one of the few movies to be released with an NC-17. Rochester's happiness was crushed by his inability to adapt to Jamaica's steamy climate and his intense relationship with his wife. The promise of the NC-17 evaporated because audiences and would-be censors failed to treat it any differently than its predecessor.

Henry and June opened on seventy-six screens—including some that would not have booked an X-rated film—on October 5, 1990. Despite the film's new NC-17 rating, there were protests at two Santa Ana, California theaters, spurred by broadcasts on Christian talk-radio station KBRT in Costa Mesa. Demonstrators expressed their fear that the NC-17 would give rise to a new flood of permissiveness in Hollywood. "I'm not protesting this particular film, but the rating in general," explained KBRT program manager Cindy Avakian. "X-rated films mean NC-17, and X-rated films do not belong in the malls."[1]

Initially the protests and the controversy over *Henry and June*'s rating helped the film. During its first weekend, it grossed about $850,000, an impressive $11,000-per-screen average. But the criticism took its toll. Two selectmen in Dedham, Massachusetts, had the film banned from the Boston suburb on the grounds that local theaters had agreed not to show X-rated fare. Although Jack Valenti criticized their action as a move

Edward Rochester and his first wife (Nathaniel Parker and Karina Lombard) explore their sexuality in John Duigan's Wide Sargasso Sea *(1993). The prequel to* Jane Eyre *is one of the few films in recent years to be released with an NC-17 rating.*

"backward into the dark ages of censorship, when witches were burned at the stake,"[2] their thinking soon spread. Many theaters, malls, and advertising outlets placed the same restrictions on the NC-17 that they had placed on the X. In addition, Donald Wildmon's American Family Association pressured Blockbuster Video into agreeing not to carry such movies (although they would continue to carry unrated films).

The immediate effect on *Henry and June* was to limit it to about one third of U.S. screens. As a result, the picture lost money at the box office, though it must be admitted that its high artistic tone, elliptical plotting, and length made it a hard sell to audiences outside the major cities.

The strictures placed on the NC-17 meant that it was business as usual for Hollywood. With *Henry and June*'s financial performance as a warning, filmmakers continued to cut their work to avoid the NC-17 label, although unrated versions, sometimes advertised as the "director's cut," were often released to home video. To escape an X, French director Louis Malle cut one minute of lovemaking from *Damage* in 1992, but it returned on the video. Jean-Jacques Annaud removed three minutes from his adaptation of Marguerite Duras's *The Lover* (1992), then added even more footage to the unrated videotape version.

A few distributors bucked the prevailing trend by releasing films theatrically with an NC-17 or no rating at all, then producing R-versions for home video. In 1992, Todd Haynes had to cut a few shots from his acclaimed debut feature *Poison* to create an R-rated version for distribution to Blockbuster and other "family" video stores. The original film had won Best Feature at the Sundance Film Festival and critical praise for its pastiche of three cinema styles—the documentary, the horror film, and the prison drama—to tell a trio of stories commenting on violence, religion, AIDS, and sexuality. But the prison story, in which a thief in a French prison rapes a fellow convict he idolizes, drew ire from the religious right, with Wildmon in particular complaining about an NEA grant that had provided about one tenth of the picture's $250,000 budget.

When video rights to *Poison* were sold to Fox/Lorber, they insisted on releasing an R-rated version. Initially, CARA demanded extensive changes. But many of the scenes they wanted cut were no stronger than anything Haynes had seen in R-rated movies and even some television dramas. He would only agree to two cuts—a shot of a man's penis while he slept and some footage of the rape victim's thigh. When he stood firm, CARA gave in and awarded the marginally cut film an R.

Ken Russell's 1991 *Whore* carried the practice of releasing alternate versions on home video to new heights. The film's original NC-17 rating had drawn flack in the press, with reviewers noting that there was little sex or nudity and that the film's overall message was a grim condemnation of prostitution. The picture had even won an endorsement from Children of the Night, a Los Angeles organization dedicated to getting young people out of prostitution.

Whore did poorly in theaters, partly because of its restrictive rating, partly because of bad reviews. The distributor, Vidmark, released it to home video in 1992, only three months after the theatrical premiere (the usual waiting period is at least six months). In all, they released four versions of the film. Along with the NC-17 version shown theatrically, Vidmark asked Russell to add two minutes of footage cut before the film's release. They sold that as the unrated director's cut. Then, to get the film into more stores, they cut five minutes from the theatrical version to win an R rating. Since this version would be pitched to family outlets, Vidmark released it with two titles. On some video boxes, the word "Whore" is covered by a long white box with the alternate title *If You Can't Say It, Just See It*. Under either title, *Whore* became Vidmark's second-most-popular release, with the unrated version drawing the most sales.

Back to *Basic*

Basic Instinct's problems with CARA ended in February 1992 when director Paul Verhoeven came up with the right combination of cuts to earn his film an R rating. In all, he removed forty-two seconds from three key scenes. During the opening murder, he cut all but one close-up of the victim being stabbed, losing a not-very-convincing shot of the ice pick going through a life-sized puppet's nose. Michael Douglas's sex scene with Jeanne Tripplehorn lost a few lines in which she tried to resist his violent lovemaking. When Douglas finally gets into bed with leading lady Sharon Stone, the R-rated sequence is missing three indications of oral sex. The scenes would return to the film for its European release and a very popular "director's cut" version on home video and laser disc.

With all the fury over *Basic Instinct*'s ratings problems, the film opened big. Thanks to Verhoeven's sharp direction and some strong performances, particularly Sharon Stone's, it stayed big, eventually grossing $385 million worldwide. The success triggered another reconciliation between Verhoeven and screenwriter Joe Eszterhas, and made Stone one of the hottest female stars in Hollywood. Although she had earned only $300,000 for her role in *Basic Instinct*, her next film, Eszterhas's adaptation of Ira Levin's steamy thriller *Sliver*, brought her $2.5 million up front and a percentage of the gross.

Basic Instinct made winners out of almost everybody connected with it. The gay protests did little to hurt the film at the box office and even triggered a backlash from feminist and lesbian critics who hailed Catherine Tramell as the most self-determined leading lady to grace a Hollywood film in years.[3] At the same time, the protests seemed

For anyone familiar with the birth of Hollywood censorship, history seemed to be repeating itself as the U.S. Congress set its sights on television violence in the mid-nineties. Fed up with increasing violence in the nation as a whole and the way television reflects and sometimes even exploits the situation, a broad range of reformers have begun demanding either more self-control within the industry or some form of regulation from the outside. The only thing not certain as this book goes to press is the form such self-control will take.

Initially television had been a blessing for young families making their personal contribution to the baby boom. But the medium's pervasiveness quickly left it vulnerable to attacks from would-be censors, particularly those concerned about the effect of television violence on the young. Critics, parents and lawmakers attacked everything from "The Untouchables" to "The Adventures of Superman," often winning major concessions from programmers.

In the eighties, however, the broadcast networks started losing their audiences to a variety of new media: home video, video games, and the less-restricted programming available through cable. In an effort to remain competitive, ABC, CBS, and NBC, joined by the Fox Network in 1987, began raising the heat levels on their own programming.

While television series explored new areas of sexuality, the television movie became increasingly violent, particularly in the depiction of real-life crime. By 1992, the production of three different movies based on the Amy Fisher-Joey Buttafuoco case and other films like *Murder in the Heartland*, a critically acclaimed miniseries about the Charles Starkweather-Carol Ann Fugate killing spree of the fifties, were drawing fire from media watchdogs.

Little of this had escaped the notice of U.S. lawmakers. After years of research that he felt demonstrated a link between violent entertainment and violence in society, Senator Paul Simon of Illinois got Congress to pass the Television Violence Act in 1990. In return for immunity from federal anti-trust prosecution, the major broadcast networks agreed to create a voluntary program for reducing television violence.

The networks took advantage of Congress's largesse for two and a half years before taking any action. As the deadline drew near, they issued a set of guidelines for the depiction of violence, but that wasn't enough for Simon. He suggested that if they didn't do more within six months, they could face serious consequences.

Some legislators wanted to restrict violent programming to time periods during which children usually did not watch. Others suggested the development of the "V-chip," a computer chip that would allow parents to program their televisions to reject any transmissions carrying a special signal warning about violent content.

Both ideas were met with fiery criticism from broadcasters, but as protests from watchdog groups like Donald Wildmon's American Family Association and Terry Rakolta's Americans for

Responsible Television grew, the broadcast networks tried to offer another solution. Finally, they created a warning to air with all violent programming "Due to some violent content, parental discretion advised." The suggestion was generally slammed as too little too late, and Wildmon and Rakolta both threatened to contact sponsors of programs bearing such warnings.

The network heads had displayed a conciliatory attitude at first, but now began fighting back. Some questioned whether television should bear all the blame for society's violence. Others pointed out that some of their staunchest congressional critics were opposed to gun control and had accepted contributions from the National Rifle Association. Finally, they noted that the legislators involved were not terribly well-informed about the medium. Even Senator Simon admitted that he had little time to watch television.

Two copy-cat tragedies in October added fuel to the fire. After watching the MTV animated series "Beavis and Butthead," a five-year-old played with his mother's cigarette lighter in imitation of the characters' fascination with fire, burning down the family's trailer home and killing his younger sister. As a result, MTV canceled the series' early-evening run, confining it to late-night hours. Imitating a scene from the theatrical feature *The Program*, teens in several states played a form of "chicken" by lying down on the center line of a highway. When three young men were killed and two others injured, the film's distributor, Touchstone, cut the scene from all prints at a cost of almost $400,000.

Shortly thereafter, U.S. Attorney General Janet Reno addressed the Senate Commerce Committee. Not only did she decry the growing violence on television (although she would later tell industry members that she never watched TV), but she advised the senators that most of their planned legislation would stand up to constitutional tests. When President Clinton echoed Reno's attitudes in his State of the Union message in January 1994, it was clearly time for action.

The timing was crucial. Congress was just beginning to consider legislation that would allow for the creation of an "information super-highway" by relaxing station-ownership rules and allowing cable and broadcast networks to develop other means of delivering services to viewers. Without some compromise on the violence issue, the networks could easily be left out in the cold or find the new technology bringing with it a series of strong content restrictions.

Late in January, the four networks accepted Simon's proposal to create an independent violence monitor. Shortly thereafter, the cable industry threw in its support as well. All sides are hoping that this will finally lay the issue to rest in a way that brings credit to all involved. As history would suggest, however, this battle, like so many others in the censorship wars, is far from over. ✄

Frank Miller

to pay off in other ways. Not only did they make homophobia, both in movies and in the culture at large, a front-page issue, but they helped spur Hollywood to tackle more gay-themed projects. The proposed film version of Larry Kramer's AIDS play *The Normal Heart* was taken off the back burner. Randy Shilts's *And the Band Played On* finally made it to the small screen. Director Jonathan Demme followed *The Silence of the Lambs*, which had been blasted in 1992 for its alleged perpetuation of homophobic stereotypes, with an AIDS story of his own, *Philadelphia*, which brought box-office leader Tom Hanks an Oscar for his performance as a gay lawyer fired when his firm discovers he has AIDS. In addition, independent and foreign productions with gay characters and themes—including Hong Kong's *Farewell, My Concubine*, France's *Savage Nights*, and the U.S. production *The Living End*—have performed impressively at the box office.

The battle is far from over, of course. *The Normal Heart* has been postponed again, despite Barbra Streisand's interest in directing and possibly costarring. Gay critics complained that *And the Band Played On* focused primarily on a straight doctor (Matthew Modine) involved in the early days of the AIDS epidemic. Despite an impressive box-office performance, *Philadelphia* also met with negative reactions from the gay community for various medical inaccuracies, the choice to give Hanks a totally supportive family (contrary to the experience of many people with AIDS), and the relatively sexless depiction of his relationship with on-screen lover Antonio Banderas.[4]

Gay stereotypes still turn up as well, with GLAAD's most recent complaints focusing on a pair of killer homosexuals in 1993's *Demolition Man*. In addition, gay characters from history and literature continue to lose their sexuality on screen. When word leaked that the leading characters in the long-awaited film version of Anne Rice's *Interview with the Vampire* were being straightened out, gay groups contemplated yet another boycott.

The one participant not helped by the *Basic Instinct* controversy was probably CARA. While the picture received mixed reviews, with some critics complaining about plot improbabilities while others hailed Verhoeven's noir-ish direction, most were in agreement that the removal of forty-two seconds had done little to make the film suitable for younger audiences. In addition, very few critics could understand how *Basic Instinct*, with its heady mix of sex and violence, was suitable for viewing by children when *Henry and June* wasn't.

Basic Instinct's success also reinforced the practice of using ratings controversies to generate free publicity. Two 1993 films, *Body of Evidence*, starring Madonna, and *Sliver*, Stone's follow-up to *Basic Instinct*, went beyond the boundaries and were threatened with NC-17 ratings. After much publicity over futile appeals and token cuts, both R-rated pictures shot to the top at the box office when they opened—and both quickly faded from sight. More than one critic complained that the distributors had capitalized on their ratings problems to pull audiences in for second-rate films. Despite the profitability of this practice, however, it merely perpetuated the stigma on the NC-17 rating.

Film as Lethal Weapon

Comparisons between *Basic Instinct* and *Henry and June* emphasize the growing backlash against violence on screen. Beyond mere quantitative objections to body counts and spilled blood, critics and many viewers have complained increasingly about action films that seem to be propaganda for using violence as a means of resolving conflicts. The spiritual children of *Death Wish*, films like the Mel Gibson-Danny Glover *Lethal Weapon* trilogy and 1993's *Judgment Night*, starring Emilio Estevez as a peaceful man lost in the Chicago slums, seem calculated to leave audiences cheering when the leading man decides to take the law into his own hands and either blow away the villain or beat him to a bloody pulp. Even such critically lauded pictures as Brian De Palma's *The Untouchables* (1987) and Martin Scorsese's *Cape Fear* (1991) have been hit with such charges.

Also causing concern has been the continued violence in theaters during the opening weekends of such gang-oriented films as Mario Van Peebles' *New Jack City* (1991), John Singleton's *Boyz N the Hood* (1991), and Ernest Dickerson's *Juice* (1992). Although similar incidents had occurred at screenings of Francis Ford Coppola's *The Godfather, Part III* (1990), Scorsese's *GoodFellas* (1990), and James Cameron's *Terminator 2: Judgment Day* (1991), negative press focused on the three black-directed, black-oriented films, opening up critics to charges of racism at a time when black filmmakers were finally beginning to make their presence felt in Hollywood.

Audience reactions to the continuing controversy over violence are difficult to gauge. While large numbers complain about too much bloodshed on screens—of six hundred respondents to an *Entertainment Weekly* poll in August 1993, 80 percent said they would like CARA to add a "V" for violence rating—large numbers also continue to buy tickets for violent movies.

The rotating panel of parents reviewing films for CARA has reflected this change in public views, at least to a limited extent. Although most of the action films derided for seeming to advocate violence continue to draw Rs, in some notable cases the reviewers have brandished the dreaded NC-17 rating to get filmmakers to tone down the on-screen mayhem. After building a strong international following with his dizzying fight scenes in such Hong Kong hits as *The Killer*, John Woo came to the U.S. in 1993 to film *Hard Target* with Jean-Claude Van Damme. He had to reedit the film seven times to escape an NC-17 for violence.

CARA's increasing sensitivity to violence may not necessarily be a good thing. The same year *Hard Target* was cut to get an R, Warner Bros. announced a twenty-fifth-anniversary reissue of *The Wild Bunch* in director Sam Peckinpah's original cut, restoring a few minutes that were excised to escape an X rating in 1969 and the thirty-five-minute cut made after the film had been rated. Even a quarter of a century later, the excised footage was too much for the ratings board. When CARA imposed an NC-17 on the new version, Warners canceled their plans.

In 1992 and 1993, two films appeared that suggested a way to make the NC-17 less of a box-office threat. Both *Bad Lieutenant* (1992) and *Wide Sargasso Sea* (1993) were made

Censorship in Your Back Yard

With their continued failure to destroy the NEA, conservatives have focused on attacking local arts funding. When two plays produced by the Theatre in the Square in Marietta, Georgia, just outside Atlanta, drew complaints from a local Baptist minister and two theater patrons in 1992, the Cobb County Commission launched an attack on the arts that made international headlines.

The two plays in question were popular successes hardly meriting the wrath poured down upon them. Henry David Hwang's *M. Butterfly* told of a French diplomat duped into a love affair with a Chinese opera star he thought was a woman. At one point, the "woman" strips on stage, revealing herself to him as a man, though the audience sees little more than his bare buttocks.

The other play, Terrence McNally's *Lips Together, Teeth Apart*, deals with the tangled relationships of two heterosexual couples spending the Fourth of July weekend in a Fire Island beach house one of the women has inherited from her gay brother. The four comment on their gay neighbors, discuss the departed brother and his lover, and wonder how they would react if one of their children were gay, but no gay characters appear on stage.

During heated public debates, artists and gay activists clashed with conservative Christians, most of whom had not seen the works in question and knew little about them. Cobb County Commissioner Gordon Wysong, who had spearheaded the attacks, refused to read the plays or view videotapes of the productions.

The Cobb County Commission got things rolling on August 10 by passing a resolution condemning the gay lifestyle. They also proposed legislation restricting public arts funding to projects

with limited budgets. Both contained adult material that was integral to their plots. And both went into theaters with an NC-17 rating. In fact, *Bad Lieutenant*'s director, Abel Ferrara, admitted to having planned his film as an NC-17 feature. Although neither was a box-office hit, their mere presence, not to mention *Bad Lieutenant*'s small financial success, suggested to filmmakers how they could work within the more restrictive rating.

Wide Sargasso Sea was a prequel to Charlotte Brontë's *Jane Eyre*, depicting the first marriage of Edward Rochester (Nathaniel Parker) and his wife's (Karina Lombard) descent into madness. Jean Rhys's novel rooted their problems in the sexual side of the relationship. Rochester experiences both a strong sexual attraction to his wife and the fear of losing himself in their emotional and physical bonding. This leads to a series of rejections that push the woman over the edge.

The sexual scenes were vitally important to the story, and when certain shots won the film an NC-17, the film's distributor, New Line Cinema, accepted the rating. Some

that support "traditional family values." When opponents threatened legal action the Commission simply voted to end all arts funding. The decision did little to effect the changes the commissioners had in mind. The Theatre in the Square had been due to receive $40,000 from the Cobb County Arts Commission to help meet its yearly budget of $800,000. Although the loss of public funding was a headache, it was hardly irreplaceable.

The commissioners defended their actions as a simple matter of economy, saying that in difficult times they had to conserve the tax-payers' money. As the Theatre in the Square considered alternative funding, or even a move to a more liberal township, that argument quickly lost validity. To save $110,000 in annual arts funding, the Cobb County commissioners had risked the loss of approximately $3.5 million in local business generated by the theater's presence.

Moreover, the Commission's actions did little to keep liberal attitudes out of the local marketplace of ideas. The legislation mobilized the gay community there as never before, leading to the creation of a political-action group and several well-attended demonstrations in the town square.

More recently, the activists have found another target, the choice of Cobb County as a venue for Olympic volleyball in 1996. A local watchdog group has alleged close ties between Wysong and one of the religious right's most reactionary factionists, while on a more personal note, Commissioner Chair Bill Byrne's daughter has come out publicly as a lesbian and denounced the Commission's anti-gay stance. Little wonder that Cobb County seems likely to be a major battleground in the cultural wars for years to come. ✂

critics even suggested that the film's frank treatment of adult materials would start a trend. That would have required a greater box-office success, however. The limited number of theaters available to an NC-17 film weren't the only problem. Although quite well made in some areas, the film suffered from a depressing story and former model Lombard's lackluster performance. In addition, the idea of a psychosexual prequel to *Jane Eyre* was far from the most salable of film concepts.

Bad Lieutenant was not cut out to become a major hit, either. This story of the last days of a police lieutenant (Harvey Keitel) addicted to drugs, sex, and gambling is a descent into hell for both the leading character and the audience. Yet the film is clearly a work of integrity. Keitel is at his best in the title role (he manages to be moving and embarrassing at the same time), while Ferrara's direction drives home the ambiguity of good and evil in a world gone mad.

There was probably no way that *Bad Lieutenant* could have been cut to achieve an R rating. The potent combination of sex, drugs, and violence, no matter how much the film seems to condemn the title character's addictions, would have been too much for CARA's panel of concerned parents to approve. Keitel dances naked with two prostitutes and blackmails two young girls into watching him masturbate. A nun is raped on an altar, then condemns herself for not being able to love her attackers enough. Keitel and his drug connection, played by cowriter Zoe Lund, spend much of the film getting high. In one long scene, he even sits for a seeming eternity with a needle sticking into his arm.

Even though Ferrara decried the way many films were cut to escape the NC-17 rating, he accepted *Bad Lieutenant*'s adults-only classification with no qualms. As he told one interviewer, "I like the look of it [the rating] on the poster, but I don't know what it means. And they don't either. If people want to see my movies, they'd go anyway."[5] He also admitted that he wouldn't want his two children—seven and four at the time—to see the picture.

Some critics complained that CARA was discriminating against independent releases and would not have slapped an NC-17 on a major studio release shot the same way. But *Bad Lieutenant*'s low budget meant that the NC-17 couldn't really do that much harm. Sparked by strong reviews and a solid core of audience support for Keitel and Ferrara, the picture appears headed for the black, which would make it the first NC-17 film to turn a profit.

With its low budget, adult treatment, and limited success, *Bad Lieutenant* prompts comparison with *Room at the Top* and *Never on Sunday*, the European films whose box-office performance inspired the X rating in the first place. It suggests that rather than risk an NC-17 with features so costly they might not survive the rating's current box-office limitations, producers and studios wishing to explore the market for serious adult movies should consider taking the plunge with less costly films.

In truth, however, the market for the NC-17 has yet to be adequately tested. To date, none of the films released with that rating has possessed anything approaching mass appeal. Of the films cut to escape the NC-17, the one most likely to have survived the restrictive rating was *Basic Instinct*. Both Paul Verhoeven and Michael Douglas wanted to take the risk, but with TriStar's insistence that Verhoeven deliver an R-rated film, the industry may have lost its best chance to date to beat the NC-17's supposed kiss of death. There is still every possibility that another high-profile, mass-market film may risk the NC-17 and score a major box-office hit. Late in 1993, Verhoeven announced plans to reteam with Eszterhas on *Showgirls*, a rock 'n' roll musical about lap dancers. Both agreed that to treat the subject properly would mean accepting an NC-17. In November, the production was bumped from Carolco's schedule by *Crusade*, an Arnold Schwarzenegger vehicle also to be directed by Verhoeven. Despite skepticism among many industry insiders, Verhoeven insisted that he would return to *Showgirls* as soon as the Schwarzenegger project was completed. Shortly before this book went to press, he did indeed finish *Crusade* and announced the resumption of pre-production work on *Showgirls*.

If *Showgirls* is never produced, however, another film will challenge the stigma on the NC-17 rating. It seems almost inevitable that some film, someday, will succeed. It's all a part of Valenti's law: "If you make a movie that a lot of people want to see, no rating will hurt you. If you make a movie that few people want to see, no rating will help you."

Censorship: The Lingering Question

Until that day comes, however, serious questions about the ratings system and its application remain. Do the ratings really provide solid advice to parents on what is and is not suitable for younger viewers? In the early days, they clearly didn't. Ratings during CARA's first few years were confusing and often contradictory as the reviewers tried to set standards for themselves, and both major and independent producers fought and cajoled their way to more favorable classifications.

With the recent change in leadership at CARA, the future of the system once again hangs in the balance. Will Richard Heffner's successor spark a new liberalism in the ratings, a shift to even more restrictive judgments, or will it be business as usual? Only one thing is sure: None of these options will satisfy all of CARA's critics.

In a broader sense, however, it is impossible for a single group, no matter how much

With the courts unwilling or unable to block what some consider indecency the radical right has found a new arena in which to make its presence known—public arts funding. The National Endowment for the Arts (NEA) had been a blessing in 1965. It marked Congress's commitment to improving the nation's cultural life and preserving its cultural heritage. At the time, Congress tried to guarantee that the new agency would not become a political football. The review process for grants was not controlled by bureaucrats, but by panels of peers in each art group who would then hand their recommendations over to the NEA chair. As a result, the agency survived attacks on such controversial works as Erica Jong's *Fear of Flying* and a production of Verdi's *Rigoletto* set in the world of organized crime.

The NEA functioned smoothly until 1989, when Donald Wildmon got wind of an exhibit originating in North Carolina. Andres Serrano had been using his work to explore the meanings of religious symbols and the evocative power of bodily fluids for years. When the Southeastern Center for Contemporary Art in Winston-Salem asked him to participate in a special show, one of the photographs he submitted was the *Piss Christ,* a shot of a plastic crucifix suspended in a container filled with urine.

Although some critics considered the work a profoundly beautiful commentary on the corruption of religion, the work seemed like a slap in the face to many Christians. One offended patron wrote Donald Wildmon about the exhibit, and that's when the troubles began.

Wildmon shared his ire with President George Bush and Senator Jesse Helms. Conservative Republicans had been trying to dismantle the NEA since President Reagan's first term. The *Piss Christ* gave them the new ammunition, and Senator Helms launched a Senate campaign against "obscene" art. Adding fuel to the fire was "Robert Mapplethorpe: The Perfect Moment," a retrospective of the late artist's photography that included homoerotic images from his personal collection. Soon Wildmon's protests were joined by complaints from other conservative groups, including Phyllis Schlafly's Eagle Forum, Concerned Women for America and the Southern Baptist Convention. When the Mapplethorpe exhibit opened at the Contemporary Arts Center of Cincinnati, police closed it down and charged the center's director, Dennis Barrie, with criminal obscenity. This marked the first such charge ever filed against a U.S. museum and its curator.

At the trial, the defense produced numerous witnesses to testify to the controversial photographs' artistic worth. The prosecution's sole expert witness claimed that the erotic pictures in the collection would encourage immoral behavior, including child molestation. At the same time, she had to concede that she was not familiar with Mapplethorpe's other work and had had little training in the visual arts. The jury found for the defense.

In 1989, Congress enacted legislation to bar the funding of obscene art, particularly "depictions of sadomasochism, homoeroticism, the sexual exploitation of children, or individuals engaged in sex acts . . ."[6] John Frohnmeyer, who had only just signed on as NEA chair, decided that the only way to enforce the legislation was by including an "obscenity oath" in all grants contracts. Rather than sign the oath, Joe Papp, director of the New York Shakespeare Festival, turned down his group's NEA grant. Choreographyer Bella Lewitzky sued over the oath and won. The courts called the obscenity bar unconstitutionally vague.

That didn't stop the protests. Members of the right felt no compunction about attacking any work that offended them, even after they were told a particular piece had not been funded by the NEA. Some also felt free to duplicate copyrighted work, sometimes out of context, in their mailings. When Wildmon did that with Donald Woynarowicz's work, the artist sued him successfully for copyright infringement and defamation of character.

In a desperate effort to save the NEA, Frohnmayer tried denying funding recommendations, but that just created more problems. When he refused grants to a quartet of controversial performance artists—Karen Finley, Holly Hughes, Tim Miller and John Fleck—the group filed suit. Shortly thereafter, Congress passed a new decency clause, and the so-called "NEA Four" amended their suit to challenge it, winning their case in June 1992.

By the time the NEA Four won their suit, Frohnmayer was out of office.[7] Following his first grant refusals, he had become more accommodating to artists, regularly defending controversial work to Congress and members of the Right. The NEA's funding of the New York literary magazine *Queer City* and presidential candidate Patrick Buchanan's attacks on other NEA projects prompted the White House to push Frohnmayer to resign on February 20, 1992.

His successor, Anne-Imelda Radice, had strong ties to President Bush. She was so notorious for denying grants that some of the peer panels refused to convene unless she could explain her actions. When she denied grants to the Massachusetts Institute of Technology's List Visual Arts Center and the Virginia Commonwealth University, playwright Jon Robin Baitz announced that he would donate his own NEA grant to the two galleries.

Radice was only in office a short time. With the transition from Republican George Bush to Democrat Bill Clinton, Clinton's choice for the NEA chair, actress Jane Alexander, sailed through her confirmation hearings in August 1993. Not only did she manage to charm most of the more conservative senators, but she stood up for creative freedom while also gently reminding the media that most NEA grants go to fund not controversial, cutting-edge artists, but programs designed to bring the arts into local communities and the schools.

Alexander's appointment didn't end criticism of the NEA. As this book goes to press, the Senate is considering a 5 percent funding cut, with disproportionately large cuts to the theater, visual arts, and inter-arts programs. The move appears to be a punishment for Alexander and the NEA's support of a performance by Ron Atley at Minneapolis's Walker Arts Center. ✄

it may seem to represent a cross-section of American parents, to provide classifications with which every audience member can agree. Certainly there are parents who would find the advocacy of violence in films like *Death Wish* and *Lethal Weapon* more offensive—and less suitable for viewing by children—than the higher levels of bloodshed or morbidity in such antiviolence films as *The Wild Bunch* or *Henry: Portrait of a Serial Killer.* But does restricting films simply because they seem to advocate or condone violence open the doors to more restrictive ratings for other films advocating unfashionable ideas?

The problem is inherent to any system of censorship or classification. Quantitative measures of cleavage, nude scenes, or acts of violence can easily degenerate into so much beancounting while ignoring a film's cumulative effect. Attempts to judge movies in terms of the overall impressions they create and the subtle messages they leave, particularly among younger minds, are open to charges of thought control. And in that realm, determining what is and is not suitable for children is a highly subjective matter.

This subjectivity is particularly troublesome when the NC-17 rating is brought into play. Unlike the other ratings, which advise parents on a film's suitability, the NC-17 is an out-and-out bar on juvenile attendance, even in the company of a parent. In the twenty-six years since the ratings began, Valenti has lost his original opposition to the most restrictive rating. As he told this writer: "Times have changed. What is being explored by filmmakers today is beyond the pale of young children, and they ought not to be exposed to it when they're not ready to absorb, to understand, to assay what they're watching. . . . With the NC-17, we are saying to parents, 'We are so confident about that rating on this movie, that we know you would be pleased to know that your children cannot see it.' "

Yet some would label that supposition premature. Might not the parents of a mature sixteen-year-old English major want their child to see *Wide Sargasso Sea* because of its use of characters from *Jane Eyre?* Couldn't the parents of a troubled fourteen-year-old experimenting with drugs use *Bad Lieutenant* as a means of opening the child's eyes to the dangers of substance abuse? In the long run, shouldn't such decisions be left in the hands of parents?

Admittedly, this places some burden on theater owners to make sure that young people attending R-rated films are indeed accompanied by a parent or adult guardian. But that's happening already. The National Association of Theatre Owners claims that the R is being enforced by 85 percent of U.S. theaters. Moreover, once a film is available on home video, there is no watchdog left to prevent a parent from showing his or her children anything at all.

Ending the stigma on the NC-17, or the rating itself, would hardly end problems with film censorship, however. The impulse to censor, to control what other people are allowed to see, hear, and think, is as old as humanity itself. It is one of our most ancient traditions and, as *Village Voice* columnist Nat Hentoff has pointed out, is far from being the exclusive province of either side of the cultural war.

The history of the Production Code and the ratings system suggests that any attempt to categorize or control works of art is almost doomed to failure. No matter how hard Will Hays, Joe Breen, and Geoffrey Shurlock fought to control film content, every subject, every issue they tried to keep off the screen has found an audience. Jack Valenti's rating system poses restrictions of its own, at least indirectly. Yet no rating can keep someone who really wants to from seeing any given film.

Over the course of more than seventy years the people behind Hollywood's self-regulation have done their best to keep state and local censors at bay. At the same time, they have consistently relaxed their standards, albeit with much heel dragging, to meet the needs of changing times. Outside Hollywood, government censors and pressure groups have often been dragged, against their wills, into a new era of screen license.

The power of ideas—liberal or conservative, traditional or unorthodox—is the one constant in the cultural wars. The American Legion could try to keep audiences from being influenced by Charles Chaplin's vision of good and evil in *Monsieur Verdoux,* but the film has found its audience through revivals, television screenings, and home-video release. Religious conservatives could keep some theaters and video stores from making *The Last Temptation of Christ* available, but audiences interested in the film's alternative view of Christianity and Martin Scorsese's artistry continue to track it down. The enemies of smut—from Joe Breen to Donald Wildmon to Catharine MacKinnon—have consistently sought to stifle views of sexuality they find offensive, only to find those views firmly entrenched in at least some corners of the marketplace of ideas.

More than two thousand years of history—from the earliest attempts to rewrite Euripides's plays to the latest film cut to reduce an NC-17 to an R—may not have proven conclusively the moral rightness or wrongness of censorship, but they have proven its futility. Ideas can be shared or kept secret. They can be sent into battle or be put on the back burner, but they can never be destroyed.

Dateline

1925

In *Gitlow* v. *New York*, the U. S. Supreme Court upholds the conviction of a New York socialist who had published a pamphlet advocating a communist revolution in this country, but agrees that First Amendment guarantees of freedom of speech and of the press can be applied to state laws.

1929

- U.S. Customs refuses to admit Voltaire's *Candide*.
- In two cases, *In re Fox Film Corp.* and *In re Vitagraph*, the Pennsylvania Supreme Court rules that sound films are no different from silents legally and are still subject to censorship.

1931

- U.S. Customs impounds a series of postcards depicting details from Michelangelo's *The Last Judgment*. This is hardly the first time the painting has been subjected to censorship. At its unveiling in 1541, Michelangelo's use of nudes was derided as "better suited to a bathroom or roadside wineshop than to a chapel of the Pope."[1] The Catholic Church tried three times—in 1541, 1566, and 1760—to purify the work by painting clothes onto the nude figures. Although successful in 1931, the U. S. Bureau of Customs would be forced to drop a similar case two years later.

1933

- In a ruling that changes the judicial definition of obscenity, Federal Judge John M. Woolsey overturns the U.S. Bureau of Customs' twelve-year ban on James Joyce's *Ulysses*, allowing Random House to publish one of the most important literary works of the twentieth century.

  Prior to the *Ulysses* decision, the definition of obscenity had been based on a British court decision in the case of *Regina* v. *Hicklin* (1868). Under the *Hicklin* Rule, a work could be ruled obscene if a single part of it could be said "to deprave and corrupt"[2] anyone, no matter how immature or mentally unbalanced.

  The *Ulysses* standard viewed a work in terms of its effect on the average person and judged the work's overall effect rather than the effect of individual sections taken out of context. By this standard, other works of literary merit and even sex-education materials were protected from prosecution.

1939

- Forest Lawn Cemetery in California unveils a reproduction of Michelangelo's *David* with a fig leaf covering one of the sculpture's most famous anatomical features. The fig leaf will remain until 1969, when it is removed over protests from local residents. Even the censored version is more forward than some would accept. Neighboring cemeteries in Glendale and West Covina have copies of the *David* made at the same time and never even put them on display.

1948

- The Christian Crusade is founded "to safeguard and preserve the conservative Christian ideals upon which America was founded . . . to oppose persons or organizations who endorse socialist or Communist philosophies, and to expose publicly the infiltration of such influences into American life . . . to oppose U.S. participation in the United Nations, federal interference in schools, housing and other matters constitutionally belonging to the states, and government competition with private business."[3] In 1967, the organization, which would grow to a membership of 250,000 families, burns Beatles albums to protest John Lennon's statement that the musical group is more popular than Christ.

1957

- The Supreme Court officially adopts the *Ulysses* standard in *Butler* v. *Michigan*, overturning the state's obscenity law on the grounds that it would "reduce the adult population . . . to reading only what is fit for children."[4]
- Although the Supreme Court sides with the government in a pair of obscenity cases (*Roth* v. *U. S.* and *Alberts* v. *California*), Justice William J. Brennan, Jr.'s majority opinion introduces the concept of "redeeming social importance"[5] as the chief factor distinguishing obscenity from protected speech. These are the first in a series of decisions in which the Court will struggle to create a legal definition of obscenity.
- The Court applies the *Roth-Alberts* standard to film for the first time in *Times Film Corp.* v. *Chicago*, determining for itself if a movie is not obscene. The case revolves around the French film *Game of Love* (1954), which the Chicago censors had banned on the grounds that its story of a young man initiated into lovemaking by an older woman violated standards of decency.
- Charles H. Keating, Jr. founds Citizens for Decent Literature in Cincinnati, Ohio. Through boycotts and letter-writing campaigns the group uses its influence to shut down pornography stores, protest questionable television programs, close

theaters, and remove racks of objectionable books from otherwise "clean" stores. By the late sixties, the CDL has 350,000 members in twenty states.

- Under pressure from the NAACP and the Urban League, the New York City Board of Education takes Mark Twain's *Huckleberry Finn* off the recommended reading list for the city's schools. This is one of the first attacks on the book as racially insensitive—attacks that continue to this day.

1959

- Libraries in Montgomery, Alabama, remove Garth Williams's 1958 children's story *The Rabbit's Wedding* from their shelves after complaints that the book is propaganda for miscegenation. The illustrations depict the marriage of a black male rabbit and a white female.

1962

- Operation Yorkville, the predecessor of Morality in Media, is founded. Under Father Morton Hill's leadership, the organization campaigns against the availability of pornography to minors; operates the National Obscenity Law Center, a clearinghouse of legal information; and publishes the *Morality in Media Newsletter* and the *Obscenity Law Bulletin*.

1964

- Comedian Lenny Bruce is convicted of public obscenity after police view three nights of his work at New York's Café Au Go Go. The conviction makes it increasingly difficult for the controversial comic to find work, eventually leading to the loss of his home. When he dies from a morphine overdose in 1966, some consider it an accident, others a suicide. In 1968, the conviction is overturned on appeal.

- Public libraries in Lincoln, Nebraska, place Hazel Bannerman's *Little Black Sambo* on reserved status after complaints from parents and the local Human Relations Council about the book's racial stereotypes.

1965

- In *Freedman* v. *Maryland*, the U.S. Supreme Court places a new barrier in the way of prior censorship. Ronald L. Freedman, a Baltimore theater owner, refuses to submit the French film *Revenge at Daybreak* to the Maryland censors in order to create a test case, and is arrested for showing the film. Even though the lower courts acknowledges that the picture, which deals with IRA activities in 1916, is far from obscene, they uphold the state board's right to require submission of all films prior to their exhibition.

Many civil libertarians hopes that the Supreme Court will use *Freedman* to finally overturn prior censorship altogether, but the Court rules more narrowly. Upholding film censorship in principle, they overturn the Maryland statute on procedural grounds because it does not ensure a speedy judicial review of all materials submitted.

The Court also imposes other restraints on censorship boards. Previously when the censors had refused to license a film, it had been up to the distributor or exhibitor to bring the case to court and prove the censors wrong. Under *Freedman*, however, a censorship board that finds a film obscene has to bring court action to prevent its exhibition, with the burden of proof falling on the censors. In addition, the censors are compelled to produce expert witnesses to support their case.

As a result of *Freedman* v. *Maryland*, several local ordinances—including those in New York, Virginia, Kansas, and Memphis, Tennessee—are ruled unconstitutional within the next few years. The case sets the precedent whereby most local censorship decisions will be overturned in the future. Maryland rewrites its censorship ordinance to guarantee a final judicial decision within five days, and the courts uphold their new law until 1981, when it becomes the last state censorship ordinance to be overturned.

1966

- Justice William J. Brennan, Jr. creates a new, three-pronged standard for pornography in his majority decision overturning a Massachusetts ban on John Cleland's eighteenth-century novel *Memoirs of a Woman of Pleasure*, also known as *Fanny Hill*. Under the Memoirs standard, a work may be ruled obscene only if it meets three requirements: "(a) the dominant theme of the material taken as a whole appeals to prurient interest in sex; (b) the material is patently offensive because it affronts contemporary community standards relating to the description or representation of sexual matters; and (c) the material is utterly without redeeming social value."[6]

1969

- The producers, distributors, and exhibitors of X-rated and erotic films pool their resources to create the Adult Film Association of America. The Los Angeles-based organization fights censorship legislation, files friend-of-the-court briefs in censorship cases and supplies legal assistance to defendants.
- The reproduction of Michelangelo's *David* at Forest Lawn Cemetery in California finally loses its fig leaf. The same year, authorities in Sydney, Australia, file obscenity charges against a bookstore for displaying a poster of the statue. The

charges are dropped when the curator of the New South Wales Art Museum points out that the original has been on public display in Florence, Italy, for almost five hundred years.

1971

- The British evangelical crusade the Festival of Light is launched at a nationwide rally attended by 215,000. The group is led by Baptist missionary Peter Hill with the help of born-again journalist Malcolm Muggeridge, censorship crusader Mary Whitehouse, and pop singer Cliff Richard. As part of the organization's campaign against pornography, they predict that the world will end in five years unless the country stamps out smut. When neither eventuality takes place, the group fades out of existence.

1975

- Phyllis Schlafly, formerly a vehement campaigner against the ERA, founds the Eagle Forum to advance a variety of conservative causes, including the battles against pornography and liberal public-school education.
- France changes its film censorship laws twice. Initially, the government stops banning films for adult audiences, using an X rating to bar children under eighteen. Public protests lead to a second change in the system, limiting X films to specialized theaters so those who don't want to be exposed to such materials won't stumble upon them by accident. The new rating hardly opens the door to adult films. X-rated films are taxed at a higher rate, with foreign pictures charged an additional import levy that keeps many such films out of the country. In addition, advertising for X-rated films is extremely limited, with no promotional clips at all allowed on television.

1977

- The Reverend Donald Wildmon enters the censorship wars by spearheading two "Turn Off Television" weeks—one in late February, another in July—to get those opposed to sex and violence on television to boycott the medium. Initially he targets NBC, at the time the lowest-rated national network. In April, he also creates the "Let Your Light Shine" campaign, urging viewers offended by overly permissive television programming to drive with their headlights on during the day. Wildmon will later head up the Coalition for Better Television and the American Family Association, pressure groups dedicated to fighting indecency in television, movies, and publicly funded art.

1978

- In one of the most unusual censorship cases ever, British activist Mary Whitehouse wins a private lawsuit against that country's *Gay News* for publishing James Kirkup's "The Love That Dares to Speak Its Name," a poem describing homosexual relations between Christ and a Roman soldier. Under British law, Whitehouse sues the newspaper as a private citizen. The jury fines the editor five hundred pounds and the paper one thousand pounds.

1979

- Jerry Falwell founds the Moral Majority, a political action group "dedicated to convincing morally conservative Americans that it is their duty to register and vote for candidates who agree with their moral principles."[7] At its height, the organization's membership includes seventy-two thousand ministers and four million lay persons. Falwell and the Moral Majority will take credit for helping sweep Ronald Reagan into the White House in 1980.

1986

- The Supreme Court of Oregon becomes the first in the nation to overturn all restrictions on obscenity. As authority, the court cites the Oregon Constitution, the failure of the original thirteen colonies to legislate against sexual obscenity, and the state's history: "Most members of the [Oregon] Constitutional Convention of 1857 were rugged individuals dedicated to founding a free society unfettered by the governmental imposition of some people's views of morality on the free expression of others."[8]

1989

- The Ayatollah Khomeini issues a death warrant against Salman Rushdie, author of *The Satanic Verses*, and offers a one-million-dollar award for his death. The book, which presents an irreverent view of Islam and numerous contemporary political figures, is banned in India, Pakistan, Saudi Arabia, Egypt, Somalia, Sudan, Malaysia, Qatar, Indonesia, and South Africa. In a display of sympathy for Rushdie, the French government decries the death sentence and promises to prosecute anyone killing the author. British prime minister Margaret Thatcher, who is portrayed in the book as "Mrs. Torture," expresses sympathy for the Muslims. In 1993, President Bill Clinton speaks briefly with Rushdie, then apologizes to representatives of Islam for doing so.

1991

- Frustrated at what he considers the failure of the ratings system to inform parents of film content, Dick Rolfe of Grand Rapids, Michigan, launches the Dove Foundation, an organization dedicated to advising parents on the suitability of films on video. Dove uses fifteen volunteers to screen and rate videos, and then sells lists of approved films to parents and video stores. The latter also receive stickers to put on films approved by the foundation. By 1993, Dove will provide its services to six hundred video outlets in the U.S. and Canada, less than 1 percent of total available stores. Dove also campaigns to get the studios to release on video the sanitized versions of films created for airline showing. In addition, in 1992 they convince McDonald's to drop its promotion of *Batman Returns* because of the PG-13 film's violence.

1992

- At a meeting in Los Angeles, Ted Baehr of Atlanta's Christian Film and Television Commission proposes the reestablishment of the Production Code. The document he distributes is virtually identical to the MPAA's original Code except for the deletion of the industry's early ban on miscegenation. The idea is largely derided by industry members and in the media.

- After years of court challenges and complaints, Dallas guts its age-classification law. Originally, the ordinance required that all films shown in the city be submitted to the Dallas Film Board for rating as to their suitability for young audiences. The board automatically labels all films rated R, X, or NC-17 unsuitable for minors, but when they extend that classification to the PG-13 *Sarafina!*, an anti-apartheid musical starring Whoopi Goldberg, the complaints are so strong that the Dallas City Council has to act. They reduce the ratings to mere recommendations and order their removal from advertising and box-office displays. A year later, they will disband the board altogether.

1993

- Donald Wildmon launches a campaign against Steven Bochco's police series "NYPD Blue" months prior to its September premiere on ABC. As originally announced, the program will be television's first R-rated series, redefining limitations on language, nudity, sex, and violence. Although a sample episode is highly praised by advertisers, almost a quarter of ABC's affiliates (fifty-seven stations) refuse to carry the show. When it scores solid ratings—thanks as much to a strong cast and solid writing as to the controversy—several affiliates decide to pick it up after all. After a few weeks, ABC offers "NYPD Blue" to independent stations in markets where affiliates have refused the show. In Dallas, the only top-twenty market not originally carrying the series, the local independent picking up "NYPD Blue" doubles its average rating for the series' time slot.

1994

- After years of delays as networks try to clean up and "de-gay" the story,

Armistead Maupin's *Tales of the City*, a faithful adaptation of the popular news-paper soap opera originally published in the *San Francisco Chronicle*, makes it to American television on PBS stations. Because of nudity, four-letter words, drug use, and the positive depiction of homosexuality, the miniseries is blacked out by several affiliates (most notably those in the Southeast) or aired in a bowdlerized version. When Georgia Public Television (GPTV) chooses to air the series in its uncensored form, the decision triggers an outcry from conservatives. One group petitions Governor Zell Miller to pull the series personally, something he cannot legally do. State legislators, many of whom have not seen *Tales of the City* and are not even aware that it is being telecast no earlier than 10:00 P.M., try to pass a motion censuring GPTV for using tax money to expose children to such adult materials. Conservatives manage to cut funding for a new production facility but fail to pass a measure prohibiting the use of state funds to produce or broadcast pornography.

• As this book goes to press, two of the first players in the Hollywood censorship wars are back in the news. A newly restored version of D. W. Griffith's *The Birth of a Nation* has been withheld from home-video release in England for two months by a ratings dispute with the British Board of Film Censors, now charged with regulating both home videos and theatrical films. The BBFC is demanding a disclaimer at the tape's start to warn viewers that the film's treatment of racial issues may cause offense, but to date has rejected two disclaimers suggested by the video's distributor. At the same time, legislation pending in Parliament could give the BBFC more control than ever over the availability of violent films on home video. Among the films whose video releases have been held up until Parliament votes is Quentin Tarantino's controversial, critically acclaimed independent pro-duction *Reservoir Dogs*.

Endnotes

INTRODUCTION

1. Will H. Hays, *The Memoirs of Will H. Hays* (Garden City, New York: Doubleday & Company, 1955), p. 370.

2. The term is derived from the "prohibition/institutions model" suggested in Annette Kuhn, *Cinema, Censorship and Sexuality, 1909–1925* (London: Routledge, 1988), p. 2.

CHAPTER ONE

1. Bernard Weinraub, "Violent Melodrama of a Sizzling Movie Brings Rating Battle," *New York Times*, January 30, 1992, p. C15.

2. Quoted in Michael Medved, *Hollywood Vs. America* (New York: HarperCollins Publishers, 1992), p. 322.

3. Quoted in Jeff Schwager, "Bad Instinct?" *Boxoffice*, March 1992, p. 8.

4. Quoted in Claudia Eller, "Verhoeven Nixes Basic Changes," *Daily Variety*, April 30, 1991, p. 15.

5. Medved, p. 323.

6. Robert W. Welkos, "Director Trims *Basic Instinct* to Get R Rating," *Los Angeles Times*, February 11, 1992, p. F1.

7. Quoted in Alex McGregor, "Sex Crimes," *Time Out*, April 22–29, 1992, pp. 19f.

CHAPTER TWO

1. Remarks attributed to Virginia Rappe, quoted in Kenneth Anger, *Hollywood Babylon* (New York: Dell Publishing Co., 1975), p. 25.

2. Quoted in Anger, p. 29.

3. Herbert S. Stone, quoted in Terry Ramsaye, *A Million and One Nights: A History of the Motion Picture Through 1925* (New York: Simon & Schuster, 1926), p. 259.

4. Quoted in Ramsaye, p. 473.

5. Quoted in Ramsaye, p. 479.

6. Quoted in Kevin Brownlow, *Behind the Mask of Innocence* (New York: Alfred A. Knopf, 1990), p. 6.

7. Quoted in Richard S. Randall, *Censorship of the Movies: The Social and Political Control of a Mass Medium* (Madison, Wisc.: The University of Wisconsin Press, 1968), p. 19.

8. Quoted in Ruth A. Inglis, *Freedom of the Movies: A Report on Self-Regulation from the Commission on Freedom of the Press* (Chicago: University of Chicago Press, 1947), pp. 83f.

9. *Message Photo-Play Co.* v. *Bell* (1917), quoted in Edward De Grazia and Roger K. Newman, *Banned Films* (New York: R.R. Bowker Company, 1982), p. 188.

10. *Pathé Exchange, Inc.* v. *Cobb* (1922), quoted in De Grazia and Newman, p. 203.

11. Hays, p. 325.

Censored Hollywood

12. Hays, p. 329.

13. Quoted in Raymond Moley, *The Hays Office* (Indianapolis: Bobbs-Merrill Company, 1945), p. 38.

14. Quoted in Homer Croy, *Star Maker: The Story of D. W. Griffith* (New York: Duell, Sloan and Pearce, 1959), p. 103.

15. Quoted in Richard Schickel, *D. W. Griffith: An American Life* (New York: Simon and Schuster, 1984), p. 283.

16. Quoted in Lillian Gish, *The Movies, Mr. Griffith, and Me* (Englewood Cliffs, NJ: Prentice-Hall, 1969), p. 158.

17. Schickel, *D. W. Griffith*, p. 294.

18. Hays, pp. 330f.

19. Quoted in Robert Sklar, *Movie-Made America: A Cultural History of American Movies* (New York: Random House, 1975), p. 132.

20. Quoted in Anger, p. 68.

21. *Message Photo-Play Co.* v. *Bell* (1917), quoted in Edward De Grazia and Roger K. Newman, *Banned Films* (New York: R. R. Bowker Company, 1982), p. 188.

CHAPTER THREE

1. Olga J. Martin, *Hollywood's Movie Commandments: A Handbook for Motion Picture Writers and Reviewers* (New York: H. W. Wilson Company, 1937), p. 17.

2. Hays, p. 344.

3. Reprinted from Gerald Gardner, *The Censorship Papers: Movie Censorship Letters from the Hays Office, 1934 to 1968* (New York: Dodd, Mead & Company, 1987), pp. 213f.

4. Quoted in Inglis, p. 116.

5. Quoted in Brownlow, p. 9.

6. Lloyd Binford, quoted in Ira H. Carmen, *Movies, Censorship, and the Law* (Ann Arbor, Mich.: University of Michigan Press, 1966), pp. 207f.

7. Quoted in Brownlow, p. 138.

8. W. Somerset Maugham, "Rain," in *The Complete Short Stories of W. Somerset Maugham* (London: Neinemann, 1951), p. 38.

9. John Colton and Clemence Randolph, *Rain* (London: Samuel French, 1923), p. 83.

10. Quoted in Gloria Swanson, *Swanson on Swanson* (New York: Random House, 1980), p. 305f.

CHAPTER FOUR

1. Lord would later claim to have written that portion of the Code on his own.

2. Jack Vizzard, *See No Evil: Life Inside a Hollywood Censor* (New York: Simon and Schuster, 1970), pp. 129f.

3. Reprinted in Leonard J. Jeff and Jerold L. Simmons, *The Dame in the Kimono: Hollywood Censorship and the Production Code from the 1920s to the 1960s* (New York: Anchor Books, 1990), p. 288.

4. Unless otherwise indicated, all citations of PCA correspondence come from the Production Code Administration Files in the Academy of Motion Picture Arts and Sciences' Margaret Herrick Library, Special Collections.

5. Unless otherwise noted, all citations from Warner Bros. scripts and advertising, as

well as correspondence not relating to Production Code matters, come from the University of Southern California's Warner Bros. Collection.

6. "*I Am a Fugitive*," *Daily Variety*, October 21, 1932.

7. Arthur Brisbane, quoted in "Hearst and Brisbane Praise Warner Film," Motion *Picture Herald*, December 3, 1932, p. 14.

8. Eugene Walter, *The Easiest Way*, in John Gassner, ed., *Best Plays of the Early American Theatre: From the Beginning to 1916* (New York: Crown Publishers, 1967), pp. 675f.

9. Quoted in Hays, pp. 448f.

10. Quoted in Maurice Leonard, *Mae West: Empress of Sex* (New York: Carol Publishing Group, 1992), p. 112.

11. Quoted in Leonard, p. 125.

12. Henry James Forman, *Our Movie Made Children* (New York: Macmillan Company, 1933), pp. 205, 219.

13. Quoted in letter from K. L. Russell to Will Hays, May, 23, 1933, Special Collections, Margaret Herrick Library.

14. Quoted in Vizzard, p. 45.

15. Quoted in Hays, p. 450.

16. Quoted in Inglis, p. 122.

17. Quoted in Vizzard, p. 50.

18. The fine was levied only twice over the course of three decades: against United Artists for releasing *The Moon Is Blue* in 1953 and against RKO for releasing *The French Line* in 1954. In neither case was the fine paid. UA quit the Association in protest, while RKO refused to pay the fine, ultimately recutting the film (see Chapter Seven).

CHAPTER FIVE

1. Martin, p. 99.

2. Thornton Delehanty, "The Films Walk Moral Tightrope," *New York Herald Tribune*, April 5, 1942.

3. Quoted in Vizzard, p. 51.

4. Quoted in Vizzard, p. 53.

5. Quoted in Hays, p. 461.

6. W. Somerset Maugham, *The Letter*, in *Best Mystery and Suspense Plays of the Modern Theatre* (New York: Avon Books, 1971), pp. 342–3.

7. Kauf., "*G-Men*," *Variety*, May 8, 1935, p. 16.

8. Arthur Pollock, "The Screen," *Brooklyn Eagle*, August 7, 1934.

9. Blade Johaneson, "Movie News," *New York Daily Mirror*, August 4, 1934.

10. "*Outcast Lady*," *Variety*, August 7, 1934.

11. "The Screen Must Not Relapse to Lewdness," *Los Angeles Examiner*, February 28, 1936.

12. "Stop Lewd Films," *Los Angeles Examiner*, February 29, 1936.

13. Frank S. Nugent, "The Screen," *New York Times*, March 12, 1936.

14. Quoted in James Robert Parrish, *The Paramount Pretties* (New Rochelle, New York: Arlington House, 1972), p. 313.

15. Joseph L. Mankiewicz, All About "*All About Eve*" (New York: Random House,

1972), pp. 148, 150.

16. Quoted in Vizzard, p. 98.

17. *Los Angeles Herald-Express*, quoted in letter from Francis Harmon to Joseph Breen, December 10, 1937.

18. Quoted in De Grazia and Newman, p. 210.

19. The FTC had begun objecting to the uncredited retitling of older films shortly after the end of World War II and had already locked horns with Breen over the reissue of *The Life and Death of Colonel Blimp*.

20. "The New Pictures: *These Three*," *Time*, March 30, 1936.

21. Phil Koury, "A Movie to Watch For," *Kansas City Star*, March 29, 1942, p. D 1.

22. In response to complaints from exhibitors, MGM also issued a version with a happy ending: Anna simply leaves Vronsky, and the two are reunited years later, after her husband's death.

23. Quoted in Greg Mitchell, *The Campaign of the Century: Upton Sinclair's Race for Governor of California and the Birth of Media Politics* (New York: Random House, 1992), pp. 415f.

24. Flin, "Three Comrades," *Variety*, May 24, 1938.

CHAPTER SIX

1. Prior to *Gone With the Wind*, Breen had allowed the word "damn" in a Warner Bros. short based on *The Man Without a Country*.

2. Quoted in Carmen, p. 46.

3. Quoted in De Grazia and Newman, p. 239.

4. Quoted in James Robert Parrish, *The RKO Gals* (New Rochelle, N.Y.: Arlington House, 1974), p. 708.

5. Adela Rogers St. John, "Why Breen Resigned from the Hays Office," *Liberty*, July 5, 1941, p. 14.

6. Quoted in James Francis Crow, "Greta Garbo's New Film Condemned by Legion of Decency," *Hollywood Citizen*, November 24, 1941.

7. James Agee, *Agee on Film*, Volume 1 (New York: Perigee Books, 1958), p. 74.

8. Quoted in Hays, pp. 534f.

9. Joseph Breen, quoted in Gardner, p. 131.

10. Quoted in Charles Chaplin, *My Autobiography* (New York: Simon and Schuster, 1964), p. 446.

11. Vizzard, p. 184.

12. W.H.M., "Film Scores Cheap Laughs at Family Life," *Tidings*, March 24, 1944.

13. "*Life Begins for Andy Hardy*," *Hollywood Reporter*, August 7, 1941.

14. Quoted in Parrish, *RKO*, p. 709.

15. Quoted in Jane Russell, *Jane Russell: My Path & My Detours* (New York: Franklin Watts, Inc., 1985), p. 72.

16. Russell, p. 18.

17. *Hughes Tool Company* v. *Motion Picture Association of America, Inc.* U.S. 224 (1946).

18. Quoted in "Judge Thunderstruck by Jane Russell in *Outlaw*; OK's Ban," *Los Angeles Herald Examiner*, September 20, 1947.

19. Russell, p. 19.

20. Congressional Record—House of Representatives, June 19, 1947, pp. 7546f.

21. Quoted in J. Mitchell Morse, "Massachusetts Court Clears *Forever Amber*," *New York Herald Tribune Weekly Book Review*, March 30, 1947.

22. "*Forever Amber*," *Life*, November 3, 1947, p. 67.

23. W.H.M., "Perfect Crime Myth Exploded," *Tidings*, August 11, 1944.

24. Quoted in Jay Robert Nash and Stanley Ralph Russ, *The Motion Picture Guide* (Chicago: Cinebooks, 1985), p. 2440.

25. Bosley Crowther, "For Better and for Worse," *New York Times*, May 5, 1946.

26. Quoted in Victor S. Navasky, *Naming Names* (Middlesex, England: Penguin Books, 1980), p. 83.

27. Brendan Bracken, quoted in "Cutting 'Salty Adjectives' From Film Stirs British," *Los Angeles Times*, December 10, 1942.

28. "O, Hollywood!," *New York Herald Tribune*, December 12, 1942, p. 14.

29. Quoted in "Stormy History of *Devil in the Flesh*," *New York Times*, March 20, 1949, p. 4X.

30. Lowell E. Redelings, "The Hollywood Scene," *Hollywood Citizen News*, October 26, 1949.

31. Eileen Creelman, "Picture Plays: Slap on Wrist May Clean Up Foreign Films," *New York World-Telegram and Sun*, March 6, 1950.

32. Bosley Crowther, "Unkindest Cut: The Code Authority's Excisions of *The Bicycle Thief* Are Upheld," *New York Times*, April 2, 1950, section 2, p. 1.

33. Quoted in A. Scott Berg, *Goldwyn: A Biography* (New York: Alfred A. Knopf, 1989), p. 418.

34. Quoted in Gardner, p. 179.

CHAPTER SEVEN

1. Quoted in Carmen, p. 45.

2. "*The Miracle*: An Outrage," *Motion Picture Herald*, January 6, 1951, p. 1.

3. Carol Trabucco, quoted in Camille M. Cianfarra, "Vatican Views *Miracle* Row," *New York Times*, February 11, 1951.

4. Roberto Rossellini, quoted in "Rossellini Appeal to Spellman on Film," *New York Times*, January 13, 1951.

5. Quoted in Crowther, "The Strange Case of *The Miracle*," *Atlantic Monthly*, April, 1951, pp. 36f.

6. Bosley Crowther, "*The Miracle* Happens," *New York Times*, June 1, 1952, Section 2, p. 1.

7. Quoted in "Freedom of the Screen Won for the Industry," *Boxoffice*, May 31, 1952, p. 9.

8. Quoted in *Boxoffice*, p. 9.

9. Quoted in *Boxoffice*, p. 10.

10. Quoted in De Grazia and Newman, p. 84.

11. Quoted in Murray Schumach, *The Face on the Cutting Room Floor: The Story of Movie and Television Censorship* (New York: DaCapo Press, 1974), p. 72.

12. Tennessee Williams, *A Streetcar Named Desire*, in Randolph Goodman, *Drama*

on Stage (New York: Holt, Rinehart and Winston, 1961), p. 354.

13. Quoted in Elia Kazan, *A Life* (New York: Alfred A. Knopf, 1988), p. 345.

14. Quoted in Kazan, p. 433.

15. Quoted in Vizzard, p. 176.

16. Quoted in Herbert Mitgang, "Transmuting a Touchy, Topical Tome," *New York Times*, June 14, 1953.

17. Martin Quigley, "Well Done!" *Motion Picture Daily*, August 14, 1953.

18. Quoted in Vizzard, p. 24.

19. Quoted in "*Moon* Cab Scene Cut, Plays Alabam'; St. Paul Solons Hold Nose, O.K. It," *Weekly Variety*, July 29, 1953, p. 4.

20. H. R. Wilkerson, "Trade Views," *Hollywood Reporter*, June 4, 1953.

21. Quoted in W. Ward Marsh, "Number of Good Pictures This Year Rises to High of 42; More Are to Come," *Cleveland Plain Dealer*, July 22, 1954.

22. Quoted in Dick Williams, "A Beef from Jane Russell," *Los Angeles Mirror*, January 14, 1954.

23. "Jane Russell Furor: Sam Goldwyn Urges New Censorship Code," *Hollywood Citizen-News*, December 29, 1953.

24. Vizzard, p. 175.

25. Quoted in Schumach, p. 45.

26. Quoted in Art Ryon, "Movie Censors Work to Improve Films, Not Simply Cut Things Out," *Los Angeles Times*, February 5, 1962, part 2, p. 1.

27. Vizzard, p. 161.

28. *Trial* was one of the few early fifties films to attempt a serious social statement. Faced with the threat of the blacklist, most writers were afraid to suggest stories that seriously challenged the status quo.

29. Gene, "*The Man with the Golden Arm*," *Daily Variety*, December 14, 1955, p. 6.

30. Quoted in De Grazia and Newman, p. 253.

31. Quoted in "High Court's Ruling on Sex in Movies," *U.S. News & World Report*, July 13, 1959, p. 50.

32. Quoted in De Grazia and Newman, pp. 264f.

33. Quoted in De Grazia and Newman, p. 265.

34. William K. Zinsser, "The New Movie: *A Farewell to Arms*," *New York Herald Tribune*, January 25, 1958.

35. Robert Anderson, *Tea and Sympathy*, in *Famous American Plays of the 1950s* (New York: Dell Publishing Co., 1962), p. 312.

36. In the sixties, the major Hollywood studios would turn increasingly to subsidiaries in order to release films rejected by the PCA and/or the Legion of Decency. Ultimately, the practice would contribute to the end of the Production Code.

37. Bosley Crowther, "Loosening the Code," *New York Times*, October 7, 1956.

38. Quoted in Gardner, p. 191.

39. Quoted in "Legion of Decency Hits Code for *Baby Doll* Okay," *Daily Variety*, November 28, 1956.

40. Vizzard, p. 206.

41. Quoted in "Spellman Denounces *Baby Doll* From Pulpit," *Hollywood Citizen News*, December 17, 1956.

42. Quoted in *Hollywood Citizen-News*, December 17, 1956.

43. Quoted in "*10 Commandments* Much More Sexy Than *Baby Doll*, Clergyman Declares," *New York Times*, December 24, 1956.

44. Quoted in "*Baby Doll* Is Approved by British Priest for Showing to Adult Roman Catholics," *New York Times*, December 21, 1956.

45. Quoted in Vizzard, p. 225.

46. The "Separate Classification" would become "A-IV" in 1963.

CHAPTER EIGHT

1. Quoted in Vizzard, p. 308.

2. Pauline Kael was one of many critics who found the device annoying. "I assumed the youngest child in the audience would get the point before he did," she wrote in *I Lost It at the Movies* (Boston: Little, Brown and Company, 1965), p. 140.

3. Powe, "*Suddenly Last Summer*," *Daily Variety*, December 16, 1959.

4. Quoted in untitled review, *Saturday Review*, February 24, 1962.

5. Quoted in Vito Russo, *The Celluloid Closet: Homosexuality in the Movies* (New York: Harper & Row, Publishers, 1981), pp. 121f.

6. Bosley Crowther, "The Screen: New *Children's Hour*," *New York Times*, March 15, 1962.

7. Russo describes most screen treatments of homosexuality from the period as mere "condescension to an amorphous 'adult' audience that Hollywood was determined to reach without offending the blue noses" (p. 119).

8. Similar notations had appeared in ads for *Elmer Gantry* (1960), *Splendor in the Grass* (1961), and *The Children's Hour* (1961), but this marked the first time the Legion had imposed such a condition on a distributor.

9. Hollis Alpert, "The Bubble Gum Siren," *Saturday Review*, June 23, 1962.

10. "Cinema: Humbert Humdrum & Lullita," *Time*, June 22, 1962, p. 94.

11. Kael, *I Lost It*, p. 208.

12. Quoted in Vizzard, p. 304.

13. Shurlock, quoted in Vizzard, p. 305.

14. Quoted in "Moral or Immoral," *Time*, December 28, 1964, p. 53.

15. Quoted in "A Kick Instead for *Kiss Me, Stupid*," *Variety*, December 9, 1964.

16. Bosley Crowther, "The Heat is on Films," *New York Times*, January 17, 1965.

17. Quoted in "Legion of Decency's Hesitation But Finally 'C's' *Pawnbroker*," *Weekly Variety*, May 12, 1965, p. 4.

18. Quoted in "Bishop Pike Endorses *Pawnbroker* Following Catholic Condemnation," *Exhibitor*, June 2, 1965.

19. Quoted in Vizzard, pp. 320f.

20. Quoted in Thomas Thompson, "Raw Dialogue Challenges All the Censors," *Life*, June 10, 1966, p. 92.

21. Quoted in Thompson, *Life*, p. 96.

22. Quoted in Thompson, *Life*, p. 96.

23. Martin Quigley, Jr., "The Code Is Dead," *Motion Picture Herald*, July 6, 1966.

24. Quoted in Vizzard, p. 323.

25. Quoted in Randall, pp. 201f.

26. Quoted in Vizzard, pp. 334f.

27. Quoted in Clyde Jeavons, "The Films of Frederick Wiseman," in Ann Lloyd, ed., *Movies of the Seventies* (London: Orbis, 1984), p. 55.

28. Quoted in "Catholic Office Rips *Blow-Up*," *Hollywood Reporter*, December 29, 1966, pp. 1–4.

29. Richard Schickel, "Harsh Moral from a Grisly Film," *Life*, July 21, 1967.

30. Bosley Crowther, "Another Smash at Violence," *New York Times*, July 30, 1967, p. 47.

CHAPTER NINE

1. Quoted in De Grazia and Newman, p. 117.

2. Quoted in Stephen Farber, *The Movie Rating Game* (Washington, D.C.: Public Affairs Press, 1972), p. 112.

3. Quoted in De Grazia and Newman, p. 130.

4. Quoted in De Grazia and Newman, p. 131.

5. Quoted in De Grazia and Newman, p. 131.

6. Marjorie Heins, *Sex, Sin and Blasphemy: A Guide to America's Censorship Wars* (New York: New Press, 1993), p. 150.

7. United Artists applied for a rating on *Midnight Cowboy* in January 1971, after it had played out its first run and won its awards. CARA then voted the film an R.

8. Quoted in Farber, pp. 85f.

9. Stern, quoted in Farber, pp. 122–123.

10. Quoted in Farber, p. 122.

11. Quoted in Farber, p. 90.

12. *Greetings* brought the MPAA its first ratings appeal; the review board simply told the distributor to discuss the situation further with Dougherty.

13. Two years later, Kubrick would trim thirty seconds from the film to win an R rating.

14. Previously, Sjöman had directed *491* (1964), the second film since *Ecstasy* to be banned by U.S. Customs. Although a jury trial upheld the Customs ban, the appeal court found that the tale of juvenile delinquents in an experimental rehabilitation program had redeeming social value and overturned the ruling.

15. Quoted in Farber, pp. 46f.

16. Quoted in Farber, p. 47.

17. Quoted in Heins, p. 157.

18. Quoted in Linda Williams, *Hard Core: Power, Pleasure, and the "Frenzy of the Visible"* (Berkeley, Calif.: University of California Press, 1989), p. 190.

19. Quoted in Heins, p. 162.

20. Quoted in Green, p. 83.

21. Quoted in Hentoff, p. 350.

22. As he told this writer, "It is the voluntarism of the ratings system that gives it its courtroom strength. It does not torment the Constitution, because nobody is forced to rate their picture."

23. Quoted in De Grazia and Newman, p. 126.

24. Quoted in De Grazia and Newman, p. 118.

25. Quoted in De Grazia and Newman, p. 346.

26. Quoted in Green, p. 189.

27. Burger, quoted in De Grazia and Newman, pp. 136f.

28. Quoted in De Grazia and Newman, p. 353.

29. Lovelace later revealed that she had been coerced into performing in the film by an abusive lover-manager. With the publication of her autobiography, *Ordeal!*, in 1980, she joined the ranks of antipornography feminists.

30. Quoted in Kenneth Turan and Stephen F. Zito, *Sinema: American Pornographic Films and the People Who Make Them* (New York: Praeger Publishers, 1974), p. 145.

31. Quoted in Richard Lacayo, "Days of Ire and Brimstone," *Time*, July 25, 1988.

32. Quoted in Amy Dawes, "Offer to Buy Pic: Christians Protest U's Christ," Daily Variety, July 18, 1988, pp. 1–6.

33. Quoted in Aljean Harmetz, "Film on Christ Brings Out Pickets, and Archbishop Predicts Censure," *New York Times*, July 21, 1988, p. C19.

34. Quoted in Jane Galbraith and Richard Gold, "Scorsese Defends *Temptation* on TV," *Daily Variety*, July 27, 1988, pp. 3–19.

35. Quoted in Aljean Harmetz, "*The Last Temptation of Christ* Opens to Protests but Good Sales," *New York Times*, August 13, 1988.

36. "Nightline," ABC Television, August 9, 1988.

37. "Nightline."

38. "Nightline."

39. Quoted in "Press Violent About Film's Violence; Prod Sam Peckinpah Following *Bunch*," *Weekly Variety*, June 24, 1969, p. 15.

40. Quoted in "Catholic Film Office Neutral on W7 R-Rated *Wild Bunch*," *Daily Variety*, July 3, 1969.

41. Quoted in "The Flick of Violence," *Time*, March 19, 1979, p. 39.

42. *Poltergeist* was originally rated R and downgraded to PG on appeal.

43. Andrew Sarris, "To Cut or Not to Cut," *Village Voice*, March 12, 1985.

44. Quoted in Michael London, "New World's *Passion* Again Fails to Pick Up R Rating," *Daily Variety*, September 24, 1984, p. 14.

45. Quoted in Desmond Ryan, "The Cook, the Actress and the 'X' Rating," *Philadelphia Inquirer*, April 15, 1990, p. 11G.

46. Quoted in "*Henry* Takes Torturous Path to Screen," *Hollywood Reporter*, April 20, 1990.

47. Quoted in Richard Huff, "MPAA Seeking Dismissal of *Tie Me Up* Lawsuit," *Daily Variety*, June 20, 1990, p. 3.

48. Quoted in "Excerpts from *Miramax* vs. *MPAA Ruling*," *Los Angeles Times*, July 21, 1990, p. F7.

49. Quoted in Jack Mathews, "Henry Miller Meets the MPAA," *Los Angeles Times*, August 27, 1990, p. F1.

50. Quoted in Stephen Farber, "A Major Studio Plans to Test the Rating System," *New York Times*, September 4, 1990.

51. He also bent to another longstanding complaint against the system, announcing that henceforth the MPAA's bulletins would briefly explain the reasoning behind all R

ratings. Two years later, they would add explanations for PG and PG-13 ratings as well.

52. Quoted in Larry Rohter, "A 'No Children' Category to Replace the 'X' Rating," *New York Times*, September 27, 1990, p. C18.

CHAPTER TEN

1. Quoted in Jack Mathews, "Sell-Out Crowds for *Henry and June*," *Los Angeles Times*, p. F12.

2. Quoted in John Voland, "Valenti: *Henry* Ban Like 'Dark Ages,' " *Hollywood Reporter*, October 8, 1990, p. 3.

3. Postfeminist critic Camille Paglia told *Vanity Fair*'s Kevin Sessums: "Women are bitches! Woman is the bitch goddess of the universe! *Basic Instinct* has to be seen as the return of the femme fatale, which points up woman's dominance of the sexual realm, and Sharon Stone's performance was one of the great performances by a woman in screen history." ("Stone Goddess," *Vanity Fair*, April 1993, p. 202.)

4. Critics have also complained that the film attacks its issues from the perspective of straight, relatively uninformed audience members. Surprisingly, most critics have overlooked several gaping plot holes, including the law firm's improbably shaky justification of Hanks's firing and the fact that two partners in the firm volunteer information about their own homophobia on the witness stand.

5. Abel Ferrara, quoted in Tom Crow, "*Lieutenant*'s General," *Village View*, January 1–7, 1993, p. 9.

6. Quoted in Heins, p. 131.

7. President Bill Clinton surprised many by authorizing the Justice Department to appeal. The action would suggest that the Clinton administration considers such decency clauses constitutionally valid. To date, the Clinton White House has not taken any other stand on the issue.

DATELINE

1. Quoted in Jonathan Green, *The Encyclopedia of Censorship* (New York: Facts on File, 1990), p. 170.

2. Quoted in Green, p. 123.

3. Quoted in Green, p. 56.

4. Justice Felix Frankfurter, quoted in Carmen, p. 70.

5. Quoted in Carmen, p. 72.

6. Quoted in Green, p. 187.

7. Quoted in Green, p. 192.

8. Quoted in Nat Hentoff, *Free Speech for Me—but Not for Thee: How the American Left and Right Relentlessly Censor Each Other* (New York: HarperCollins Publishers, 1992), p. 318.

Bibliography

GENERAL SOURCES

"Aaron Stern Joins Columbia; He and Hirschfield Plot Duties; M.D. Got Along With Distribs." *Variety*, December 5, 1973, pp. 3:29.

Adler, Mortimer J. *Art and Prudence: A Study in Practical Philosophy*. New York: Longmans, Green and Co., 1937.

"Alexander May Face Tough NEA Role." *Atlanta Journal-Constitution*, August 9, 1993, p. B7.

Alexander, Kathey. "Cobb Board Votes to Kill Arts Funding." *Atlanta Journal-Constitution*, August 25, 1993, p. A1.

——— and Cathy Cleland-Pero. "Severed Ties Likely Won't End Dispute." *Atlanta Journal-Constitution*, August 25, 1993, pp. C1:C8.

Anger, Kenneth. *Hollywood Babylon*. New York: Dell Publishing Co., 1975.

Atkins, Thomas R., ed. *Sexuality in the Movies*. Bloomington, Ind.: Indiana University Press, 1975.

Baxter, Tom. "Cobb's Vote is Full of Consequences." *Atlanta Journal-Constitution*, August 26, 1993, p. C2.

Behlmer, Rudy. *Behind the Scenes*. Hollywood, California: Samuel French, 1982.

———. *Memo from David O. Selznick*. New York: Viking Press, 1972.

Berg, A. Scott. *Goldwyn: A Biography*. New York: Alfred A. Knopf, 1989.

Berman, Sam. "The Hays Office." *Fortune*, December 1938, pp. 68–72.

"Breen Sees Cleaner Films." *Los Angeles Times*, July 15, 1934.

"Breen—The Man & His Cause." *Motion Picture Herald*, December 22, 1965, p. 1.

Brockett, Oscar G. *History of the Theatre*. Fourth Edition. Boston: Allyn and Bacon, 1982.

Brownlow, Kevin. *Behind the Mask of Innocence*. New York: Alfred A. Knopf, 1990.

Carmen, Ira H. *Movies, Censorship, and the Law*. Ann Arbor, Michigan: University of Michigan Press, 1966.

"CBS Blasts House Bill Requiring TV 'V-Chip.'" *Atlanta Journal-Constitution*, August 6, 1993, p. C6.

Cleland-Pero, Cathy. "Woodward, Newman Give $20,000 to Help Cobb Theater Stay on Stage." *Atlanta Journal-Constitution*, September 23, 1993, p. G1.

"Clergy Sees Reform by Hollywood Studios." *Los Angeles Times*, July 15, 1934.

Coakley, Mary Lewis. *Rated X: The Moral Case Against TV*. New Rochelle, NY: Arlington House Publishers, 1977.

Corkis, Jim, and John Cawley. *Cartoon Confidential*. Westlake Village, California: Malibu Graphics, 1991.

De Grazia, Edward, and Roger K. Newman. *Banned Films: Movies, Censors and the First Amendment*. New York: R.R. Bowker Company, 1982.

Ernst, Morris L., and Pare Lorentz. *Censored: The Private Life of the Movies*. New York: Jonathan Cape and Harrison Smith, 1930.

Farber, Stephen. *The Movie Ratings Game*. Washington, D.C.: Public Affairs Press, 1972.

"Film Industry Snubs Joe Breen's Funeral." *Variety*, December 15, 1965.

Forman, Henry James. *Our Movie Made Children*. New York: Macmillan Company, 1933.

Frohnmayer, John. *Leaving Town Alive: Confessions of an Arts Warrior*. Boston: Houghton Mifflin Company, 1993.

Gardner, Gerald. *The Censorship Papers: Movie Censorship Letters from the Hays Office, 1934 to 1968*. New York: Dodd, Mead & Company, 1987.

Goldman, Kevin. "Networks' Plan for TV Program Warnings May Backfire." *Wall Street Journal*, July 1, 1993.

Green, Jonathon. *The Encyclopedia of Censorship*. New York: Facts on File, 1990.

Hadleigh, Boze. *The Lavender Screen*. New York: Citadel Press, 1993.

Hay, Peter. *MGM: When the Lion Roars*. Atlanta: Turner Publishing, 1991.

Hays, Will H. *The Memoirs of Will H. Hays*. Garden City, New York: Doubleday & Company, 1955.

Heins, Marjorie. *Sex, Sin, and Blasphemy: A Guide to America's Censorship Wars*. New York: New Press, 1993.

Hentoff, Nat. *Free Speech for Me—but Not for Thee: How the American Left and Right Relentlessly Censor Each Other*. New York: HarperCollins Publishers, 1992.

Inglis, Ruth A. *Freedom of the Movies: A Report on Self-Regulation from the Commission on Freedom of the Press*. Chicago: University of Chicago Press, 1947.

"Joe Breen's Film Censor Duties at End." *Hollywood Citizen-News*, June 18, 1941, p. 1.

Jubera, Drew. "Backlash Against Television Violence." *Atlanta Journal-Constitution*, October 21, 1993, pp. A1–A8.

Kael, Pauline. *I Lost It at the Movies*. Boston: Little, Brown and Company, 1965.

Katz, Ephraim. *The Film Encyclopedia*. New York: Perigee Books, 1979.

Kazan, Elia. *A Life*. New York: Alfred A. Knopf, 1988.

Kuhn, Annette. *Cinema, Censorship and Sexuality, 1909–1925*. London: Routledge, 1988.

Leff, Leonard and Jerrold L. Simmons. *The Dame in the Kimono: Hollywood Censorship and the Production Code from the 1920s to the 1960s*. New York: Anchor Books, 1990.

Leonard, Maurice. *Mae West: Empress of Sex*. New York: Carol Publishing Group, 1991.

Maltin, Leonard. *Movie and Video Guide 1994*. New York: Signet Books, 1993.

Martin, Olga J. *Hollywood's Movie Commandments: A Handbook for Motion Picture Writers and Reviewers*. New York: H.W. Wilson Company, 1937.

McAvoy, Kim. "Networks Adopt Violence Warning." *Broadcasting & Cable*, July 5, 1993.

McCarthy, Todd, and Charles Flynn, eds. *Kings of the Bs: Working Within the Hollywood System*. New York: E.P. Dutton & Co., 1975.

Medved, Michael. *Hollywood vs. America*. New York: HarperCollins, 1992.

Miller, Don. *"B" Movies: An Informal Survey of the American Low-Budget Film, 1933–1945*. New York: Curtis Books, 1973.

Mitchell, Greg. *The Campaign of the Century: Upton Sinclair's Race for Governor of California and the Birth of Media Politics*. New York: Random House, 1992.

Moley, Raymond. *Are We Movie Made?* New York: Macy-Masius, 1938.

———. *The Hays Office*. Indianapolis: Bobbs-Merrill Company, 1945.

Nash, Jay Robert, and Stanley Ralph Russ. *The Motion Picture Guide*. Chicago: Cinebooks, 1985.

Navasky, Victor S. *Naming Names*. Middlesex, England: Penguin Books, 1980.

O'Briant, Don. "Theater Benefits Marietta in Many Ways, Square's Merchants Say." *Atlanta Journal-Constitution*, August 20, 1993, p. C7.

Otto, Mary. "Clinton's First Test Looms in Culture Wars." *Atlanta Journal-Constitution*, August 27, 1993, p. E7.

Parrish, James Robert. *The Paramount Pretties*. New Rochelle, New York: Arlington House, 1972.

———. *The RKO Gals*. New Rochelle, New York: Arlington House, 1974.

——— and Don E. Stanke. *The Glamour Girls*. New Rochelle, New York: Arlington House, 1975.

Perry, George. *The Great British Picture Show: From the '90s to the '70s*. New York: Hill and Wang, 1974.

Ramsaye, Terry. *A Million and One Nights: A History of the Motion Picture Through 1925*. New York: Simon & Schuster, 1926.

Randall, Richard S. *Censorship of the Movies: The Social and Political Control of a Mass Medium*. Madison, Wisconsin: University of Wisconsin Press, 1968.

Robertson, James C. *The British Board of Film Censors: Film Censorship in Britain, 1896–1950*. London, Croom Helm, 1985.

Russell, Jane. *Jane Russell: My Path and My Detours*. New York: Franklin Watts, Inc., 1985.

Russo, Vito. *The Celluloid Closet: Homosexuality in the Movies*. New York: Harper & Row, 1981.

Ryon, Art. "Movie Censors Work to Improve Films, Not Simply Cut Things Out." *Los Angeles Times*, February 5, 1962, Part II, pp. 1:12.

St. John, Adela Rogers. "Why Breen Resigned from the Hays Office." *Liberty*, July 15, 1941, pp. 15–16, 43–44.

Schumach, Murray. "The Censor As Movie Director." *New York Times Magazine*, February 12, 1961, pp. 15–36.

———. *The Face on the Cutting Room Floor: The Story of Movie and Television Censorship*. New York: Da Capo Press, 1974.

Sklar, Robert. *Movie-Made America: A Social History of American Movies*. New York: Random House, 1975.

Smith, Ben, III, and Kathey Alexander. "Controversy Puts County on the Map." *Atlanta Journal-Constitution*, August 25, 1993, p. C8.

Solomon, Charles. *The History of Animation: Enchanted Drawings*. New York: Alfred A. Knopf, 1989.

"Stern Quitting as Code Chief." *Daily Variety*, December 3, 1973, pp. 1–4.

Thomson, David. *Showman: The Life of David O. Selznick*. New York: Alfred A. Knopf, 1992.

Turan, Kenneth, and Stephen F. Zito. *Sinema: American Pornographic Films and the People Who Make Them.* New York: Praeger Publishers, 1974.

Vale, V. and Andrea Juno, eds. *Re/Search #10: Incredibly Strange Films.* San Francisco: Re/Search Publications, 1986.

Vizzard, Jack. *See No Evil: Life Inside a Hollywood Censor.* New York: Simon and Schuster, 1970.

Williams, Linda. *Hard Core: Power, Pleasure, and the "Frenzy of the Visible."* Berkeley, Calif.: University of California Press, 1989.

SOURCES FOR SPECIFIC FILMS

All About Eve (1950)

Mankiewicz, Joseph L. *More About "All About Eve."* New York: Random House, 1972.

Anatomy of a Murder (1959)

"Preminger KO's Chicago Censors." *Daily Variety,* July 9, 1959.

"Too Much Anatomy." *Richmond News Ledger,* August 5, 1959, p. 50.

And God Created Woman (1957)

Flynn, Hazel. "Bardot, the Babe!!!!" *Beverly Hills Citizen,* January 2, 1958, p. 5.

"Indies Account for Four Films Rated by MPAA." *Daily Variety,* April 26, 1978.

Baby Doll (1956)

"*Baby Doll* Is Approved by British Priest for Showing to Adult Roman Catholics." *New York Times,* December 21, 1956.

"Legion of Decency Hits Code for *Baby Doll* Okay." *Daily Variety,* November 28, 1956, pp. 1–10.

"MPAA 'Wonders' How *Baby Doll* Got Code Seal; Regrets Okay Can't Be Rescinded." *Daily Variety,* December 7, 1956.

"Paris Cardinal Refuses to Condemn *Baby Doll*," *Los Angeles Times,* January 7, 1957.

"Spellman Denounces *Baby Doll* from Pulpit." *Hollywood Citizen-News,* December 17, 1956.

"*10 Commandments* Much More Sexy Than *Baby Doll*, Clergyman Declares." *New York Times,* December 24, 1956.

Williams, Dick. "Passion, Revenge and Hate Among South White Trash." *Los Angeles Mirror-News,* December 27, 1956.

Bad Lieutenant (1992)

Crow, Tom. "*Lieutenant*'s General." *Village View,* January 1–7, 1993, pp. 9–15.

Basic Instinct (1992)

Ansen, David. "Kiss Kiss Slash Slash." *Newsweek,* March 23, 1992.

Eller, Claudia. "Verhoeven Nixes Basic Changes." *Daily Variety,* April 30, 1991, pp. 12–15.

Grant, Steve. "Divide and Conquer." *Time Out,* April 22–29, 1992, pp. 19–21.

Harwood, Jim. "31 Protesters Busted at S. F. *Basic* Location." *Daily Variety,* May 1, 1991, pp. 3–10.

McGregor, Alex, "Sex Crimes." *Time Out*, April 22–29, 1992, pp. 18–21.

Schruers, Fred. "Stone Free." *Premiere*, May 1993, pp. 58–62.

Schwager, Jeff. "Bad Instinct?" *Boxoffice*, March 1992, pp. 8f.

Sessums, Kevin. "Stone Goddess." *Vanity Fair*, April 1993, pp. 156–161.

Simpson, Janice C. "Out of the Celluloid Closet." *Time*, April 6, 1992, p. 65.

Weinraub, Bernard. "Violent Melodrama of a Sizzling Movie Brings Rating Battle."
New York Times, January 30, 1992, pp. C15–19.

Welkos, Robert W. "Director Trims *Basic Instinct* to Get R Rating." *Los Angeles Times*,
February 11, 1992, pp. F1–F5.

Wells, Jeffrey. "What Was Cut: Turning Down the Heat." *Entertainment Weekly*,
April 3, 1992, p. 20.

Belle of the Nineties (1934)

Abel. *"Belle of the 90's." Variety*, September 25, 1934.

"Belle of the Nineties." Motion Picture Daily, August 20, 1934.

The Bicycle Thief (1949)

Creelman, Eileen. "Picture Plays: Slap on Wrist May Clean Up Foreign Films." *New
York World-Telegram and Sun*, March 6, 1950.

Crowther, Bosley. "Unkindest Cut: The Code Authority's Excisions of *The Bicycle Thief*
Are Upheld." *New York Times*, April 2, 1950, section 2, p. 1.

Quigley, Martin, Jr. *"The Bicycle Thief." Motion Picture Herald*, December 24, 1949.

"Skouras Chain Flouts Pic Code." *Daily Variety*, October 23, 1950, p. 5.

"Spot on the Wall." *Motion Picture Herald*, March 11, 1950.

The Birth of a Nation (1915)

Clarke, Steve. "U.K. Violence Regs Put Video 'Birth' on Hold." *Variety*, May 23–29, 1994,
pp. 27–29.

Croy, Homer. *Star Maker: The Story of D. W. Griffith*. New York: Duell, Sloan and
Pearce, 1959.

Gish, Lillian. *The Movies, Mr. Griffith, and Me*. Englewood Cliffs, New Jersey:
Prentice-Hall, 1969.

Schickel, Richard. *D. W. Griffith: An American Life*. New York: Simon and Schuster,
1984.

Blow-Up (1966)

"Blow-Up Director Puts MGM in Code Hang-Up; Catholics Views Pend." *Variety*,
December 14, 1966, pp. 3–17.

"Catholic Office Rips *Blow-Up.*" *Hollywood Reporter*, December 29, 1966, pp. 1–4.

"Gross of $7 Million." *Hollywood Reporter*, July 21, 1967.

"Pastor Leads His Flock to *Blow-Up.*" *Variety*, May 31, 1967.

Caged (1950)

Eager, Helen. "Writer Went to Prison to Get Facts for Story." *Boston Traveler*, April 13,
1950.

Casablanca (1942)
Miller, Frank. *Casablanca: As Time Goes By*. Atlanta: Turner Publishing, 1992.

The Children's Hour (1961)
Crowther, Bosley. "The Screen: New *Children's Hour*." *New York Times*, March 15, 1962.
Untitled Review. *Saturday Review*, February 24, 1962.

Citizen Kane (1941)
Kael, Pauline. *The Citizen Kane Book*. Boston: Little, Brown and Company, 1971.

The Cook, the Thief, His Wife and Her Lover (1989)
Corliss, Richard. "X Marks the Top." *Time*, April 9, 1990.
Ryan, Desmond. "The Cook, the Actress and the 'X' Rating." *Philadelphia Inquirer*, April 15, 1990, pp. 1G–11G.

Crimes of Passion (1985)
"*Crimes of Passion* Revisited." *Variety*, October 17, 1984, pp. 7–30.
Klein, Richard. "New World's *Passion* Again Fails to Pick Up R Rating." *Daily Variety*. September 24, 1984, p. 15.
London, Michael. "Film Clips: Russell's Crimes Stirs Passion Over Its Rating." *Los Angeles Times*, September 21, 1984, pp. 1–14.
Sarris, Andrew. "To Cut or Not to Cut." *Village Voice*, March 12, 1985.

Deep Throat (1972)
Farley, Ellen and William K. Knoedelseder, Jr. "The *Deep Throat* Payoff: Suitcases Full of Cash." *Los Angeles Times Calendar*, June 13, 1982, , pp. 7–9.
Hentoff, Nat. "The *Deep Throat* Conspiracy Case, Part I: How to Make the First Amendment Obscene." *Village Voice*, June 28, 1976, pp. 27–30.
Hill, Richard. "My Linda Lovelace Problem (and Yours). *Oui,* February 2, 1973, pp. 71–72.
"N.Y. News Sticks to *Deep Throat* Nix." *Variety*, August 27, 1972.
Oelsner, Lesley. "Obscenity: What's Really Deep Is the Logic." *New York Times*, December 31, 1972.
"UN & Show Types Dig *Deep Throat*." *Variety*, August 23, 1972, pp. 1–62.

Devil in the Flesh (1946)
Redelings, Lowell E. "The Hollywood Scene." *Hollywood Citizen News*, October 26, 1949.
"Story History of *Devil in the Flesh*." *New York Times*, March 20, 1949.

Double Indemnity (1944)
"*Double Indemnity*." *Hollywood Reporter*, April 24, 1944.
Hanna, David. "Hayes Censors Rile Jim Cain." *New York Daily News*, February 14, 1944.

Scheuer, Phillip K. "Film History Made by *Double Indemnity*." *Los Angeles Times*, June 6, 1944, pp. 1–2.

W.H.M. "Perfect Crime Myth Exploded." *Tidings*, August 11, 1944.

Duel in the Sun (1946)

"Cantwell Warns People Against *Duel in the Sun*." *Los Angeles Times*, January 16, 1947.

"Churches Hit *Duel in the Sun*." *Los Angeles Herald Examiner*, January 15, 1947.

Congressional Record—House of Representatives, June 19, 1947, pp. 7546f.

"Hog-Wash Served in Golden Canteen." *Tidings*, January 3, 1947.

The Easiest Way (1931)

Walter, Eugene. *The Easiest Way*. In Gassner, John, ed. *Best Plays of the Early American Theatre: From the Beginning to 1916*. New York: Crown Publishers, 1967.

Ecstasy (1933)

"*Ecstasy*: The Movie That Caused a 'War.'" *Look*, March 1937, pp. 28–31.

McKenny, Ruth. "*Ecstasy* Is a Film, Not Husband's State of Mind." *New York Post*, December 17, 1935, p. 19.

Silber, Fritz. "U.S.A. Censors Evidently O.K. *Ecstasy*." *Washington Daily News*, April 25, 1936.

Every Day's a Holiday (1938)

Barnes, Howard. "*Every Day's a Holiday*." *New York Herald Tribune*, January 27, 1938.

Patrick, Corbin. "*Hurricane* Is Terrific; Mae West Toned Down." *Indianapolis Star*, January 15, 1938.

"Views and Reviews." *Los Angeles Examiner*, January 4, 1937.

A Farewell to Arms (1957)

Zinsser, William K. "The New Movie: *A Farewell to Arms*." *New York Herald Tribune*, January 25, 1958.

Forever Amber (1947)

"Allied Warns on *Amber*." *Daily Variety*, November 10, 1947, pp. 1–10.

"*Amber*'s Roxy Gross 328G for Two Weeks." *Hollywood Reporter*, November 6, 1947, p. 1.

"*Forever Amber*." *Life*, November 3, 1947, pp. 67–68.

"Kathleen Winsor." *Life*, October 30, 1944, p. 41.

"Legion Condemns *Amber* but Beaux Stand in Line." *Daily Variety*, October 23, 1947.

"Legion Grants 'B' Status to *Amber* After Revisions." *Hollywood Reporter*, December 9, 1947.

"Ohio Archbishop Condemns *Amber*." *Hollywood Reporter*, November 5, 1947.

Nugent, Frank. S. "*Forever Amber* or 'Crime Doesn't Pay.'" *New York Times Magazine*, August 4, 1946, pp. 12–44.

The French Line (1954)
"Jane Russell Furore: Sam Goldwyn Urges New Censorship Code." *Hollywood Citizen-News*, December 29, 1953.
Williams, Dick. "A Beef from Jane Russell." *Los Angeles Mirror*, January 14, 1954.

From Here to Eternity (1953)
"Censored." *Look*, August 25, 1953.
"From Here to Obscurity." *Life*, April 16, 1951.
Mitgang, Herbert. "Transmuting a Touchy Topical Tome." *New York Times*, June 14, 1953.
"New Films." *Newsweek*, August 10, 1953.
Quigley, Martin. "Well Done!" *Motion Picture Daily*, August 14, 1953.

G-Men (1935)
Kauf. "*G-Men*." *Variety*, May 8, 1935, p. 16.

Gigi (1958)
Fordin, Hugh. *The Movies' Greatest Musicals*. New York: Fredcrick Ungar Publishing Co., 1984.

The Girl from Missouri (1934)
Johaneson, Bland. "Movie News." *New York Daily Mirror*, August 4, 1934.
Pollock, Arthur. "The Screen." *Brooklyn Eagle*, August 7, 1934.

Happy Anniversary (1959)
"'Broad-Minded' Code Board to Hear *Happy* Appeal Nov. 4th." *Daily Variety*, October 30, 1959, pp. 1–18.
"A Sentence Redeems H*appy Anni*; Paradoxes Galore in Predicament of Those 'Judging' United Artists." *Variety*, November 11, 1959, pp. 2–20.

Henry and June (1990)
Farber, Stephen. "A Major Studio Plans to Test the Rating System." *New York Times*, September 4, 1990.
"Flicks Nix X Pix; Lids on Kids." *Newsweek*, October 8, 1990, p. 73.
Kissinger, David. "X-Rated *June* Could Ignite Major Revolt Against MPAA." *Variety*, September 10, 1990, pp. 3–8.
Mathews, Jack. "Henry Miller Meets the MPAA." *Los Angeles Times*, August 27, 1990, pp. F1–F10.
_____. "Sell-Out Crowds for *Henry & June*." *Los Angeles Times*, October 8, 1990, pp. F1–F12.
Rohter, Larry. "A 'No Children' Category to Replace the 'X' Rating." *New York Times*, September 27, 1990, pp. A1–C18.
Tusher, Will. "Boston 'Burb Bans U's *Henry and June*." *Daily Variety*, October 5, 1990, pp. 1–39.
Voland, John. "Valenti: *Henry* Ban Like 'Dark Ages.'" *Hollywood Reporter*, October 8, 1990, pp. 3–18.

Henry: Portrait of a Serial Killer (1990)
Berman, Marc. "MPI Takes Another Stab at an R Rating for *Henry*." *Variety*, June 22, 1992.
O'Grady, Dominic. "*Henry* Re-Edited in Hopes of Getting Censor Approval." *Hollywood Reporter*, February 25, 1992.
Sabatini, Vicki. "Henry Producers Taking MPAA to Court Over X Rating." *Hollywood Reporter*, May 18, 1990, pp. 1–98.

Heroes for Sale (1933)
Hoberman, J. "Just the Low Points." *Village Voice*, January 28, 1992, p. 58.

Hitler's Children (1943)
"A Fairy Tale That Happens to Be True." *New York Herald Tribune*, March 7, 1943, pp. 3f.
Levitas, Louise. "*Hitler's Children.*" *PM Magazine*, January 3, 1943.

I Am a Fugitive from a Chain Gang (1932)
Abel. "*I Am a Fugitive.*" *Variety*, November 15, 1932.
"Hearst and Brisbane Praise Warner Film." *Motion Picture Herald*, December 3, 1932, p. 14.
Higham, Charles. "When Muni Wore Chains and Bogart Wore a Black Hood." *New York Times*, July 1, 1973, pp. 9–17.
"*I Am a Fugitive.*" *Daily Variety*, October 21, 1932.
"Page Will Hays." *La Grange (Ga.) News*, April 17, 1932.

I Am Curious (Yellow) (1967)
Mayer, Michael. "A Not So Curious Result." *Motion Picture Herald*, January 29, 1969, pp. 13f.
Schickel, Richard. "It Hides Nothing but the Heart." *Life*, March 21, 1969.

In Which We Serve (1942)
"Cutting 'Salty Adjectives' from Film Stirs British." *Los Angeles Times*, December 10, 1942.
"O Hollywood!" *New York Herald Tribune*, December 12, 1942, p. 14.

Indiana Jones and the Temple of Doom (1984)
Harmetz, Aljean. "Rating of *Indiana Jones* Questioned." *New York Times*, May 21, 1984.
Pry. "*Indiana Jones* and the Temple of Free Speech." *Daily Variety*, May 31, 1984, p. 2.
"Valenti Rejects *Jones* Rating Criticism." *Daily Variety*, May 31, 1984, pp. 2–4.
Zogli, Richard. "Gremlins in the Rating System." *Time*, June 25, 1984, p. 78.

King Kong (1933)
MacQueen, Scott. "Old *King Kong* Gets Face Lift." *American Cinematographer*, January 1989, pp. 78–83.

Kings Row (1942)
Koury, Phil. "A Movie to Watch For." *Kansas City Star*, March 29, 1942, p. D1.

Kiss Me, Stupid (1964)
Crowther, Bosley. "The Heat Is on Films." *New York Times*, January 17, 1965.
———. "Moral Brinksmanship." *New York Times*, December 13, 1964.
"A Kick Instead for *Kiss Me, Stupid.*" *Variety*, December 9, 1964.
"Moral or Immoral." *Time*, December 28, 1964, pp. 53–54.
"Public Outcry Cancels Stupid *Columbus* Dates." *Exhibitor*, June 2, 1965.
Scheuer, Philip K. "Censor Rumblings Increase Steadily." *Los Angeles Times*, December 30, 1964.
Thompson, Thomas. "Wilder's Dirty-Joke Film Stirs a Furor." *Life*, January 15, 1965.

Klondike Annie (1936)
"Lewd Films Invite Federal Censorship." *Los Angeles Examiner*, March 7, 1936.
Nugent, Frank S. "The Screen." *New York Times*, March 12, 1936.
"The Screen Must Not Relapse to Lewdness." *Los Angeles Examiner*, February 28, 1936.
"Stop Lewd Films!" *Los Angeles Examiner*, February 29, 1936.

Lady Chatterley's Lover (1957)
Crowther, Bosley. "Victory for Ideas." *New York Times*, July 5, 1959.
"High Court's Ruling on Sex in Movies." *U.S. News & World Report*, July 13, 1959, p. 50.

Last Tango in Paris (1973)
"The Ban Is Lifted on *Last Tango* in Italy." *Variety*, February 11, 1987, pp. 2–92.
"Italy Acquits Brando of Obscenity in Film." *Los Angeles Times*, March 3, 1973.

The Last Temptation of Christ (1988)
Dawes, Amy. "Offer to Buy Pic: Christians Protest U's *Christ.*" *Daily Variety*, July 18, 1988, pp. 1–6.
———. "Protest Continues: Wasserman Picketed Over *Temptation.*" *Daily Variety*, July 21, 1988, pp. 6–15.
Ebert, Roger. "*Last Temptation* Censorship Lacks Divine Inspiration." *Chicago Sun-Times*, July 24, 1988.
Galbraith, Jane and Richard Gold. "Scorsese Defends *Temptation* on TV." *Daily Variety*, July 27, 1988, pp. 3–19.
Harmetz, Aljean. "Film on Christ Brings Out Pickets, and Archbishop Predicts Censure." *New York Times*, July 21, 1988, p. C19.
———. "*The Last Temptation of Christ* Opens to Protests but Good Sales." *New York Times*, August 13, 1988.
———. "Scorsese *Temptation* Gets Early Release." *New York Times*, August 5, 1988.
———. "7,500 Picket Universal Over Movie About Jesus." *New York Times*, August 12, 1988, p. C4.
"*Last Temptation* Controversy." "Nightline," ABC Television, August 9, 1988.
Locayo, Richard. "Days of Ire and Brimstone." *Time*, July 25, 1988.

London, Michael. "Film Clips: Paramount Decides to Resist *Temptation*." *Los Angeles Times Calendar*, January 6, 1984, pp. 1–10.

Schwartz, Amy E. "A Personal View: The *Temptation* Resistance." *San Francisco Chronicle*, August 9, 1988, p. E1.

Shaver, Jessica. "*Temptation* Presents a False Picture of Jesus." *Long Beach Press-Telegram,* July 28, 1988, p. B7.

The Letter (1929/1940)

Maugham, W. Somerset. *The Letter.* In *Best Mystery and Suspense Plays of the Modern Theatre.* New York: Avon Books, 1979.

Life Begins for Andy Hardy (1941)

"The Hardy Series Goes Adult." *Motion Picture Herald*, August 16, 1941.

"*Life Begins for Andy Hardy.*" *America*, September 6, 1941.

"*Life Begins for Andy Hardy.*" *Hollywood Reporter*, August 7, 1941.

Lolita (1962)

Alpert, Hollis. "The Bubble Gum Siren." *Saturday Review*, June 23, 1962.

"Cary Grant, Harris-Kubrick Cross Verbal Swords in Duel Over *Lolita*." *Hollywood Reporter*, October 10, 1958.

"Cinema: Humbert Humdrum & Lullita." *Time*, June 22, 1962, p. 94.

Lawrenson, Helen. "The Man Who Scandalized the World." *Esquire*, August 1960, pp. 70–73.

"Nymphet Found." *Time*, October 10, 1960.

Thomas, Bob. "Cary Grant Spurns Bid to Play Lead in *Lolita*." *Los Angeles Mirror-News*, October 6, 1958.

The Man with the Golden Arm (1955)

Gene. "*The Man with the Golden Arm*." *Daily Variety*, December 14, 1955, p. 6.

"UA Execs Flex Arm at Production Code; 'Confident' Pic Can Win Precedental Seal." *Daily Variety*, November 8, 1955, pp. 1–10.

Mildred Pierce (1945)

Barnes, Howard. "On the Screen: *Mildred Pierce*." *New York Herald Tribune*, September 29, 1945.

McManus, John T. "James Cain's Ugly America." *PM*, September 30, 1945.

The Miracle (1949)

"Ban Is Denounced; Film Is Withdrawn." *New York Times*, February 17, 1951.

"Burstyn Enthuses." *Daily Variety*, May 27, 1952, p. 1.

Cianfarra, Camille M. "Vatican Views *Miracle* Row." *New York Times*, February 11, 1951.

Crowther, Bosley. "*The Miracle* Happens." *New York Times*, June 1, 1952, Section 2, p. 1.

———. "The Strange Case of *The Miracle*." *Atlantic Monthly*, April 1951, pp. 35–39.

"Crowther Rap Over *Miracle* Stirs MPAA Bd." *Variety*, February 28, 1951, pp. 3–63.

"Freedom of the Screen Won for the Industry." *Boxoffice*, May 31, 1952, pp. 8–10.

"*The Miracle*: An Outrage." *Motion Picture Herald*, January 6, 1951, p. 1.

"*The Miracle* Decision." *Tablet*, May 31, 1952.

"*The Miracle*—Why It Is Blasphemous and Sacrilegious." Pamphlet on file with MPAA
  Letters, Special Collections, Margaret Herrick Library, January 1951.

"Rossellini Appeal to Spellman on Film." *New York Times*, January 13, 1951.

"Supreme Court Upholds Ban on *The Miracle*." *New York Times*, May 12, 1951.

The Miracle of Morgan's Creek (1944)

Agee, James. *Agee on Film, Volume 1*. New York: Perigee Books, 1958.

W.H.M. "Film Scores Cheap Laughs at Family Life." *Tidings*, March 24, 1944.

Spoto, Donald. *Madcap: The Life of Preston Sturges*. Boston: Little, Brown and
  Company, 1990.

Monsieur Verdoux (1947)

Chaplin, Charles. *My Autobiography*. New York: Simon and Schuster, 1964.

The Moon and Sixpence (1942)

Delehanty, Thornton. "The Films Walk Moral Tightrope." *New York Herald Tribune*,
  April 5, 1942.

"*The Moon and Sixpence*." *Motion Picture Herald*, September 19, 1942.

Wright, Virginia. *Los Angeles Daily News*, April 8, 1942, p. 21.

The Moon Is Blue (1953)

"Binford Ban Backfires; *Moon* Shines With SRO in his Native State." *Variety*,
  September 9, 1953.

"Chains Flout Code, Book *Blue*." *Daily Variety*, June 30, 1953, p. 1.

Marsh, W. Ward. "Number of Good Pictures This Year Rises to High of 42; More Are
  to Come." *Cleveland Plain Dealer*, July 22, 1954.

"*Moon* Cab Scene Cut, Plays Alabam'; St. Paul Solons Hold Nose, O.K. It." *Variety*,
  July 29, 1953, p. 4.

Wilkerson, H. R. "Trade Views." *Hollywood Reporter*, June 4, 1953.

"NYPD Blue" (TV series, 1993)

"Channel Surfing," *Atlanta Journal-Constitution*, October 11, 1993, p. C6.

"Channel Surfing," *Atlanta Journal-Constitution*, October 13, 1993, p. E10.

Jubera, Drew. "Bochco's Calm Amid the Furor Over Steamy 'NYPD Blue.' " *Atlanta
  Journal-Constitution*, July 26, 1993, pp. B1–2.

——— and Phil Kloer. " 'NYPD' Too Blue for Many Stations." *Atlanta Journal-
  Constitution*, September 7, 1993, p. F6.

Outcast Lady (1934)

Blackford. "Iris March." *Billboard*, September 1, 1934.

"*Outcast Lady*." *Daily Variety*, August 7, 1934.

The Outlaw (1941)
"History in the Making." *Hollywood Reporter*, January 14, 1947, pp. 1–4.
"Hughes Asks High Court to Break N.Y. *Outlaw* Blockade." *Hollywood Reporter*, November 20, 1946.
Hughes Tool Company v. *Motion Picture Association of America, Inc.*, U.S. 224 (1946).
"Judge Thunderstruck by Jane Russell in *Outlaw*; OK's Ban." *Los Angeles Herald-Examiner*, September 20, 1947.
"The Ohio Censor Finally Passes *Outlaw*, RKO Has No Plan to Release Pic There." *Daily Variety*, June 16, 1954.
"*Outlaw* Gets New Legion Category." *Hollywood Reporter*, October 10, 1949.
Sammis, Fred R. "The Case Against *The Outlaw*." *Photoplay*, September 1946.

The Pawnbroker (1965)
"AIP Bows to Catholic Office; Sees 5,000–10,000 Added Playdates for *Pawnbroker* with Bosom Scene Out." *Variety*, August 3, 1966.
"Albany to See a 'C' Film." *Variety*, September 15, 1963.
"Bishop Pike Endorses *Pawnbroker* Following Catholic Condemnation." *Exhibitor*, June 2, 1965.
"Legion of Decency's Hesitation but Finally 'C's' *Pawnbroker*." *Variety*, May 12, 1965, p. 4.
"*Pawnbroker* Nude Scenes Stay, Even If Seal Refused: Landau." *Variety*, March 18, 1965.

Poison (1991)
Williams, David E. "Banned First Hand: An Interview with Todd Haynes." *Film Threat Video Guide*, number 7 (1993), pp. 50–55.

The Postman Always Rings Twice (1946)
Crowther, Bosley. "For Better and for Worse." *New York Times*, May 5, 1946.
Maslin, Janet. "The Story Is the Same but Hollywood Has Changed." *New York Times*, April 26, 1981.

Re-Animator (1985)
"Empire's *Re-Animator* Finds Good Press, Ad Restrictions." *Daily Variety*, October 28, 1985, pp. 1–14.
"MPAA's Long Rating Arm Finally Tags *Re-Animator*." *Daily Variety*, June 17, 1986, p. 8.

Sadie Thompson (1928)
Colton, John, and Clemence Randolph. *Rain*. London: Samuel French, 1923.
Maugham, W. Somerset. "Rain." In *The Complete Short Stories of W. Somerset Maugham*. London: Neinemann, 1951.
Swanson, Gloria. *Swanson on Swanson*. New York: Random House, 1980.

She Done Him Wrong (1933)
Watts, Richard, Jr. "On the Screen." *New York Herald Tribune*, February 10, 1933.

Spartacus (1960)
Adair, Gilbert. "Violence and Sex." *Connoisseur*, April 1991, pp. 136f.
"Legion of Decency 'Negotiating' with U-I on Spartacus." *Daily Variety*, October 17, 1960.

The Story of Temple Drake (1933)
Aaronson. "*The Story of Temple Drake*." *Motion Picture Herald*, May 13, 1933.
Abel. "*Temple Drake*." *Daily Variety*, May 9, 1933.
"*The Story of Temple Drake*." *Film Daily*, May 6, 1933.

A Streetcar Named Desire (1951)
Kazan, Elia. "Pressure Problem." *New York Times*, October 21, 1951.
"Kazan Article Explains *Streetcar* Cutting in Rap at Warners, Legion." *Variety*, October 24, 1951, pp. 6–13.

Suddenly Last Summer (1959)
Powe. "*Suddenly Last Summer*." *Daily Variety*, December 16, 1959.
"*Suddenly Last Summer*." *Time*, January 11, 1960.

Tea and Sympathy (1956)
Crowther, Bosley. "Loosening the Code." *New York Times*, October 7, 1956.
"If Metro Can't Brew *Tea* to Suit Production Code, Author Still Gets 100G." *Daily Variety*, September 22, 1954.
Schallert, Edwin. "*Tea and Sympathy* Likely to Provoke Mixed Reaction." *Los Angeles Times*, October 4, 1956.
"*Tea, Sympathy* May Duck the Code." *Variety*, December 16, 1953.

These Three (1936)
"The New Pictures: *These Three*." *Time*, March 30, 1936.

Three Comrades (1938)
Flin. "*Three Comrades*." *Variety*, May 24, 1938.

Tie Me Up! Tie Me Down! (1990)
Brown, Rich. "MPAA Asks Court to Untie Miramax Suit Over X Rating." *Hollywood Reporter*, June 20, 1990. pp. 1–25.
Collins, Glenn. "Judge to Rule in July on X Rating for *Tie Me Up!*" *New York Times*, June 22, 1990.
"Excerpts from *Miramax* vs. *MPAA Ruling*." *Los Angeles Times*, July 21, 1990, p. F7.
Fox, David J. "Rating System Faces Challenges on Two Fronts." *Los Angeles Times*, July 21, 1990, pp. F1–F7.

Titticut Follies (1967)
Jeavon, Clyde. "The Films of Frederick Wiseman." In Lloyd, Ann, ed. *Movies of the Seventies*. London: Orbis, 1984.

Two-Faced Woman (1941)
Crow, James Francis. "Greta Garbo's New Film Condemned by Legion of Decency." *Hollywood Citizen*, November 24, 1941.
"Page Our Mr. Hays." *Indianapolis News*, December 1, 1941.
"Prelate Raps Film Garbo." *Los Angeles Herald and Express*, November 27, 1941.

Whore (1991)
Fox, David J. "Movie on Prostitution Still Gets an NC-17 Rating." *Los Angeles Times*, September 9, 1991.
Hunt, Dennis. "Ken Russell's Movie Available in Four Versions." *Los Angeles Times*, January 31, 1992.

Who's Afraid of Virginia Woolf? (1966)
Quigley, Martin, Jr. "The Code Is Dead." *Motion Picture Herald*, July 6, 1966.
"Report WB *Woolf* Decision Cued by NCOMP's Rating." *Daily Variety*, May 27, 1966.
"Reveal WB Did Delete 2 Dialog Ejaculations to Get *Woolf* Code Seal." *Daily Variety*, July 13, 1966.
Thompson, Thomas. "Raw Dialogue Challenges All the Censors." *Life*, June 10, 1966, pp. 92–98.
"*Virginia Woolf* Adults Policy Called Success." *Motion Picture Exhibitor*, September 28, 1966.

Wide Sargasso Sea (1993)
Cohn, Lawrence. "*Wide Sargasso Sea.*" *Variety*, April 19, 1993, p. 45.

Appendix

Particular Applications of the Code {Addenda to 1930 Code}

GENERAL PRINCIPLES

1. No picture shall be produced which will lower the moral standards of those who see it. Hence the sympathy of the audience shall never be thrown to the side of crime, wrong-doing, evil or sin.
2. Correct standards of life, subject only to the requirements of drama and entertainment, shall be presented.
3. Law, natural or human, shall not be ridiculed, nor shall sympathy be created for its violation.

PARTICULAR APPLICATIONS

I. Crimes against the law:

These shall never by presented in such a way as to throw sympathy with the crime as against law and justice or to inspire others with a desire for imitation.

The treatment of crimes against the law must not:

  a. Teach methods of crime.

  b. Inspire potential criminals with a desire for imitation.

  c. Make criminals seem heroic and justified.

I. MURDER

  a. The technique of murder must be presented in a way that will not inspire imitation.

  b. Brutal killings are not to be presented in detail.

  c. Revenge in modern times shall not be justified. In lands and ages of less developed civilization and moral principles, revenge may sometimes be presented. This would be the case especially in places where no law exists to cover the crime because of which revenge is committed.

2. METHODS OF CRIME shall not be explicitly presented.

  a. Theft, robbery, safe-cracking, and dynamiting of trains, mines, buildings, etc., should not be detailed in method.

  b. Arson must be subject to the same safeguards.

  c. The use of firearms should be restricted to essentials.

  d. Methods of smuggling should not be presented.

3. ILLEGAL DRUG TRAFFIC must never be presented.

Because of its evil consequences, the drug traffic should never be presented in any form. The existence of the trade should not be brought to the attention of audiences.

4. THE USE OF LIQUOR in American life, when not required by the plot or for proper characterization, should not be shown.

The use of liquor should never be excessively presented even in picturing countries where its use is legal. In scenes from American life, the necessities of the plot and proper characterization alone justify its use. And in this case, it should be shown with moderation.

Frank Miller

II. Sex

The sanctity of the institution of marriage and the home shall be upheld. Pictures shall not infer that low forms of sex relationship are the accepted or common thing.

1. ADULTERY, sometimes necessary plot material, must not be explicitly treated, or justified, or presented attractively. Out of regard for the sanctity of marriage and the home, the triangle, that is, the love of a third party for one already married, needs careful handling. The treatment should not throw sympathy against marriage as an institution.

2. SCENES OF PASSION must be treated with an honest acknowledgment of human nature and its normal reactions. Many scenes cannot be presented without arousing dangerous emotions on the part of the immature, the young or the criminal classes.
a. They should not be introduced when not essential to the plot.
b. Excessive and lustful kissing, lustful embraces, suggestive postures and gestures, are not to be shown.
c. In general, passion should be so treated that these scenes do not stimulate the lower and baser element.

3. SEDUCTION OR RAPE
a. They should never be more than suggested, and only when essential for the plot, and even then never shown by explicit method.
b. They are never the proper subject for comedy.

4. SEX PERVERSION or any inference to it is forbidden.

5. WHITE SLAVERY shall not be treated.

6. MISCEGENATION (sex relationship between the white and black races) is forbidden.

7. SEX HYGIENE AND VENEREAL DISEASES are not subjects for motion pictures.

8. SCENES OF ACTUAL CHILDBIRTH, in fact or in silhouette, are never to be presented.

9. CHILDREN'S SEX ORGANS are never to be exposed.

III. Vulgarity

The treatment of low, disgusting, unpleasant, though not necessarily evil, subjects should be subject always to the dictate of good taste and a regard for the sensibilities of the audience.

IV. Obscenity

Obscenity in word, gesture, reference, song, joke, or by suggestion (even when likely to be understood only by part of the audience) is forbidden.

V. Profanity

Pointed profanity (this includes the words, God, Lord, Jesus, Christ—unless used reverently—Hell, S.O.B., damn, Gawd), or every other profane or vulgar expression however used is forbidden.

VI. Costume

1. COMPLETE NUDITY is never permitted. This includes nudity in fact or in silhouette, or any lecherous or licentious notice thereof by other characters in the picture.

2. UNDRESSING SCENES should be avoided, and never used save where essential to the plot.

3. INDECENT OR UNDUE EXPOSURE is forbidden.

4. DANCING COSTUMES intended to permit undue exposure or indecent movements in the dance are forbidden.

VII. Dances

1. DANCES SUGGESTING OR REPRESENTING SEXUAL ACTIONS or indecent passion are forbidden.

2. DANCES WHICH EMPHASIZE INDECENT MOVEMENTS are to be regarded as obscene.

VIII. Religion

1. NO FILM OR EPISODE MAY THROW RIDICULE on any religious faith.

2. MINISTERS OF RELIGION IN THEIR CHARACTER AS MINISTERS of religion should not be used as comic characters or as villains.

3. CEREMONIES OF ANY DEFINITE RELIGION should be carefully and respectfully handled.

IX. Locations

Certain places are so closely and thoroly [sic] associated with sexual life or with sexual sin that their use must be carefully limited. Brothels and houses of ill-fame are not proper locations for drama.

X. National feelings

The just rights, history, and feelings of any nation are entitled to consideration and respectful treatment.

1. The use of the Flag shall be consistently respectful.

2. The history, institutions, prominent people and citizenry of other nations shall be represented fairly.

XI. Titles

Salacious, indecent, or obscene title shall not be used.

Index

Acknowledgments

Unlike the history of censorship over the last century, the history of this book has been smooth and far from contentious. For that, I owe deep thanks to the many people at Turner Publishing who helped me through the research and writing of *Censored Hollywood*, particularly Michael Reagan, Walton Rawls, Kathy Buttler, Larry Larson, Karen Smith, Vivian Lawand, Zodie Spain, Marty Moore, Michael Walsh, Tammy Winter, Caroline Harkelroad, and Patrick Dillon.

Special thanks are also owed to Jack Valenti, president of the Motion Picture Association of America and the creator of the current ratings system, who made himself available to me for two interviews. Nadine Strossen, president of the American Civil Liberties Union, took the time to review the text and provide much appreciated input. I received invaluable research assistance from the George Eastman House in Rochester, New York; Linda Maher, Robert Cushman, and all of the staff at the Margaret Herrick Library of the Academy of Motion Picture Arts and Sciences; and from Leith Adams and Stuart Ng of the Warner Bros. Collection of the University of Southern California School of Cinema-Television. I am particularly grateful to Stuart Ng for suggesting I look into the censorship files on Warner Bros.' *Caged*. In addition, Roger Mayer, Dick May, Cathy Manolis, and Mary Beth Verhunce of Turner Entertainment Company helped with hunting down information and pictures and with contacts throughout the industry.

Gregory C. Lisby and Gary Moss of Georgia State University were kind enough to share with me the research for their upcoming book on film censorship in Atlanta. Ted and Gloria Maloof and Louise Collins shared their memories of life in Atlanta under local censor Christine Smith Gilliam. Lee Tsiantis of 20th Century–Fox's Atlanta public relations office helped me track down some of the films I screened for this book. Among the friends who provided a sounding board, gave me feedback on portions of the manuscript, or kept me company through dozens of screenings are Valetta Anderson, Eleanor Brownfield, Becky Harris, Lynne Hatcher, Brad Lapin, Lorraine Lombardi, Janet Metzger, and particularly Beverly Thrasher, who spent the better part of her Christmas holidays going over the first draft with me. In addition, my colleagues at Turner Broadcasting—Mary Kay Fiorillo, Kevin Little, Jeff Matteson, and Misty Skedgell—helped me juggle two full-time careers.

Final—and deepest—thanks go to my research assistant, Woolsey Ackerman. In addition to compiling the photographs for this volume, he helped me sift through the hundreds of Production Code files at the Margaret Herrick Library and compiled an impressive collection of press clippings on the films covered in this book. Without his unstinting commitment and his own encyclopedic knowledge of Hollywood history, this volume would have been impossible to complete.

Photo Credits

Cover: Courtesy of Turner Entertainment Company

Title page: Courtesy of Turner Entertainment Company

Introduction, p. 7: Courtesy of Turner Entertainment Company

Chapter One, p. 13: Courtesy of Universal City Studios, Inc.,
Courtesy of MCA Publishing Rights, a Division of MCA, Inc.

Chapter Two, p. 21: Courtesy of Turner Entertainment Company

Chapter Three, p. 37: Courtesy of Kino International

Chapter Four, p. 49: Courtesy of Universal City Studios, Inc.,
Courtesy of MCA Publishing Rights, a Division of MCA, Inc.

Chapter Five, p. 85: Courtesy of Turner Entertainment Company

Chapter Six, p. 113: Courtesy of Turner Entertainment Company

Chapter Seven, p. 147: Courtesy of Warner Bros. TV

Chapter Eight, p. 183: Courtesy of Warner Bros. TV

Chapter Nine, p. 211: Courtesy of Photofest

Chapter Ten, p. 247: Courtesy of New Line Cinema